The Making of Modern Japan

Studies in Critical Social Sciences Book Series

Haymarket Books is proud to be working with Brill Academic Publishers (www.brill.nl) to republish the *Studies in Critical Social Sciences* book series in paperback editions. This peer-reviewed book series offers insights into our current reality by exploring the content and consequences of power relationships under capitalism, and by considering the spaces of opposition and resistance to these changes that have been defining our new age. Our full catalog of *SCSS* volumes can be viewed at https://www.haymarketbooks.org/series_collections/4-studies-in-critical-social-sciences.

Series Editor
David Fasenfest (Wayne State University)

New Scholarship in Political Economy Book Series

Series Editors
David Fasenfest (Wayne State University)
Alfredo Saad-Filho (King's College London)

Editorial Board
Kevin B. Anderson (University of California, Santa Barbara)
Tom Brass (formerly of sps, University of Cambridge)
Raju Das (York University)
Ben Fine ((emeritus) soas University of London)
Jayati Ghosh (Jawaharlal Nehru University)
Elizabeth Hill (University of Sydney)
Dan Krier (Iowa State University)
Lauren Langman (Loyola University Chicago)
Valentine Moghadam (Northeastern University)
David N. Smith (University of Kansas)
Susanne Soederberg (Queen's University)
Aylin Topal (Middle East Technical University)
Fiona Tregenna (University of Johannesburg)
Matt Vidal (Loughborough University London)
Michelle Williams (University of the Witwatersrand)

The Making of Modern Japan

Power, Crisis, and the Promise of Transformation

Myles Carroll

Haymarket Books
Chicago, IL

First published in 2021 by Brill Academic Publishers, The Netherlands
© 2021 Koninklijke Brill NV, Leiden, The Netherlands

Published in paperback in 2022 by
Haymarket Books
P.O. Box 180165
Chicago, IL 60618
773-583-7884
www.haymarketbooks.org

ISBN: 978-1-64259-797-4

Distributed to the trade in the US through Consortium Book Sales and Distribution (www.cbsd.com) and internationally through Ingram Publisher Services International (www.ingramcontent.com).

This book was published with the generous support of Lannan Foundation and Wallace Action Fund.

Special discounts are available for bulk purchases by organizations and institutions. Please call 773-583-7884 or email info@haymarketbooks.org for more information.

Cover design by Jamie Kerry and Ragina Johnson.

Printed in the United States.

10 9 8 7 6 5 4 3 2 1

Library of Congress Cataloging-in-Publication data is available.

Contents

Acknowledgements VII
List of Illustrations IX

1 Introduction 1
   1 Analytical Approach 3
   2 Outline of the Argument 5
   3 Outline of the Chapters 6

2 Lineages of Japanese Political Economy 14
   1 Creative Conservatism and the Developmental State: Japan's Post-war Boom 14
   2 Institutional Approaches to the Study of Japanese Politics 22
   3 The Long Decline: Theorizing Crisis in Heisei Japan 24
   4 The Welfare State and Social Reproduction in Post-war Japan 33
   5 Conclusion 40

3 Towards a Gramscian Understanding of Japanese Political Economy 42
   1 Historical Materialist Methodology 43
   2 Hegemony 46
   3 Hegemony and Hegemonic Order 47
   4 Social Reproduction 48
   5 Conditions for Hegemonic Order 50
   6 Historic Bloc 52
   7 Explaining Change: Conjunctural and Organic 54
   8 Organic Crisis 55
   9 World Order, Forms of State, Social Forces 56
   10 Relations of Force 58
   11 Caesarism, Passive Revolution and Trasformismo 59
   12 Counter-hegemony and the (Post-) Modern Prince 61
   13 Political Ecology 62
   14 Towards a Gramscian Feminist Approach to the Japanese Post-war Order 63
   15 Conclusion 68

4 The Post-war Hegemonic Order 70
   1 The Post-war Hegemonic Order 71
   2 Conditions of Post-war Hegemonic Order 74
   3 The Post-war Japanese Historic Bloc 104
   4 Conclusion 108

5 Contradictions and Transitions of the Late Shōwa Era 109
1. Structural Changes to World Order 110
2. Structural Demographic Changes 115
3. Political Changes 118
4. Institutional Changes 124
5. Implications of these Changes for Hegemonic Order 133
6. Conclusion 136

6 The Organic Crisis of the Heisei Era 139
1. Historical Background to the Crisis 140
2. Conditions of the Crisis 153
3. Implications of the Crisis 171
4. Conclusion 173

7 Caesarism, Passive Revolution and the Return of the LDP under Abe 176
1. Abe's Political Comeback 177
2. Breaking the Deadlock: The Caesarism of "Abenomics" 179
3. The Real Abe? Passive Revolution, Militarism and Soft Authoritarianism 186
4. Consequences of Abe's Reign for the Hegemonic Order? 193
5. Conclusion 199

8 Whither Post-Abe Japan? Four Scenarios for the Future 202
1. The Neo-conservative Option 203
2. The Neo-liberal Path 209
3. Back to the Future: Neo-communitarianism? 215
4. Counter-hegemony and a Democratic Socialist Future 221
5. Conclusion 229

9 Conclusion 231
1. Conditions for Hegemonic Order: Political Legitimation 231
2. Conditions for Hegemonic Order: Capital Accumulation 234
3. Conditions for Hegemonic Order: Social Reproduction 237
4. Overarching Theoretical Implications of the Argument 241
5. Towards a Gramscian Political Economy of Modern States 243

Bibliography 245
Index 261

Acknowledgements

Though I take full responsibility for any remaining errors or oversights in this book, I could not have carried out this research or written this book without the love, support and kindness of many people.

Stephen Gill has been an intellectual inspiration to me since my undergraduate years, and it was in many ways a dream come true to have him as my supervisor. Stephen provided immense support, not only in helping me develop this project and fine-tune it as a dissertation in the final months, but also through his apt advice and dutiful letter-writing, which enabled me to win strong funding for every year of my doctoral studies. Without this support, this project – which involved extensive fieldwork in Japan – would have been impossible. Moreover, Stephen provided me with invaluable connections in Japan that enabled me to live and work there as well as early opportunities to publish elements of this research. I owe very much to Stephen.

Isa Bakker was also immensely supportive as my dissertation second reader, while also providing a central inspiration for the theoretical approach I developed (along with Stephen), as well as many crucial insights and points of advice as I developed the project. I thank Isa as well for spearheading the *Capital & Class* special issue, in which I was able to publish an article that came out of this project. David McNally was also extremely helpful as a committee member, posing challenging and compelling questions, which helped me clarify many key issues that I likely would have never even thought about without his critical insights.

I would also like to give a special thank you to Seiji Endo, Vice President at Seikei University, who served as my field supervisor in Japan for two years. In addition to helping me obtain a position as Visiting Scholar in Seikei University's Faculty of Law, Seiji provided me with immense support in developing the blueprint of my project, refining it (in response to some of his concerns) and turning it into the finished copy. He also introduced me to various key Japanese language (as well as English) texts and leading scholars in Japan, all of which have helped strengthen the depth and scope of the analysis of this book. His support with this project was of immeasurable significance.

Very special thanks are also due to David Fasenfest, who has been the most helpful and kindest editor I ever could have hoped for. David's patience, guidance and support have been crucial in enabling me to bring this project to fruition and helping me get over the final series of hurdles in converting this manuscript from a doctoral dissertation into a full-fledged book. I am very grateful to him for that.

I also want to thank a number of people from Japanese and Canadian academia, including Heidi Gottfried, Hideo Aoki, Shannon Bell, Derek Hall, Stefan Kipfer, Naoaki Kobayashi, Tokuoh Konishi, Makoto Itoh, Yahilo Unno and Nobuharu Yokokawa for their advice and insights as I developed this project.

Thanks are also due to a number of institutions, which provided various forms of support, including both monetary and non-monetary. York University gave me strong funding in my first year of doctoral studies while also supporting my various external funding applications. The Social Science and Humanities Research Council of Canada then provided extensive funding for the final four years of my studies, without which it would have been impossible to conduct fieldwork in Japan. Seikei University provided significant institutional support, including office space and full access to their library. Many thanks are also due to Ochanomizu University, where I have been employed as Assistant Professor since April 2020. Despite the extenuating circumstances of the Covid-19 global pandemic, my institutional supports at Ochanomizu, as well as the quiet space offered by my office, have been especially helpful in enabling me to concentrate on the final stages of revising this book.

Finally, I would also like to thank my family for their unwavering support and love. As always, my parents Anne Preyde and Bill Carroll provided tremendous emotional support, even in my moments of self-doubt, every step of the way. Particular thanks are due to my father for all his insightful comments and probing questions along the way and especially those that helped to bring this book to fruition. My brother Wes Carroll also provided significant moral support, and there was nothing like listening to his music when I needed a break.

Most of all, however, I want to thank my wife Yasuka Kanoh and son Tomohisa for truly being the sparkling diamonds in my life. When I started this project, Yasuka and I had just met and Tomo had not yet entered this world. It is hard to believe how far we have come as a family in these past three years, just as this project has come to fruition. I could never have done any of it without these two, and I dedicate this book to Yasuka and Tomo.

Illustrations

Figures

1   The post-war Japanese historic bloc (left triangle) and the groups excluded from it (right circle)   54
2   Results of the 2012, 2014 and 2017 Lower House elections   198
3   A political compass of the four ideal type future scenarios of Japanese ruling regimes   222

Table

1   Types of labour categories in Japan   163

CHAPTER 1

Introduction

Thirty years after the 1989 crash of the Nikkei Tokyo Stock Exchange, the Japanese post-war boom seems now to be little more than a distant memory. Today crisis defines Japanese politics and may do so for many years to come (Noble 2012). This crisis has economic, political, social and ecological dimensions. More than two decades of economic stagnation have led to an unraveling of Japan's post-war class compromise including its famed lifetime employment system (Osawa et al. 2012; Schoppa 2006). The cost of stagnation to the state has been high: public debt is now 2.5 times GDP, the highest level in the world (MOF 2017). Moreover, poverty, income inequality and precarious employment have increased markedly since the late 1980s (Wakatabe 2015). Politically, after 38 years of stable Liberal Democratic Party (LDP) rule, the 1990s and 2000s witnessed unprecedented political turmoil, with various periods of rule by non-LDP coalition governments and "reformist" LDP leaders. This culminated in the landslide victory for the Democratic Party of Japan (DPJ) in 2009 yet was followed only three years later by voters' staunch rejection – and the subsequent self-destruction – of the DPJ. Socially, Japan faces the challenge of a shrinking and aging population (a phenomenon known as *shōshikōreika*) (Noble 2012), as many Japanese youth see the traditional family as either unappealing or unviable (Nemoto 2008; Ratherford et al. 2001; Schoppa 2006), dynamics that also deepen the economic malaise. Moreover, as the ratio of elderly people to working age people increases, the costs of health care and social security are increasing just as the size of the tax base from which to pay for those programs declines (Itoh 2000).

This situation is sharpened by gender dynamics. Women have traditionally been disadvantaged in the public sphere (Nemoto 2013; North 2009). Yet public officials are now calling upon them to fill labour shortages whilst returning to their traditional roles as mothers, to revive Japan's sagging birthrate (Kawai 2009). Ecologically, Japan must determine how to negotiate the energy challenges posed by climate change in the aftermath of the Fukushima nuclear situation and the anti-nuclear movement it begat (Calder 2013; Koyama 2013). While some elements of the crisis, including Fukushima, are recent, the crisis itself is not new (Katz 1998). And yet, though these problems suggest the need for broad changes in Japanese political economy, the crisis has so far created little impetus for systemic change. Even when the government has acknowledged the need for significant changes, such as under the Abe and Suga administrations, it has thus far failed to deliver policies capable of overcoming these daunting challenges.

In academic research, it has often been the case that separate aspects of the crisis have been taken up in separate literatures (for exceptions see Itoh 2000; Gao 2001; Schoppa 2006). For example, much has been written about the implications of the economic crisis and the class implications of Japan's shift towards economic liberalism (Cerny 2005; Grimes 2012; Kawai 2009; Lechevalier 2014; Reitan 2012; Watanabe 2007). Similarly, a great deal of research has examined the gender implications of shifting social norms surrounding production and reproduction in the face of the crisis (Hanochi 2003; Liddle and Nakajima 2004; Mackie 2013; Miura 2012; Nemoto 2013; North 2009; Osawa 2013; Takeda 2005; Yoda 2006). Other work has examined the transformations to Japan's political institutions in response to (and as part of) the crisis (Curtis 1999; Krauss and Pekkanen 2010). Finally, a fair amount of attention has been paid to the cultural and political implications of *nihonjinron*, or Japan's nationalist cultural ideology of uniqueness, exceptionalism and most importantly, ethnic homogeneity (*tan'itsu minzoku*), including how it relates to the crisis (Befu 2009, 2001, 1993; Lebra 2004; Oguma 2002; Revell 1997; Sugimoto 2010).

The underlying premise of this book is that these various economic, political, social and cultural crises contemporary Japan faces are inherently interrelated. Not only can our understanding of each be enhanced by an investigation into their interrelatedness, absent this attempt to investigate and understand connections, our understanding of each crisis – whether economic, political or social – will be incomplete. Yet if the task of understanding Japan's economic, political and social systems on their own is a daunting one, the task of weaving together the intricacies of each of them into a cogent analysis is nigh impossible. Nonetheless, this is the task that this book sets for itself. If it is successful – a question for which readers will be the judge – it will represent one of the first attempts to integrate our understanding of social, economic and political conditions in Japan from the post-war to the present. If it is unable to legitimately claim such a grandiose achievement, it will at least provide one of the first attempts to use Gramscian, feminist political economic and other historical materialist theoretical tools to systematically explore Japan's crisis as a multifaceted, complex and long-term "organic crisis," to use the Gramscian term used throughout the book to describe the crisis (Gramsci 1992).

It is difficult to exaggerate the gravity of the crisis explored in this book. This is not only for Japan but also for other countries that are home to social, economic and political dynamics and contradictions similar to Japan. While Japan's economy has remained stagnant for nearly twenty-five years, public debt has soared and continues to grow. Yet as the population ages and declines, the tax base is shrinking and the costs of caring for a rapidly aging population will likely continue to grow for decades unless drastic measures are taken. It is thus clear that Japan is facing a deep crisis with both political-economic and socio-cultural roots. This book therefore explores the complicated web of factors that underlie this crisis, demonstrating how it has evolved and why leading actors within the state and civil society have thus far been unable to adequately resolve its contradictions. It provides not only a thorough analysis of these complicated challenges facing contemporary Japan but also uses Japan as the empirical focus of research that dialogues with wider theoretical discussions about production, social reproduction, hegemony and crisis in the contemporary global political economy. Moreover, while Japan is the focus of this book, many of the dynamics observed in Japan, including population aging, economic stagnation and the structural debt crisis, are also present in other countries, whether Western European countries such as Germany and Italy or East Asian newly industrialized countries such as Taiwan and South Korea. This book therefore has wider comparative and international relevance beyond Japan as well.

1   Analytical Approach

In exploring the lineages and consequences of the current conjuncture in Japanese political economy and society, the argument of this book is centered on the following questions: First, *how can we understand the crisis facing contemporary Japan as the result of contradictions emergent within Japan's post-war order*? Second, *what are the implications of the crisis for the future of Japanese society and political economy and for the continued viability of Japan's post-war hegemonic order*?

As it traces the lineages of the current crisis and how it can be explored in the context of a specific set of ruling relations within Japanese society and political economy, this book is primarily animated by an engagement with two interlocking theoretical approaches: Gramscian political economy and feminist political economy. It engages with theoretical debates on political power, focusing on how ruling elites maintain power and popular support during periods of crisis, particularly through the dissemination of cultural, political and economic ideas that justify their authority within society (see, for example, Gramsci 1992). It also considers historical evidence of the nature of the global shift *away from* the mixed economies of the post-war era and *towards* neoliberalism since the 1980s and assesses the significance of this transformation for Japanese political economy (Ruggie 1982). This is not to assume that Japan has merely followed Britain, the United States and other countries in adopting neoliberal policies and principles but to explore how the global neoliberal context has impacted Japan's specific political economic order, variously described as creative conservatism (Pempel 1982) and developmentalism (Johnson 1982). Finally, it engages with feminist discussions of the significance of the gendered division of labour for production and social reproduction in Japan and other developed countries (Bakker 2007, 2003; Vogel 1983).

As it traces the contours of Japan's hegemonic order, what Gramsci would term its ruling historic bloc, the book draws on the theoretical contributions of not only Antonio Gramsci (1992) but also a number of important neo-Gramscian thinkers who have applied Gramsci's ideas to the post-war global political economy (Cox 1987, 1996; Gill 1993, 2008, 2012). In particular, Robert Cox's *Production, Power and World Order* (1987) represents a major theoretical and methodological influence for this work. Cox reworks many of Gramsci's theoretical insights into a more systematic analysis that is perhaps more applicable to post-war and contemporary political economy than Gramsci's original works. However, rather than attempting to uncritically shoehorn the Japanese case into the conceptual spaces offered by Gramsci, Cox and other theories, this book seeks to re-appropriate and nuance them in dialogue with the existing literature on Japanese political economy and the empirical findings of this research.

Beyond using this Gramscian theoretical framework to orient our understanding of power and hegemony in post-war Japan, this book engages directly and critically with existing literature on the political economic development of post-war Japan (see, for example, Itoh 2000; Johnson 1995, 1982; Katz 1998; Murakami 1984, 1996; Okimoto 1989; Schoppa 2006; Vogel 2006). In that sense, it provides an updated account of the rise (and fall) of Japan in the post-war era, building on the empirical and conceptual work laid down by previous authors. Yet part of the book's task is also to demonstrate shortcomings and limitations in this literature and how they can be overcome through the theoretical framework that it uses.

Because questions of gender and social reproduction represent a significant part of my understanding of the crisis, the book also draws on discussions relating to these themes from feminist political economy literature (Bakker 2007; Bakker and Silvey 2008; Gill and Bakker 2003a, 2003b). In particular, it engages with feminist theorizations of the contradictions between capitalist production and social reproduction that are manifest under capitalism. The book provides a robust empirical demonstration of how these contradictions have been manifest in Japan. In so doing it produces new insights into the nature and causes of crises of social reproduction under contemporary capitalism, while building on Gill and Bakker's (2003a, 2003b) seminal work in this area.

2 Outline of the Argument

In formulating a hypothesis about the nature of Japan's post-war order and its implications for both the post-war boom and subsequent and ongoing organic crisis, the book develops an argument about the dominant or hegemonic social forces behind Japan's post-war order. Following Robert Cox (1996), I understand hegemony to include material, institutional and ideological dimensions. Based on this conceptual blueprint, I want to suggest that the core of Japan's hegemonic ruling elite or historic bloc has consisted of a triad of actors. These include 1) the LDP; 2) the state bureaucracy (especially the Ministry of Finance (MOF) and former Ministry of International Trade and Industry (MITI), now the Ministry of Economy, Trade and Industry) and 3) *keiretsu* business conglomerates and business organizations such as the *keidanren* (Japanese Business Federation), with supporting roles played by well-organized groups in other segments of the economy, in particular the *petit bourgeoisie* of small businesses and farmers (Okimoto 1989; Vogel 2006). Moreover, I argue that the hegemony of this triadic formation has been held in place ideologically not only by certain ideas about politics and economics but also by ideas about gender, class and nation.[1]

Ultimately, however, there were contradictions within this model, and it has slowly unraveled due to both these internal contradictions and external pressures (Itoh 2000; Katz 1998. Yet policymakers have appeared unsure of how to deal with the crisis, partly, I argue because of the complexity and depth of the contradictions that have exacerbated it. Therefore, part of what is at stake in understanding the crisis is to understand how a complex and interlocking web of cultural, social, political and economic ideas, institutions and power relations collectively helped produce a stable and hegemonic post-war order, ensuring the continuity of a rapidly expanding capitalist economy, a stable regime of social reproduction and a relatively hegemonic political order led by the LDP and bureaucracy. Yet these forces have ultimately been driven by

---

1 For example, the lifetime employment system was only possible because of the gendered division of labour; the "traditional family" model of a breadwinner husband and housewife (*kindai kazoku*); and certain migration policies that tended to be exclusive; among other gendered and raced cultural constructs, including the notion of Japan as a homogeneous ethnonation, or *tan'itsu minzoku*.

internal contradictions that have led to the current conjuncture of organic crisis. The resolution to this crisis cannot be achieved simply by addressing one or two linkages in isolation from the others.

As far as the implications of this crisis for the future of Japan, it is likely that the contradictions that have led to the crisis and the crisis itself will only worsen, as long as its underlying causes are not tackled. Moreover, as Chapter Seven shows, tepid or superficial reform policies such as those attempted thus far will only postpone or displace further crisis. As we will see in Chapter Eight, only fundamental structural changes that resolve the deep class and gender contradictions of society can allow Japan to permanently overcome the crisis. While the coming decades will likely see a struggle over competing solutions to the crisis and competing visions for Japan that empower some social groups while excluding others, without these changes the crisis will ultimately only deepen and its contradictions will only become more difficult to defer and displace.[2] Ultimately, part of the argument developed in this book is that post-war Japanese capitalism was successful up until the 1990s by externalizing a number of its contradictions related to the international political economic, class-based, gendered and environmental effects of production, social reproduction, industrialization and development. Considered in this way, then, the crisis that Japan has experienced since the 1990s is an expression of many of these contradictions inherent to Japan's post-war political economic (and social) order. In other words, the crisis did not simply "begin" in 1990: its seeds were already being sown decades before then (Itoh 2000). To transcend the crisis, it is likely that a system that can overcome or at least better internalize these contradictions in a way that is stable and socially just will be needed.

3   Outline of the Chapters

Seven chapters follow this introductory chapter. Chapter Two provides a review of existing approaches to the study of Japanese political economy in the post-war era. It surveys the works of a range of thinkers, focusing primarily (though not exclusively) on English-language contributions. The chapter considers primarily how existing approaches have sought to explain the causes of Japan's

---

2   For example, the state has so far introduced some modest social welfare policies that have softened the blow of long-term stagnation to the working class, preventing income inequality, immiseration and the rise of precarious work from being greater challenges than they otherwise might have been. Yet this it has only slowed rather than reversed these trends and at the same time incurred a growing budgetary deficit.

post-war boom on the one hand, and the more recent period of crisis on the other, while also giving space to different characterizations of Japan's model of welfare provisioning and social reproduction, a dynamic often missing from dominant explanations of both the economic boom and the crisis. The chapter surveys a range of approaches to understanding the post-war boom and post-1990s crisis, including institutionalist, Weberian, neoliberal, feminist and *régulationist* approaches. It finds that while many of them have merit, none are convincing in their ability to account for *both* the period of economic boom *and* the more recent turn to crisis. Nonetheless, the chapter finds one contribution – that of Marxist political economist Makoto Itoh (2000) – to be more convincing in its account of the underlying structural bases for the changing conditions of the entire post-war era. Many parts of Itoh's argument are ultimately incorporated into the argument of the book. However, the argument developed here also differs from Itoh's significantly by emphasizing not only the structural economic conditions of the post-war order (and the contradictions that emerged within them and gave rise to the crisis) but also the underlying cultural, social and political conditions that underlay Japan's post-war hegemonic order and the way these other dynamics interacted with the economic structural factors in both complementary and, ultimately, contradictory ways.

Building on the analysis of existing approaches to the study of Japanese political economy in Chapter Two, Chapter Three gives an overview of the theoretical framework used in the book. While the argument ultimately accepts many of the empirical premises explored in the preceding chapter, including but not only those of Itoh, this chapter is more concerned with developing in abstract terms the underlying theoretical underpinnings of the approach taken. Taking the survey of existing approaches to post-war Japanese political economy conducted in Chapter Two as its point of departure, it demonstrates how this overarching theoretical approach can form the basis of a concise overarching original argument about Japanese hegemonic order in the post-war era. First, it acknowledges the underlying methodological point of departure for the book as a whole, as rooted in the dialectical historical materialism of Karl Marx's philosophy of praxis. Second, it adopts an understanding of political economy rooted in the thinking of Antonio Gramsci that draws on a wide range of Gramscian concepts, including those of hegemony, historic bloc, relations of force, organic crisis, *trasformismo* modern prince, passive revolution and Caesarism. Third, in its treatment of Gramsci's concept of hegemony, it develops a framework of the conditions necessary for hegemonic order. To that end it builds on the work of James O'Connor (2003) to see political legitimation and capital accumulation as two conditions necessary for stable capitalist hegemony. However, it seeks to go beyond this by positing a third condition of hegemonic order. Drawing on the work of Isabella Bakker and Stephen Gill (2003), it sees social reproduction as a further condition (dialectically integrated with the others) of hegemonic order that requires special consideration.

Fourth, building on these Gramscian foundations it considers Robert Cox's understanding of the dialectical interaction of world order, domestic social forces, and the state as the basis for exploring conditions of political order and hegemonic rule, while adding social reproduction as a fourth level of social praxis through which hegemonic orders are contested and maintained. Fifth, it includes recognition of the importance of political ecological questions to the understanding of political economy and hegemony and the inherently contradictory relationship between processes of capital accumulation and ecological vitality. Finally, drawing on both the insights of Bakker and Gill (2003a, 2003b) and those of James O'Connor (2003), it develops an original understanding of the basis for hegemonic order as rooted in a ruling regime's ability to maintain three conditions of political legitimation, capital accumulation and social reproduction. Exploring the theoretical underpinnings of these concepts and their relevance to Japanese political economy and society, the chapter ends by presenting a basic sketch of the overall argument of the book.

Four historical chapters then follow this sketch of the theoretical approach. Chapter Four examines conditions in the post-war period from 1950 to 1972, the height of Japan's post-war hegemonic order. It argues that key to Japan's post-war success was the establishment of a hegemonic order led by a historic bloc that represented a wide range of societal interests and that was therefore able to successfully balance requirements of capital accumulation, political legitimation and social reproduction. It first considers the degree to which this period saw the three requirements for stable hegemonic order maintained, finding that in general, the high rate of economic growth and investment, the high degree of egalitarian growth in incomes, political participation and support for the LDP, the robust birth rate and rapidly improving health indicators and rates of education attainment suggest that all three requirements – capital accumulation, social reproduction and political legitimation – were maintained.

Second, it explores the reasons for the success of this hegemonic order, considering eleven overarching conditions for its successful maintenance during this period. These eleven conditions cover the following areas: 1) global geopolitical conditions; 2) global political economic conditions; 3) the electoral and party system; 4) the state form and the bureaucracy; 5) production and the role of capital; 6) production and the role of the working class; 7) production and the role of the *petit bourgeoisie*; 8) institutions relating to social reproduction and the family; 9) structural demographic conditions and welfare institutions; 10) the role of post-war nationalism and cultural ideology; 11) political ecological conditions. The chapter thus explores dynamics within each of these areas and the role played by conditions within each in reinforcing and maintaining the hegemonic order. Third, it posits that in the context of the above conditions, the post-war hegemonic order was characterized by a historic bloc that was led by the LDP, bureaucracy and corporations but that incorporated the interests of a range of social forces, including blue- and white-collar workers and the *petit bourgeoisie*. This historic bloc was thus the backbone of Japan's post-war hegemonic order and a major underlying basis for its success.

Chapter Five then explores dynamics of the late Shōwa Period from 1972 to 1989. It argues that beginning in the 1970s Japan's post-war hegemonic order began to slowly encounter changes to the underlying conditions that supported it. These changes gradually accumulated, and ultimately led to growing contradictions between the roles performed by Japan's social, political and economic institutions and the roles they were supposed to perform. The chapter is divided into two parts. The first part of the chapter outlines key changes to conditions of hegemonic order and considers three types of change that are significant in this period. First, structural changes include not only changes to the structural conditions of global political economy due to globalization, technological innovation and the end of the Dollar-Gold Standard but also changing demographic conditions. In both cases, these changes affected underlying structural conditions and occurred largely beyond the control of the Japanese state.

Second, political changes refer to significant policy changes, either in response to changing structural conditions or as a response to challenges of Japan's original post-war order, and include, most prominently, welfare expansion under Tanaka Kakuei (1972–4), fiscal retrenchment under Suzuki Zenkō (1980–82), and neoliberal reform under Nakasone Yasuhiro (1982–87). Third, what I call institutional changes but also referred to as path-dependencies or institutional drift (Hacker et al. 2015), represent a slow shift in the function or nature of institutions to the point that they no longer perform their original role. In some cases, this can lead institutions to shift from a complementary to a contradictory relationship with other institutions and with the hegemonic order as a whole. Such changes include the mounting costs of Japan's lifetime employment system to firms; the growing costs (and diminishing returns) of infrastructure spending; and the negative repercussions of Japan's mixed member electoral and LDP-dominated party system. The second part of the chapter outlines the implications of these transformations for hegemonic order; for its ability to fulfill requirements of political legitimation, capital accumulation and social reproduction; and for the relations of force within Japan's historic bloc.

Chapter Six considers the Heisei Period from 1989 to 2012. This era marked the onset of a deep seated and multifaceted organic crisis that had implications for all three requirements of hegemonic order: political legitimation, social reproduction and capital accumulation. Politically, the 1990s and 2000s saw a constant push for political reform, including the election of the first non-LDP led government (in 1993–1996), as well as LDP governments led by the reformist Hashimoto Ryūtarō (1996–1998) and the anti-establishment Koizumi Jun'ichirō (2001–2006). Finally, in 2009, voters emphatically rejected the LDP, electing the rival DPJ to power in a landslide. Yet even the DPJ proved incapable of managing Japan's arcane political and administrative system and were swept out of power just three years later in 2012.

Economically, in the aftermath of the end of the economic bubble in the early 1990s Japan entered a period of nearly continuous economic stagnation – very low growth punctuated by periods of recession – that has more or less continued into the present. This is despite numerous efforts to restore conditions for profitable accumulation that have oscillated between neoliberal deregulation policies on one hand and pump-priming Keynesian stimulus spending on the other. Finally, with regard to social reproduction, Japan's fertility rate cratered in the 1990s, while the size of the workforce temporarily[3] peaked in 1995. Indeed, the total population began to shrink in 2008, while ballooning welfare costs could only be covered fiscally by an ever-growing deficit. This chapter then argues that paradoxically, the causes of this crisis can be found in the same eleven conditions given for the earlier period of success in the post-war era. Due to changing political, demographic and structural economic dynamics, many of these conditions now served as reasons for the entrenchment and intractability of the crisis. In other words, the conditions that initially supported Japan's hegemonic order came to account for its unraveling and the obstinacy of the crisis that followed. Moreover, attempts to reform institutions without attempting to structurally reorder the balance of forces within Japan's ruling historic bloc only made things worse.

Chapter Seven then examines developments since the return of Abe Shinzō, Prime Minister from 2012 to 2020. It argues that Abe's unlikely return to power (he was briefly Prime Minister in 2006–7) after three years of rule under the DPJ represented arguably the most successful attempt to reorder hegemonic

---

3   After declining for several years in the 1990s and 2000s, the size of the workforce began to grow again in recent years due to the rapid increase in women's labor force participation rate (as well as, to a lesser extent, that of seniors), passing the 1995 level.

ruling relations since the onset of crisis. It explores the curious ways in which Abe restored the LDP's stranglehold on power – helped by a thoroughly disorganized opposition – and generated public support for a policy agenda that was widely heralded as bold and courageous. It holds that in the period since the return of Abe in 2012, the LDP-led hegemonic order has – at least on the surface – reasserted itself, largely breaking the political impasse that had existed for the previous two decades and winning six consecutive elections with nearly a two-thirds' majority of seats between the LDP and its coalition partner Kōmeitō. At least initially, Abe's return brought not only renewed LDP dominance but also a renewed optimism about the future for many Japanese.

It sees the high degree of political stability that Abe achieved as a stark contrast to the preceding two decades of Japanese politics and asks what accounts for Abe's success in restoring LDP dominance? In answering this question, the chapter argues that Abe executed a strategy that combined Caesarist policies aimed at "breaking the deadlock" of the past twenty years along with measures designed to entrench Abe and his party's political control through covert means, akin to Gramsci's concept of "passive revolution". The former involved economic and social policies including his "Abenomics" economic program and various social welfare policies that were designed to appear both capable of resolving the myriad economic and social challenges facing Japan and responsive to the varying needs of different social groups, thus appearing to broadly represent the interests of society at large. In contrast, the latter involved various security and administrative policies that enabled the Abe government to dramatically increase its power while silencing or disarming potential rivals and critics, especially in the media and bureaucracy.

However, while this combined strategy of Caesarism and passive revolution may have been effective in restoring LDP-led political dominance – on more conservative terms than before – it cannot provide a long-term solution to Japan's crisis as long as underlying structural contradictions continue to go unresolved. This chapter begins by outlining the ways in which Abe tried to "break the deadlock" of the Heisei era organic crisis through a bold Caesarist reform program rooted in an unorthodox mix of Keynesian, neoliberal and even social democratic policies. Next, it examines how this Caesarist program was pursued in parallel to a more conservative, even authoritarian approach to defense, administrative and domestic security policy – albeit under the radar – akin to Gramsci's concept of passive revolution. Then, it considers the consequences of the Abe administration's policies for Japan's hegemonic order. It asks whether contradictions exist between these policies, such as the commitment to a renewed nationalism on one hand and the transformation of Japan into a country that is increasingly open to immigrants on the other. Lastly, the chapter shows why Abe's agenda ultimately failed to resolve the organic crisis insofar as his approach largely addressed only the superficial consequences of the crisis rather than the underlying structural contradictions that have prevented its resolution thus far.

In light of the analysis of Japanese political economy and hegemonic order in both the past and present as developed in the preceding chapters, Chapter Eight looks to the future. It discusses four different "ideal-type" scenarios for what future awaits Japan, considering the political, economic and social consequences of each of them. It explores how each scenario might fulfill requirements for social reproduction, political legitimation and economic accumulation, while considering the barriers and contradictions inherent in each model. First, it lays out a scenario whereby more traditional gender and cultural norms and identities are promoted – and their corresponding social policies implemented – through a sort of nationalist conservatism, or neo-conservatism. This policy program in some ways reflects core elements of Abe's agenda and the direction the LDP has taken over the past twenty years while also harkening back to the political program of former Prime Minister Nakasone. Second, it proposes a more neoliberal model that has political antecedents in Koizumi Jun'ichirō's (2001–2006) policies as well as those proposed by the regulatory reform advisory panel of the early 1980s known as Rinchō II. An ongoing neoliberal shift was also reflected in some of Abe's policies, particularly the third arrow of his Abenomics economic policy, which stressed trade liberalization, American-style corporate reform and labour market and agricultural deregulation, among other things.

Third, it proposes a return to the good old days under a revival of the communitarian model that dominated throughout most of the post-war era, until the 1980s. This approach continued to have a significant amount of support until at least the postal privatization of 2007, which partially dismantled the system for financing pork-barrel spending through the postal savings system. Moreover, it still carries much weight among elements of the LDP, including among lawmakers affiliated with agricultural and construction sector interests, but looks increasingly unlikely given the contradictions that emerged from this model previously and its incompatibility with economic globalization. Finally, a democratic socialist or social democratic path remains the most difficult but best option for Japan's future from the perspective of progressive social reproduction. After long existing on the margins and mainly supported by minor parties such as the Japanese Communist Party (JCP) and now-defunct Japanese Socialist Party (JSP), the 2009 landslide electoral victory for the DPJ brought elements of this program into the mainstream. At the current conjuncture, however, such a project seems highly unlikely to emerge as dominant but given precedents of successful social movement and community organizing in Japan, as well as the deepening severity of structural challenges, it may be more likely to emerge in the future.

The book ends with a brief concluding chapter that considers some overarching conclusions of the research, engaging with a number of core themes that span multiple chapters and assessing the implications of these findings for our understanding of Japanese political economy in the post-war era as a whole.

CHAPTER 2

Lineages of Japanese Political Economy

This chapter discusses the evolution of post-war Japanese political economy through a survey of some of the most significant contributions to our understanding of Japanese economics, politics and society.[1] In doing so it explores four issues, all of which serve as starting points for the overarching problems explored later in the book. First, it considers how existing scholarship has accounted for Japan's post-war economic success, particularly until the early 1970s but in some cases until as late as the 1990s. To this end, it focuses on the varying explanations given for Japan's post-war boom, critically assessing their merits and limitations. Second, it considers a range of leading analyses of Japan's post-war political order. Specifically, these works focus on the relationship between Japan's post-war electoral and political system and the 38-year period of unchallenged LDP one-party rule that lasted from 1955 to 1993. Third, it considers leading accounts of the period of economic crisis facing Japan since at least the 1990s. Fourth, it considers several leading approaches to the analyses of social reproduction and the welfare state in Japan.

This chapter serves as the point of departure for the development of the original analytical framework used in this book, which will be the focus of the next chapter. The chapter is thus intended less as a comprehensive literature review and more as an attempt to familiarize readers with many of the problems and puzzles that collectively serve as the starting point for the understanding of Japanese post-war order and crisis that is developed in this book.

1   Creative Conservatism and the Developmental State: Japan's Post-war Boom

During the post-war era Japan's economy grew more rapidly than almost any economy in history. Between 1946 and 1976, the economy grew 55-fold (Johnson 1982). GDP grew faster than ten percent per year through the 1950s and 1960s and then by four percent per year during the 1970s and 1980s (Itoh 2000). Through this rapid transformation Japan emerged as not only one of the wealthiest but also one of the most equitable societies in the world. Moreover,

---

1   Parts of this chapter draw upon an earlier article, "Production, reproduction and crisis in Heisei Japan", published in *The Japanese Political Economy* in 2018.

it did this while simultaneously maintaining among the lowest rates of public welfare expenditures in the world (Schoppa 2006). Though there were always limitations to the Japanese model of development, the remarkable success of Japan's post-war growth is hard to deny. However, the reasons for these successes are far from obvious. Within North American political science discourse at least, dominant explanations for Japan's post-war economic miracle have tended to fall within two broad camps: traditionalism and revisionism (Katz 1998). While traditionalists argue that nothing fundamentally differentiates Japan's model of economic development from those of other major capitalist countries, revisionists claim that certain features of Japanese political economy and society and culture more generally fundamentally differentiate it from other industrialized countries and thus necessitate a different foreign policy response from the perspective of the American state.[2] However, particularly since the 1970s, it has been the revisionist paradigm that has assumed a greater degree of legitimacy and explanatory purchase. While this perspective originated with James Abegglen's (1958) *The Japanese Factory* and was popularized with Ezra Vogel's (1979) *Japan as Number One*, it was especially with Chalmers Johnson's (1982) *MITI and the Japanese Miracle* that this position came to be robustly theorized and empirically documented.

In *MITI and the Japanese Miracle*, Johnson (1982) seeks to provide an institutional explanation for Japan's post-war economic growth, arguing that the state played a significant role in creating the conditions for rapid industrialization and economic growth. However, in contrast to James Abegglen's "Japan Incorporated" thesis, Johnson rejects cultural essentialist explanations for Japanese success. Decrying claims by Abegglen and others of some innately Japanese propensity to work hard, sacrifice personal gain for the good of the nation, cooperate with coworkers and obey superiors, Johnson argues that Japan's developmental model emerged as a response to the pressures of catch-up development, late industrialization and a lack of access to resources. Moreover, in the postwar context, the consensus around economic growth and economic mobilization emerged as a result of the horrors of war, depression, and occupation. Johnson also disputes rational choice explanations of Japan's period of rapid economic growth that reject the role of the state in enabling rapid growth and instead locate it solely with the hard work and optimal decision-making of individuals and firms. Instead, Johnson's institutionalist model recognizes the importance of three distinctly Japanese practices

---

2 Virtually all scholarship on Japanese political economy written by American academics implicitly assumes an American perspective, evaluating Japanese institutions and policies according to American standards and values and evaluating Japan's post-war rise in terms of American interests, what Gill (2012) calls "imperial common sense" (506).

of labour management (lifetime employment, enterprise unionism and the seniority wage system) but goes further to emphasize a particular role of the state, orchestrated through the bureaucracy, quite distinct from those of other countries: the developmental state.

Johnson (1982) understands the developmental state as a state form that prioritizes economic growth and industrialization over all other policy areas. Moreover, and in contrast to both the American and Soviet models of economic development, Johnson characterizes Japan's model as plan-rational. Unlike the American market-rational approach, the state is expected to play a much greater role in the economy, directly managing industrialization and commerce at the national level through both macro-economic policy creation and micro-level direct management and guidance of firm-level activity. However, unlike the Soviet plan-ideological model, government and bureaucracy-led planning is not seen as an end in itself but simply a means to the end of economic growth and industrialization.

Johnson (1982) draws our attention to four elements of the developmental state that he sees as integral to Japan's success. First, the developmental state has a small and inexpensive, but elite bureaucracy staffed by the best managerial talent available. Indeed, Japan's bureaucracy may have been more powerful and more effective in industrial policy direction than other countries, but it was actually smaller in terms of personnel and budget. Therefore, the second element of this model is a political system in which the bureaucracy is given sufficient scope to take initiative and operate effectively. Johnson suggests, "this means effectively that the legislative and executive branches of government must be restricted to 'safety valve' functions" (1982: 313). The third element of the model is the perfection of market-conforming methods of state intervention in the economy. In implementing its industrial policy, the state must take care to preserve competition. Johnson sees excessive intervention and a failure to ensure that the economy retained its basic competitive market form as factors that led to the crisis of the 1940s. The final element is a pilot organization: The Ministry of International Trade and Industry (MITI). Johnson argues that MITI had the right balance of powers in order to be effective without being all-powerful; carefully orchestrating industrial, financial, and trade policy in concert with the Cabinet, Bank of Japan, Ministry of Finance (MOF), and *keiretsu* (business conglomerates)[3] while maintaining a balance of power between these institutions and itself.

While Johnson's idea of the developmental state, and the role of the bureaucracy in Japanese economic development is significant, we must also consider

---

3   *Keiretsu* refers to the business conglomerates that emerged after the post-World War II breakup of the family-owned *zaibatsu*. *Keiretsu* involve groups of businesses, often centered

the role played by other forces within the state and political elites, including the LDP. Pempel's (1982) notion of "creative conservatism," or the pragmatic approach to politics taken by Japan's ruling elite must also be seen as a driver of Japan's post-war success, not only economically but also politically, as I will explore in more depth in Chapter Four. Pempel argues that "what sets off the politics of public policy in Japan is a twofold combination: first, the conservative nature of the social support base of government in Japan; and second, the relative strength and cohesiveness of the Japanese state apparatus" (11). However, key to maintaining such a cohesive political project has been the creative, fluid and flexible creation of policies and setting of priorities. In other words, the overall operative framework of the regime is conservative, but it is nonetheless highly adaptive and dynamic in the face of challenges. This creative conservatism is reflected in the tension between consensus and conflict: while decision-making processes are highly consensus-driven and the value ascribed to consensus leads many to forego private gain for the sake of social harmony, consensus is not permanent but is periodically punctuated by moments of conflict. The tendency for unions to largely acquiesce to the demands of capital – except during the annual *shuntō* spring offensive, when they formed a united offensive in pushing for sectoral wage increases – is indicative of this dynamic. While the narrow focus of the labour movement within enterprise unionism prevented it from assuming a greater social or political role and thus from becoming an effective voice within the LDP, its periodic militancy helped cement the lifetime employment model, state policies geared at full employment and a fairly equitable distribution of income throughout most of the postwar era (Pempel 1982).

However, though this periodic labour militancy and the relative strength of unions within the narrow confines of the individual firm facilitated a more egalitarian and communitarian model of development, the absence of a coherent unified workers movement and especially the relative insignificance of workers to the LDP's electoral coalition led to a relatively minimalist welfare state until at least the 1970s. The state focused on development and industrialization

---

around a major bank and with interlocking boards of directors. The main types of *keiretsu* include horizontal *keiretsu*, which often included members corresponding to each major industry (steel, chemicals, shipping, trading, insurance and banking, though often including electronics, food and beverages and other industries as well) or groupings of firms from various industries, and vertical *keiretsu*, or a grouping along a supply chain (e.g., Toyota as the lead firm with many smaller parts manufacturers and other auto industry firms as subordinate members of its group). While there were six main horizontal *keiretsu* until the 1990s, the 2000s have seen various mergers result in only three, focused around the three main banks, Mitsubishi UFG, Sumitomo-Mitsui and Mizuho (see also Murakami 1996).

without significant welfare spending and with a tax base that was far lower than other industrialized countries. Nonetheless, Pempel reminds us that this conservatism was also "creative." The regime's ability to respond boldly and swiftly to policy challenges, such as by implementing strong measures to deal with pollution and other environmental problems in the 1970s or by rapidly expanding social security programs in the 1970s (and more significantly in the 1990s), is strong evidence of this (Schoppa 2006). As we will explore later on, the nature of class power relations inherent in this creative conservatism – enough accommodation of working-class interests to ensure political legitimacy for the ruling regime, not so much as to directly challenge the balance of class forces – was highly conducive to the maintenance of hegemony in Japan's post-war order.

While Johnson's focus on the role bureaucracy and Pempel's consideration of the role of the LDP in and its creative conservatism, we must also consider the role played by capital within Japan's post-war order, as well as its relations with various elements of the state. Cognizant of these issues, Okimoto (1989) has argued for a nuanced perspective that attributes equal importance to the directive role played by MITI in industrialization and to the space left to corporations' strategies of flexible accumulation. Okimoto's work involves a specific focus on how MITI was able to guide the creation of a globally competitive high technology sector in the 1980s. Yet in many ways his contribution is to expand on the basic theorization of the developmental state laid down by Johnson, not only to show how it evolved in the 1970s and 1980s but also to "bring capital back in." Implicitly at least, Okimoto locates the *keiretsu*, MITI and the stability of LDP rule as three fundamental underlying factors behind the success of the developmental state. While Okimoto provides a systematic account of what made MITI such a successful and influential institution, many of his points reiterate Johnson's groundbreaking work. However, for our purposes his analysis of the roles played by the *keiretsu* and LDP are worth considering in depth, as they provide an important basis for the understanding of ruling relations in post-war Japan developed in this book.

As Chapter Four will discuss in greater depth, each of Japan's post-war horizontal *keiretsu* developed as a network of firms anchored around a "main bank." Okimoto shows how the *keiretsu* system enables main banks to finance their own *keiretsu* affiliate firms in times of crisis rather than forcing them to rely on government bailouts as in the United States. Under this system, downstream and upstream small and medium enterprises (SMEs) affiliated with the lead firms have to absorb much of the shock in the system to keep it smooth for lead firms but they also draw enormous benefits from the direct links and easy access to financing and markets. The ability of these subordinate firms to absorb shocks (through the cancellation or suspension of contracts) was one factor that enabled the success of the lifetime employment system. While their patterns of boardroom interlocking and reciprocal financing arrangements are much more coordinated than the free enterprise model of American capitalism, *keiretsu* are not monolithic and differ markedly from the pre-war *zaibatsu*. Interlocking ownership occurs across *keiretsu*: for example, Mitsubishi has shares in and makes loans to Sumitomo *keiretsu* members (see also Grbic 2007). Okimoto argues that the *keiretsu* system was probably necessary for MITI to orchestrate the industrial policy efforts that it made; certainly, a high level of concentration and coordination within industry was necessary for the consensus-based model across industry that MITI relied on to be effective.

In addition to the roles played by MITI and the *keiretsu*, a third factor in Japan's successful developmentalism has been the LDP, which has ruled Japan nearly continuously and with only two breaks since 1955. Okimoto argues that the LDP's success can be understood as a result of its pursuit of two overarching goals: industrialization and the maintenance of political power. In the first case, it left much of the leeway of policymaking to MITI. In the second case, it sought to simultaneously reward its supporters through economically inefficient subsidies (to farmers and small business) while at the same time constantly modernizing and updating its approach in the face of a rapidly developing and changing domestic political economy. As farmers became less numerically significant and more financially burdensome, the LDP was able to greatly reduce their subsidies without losing their political support in the 1970s. Rival factions in the LDP prevented it from becoming enough of a unified and centralized institution to try to monopolize party control over the state and bureaucracy. Yet because factions were not rooted in ideology or social cleavages but in personal and historical rivalries, they never threatened to split the party. Okimoto sees that there were four elements of LDP's grand coalition: clientelist relations with farmers, doctors and small businesses; patronage to industry; big business lobbying; and generalized voter support. While the LDP long used various policies of preferential subsidies or pork barrel spending to shore up support from the first three groups, recent decades have seen an increasing importance of generalized voters in cities, leading the LDP to become more of a mass party. The shift to policy areas more important to urban voters such as social welfare, environmental protection and quality of life led to a resurgence of the LDP in the 1970s as other parties failed to capitalize on the opportunities posed by the contradictions of Japanese industrialization.

These three accounts – Johnson's developmental state; Pempel's creative conservatism and Okimoto's triad of power rooted in the bureaucracy, *keiretsu* and LDP – share two main things in common: an institutionalist methodological approach and an emphasis on the role of the state in fostering and maintaining conditions for successful development. Taken together, they offer three insights: First, they demonstrate the importance of significant state intervention in the economy through the bureaucracy, and in particular through MITI and its highly effective and targeted industrial policy. Second, they point to the critical role played by the LDP as a political force that was conservative yet creative, able to maintain control and adapt to changing dynamics and sustain its overall grip on power by being flexible, recognizing the need to cater to a wide range of stakeholders (i.e., big business, farmers, and small business) while pursuing policies that benefited workers economically (especially with the lifetime employment system) without giving space to them politically. Third, they speak to the importance of a cohesive and collaborative relationship both between the state and industry and within industry, through the *keiretsu* system, *shingikai* government-business councils (that sometimes included organized labour as well) and the *dangō* system of intra-industry collusive government contract negotiations (that reinforced clientelistic relationships between small businesses and government officials) (Okimoto 1989; Johnson 1995).

On their own, these explanations are useful in accounting for the successes Japan enjoyed in the post-war era, at least through the 1970s. Their shortcomings lie less in their inability to explain the success of the high-growth period than in the way these explanations appear incompatible with the following twenty years of economic decline, suggesting that these accounts on their own are unable to explain contradictions in the Japanese model that ultimately led to the long-term crisis. The rest of this chapter will indirectly draw our attention to the problems with this regime of accumulation[4] by examining the various ways in which the crisis has been explained thus far. After considering a number of institutionalist and neoliberal accounts of Japanese political economy in the post-bubble period, I will sketch the blueprint of a synthetic theoretical approach rooted in historical materialism that is able to integrate some of the insights of earlier theories while embedding them within an overarching framework of capitalist contradiction and organic crisis.

However, though their influence has been significant and many of their insights difficult to deny it is important to note that not all leading

---

4   Here, a regime of accumulation refers to the set of economic, political and social institutions and relations, both formal and informal, state and non-state, that exist to aid the process of production and capital accumulation in a given society, including regulations and policies aimed at firms and relations both among firms and between firms, the state, and labour groups.

institutionalist analyses of the post-war Japanese model share the assumptions developed by Johnson, Pempel and Okimoto. Within Japan, Yasusuke Murakami's (1996, 1984) has provided a somewhat contrarian approach to understanding the period of rapid economic approach. Murakami's neo-Weberian approach highlights the role of the state in providing conditions for rapid economic growth, but from a perspective that nonetheless recognizes the fundamental significance of favorable structural global economic conditions. To start with, Murakami considers the influence of cultural factors on the Japanese development model, the "Japan Inc." thesis of Abegglen as largely unsatisfactory for explaining Japan's post-war boom. Murakami (1984) claims that post-war industrial development was buttressed by general structural conditions of gradually falling costs of production, and that this was the fundamental driver of growth. The demand provided by the American market and technology transfers from the United States were among the primary causes of this.

Murakami's argument thus contrasts with those of Pempel and Johnson, who have emphasized the role of the state as a more fundamental driver of growth. Nonetheless, Murakami argues that under these overall conditions favorable to growth, the state still had a role to play in limiting the contradictions that emanated from these conditions. In particular, the state played a crucial role in reducing the tendency toward over-competition that was caused by the general trend of falling costs of production. It did this by promoting cartelization (setting up barriers to competition that would prevent bankruptcy and help restore conditions for profitable accumulation) and export-oriented dumping-like policies (which serve to spur a rebound in domestic production, thus promoting accumulation) on an industry-specific basis during periods of economic stagnation. Conversely, it promoted domestic demand-driven production and market competition during periods of economic growth.

Murakami argues that this overall developmentalist approach kept Japanese capitalism in a state of stability and balance. This balance meant that it never become too market-driven to become unstable (through a constant wave of start-ups and bankruptcies, hirings and firings). Yet it also and never become so state-controlled as to stifle market-driven innovation and international competitiveness. He emphasizes how this produced a remarkable degree of stability in Japanese industry. In steel, automobiles and synthetic fibers, there was very little change in the rank order in size of the ten largest firms from the early 1950s to the mid-1960s, even as the scale of production increased tenfold (in the case of steel). Nonetheless, Murakami recognizes that this had a negative effect on firms in many countries outside of Japan and argues that the protectionist barriers that ensured this stability existed far longer than they were necessary economically or justified politically by Japan's relative economic backwardness. Either way, Murakami shows how Japanese state-led developmentalism was an important part of the post-war boom, though perhaps more as a means of ensuring systemic stability than in actually promoting rapid accumulation.

2 Institutional Approaches to the Study of Japanese Politics

Aside from the focus given to political economic structures and institutions in explanations of Japan's post-war order, a number of approaches have considered the institutional logic of Japan's post-war political and electoral system. These approaches have often understood political institutions as providing the basis for political stability, anchoring ruling relations while also structuring the distribution of power and goods in Japanese society at large. While these three approaches to understanding Japan's political institutions are not meant to represent explanations for the economic successes of the post-war period, they do provide implicit arguments about the ways Japan's political institutions operated to produce several decades of stable political order under LDP one-party rule, a question that is highly relevant to our consideration of the causes of Japan's stable and hegemonic post-war order overall. Indeed, as Chapter Four will show, it is impossible to understand the unparalleled dominance of the LDP from the 1950s to the 1990s (and beyond) without understanding the structural advantages afforded to it by Japan's post-war electoral system and the political relations it generated.

One of the leading approaches in this respect has been Curtis's (1988) survey of the Japanese political system from the 1950s to the 1980s, which points to several features of Japan's political institutions that promoted stability and thus facilitated economic growth and development. Curtis argues that even though the LDP maintained power, the political system changed significantly between the 1950s and 1980s. In particular, he posits that there was a move from confrontational and polarizing politics in the 1950s to consensual and moderate politics in the 1980s, which enabled the LDP to retain its dominance even in the face of changes to its core support groups, such as farmers and small business owners, which declined in number throughout the postwar period.

Similar to Curtis, Ramseyer and Rosenbluth (1993) offer a rational choice institutionalist explanation of Japanese political and social order that eschews cultural explanations for Japanese social conditions, instead arguing that Japanese function like all other humans as rational actors attempting to maximize gains within the institutional structure of the given political system. Rather than reflecting any primordial Japanese cultural characteristics (such as groupism or respect for authority), the way agents act within Japanese politics is conditioned by the particular characteristics of Japanese political institutions. The *de facto* one-party rule of the LDP up to 1993 then was less a product of the Japanese electorate's preference for one party rule than of the institutional advantages that accrued to the LDP via the electoral system.

Consequently, the authors predicted that with the electoral reforms of 1993, which brought about the end of the multi-member electoral system and its replacement with a hybrid system combining single member districts and proportionate representation, Japanese politics would be transformed, and the era of LDP dominance would definitively end. At the same time, they predicted that many of the institutions that the LDP and other parties developed internally to help win elections, including candidate-centered political support groups called *kōenkai*, the highly decentralized policymaking body of the LDP called the Policy Affairs Research Council (PARC), and the LDP's intraparty factions, would disappear, no longer relevant in the context of a transformed political system. However, as Chapter Six will show, many of Ramseyer and Rosenbluth's predictions ultimately proved wrong, forcing us to look deeper for the roots of contradictions within Japan's political system, and the problems it has faced since the 1990s (and earlier).

In some ways trying to overcome the limits of the understanding of Japan's electoral and political system offered by Ramseyer and Rosenbluth, Krauss and Pekkanen (2010) have argued that rather than declining, many of the key institutions of the LDP – the PARC, *kōenkai* and factions – remain relevant to the LDP even after electoral reform. Unlike Ramseyer and Rosenbluth, Krauss and Pekkanen reject the idea that these institutions exist solely to help win elections and distribute powerful positions (both nationally and within the party) in relation to the constraints and incentives posed by the Japanese electoral system. Instead, they argue that these internal LDP institutions developed for particular historical reasons, not simply as effects of the electoral system. Krauss and Pekkanen then give evidence that these institutions have not declined in importance since electoral reform. Indeed, at the time of writing (2021), it appears that at least the PARC and factions are witnessing a renaissance within the LDP, even if central party organs for fundraising and political support have reduced the power of *kōenkai*.

3 The Long Decline: Theorizing Crisis in Heisei Japan

Though many of the theorizations of Japan's post-war boom, including those of Johnson, Okimoto, Murakami and Pempel, were successful in explaining dynamics in Japanese political economy until the 1990s, events since then force us to reconsider many of their insights. While the period up until the 1990s saw rapid and then moderate GDP growth, the period since the 1990s has seen Japan's economy virtually stand still: Japan's nominal GDP (measured in yen) in 2014 was less than in 1996 (Sekai Keizai n.d.). Moreover, unemployment and inequality have grown while public debt has skyrocketed (Wakatabe 2015). Now three decades old, Japan's prolonged economic crisis greatly overshadows the preceding period of rapid industrialization. What accounts for this seemingly sudden change in economic fortunes for Japan and why has this crisis proven so intractable? According to Vogel (2006), explanations for Japan's current conjuncture of crisis fall into two camps. On one hand, policy-centric analysts such as Pempel (1998), Johnson (1995) and Vogel himself tend to associate the long period of economic stagnation since the 1990s with relatively superficial, incidental or easily reconcilable failures of policy (see also Posen 1998; Krugman 1998; Harada 1999).[5] According to Vogel, this position sees the extended crisis as the result of a culmination of technical policy mistakes over narrow problems. For example, he sites ill-timed changes to the Bank of Japan interest rate both before and after the bubble; the delayed implementation of banking regulation in the 1990s; and consumption tax hikes that were poorly timed to coincide with the 1997 Asian Financial Crisis as relatively simple and technical policy errors that could easily have been done differently in hindsight. According to this perspective, then, Japan's model remains no less suited to the contemporary world than to that of forty years ago and can be made to work again if only it can be slightly tweaked to adjust to the narrowly circumscribed new challenges of the world today.

On the other hand, a number of thinkers on both the left and the right have attributed Japan's problems to far deeper structural challenges (see, for example, Itoh 2000; Katz 1998). They have argued that Japan's continued economic growth after the mid-1970s (when other developed countries faced serious crises of stagflation) came about not because of but in spite of its development model, or that the model consistently overshadowed or exacerbated deep contradictions, only postponing an inevitable crisis. According to these

---

5 It is likely not a coincidence that all of these publications date to the 1990s, when the crisis was only just beginning.

explanations, Japan's period of growth in the 1950s through to the 1970s and not the period of crisis since the 1990s is what must be seen as an historical anomaly. Moreover, Japan's developmentalist model poses significant barriers to overcoming the crisis and must be substantially overhauled if the crisis is to be overcome. After reviewing the arguments of the policy-centric perspective I will examine these structural explanations of the crisis.

In his sociological institutionalist sketch of reform in the 1990s, Vogel (2006) argues that far from standing still in the face of growing challenges, Japan has chosen a path to reform that follows the path dependencies of the old system, keeping certain elements of it intact while remodeling others and forcefully rejecting any wholesale adoption of the American neoliberal model. However, unlike some of the structuralist critiques developed below, Vogel does not see the lack of deep structural reform and liberalization as a result of unresponsive institutions or stubbornly laggard politicians. Instead, he characterizes the modest reforms that have taken place as adequate and appropriate responses to the challenges of the contemporary world. He asserts: "Japanese politicians and bureaucrats and the Japanese people just do not want reforms that would make Japan ... more competitive yet less stable or that would attack structural problems at the expense of massive unemployment or other social dislocation ... why should we expect the Japanese political system to deliver reforms that the Japanese people do not want?" (45). Vogel points to an array of policy changes in labour relations, corporate governance and finance and argues that these changes have been brought about through a combination of rational economic, institutional and sociological incentives.

Vogel argues that with regard to policy reform, "the government pursued incremental reforms; packaged delicate political compromises, with considerable compensation to the potential losers; and designed reforms to preserve the core institutions of the Japanese model in the face of new challenges and to build on the strengths of those institutions as much as possible" (218). At the same time, corporations "strived to adjust as much as possible without undermining ... cooperative relations [with workers, banks and suppliers] and to leverage the benefits of these relationships to overcome their problems" (218). To the extent that liberalization has happened, in all of these areas, it has been executed carefully so as to cause as little disruption as possible. Vogel predicts a continuation of this trend of gradual reform and policy drift within the overarching contours of the existing model.

Ultimately, while there is value in Vogel's mobilization of a sociological lens and engagement with the varieties of capitalism literature in challenging the assumed virtues of a liberalization model for Japan, there are major limits to Vogel's rather rose-tinted appraisal of the status quo. Regardless of how Japanese people and bureaucrats may feel about the current conjuncture, and regardless of whatever affinity they may have for the existing system, there are obvious contradictions with the existing model that Vogel's policy-focused analysis misses. The public may be satisfied with a system that has been kept mostly intact, albeit under conditions of economic stagnation, but insofar as this status quo has only been preserved in the face of ballooning public debt, a rapidly shrinking workforce and social security and healthcare costs that are projected to skyrocket, it is unclear how much longer such a model will be sustainable, something that Vogel's relatively narrow focus obfuscates.

In a similar vein, Pempel (1998) explored the implications of creative conservatism in the 1990s, reaching similar conclusions as Vogel. Pointing to electoral reform, the increase in welfare spending and the reduced role of bureaucratic industrial policy, Pempel argued that a regime shift had already taken place and that Japan in the 1990s would be different from Japan in the 1960s. However, as with Vogel, this frame of analysis is concerned with superficial policies and institutions and misses the importance of structural political economic conditions. Pempel may recognize the superficial problems facing Japan (the flawed multi-member district electoral system, the lack of adequate eldercare institutions for a rapidly aging society and the fiscal and financial problems associated with the bubble economy and the bad debt crisis). Yet his approach fails to understand these as mere symptoms of deeper problems. In that context, while the changes that have taken place appear to Pempel as a regime shift, in reality, the underlying structures that brought about many of these problems remain largely unchanged.

Ultimately, it is hard to justify the perspective that Japan has already remodeled itself or gone through a regime shift, or a transformation in the core power relations among major social forces within the state, economy and society. Although certain reforms have succeeded in addressing superficial symptoms of the crisis as they have appeared, as I will show below fundamental contradictions underlying the crisis remain largely unresolved. For Pempel and Vogel, the changes to Japanese political and economic institutions needed to overcome the crisis were already made in the 1990s. However, more than twenty years later, the idea that Japan reformed a little bit – just the right amount – in response to a relatively circumscribed set of challenges appears increasingly untenable.

In contrast to this policy-centered approach, a number of theorists have stressed the need for a structuralist accounting of Japan's economic malaise. Writing from a more neoliberal perspective, Katz (1998), for example, argues that the crisis is fundamentally rooted in deep structural flaws in the Japanese model of capitalism. The same developmentalist approach to industrial policy that enabled rapid economic growth in the 1950s and 1960s led to the development of an unbalanced and in many ways inefficient economy since the 1970s. Katz recognizes that the Japanese state played an important role in the early stages of industrialization through an industrial policy that promoted the development of fledgling industries through subsidies and protections and therefore hastened the speed of industrialization. Yet he argues that these policies since became outdated and incompatible with the mature and declining industries of the post-1970s era. Instead, weak, uncompetitive industries are kept afloat at the expense of internationally competitive ones and the economy as a whole is dragged down by their weight.

Katz (1998) argues that at around the time of the first oil shock in 1973, Japan's leading exporters had already reached a high level of international competitiveness and that the phase of MITI-led catch-up development should have ended and been replaced with a more liberal, regulatory approach to state intervention in the economy without protections and barriers to imports. However, this did not happen, and the state instead maintained its *dirigiste* approach to the economy, continuing to restrict imports and providing protections to declining industries in sectors such as construction, retail, and shipbuilding. While imports rose faster than GDP during the industrialization of most now-developed countries, in Japan they grew slower; imports in 1990 were lower as a percentage of GDP than they had been in 1950. By the 1980s, Japan was exceptional in its virtual lack of imports for anything other than crude natural resources that did not exist in Japan, such as oil and coal. By refusing to open up other industries to foreign competition, MITI protected domestic firms in those industries from pressures that might have curtailed corruption, domestic price gouging and industry collusion. Instead, with declining productivity in many protected uncompetitive industries, the Japanese economy could only grow by bolstering its trade surplus and borrowing. By setting up restrictions in imports, the state (through MITI and the Fair Trade Commission) allowed domestic cartels to charge high prices domestically and use their inflated revenues to sell their products abroad for below-market prices. Super-competitive exporting firms gave the image of a highly advanced economy overseas, but domestically the economy was riven by contradictions and problems. For Katz, the crisis of the bubble economy was thus a culmination of this downward spiral that began in the 1970s. Domestically, high prices dampened consumption and led firms to re-invest a significant share of revenue each year for export-oriented production. It is out of this dynamic that the popular phrase "rich Japan, poor Japanese" emerged.

In arguing the need to fully abandon the protectionist model, Katz (1998) claims that the solution to the crisis is not for Japan to simply emulate the United States. Concretely, however, his four policy prescriptions closely resemble this. First, he argues that Japan must move to a more competitive electoral system less captured by interest groups and more driven by the interests of the middle-class electorate. Second, Japan must establish a more competitive and less cartelized domestic economy. Third, it must remove barriers to imports and inward FDI so that uncompetitive sectors can face the pressures of competition and improve their efficiency (or lose out). Finally, it must create a financial system where risk is borne by individuals rather than shared or dispersed throughout a financial grouping as the *keiretsu* system allowed (and most companies' bad decisions or liquidity crises were bailed out either by their *keiretsu* banks or by the state). Katz admits that such a system would lead to a significant rise in unemployment but argues that within a few years the ten million or so jobs lost by the shock of liberalization would be back (though we might assume that global competitive pressures would make it unlikely that these jobs would be high-paying or protected through the lifetime employment system).

Making an argument similar to Katz, Anchordoguy (2005) has argued that Japan's period of economic stagnation since the 1990s can be explained by its inability to effectively reform a highly interventionist economic system no longer compatible with a globalizing world economy. Like Katz, she argues that Japan's model of "communitarian capitalism" involves a highly inefficient system of protections for inefficient firms and unproductive workers that hold back more productive firms and workers, undermining the competitiveness of the economy as a whole. While this may produce a relatively high degree of equality of outcomes (something that Anchordoguy does not seem to value very highly), it stifles the entrepreneurial energy of Japanese people and renders Japanese firms less competitive than they otherwise would be in world markets. Moreover, lacking proper means to reward bold, risk-taking activity (such as through significant dividend payouts to executives), the system stifles risk-taking, holding back Japanese leadership in cutting-edge industries such as information technology and biotechnology, while incentivizing firms to make low-risk, low-reward decisions only. Anchordoguy acknowledges that the communitarian capitalist system may have been effective in an era of Fordist mass production where Japan could easily benefit from new technologies provided by more advanced economies (in particular the US). Yet she argues that these institutions are not effective in promoting growth and innovation in the economies of leading countries who need to develop cutting edge technologies themselves. In response, like Katz, Anchordoguy calls for greater liberalization and deregulation of the Japanese economy, removing protections and supports for inefficient producers and workers and for vested interests, and creating new incentives for productive workers, executives and firms. Anchordoguy thus implicitly calls for the abandonment of Japan's coordinated market economy form and convergence with the American style liberal market economy form discussed in the varieties of capitalism literature (see also Hall and Soskice 2001).

With parallels to Katz and Anchordoguy, Schoppa (2006) has tried to explain why the Japanese state has been relatively slow to respond to long-term problems of industrial hollowing out and demographic decline that are symptomatic of the crisis (for a similar argument see also Gao 2001). Though different in many respects, Schoppa implicitly shares many of Katz's assumptions about the causes of the crisis. He argues that the Japanese economy is over-regulated, the labour costs of the lifetime employment system make it uncompetitive, the state and lead firms distort the market by propping up inefficient sectors, state spending on infrastructure is too high and the lack of an external, fluid labour market poses barriers to global competitiveness. Unlike Katz and Anchordoguy, Schoppa shies away from advocating a full neoliberalization of Japanese economy and raises concerns about the American or British model. Yet there should be no doubt that his Third Way prescriptions would have severe consequences for the working class, exacerbating already worrying trends of growing poverty, inequality and unemployment (Wakatabe 2015). Moreover, in deriding infrastructure spending in transportation and construction, he misses the way this has served as an integral element of Japan's "welfare through work" strategy, discussed below (Miura 2012). Therefore, while the neoliberal critiques of Katz, Anchordoguy and to a lesser extent Schoppa are correct in pointing to deep structural contradictions in the Japanese political economy, the root causes of this structural crisis must be located not in Japan's interventionist or protectionist industrial policy but in capitalism itself, among other things.

In contrast to these neoliberal critiques, Makoto Itoh (2000, 1992, 1990) has made a forceful argument about deep-rooted flaws in the Japanese political economy, but from a perspective rooted in the thinking of Marxist political economist Kōzō Uno. To begin, in stark contrast with Johnson, Okimoto and others who continued to extol Japan's system well into the 1990s, Itoh shares the long-term structural crisis perspective of Katz, arguing that "the Japanese economy has been in continuous downturn since 1973, initiated by the inflationary crisis of 1973–75" (Itoh 2000: 1).

Itoh understands the high growth period until 1973 as being historically exceptional and contingent on at least four conditions: 1) a favorable international environment led by easy access to the American market and the guarantee of security under the US security umbrella; 2) the availability of new technologies, mainly from the United States, which enabled easy industrial upgrading; 3) favorable conditions of trade, especially cheap oil and other raw materials which Japan needed to import; 4) the availability of cheap and docile (male) labour, ensured by the steady movement of mostly young people from the countryside to the cities. The fourth point is especially important in how it relates to Japan's famed lifetime employment system. Companies could pay workers a very low starting salary while guaranteeing them permanent employment and annual pay rises. Given the relative youth of the Japanese workforce, this system of overexploiting young workers (while overpaying older workers) helped to guarantee firms a very high rate of accumulation (as long as the workforce remained young) while simultaneously providing workers with the conditions of job security and life-course stability needed to ensure worker loyalty and dedication to the firm.

Under these labour conditions, patterns of accumulation for manufacturing capital were able to raise labour productivity by nearly ten percent a year during the 1950s and 60s, more than making up for the six percent nominal annual increases in wages. Firms also made rapid investments in capital equipment to the tune of 22 percent a year, facilitating future growth in labour productivity and accumulation (Itoh 2000). Moreover, high private savings among Japanese workers enabled the Bank of Japan to keep interest rates low, which ensured that banks could maintain easy access to credit. However, this model, and in particular the favorable conditions that had underscored it, eventually eroded.

Itoh argues that the decision of the Nixon Administration to abandon the Dollar-Gold Standard, in part a response to the export threat of Japan and Germany, led to inflationary crises around the world (Itoh 2000). This, coupled with the oil shock of 1973, led to a substantial increase in raw materials costs, which Japan relied on heavily as imports. At the same time, as the flow of workers from the countryside to the cities slowed, workers found themselves in a stronger position to negotiate wage increases. While this led to an expansion in workers' purchasing power during the 1970s, it led to a contraction in the rate of accumulation. These dynamics underscored the initial decline in Japan's rate of growth from ten percent over the period from 1955 to 1973 down to four percent from 1974 to 1990.

Itoh (2000) suggests, then, that the crisis did not begin in 1990 with the bursting of the real estate bubble but in 1973 with the breakdown of the Dollar-Gold Standard and the first oil crisis that massively increased its import costs. Consequently, the period from 1973 until the bursting of the bubble in 1990 was marked by a succession of policies designed to restore conditions for profitable accumulation. Initially, by embracing emergent technologies and shutting down old plants, Japanese industry was able to increase exports to the US, restore a trade surplus and renew conditions of productivity growth as well as GDP growth in the late 1970s. However, this period was punctuated by the second oil shock of 1979, as well as the end of the US Dollar-Gold standard and the revaluation of the yen that ensued, factors that ultimately undermined exports and stifled growth. While the mid-1980s saw a return to growth and a greater export surplus, it was quickly undermined by the effects of the 1985 Plaza Accord and the soaring yen, which led to depressed profits in manufacturing, growing unemployment and reduced GDP growth. Subsequently, while the late 1980s period of the real estate and financial asset bubble brought back strong GDP growth and profits for firms, as well as a decline in the budget deficit, it only occurred through the rapid expansion of asset values (especially in real estate) and not through real growth in the productive economy.

For Itoh, then, while the period up until the early 1970s was marked by robust GDP growth, increasing wages and rising labour productivity, a variety of factors destabilized this regime of accumulation. Such factors included the breakdown of the Bretton Woods Dollar-Gold standard and the system of fixed exchange rates, economic globalization and the decline in the rate of profit. The 1970s and 1980s was thus a volatile period in which the state attempted to adjust to the new reality whilst maintaining much of the old system, managing to mostly hold things together superficially while structural contradictions deepened beneath the surface. Ultimately, however, these contradictions could not be displaced and in the wake of the bursting of the asset bubble, a prolonged period of economic stagnation set in.

For Itoh (2000), the period since the 1990s has been characterized by five significant structural challenges to the Japanese political economic order. First, the deflationary spiral in stocks and asset prices severely depressed investment and recovery through most of the 1990s. Even today, we can see this tendency continuing, as the government has lowered the interest rate below zero and yet still cannot induce significant borrowing and investment on the part of capital. Second, and reiterating the point made by Schoppa (2006) and Katz (1998), the 1990s and 2000s have been beset by an industrial hollowing out, as major firms have moved many and in some cases all of their export-oriented production overseas. Third, consumer confidence has continued to be stagnant, falling continuously even before the scheduled consumption tax hike that has already been postponed until fall 2019. A public unwilling to spend even under conditions of comparatively low consumption taxes has severely undermined the capacity for the economy to escape deflationary pressures.[6] Fourth, the ballooning public debt, which now accounts for over 930 trillion yen and more than 200 percent of GDP (MOF 2016) not only raises challenges for the long-term fiscal viability of the state but also consumes an increasing share of the state budget for interest payments (Itoh 2000). Finally, and most significantly, the decline in Japan's population, exacerbated by a low birth rate and rapidly aging society has further reduced labour productivity while additionally burdening the state with rapidly escalating welfare and social security costs. With Itoh, we can thus see the progression from a period of genuine expansion until the early 1970s to a transitory period of moderate growth that was beset by contradictions and finally to a period beginning in the 1990s where the contradictions deepened, conditions for growth diminished, and the crisis became entrenched.

In addition to Itoh's Marxian analysis of the crisis, another critical approach to understanding it has come from the French *régulation* school, including Robert Boyer (2014) and Sebastien Lechevalier (2014). In particular, Lechevalier (2014) has argued that Japan's economic crisis came about primarily as a result of neoliberal restructuring that began in the 1980s under Nakasone. Despite rhetoric to the contrary, Lechevalier argues that such restructuring of the economy was actually unnecessary at the time and done for political as well as ideological reasons. Lechevalier then contends that the economic bubble and subsequent crash, as well as the social disruptions caused by the economic crisis came about because of an incoherent transition away from the old model of Japanese capitalism without a coherent plan to replace it with something of a functional equivalent. Instead of fully reordering its political economic regulatory regime along American lines, for example, the transition involved an uneven shift towards American style institutions in some areas, while retaining Japanese style institutions in other areas and even reforming institutions in a continental European style in others. This institutional incoherence has thus replaced the high degree of institutional synergy that previously existed,[7] causing contradictions that have prevented a return to profitable conditions for accumulation, thus precluding any return to consistent growth.

---

6 And low rates of domestic consumption have not been counterbalanced by high rates of consumption abroad either: the number of outward tourists is virtually unchanged since 1996 (despite more than quintupling in the two decades prior to 1996) (JTB 2019).

7 Such synergies include the relationship between the long-term and secure financing relations between firms and lead banks within a business network on the one hand and the long-term and secure relationship between labor and capital characterized by lifetime employment on the other.

While there is certainly much of merit with the approach of the *régulation* school, and the analysis of this book draws much insight from the approach, Lechevalier's analysis is nonetheless excessively charitable to the realities of Japanese political economy in the 1970s and 1980s. The neoliberal direction (inconsistent as it may have been) that Japan began to chart under Nakasone is no doubt partially to blame for the bubble economy and for the chronic underconsumption and deflation that has followed (as well as mounting social problems). Yet it would be a mistake to argue, as Lechevalier implicitly does, that there was nothing fundamentally wrong with the traditional Japanese regulatory regime up until the 1980s. As my analysis will show, the success of this model was overdetermined by favorable structural conditions, notably a young population and favorable global conditions, that overshadowed gaping inefficiencies inherent to the model. With the right reforms, the conditions of crisis that emerged in the 1990s and 2000s could have been averted. At the same time, neither a continuation of the status quo of Japanese style political economy nor a shift to neoliberalism (whether fragmentary or consistent) could have ameliorated the underlying structural contradictions inherent in the Japanese model. Needless to say, there are reasons, rooted primarily in the nature of Japan's political order, why a different type of transformation that in hindsight might have worked was not pursued.

4 The Welfare State and Social Reproduction in Post-war Japan

The approaches of Itoh and Lechevalier provide important insights into the contradictions that emerged out of the post-war model. This is both in terms of its growing incompatibility with neoliberal globalization and regarding its increasing inability to ensure that the capitalist and working classes could each continue to benefit. However, despite the merits of these approaches, neither directly considers the consequences of Japanese political economy from the perspective of gender and social reproduction, either during the period of economic growth and political stability or in the later period of crisis and stagnation. How have feminists integrated the role of gender and reproduction into their understanding of Japanese political economy? Before we can explore how the roles of gender and reproduction are integrated into understandings of political economy in general, it is necessary to consider how the post-war Japanese welfare state has been theorized and what its gendered implications have been. Mari Miura has produced one of the most innovative models for explaining the relationship between production and reproduction in post-war Japan, using a model that she calls "welfare through work" (Miura

2012). Miura's concept of "welfare through work," the Japanese system of social welfare, takes as its point of departure the welfare state schematic famously developed by Gøsta Esping-Andersen (1990) that posits a three-world model of welfare states under capitalism.

Esping-Andersen argues that welfare states emerged as a result of different configurations of class interests in government, particularly in the early twentieth century. Across Europe and North America, three different models of welfare states emerged, depending on prevailing configurations of class forces. In North America and the UK, where the capitalist class was most politically dominant, limited, residual welfare states emerged that provided limited provisioning and left as much room as possible market forces. In contrast, in continental Europe, more conservative, statist and landed interests achieved political dominance, along with the more subordinate consent of less well-established bourgeois classes. Less wedded than their Atlantic compatriots to the values of free markets, and driven to achieve a modernization project that could keep the social fabric of traditional class society intact, they instituted programs that were more expansive than their liberal counterparts but highly stratified, designed to entrench rather than overcome traditional class differences and gender roles whilst pacifying and coopting subordinate classes into the overall state-building project. Finally, in Nordic Europe, organized labour and their social democratic parties were able to achieve political ascendancy in the early 20th century, buttressed by class coalitions with agrarian interests that were far more inchoate than on the continent. These red-green coalitions built social democratic welfare states characterized by high levels of spending on programs that were universal in scope and designed to promote social equality and human freedom, dismantling rather than entrenching traditional social hierarchies and gender divisions.[8]

While Esping-Andersen's model has been highly influential, it has been criticized for being unable to adequately categorize the Japanese model. Esping-Andersen himself has admitted difficulty in finding a place for Japan in his model in later work, characterizing it as an outlier, or a liberal-conservative hybrid. Miura takes Esping-Andersen's basic three-category model as a starting point, locating each category as the meeting point of two axes: on one axis is the extent to which the state provides support for income maintenance, through programs such as unemployment insurance, social security, disability

---

8   While "red-green" has in recent decades signified electoral alliances between social democratic and ecologist political parties, in pre-war and early post-war Scandinavia, the term signified alliances between social democratic and centrist agrarian political parties (see also Esping-Andersen 1990).

pay and bereavement pay; on the other is the extent to which the state actively supports employment maintenance, actively intervening in the economy in order to keep unemployment to a minimum, through infrastructure spending, protections against dismissal, and other proactive make-work policies.

Though far simpler than Esping-Andersen's model, this two-axis model of Miura's largely replicates his categories. Miura characterizes countries that generally provide low levels of income maintenance and employment maintenance as "workfare" states, which correspond with the market-based liberal welfare model characteristic of the Anglo countries. She lists countries that provide low levels of employment maintenance but high levels of income maintenance and similarly mirror the conservative welfare model of continental Europe as "welfare without work". Countries that provide high levels of both income maintenance and employment maintenance cohere with the social democratic welfare model of Scandinavia. Miura terms these countries "welfare with work." However, based on her two-by-two model, a fourth category not present in Esping-Andersen's model appears, one that provides low levels of income maintenance (i.e., relatively little funding for unemployment insurance, old age security and disability pay) but high levels of employment maintenance. She terms this model "welfare *through* work" and cites it as the welfare model of Japan (as well as Switzerland).

How have the Japanese state and capital mediated the tension between capitalist tendencies to maximally exploit labour – beyond its ability (or willingness) to reproduce itself – and its need for human labour to be reproduced intergenerationally? How has the current crisis come to manifest the state's increasing inability to effectively mediate this contradiction? Though a comprehensive answer is beyond the scope of this chapter, in part, they have done so through a rigorously enforced and protected gendered division of labour geared at producing and safeguarding stable male breadwinner families whereby women could be relied on wholly to take care of domestic labour including childrearing (and occasionally fill gaps in the labour market as an industrial reserve army). This policy regime can best be characterized as "welfare through work" and has included several critical elements (Miura 2012), including (nearly) full male employment, lifetime employment, housewife tax incentives, and barriers to women's full participation in the workforce.

First, through make-work projects, the state has actively sought to maintain full male employment through public financing, giving contracts away to companies in the construction industry in particular in order to re-employ working-age men during periods of economic downturn and heightened unemployment (Miura 2012). Second, through the lifetime employment system, companies have historically guaranteed permanent employment and progressive pay rises as long as their workers stay fully loyal to the company, accepting job transfers and long overtime hours (Miura 2012; Vogel 2006). Importantly, both of these policies have been implemented in lieu of generous welfare or unemployment insurance transfers, which have traditionally been minimal by international standards.

Third, by providing tax deductions for secondary incomes under 1,030,000 yen (the equivalent of a 20-to-25-hour work week at or near the minimum wage), the state has promoted women's roles as housewives by incentivizing them to stay home or only work part time (and in the process penalized dual breadwinner households)[9] (Miura 2012). Finally, by imposing barriers, both implicit and explicit, to women's full employment as permanent, career-track workers along the lifetime employment model,[10] the state has tried to ensure that for most women, getting married was almost invariably the easiest means of ensuring economic security. Through all these policy measures, the state has rigorously enforced a gender division of labour that reinforces women's economically subordinate relationship to their working husbands and entrenches their role as domestic workers. The system was thus designed specifically both to guarantee the stability of the male breadwinner/female housewife model and to make alternative arrangements difficult for women. While this produced a highly patriarchal social system that was oppressive to women (as well as to men, who were expected to work tremendously long hours), this system was successful in providing women with both the expectation and the means of bearing the burden of social reproduction work, including, crucially, child-rearing.[11] As a result, the Japanese state was able to ensure a birth rate capable of sustaining the domestic workforce.[12]

A further contribution to the study of social reproduction in post-war Japan of note is that of Margarita Estevez-Abe (2008). Estevez-Abe's argument in

---

9 While less than five percent of men aged 25 to 55 worked in non-regular jobs (including part time, contract and dispatch jobs), nearly half of all women worked in non-regular jobs in 2000 (Miura 2012).

10 Initially there were firm legal barriers that prevented women from being forced to work overtime which paradoxically reduced their employability; but otherwise, there were always cultural expectations that they would only work until marriage or the birth of their first child so they were put on an employment track that made it impossible to be a breadwinner (see also Itoh 2000).

11 This tendency is demonstrated by Japan's "M-curve," where female employment is initially high for women in their early to mid-twenties, but then dramatically drops during the childbearing years in the late twenties to mid-forties before rising again, albeit only in a non-regular capacity (Itoh 2000; Schoppa 2006).

12 For example, in 1973, the fertility rate in Japan was 2.1 (MHLW 2012).

many ways corresponds with that of Miura in seeing programs for employment maintenance and the tendency to make access to welfare conditional on employment as hallmarks of Japan's welfare regime. Estevez-Abe argues that the development of Japan's welfare system had much to do with the postwar electoral system. While this system will be explained in greater detail in Chapter Four, under Japan's multi-member district, single non-transferable vote system, the LDP was enabled (and required) to run multiple candidates against each other in the same district. This system encouraged campaigning based on candidates' personal appeal rather than simply the party label, since party label alone would not help specific candidates within a party get elected. Ultimately, this meant that the party was relatively weak institutionally, and struggled to control the impulses of LDP lawmakers anxious to win favor among their constituents with targeted (rather than universal) spending, particularly through public works and agricultural subsidies. Moreover, Estevez-Abe argues that since this electoral system tended to produce stable LDP majority governments, the LDP had a disincentive to raise taxes,[13] and thus had little means for funding universal programs, instead favoring more direct copayment arrangements as well as tax subsidies. Estevez-Abe shows how this system came to be increasingly tenuous after the 1970s, when economic growth slowed and population aging (combined with electoral threats from the left) necessitated greater social spending and the deficit quickly ballooned.

Ultimately, however, due to the inertia caused by an electoral system that made credible promises of constituency-targeted pork-barrel spending the easiest guarantee of victory for individual candidates, things were slow to change. Indeed, things only began to shift in the 1990s when electoral defeat for the LDP enabled a new coalition of parties that eventually coalesced into the DPJ, the main opposition to the LDP since the 2000s, to govern. Instituted in 1993, the new electoral system combined first past the post with proportional representation. This produced a series of LDP-led coalition governments that were more responsive to the need for both tax raises and the expansion of universal programs as well as ultimately more willing to make cuts to agricultural and small business subsidies as well as restrain public works spending, measures that hurt the traditional base of the LDP. Estevez-Abe posits that electoral reform has gone some way to resolve contradictions in Japanese political economy, which she primarily equates with the electoral system and the clientelist and inefficient system of public administration and economic management

---

13 Estevez-Abe argues that unpopular though necessary policies such as taxes are likely to result in electoral losses for majority governments and are therefore more likely to be implemented by minority or coalition governments where blame can be shared.

it produced. Nonetheless, she also cautions that insofar as Japan has shifted to a more explicitly Westminster style electoral system with strong cabinet authority (rooted in the Prime Minister), more robust party affiliation and a weakened bureaucracy, it is at risk of seeing a shift to more neoliberal political order, as electoral incentives now strongly favor tax cuts, even if reduced state revenue necessitates spending cuts.

Estevez-Abe's approach holds merits in pointing to the contradictions caused by an electoral system that strongly oriented the LDP towards building an electoral coalition with relatively well-organized *petit bourgeois* interests (particularly in the underdeveloped countryside) that was ultimately neither very responsive to working class interests (as in social democratic countries) nor to those of capital (as in the US and UK). However, there is little evidence that electoral reform has done much to help Japan escape systemic political economic crisis. Indeed, it is now twenty-five years since electoral reform and economic growth remains lethargic while social problems, including poverty and inequality have only worsened. Moreover, there is little evidence that the institutional political problems caused by the old system have been solved despite the shift to a new, pseudo-Westminster style electoral system. This includes not only corruption and the excessive influence of factional politics in the LDP's internal dynamics but also the lack of a credible electoral alternative to the LDP. While electoral reform clearly had a major impact on Japanese politics in the immediate moment, it is clear, particularly in the aftermath of the DPJ's disastrous three-year reign (2009–2012), that the reforms did little to upend the underlying structures of Japanese political order. On the contrary, as this book will show recent years under Prime Minister Abe Shinzō (2012–2020) have seen in many ways a return to the old patterns of factionalism, corruption, bureaucratic rule and clientelism.

Within Japan, another influential voice on welfare politics has been that of Mari Osawa (2013). Osawa has argued that Japan's welfare system can be characterized as following a "male breadwinner model," which she contrasts with the "dual support model" of Scandinavia and the "market-oriented model" of the Anglo countries. In this sense, her formulation reflects Esping-Andersen's three-group typology, rather than Miura's four-group typology, and places Japan with what Esping-Andersen characterized as the conservative or Christian democratic countries of continental Europe. Osawa shows how Japan's welfare system developed on the premise of single income breadwinner families, and shares with Miura an understanding of how this model was supported through a range of welfare policies.

However, arguably providing a more critical edge to her analysis than Miura, Osawa also shows how this model only served to exacerbate the insecurity of families and households who did not enjoy a male breadwinner income, including low-income, dual income families and single-mother households. Osawa further shows how despite having the most egalitarian distribution of income based on market income alone (before transfers) of any country, Japanese welfare programs did little to combat inequality and poverty, and Japan's after-transfer distribution of income was more unequal than most developed countries. Osawa points to how Japan has consistently had among the highest rates of child poverty, and how compared to other countries, an extremely high percentage of households below the poverty line have two working parents. Overall, Osawa's largely empirical analysis suggests that in addition to providing carrots to incentivize the male breadwinner, female housewife model that Miura discusses, Japan's welfare system produced intense pressures on families that strayed from that norm. Osawa shows how measures driven by Ministry of Health and Welfare bureaucrats in the 1980s and 1990s attempted to challenge this dynamic by creating more robust social supports for working mothers in particular. Yet these efforts were generally rebuffed by more powerful bureaucrats in Finance and Construction ministries already committed to the infrastructure spending of the construction state. In other words, unlike its myriad institutions of employment support, particularly for male workers (the "welfare through work" component), Japan's traditional welfare system was in no way designed to promote stability and egalitarian outcomes. Rather, Osawa suggests that it only acted as a last-minute safety-valve to support people living in poverty from destitution, not actually to pull them out of poverty. However egalitarian the Japanese social order may have been in the post war period, Osawa's analysis suggests that it was in spite of, rather than because of, the Japanese welfare state.

In some ways reflecting Osawa's analysis, Gottfried (2008, 2015) and Shire (2008) have each contributed important insights to our understanding of social reproduction in Japan. In ways similar to Miura (2012) and Osawa (2013), Gottfried (2015) has argued that Japan's post-war boom was dependent on a rigid gender division of labor under which men worked long hours in exchange for breadwinner wages. In contrast, women were required to shoulder the burden of unpaid domestic work, while also filling shifting demand for labor through paid employment in low-wage and precarious jobs. While this system served as an anchor for Japan's post-war growth, Gottfried argues that it has since been a barrier to economic expansion, while also undermining the economic and social security of Japanese workers.

Similarly, while Shire (2008; see also Shire and Nemoto 2020) acknowledges the significance of the gender dual system and the security provided to men directly and to women (and only married women) indirectly through the lifetime employment system, she reminds us that this model only ever applied to those men who worked for large firms, while in households where husbands worked for small and medium sized enterprises, women were often required to work as well (see also Gao 2001). Moreover, since the 1990s, labor deregulation and economic stagnation have led to the dismantling of the lifetime employment system among a portion of large firms has further undermined the institutional basis for stable social reproduction in Japan, and with it the material basis for livelihood security for a large number of workers.

Overall, then, we can see how interpretations have varied over the roles of Japan's welfare institutions, both formal and informal, in anchoring political and economic order, not only the period of successful and stable hegemonic order until the 1990s but also during the period of crisis that has continued since then. The next chapter will seek to anchor some of the empirical and theoretical insights about the Japanese welfare regime within a broader discussion of social reproduction under capitalism in its overall presentation of the theoretical framework used in this book.

5   Conclusion

This chapter has explored a range of approaches addressing some of the most significant puzzles and problems pertaining to our understanding of post-war Japanese political economy. It has considered the problem of Japanese political economy through an engagement over four main questions: 1) what were the causes and conditions of Japan's post-war boom? 2) what roles have Japan's political institutions played and how have they influenced Japanese political economy overall? 3) what conditions can account for Japan's period of crisis since the 1990s? and 4) what factors characterize Japan's model of welfare and social reproduction? It has considered how these various research questions have been considered from a range of theoretical perspectives, including institutionalist, neoliberal, Weberian, Marxist and feminist perspectives. Yet while the discussion developed in this chapter has highlighted a range of critical insights into each of these four questions separately, this chapter has also demonstrated the tendency for each of these questions to be addressed in isolation from the others. Building on this discussion, then, the rest of the book will provide an analysis of Japan's post-war order that attempts to integrate these four issues. The next chapter will lay out an original analytical framework for this analysis of post-war Japanese political economic order that is primarily rooted in the work of Antonio Gramsci. After presenting this analytical framework in Chapter Three, the four chapters that follow it will each use that perspective to explore the causes, conditions and consequences of political economic order of different eras of post-war Japanese history.

CHAPTER 3

Towards a Gramscian Understanding of Japanese Political Economy

Building on the analysis of existing approaches to Japanese political economy offered in the previous chapter, this chapter seeks to develop an original perspective for the analysis of Japan's post-war political economy.[1] In doing so, it proposes six elements of this framework, going through them in turn before providing an overall analysis of the theoretical perspective as a whole for our understanding of Japanese political economy. First, it explores the basic methodological point of departure of this original work in historical materialism, borrowing from Gill (1993) and others to sketch out some of the underlying philosophical assumptions behind this approach. Second, within the Marxist canon in general it locates inspiration with the work of Antonio Gramsci (1992) in particular and provides an analysis of the work of Gramsci, including an exploration of Gramsci's concept of hegemony.

Third, building on the basic formulation for hegemony provided by Gramsci, it seeks to parse out an original interpretation of the conditions necessary for hegemonic order. It finds part of the answer to this problem in James O'Connor's (2003) explanation of political legitimation and capital accumulation as conditions necessary for hegemonic order. Yet it sees this framework on its own as insufficient for understanding the conditions necessary for hegemonic projects to succeed in the long term. In addition to capital accumulation and social reproduction, it thus adds social reproduction as a third condition, for reasons that will become clear below. Thus, the chapter's fourth aim is to provide an orientation towards feminist political economic understandings of social reproduction under capitalism.

After this segue into a review of feminist political economic discussions of social reproduction it returns to its engagement with Gramsci. It explores Gramsci's notions of historic bloc, relations of force and considering their relevance to the analysis of post-war Japan. It then takes the Gramscian lens further into the post-war era through the neo-Gramscian approach of Robert Cox (1987). It outlines Cox's understanding of dialectical interplay between world order, the

---

1 Parts of this chapter draw upon an earlier article, "Production, reproduction and crisis in Heisei Japan", published in *The Japanese Political Economy* in 2018.

state and domestic social forces in the building and maintaining of a hegemonic order, detailing the relevance of this conception for our understanding of Japan. It also provides an explanation of Cox's adaptation of Gramsci's concept of the relations of force, which will be of use to our analysis in Chapter Eight.

Next, the chapter returns to consider a number of additional Gramscian concepts that are significant to the analysis of later chapters, including Caesarism, passive revolution, *trasformismo* and the Modern Prince. Finally, it briefly considers the importance of incorporating a political ecological lens to the study of political economy and hegemony, not least in the context of global climate change. After developing these various elements of the theoretical framework, it considers some of their implications for Japan, synthesizing them into a cohesive theoretical framework and concretizing them in the context of post-war Japanese political economy. The chapter thus ends with a brief overview of the overall argument of the book written through the theoretical framework developed here.

1   Historical Materialist Methodology

In contrast to many of the prevailing approaches to the study of Japanese political economy, which have predominantly been institutionalist or neoliberal in their orientation, this book is anchored methodologically in a commitment to historical materialism. Historical materialism takes as its starting point a rejection of positivist, reductionist and methodological individualist assumptions of realism and liberalism (Gill 1993; Maclean 1981). Rather than understanding theory and research as practices of detached objectivity, it sees theory as dialectically interwoven with praxis. As we study the world, we shape it, and it, in turn, shapes us. This is, however, different from some variants of post-structuralism that may reject entirely the notion of a world independent of discourse. For historical materialists, there is a real, material world, conditioned by human ideation as well as by extra-discursive structural and historical conditions that set the conditions of possibility for human action. However, for Gramsci, if the relationship between theory and praxis is not unilinear but dialectical, then we have an obligation not only to understand the world but also to intervene in it ethically (Gill 1993). The social justice dimension of historical materialist theory is thus not merely a kind afterthought but rooted in its very epistemological foundations.

Thus, the dialectical approach of historical materialism leads us to an epistemology that rejects the positivist separation of theory and praxis while also rejecting the anti-foundationalism of some other post-positivist approaches. Moreover, we see how these epistemological commitments lead directly to an understanding of theory (united with praxis) as an inherently ethical project. However, in addition to its opposition to the positivist underpinnings of many realist and liberal approaches that take natural science as their template for understanding the social world, historical materialism is founded on a rejection of methodological individualism and reductionism. Instead, it seeks to understand social reality as a dialectically interwoven totality (Gill 1993). Rather than seeing objects of inquiry as discrete, homogeneous individual units, historical materialists see them as necessarily parts of a greater whole, as well as a whole in their own right with their own constitutive parts. This is no truer than in historical materialists' understanding of the state. Rather than assuming states to be unitary and independent actors, exogenous to the international system and functionally detached from their domestic political spheres (as some realists may assume), historical materialists see states as deeply imbricated with other actors and social forces, domestically, internationally and transnationally. Their interests and identity are never given but always in flux through dynamic engagement with the wider world.

Historical materialism thus rejects the subject-object dualism of positivism and the reductionist underpinnings of other structuralist approaches. But how does it actually explain social reality? Perhaps the best way to answer this question is to consider the historical materialist approach to four issues: history, power, continuity and change.

Historical materialists generally believe, to paraphrase Marx, that people make their own history, but not under conditions of their own choosing.[2] In any given era, human agency is constrained by history: the conditions of the possible are historically given, though the direction towards which they are pushed is never pre-determined. The course of history is shaped by structural dynamics, themselves the distilled effect of past processes and struggles. History thus poses constraints on human action but does not rigidly determine it. One of the most important insights of historical materialism, beginning with Marx but perhaps reaching its apex with Braudel (1980), has been an appreciation of the ultimate historicity of even the most seemingly permanent structural conditions. Braudel's theory of history shows how the global political economy has always been embedded in deep structural foundations that largely go unnoticed and set the conditions of possibility for social life in any given moment, but that gradually change over the course of history and cannot be taken as permanent and unending conditions. Nevertheless, "history," in this way, poses real structural constraints to human action that are not eternal and

---

2 Though stated most famously by Marx, as Williams (1983) has noted, this conception of history and human agency can be traced at least as far back as eighteenth century Italian philosopher Giambattista Vico.

universal but that may nonetheless be deeply embedded in practices of daily life. Braudel's conception of history thus enables us to understand elements of both continuity and change in world politics. Rather than understanding history as a simple linear process, Braudel draws our attention to the importance of different conceptions and rhythms of time. Both the events-time that we can perceive over the course of a year or a human lifespan and the *longue durée* of slow-moving time that may appear as permanent but, in reality, is dynamic. Neither the *longue durée* nor events-time alone can explain the course of continuity and change in history; the two are in practice co-constitutive in particular conjunctures.

A further question for historical materialists relates to cause and effect. While positivists assume that there exists a simple and linear relationship between the two, historical materialists understand the relationship to be much more complex and dialectical (see also Harvey 1996). To posit cause and effect is to assume that either of these can simply be isolated, separated from the web of social relations that gives them life, without destroying the very concreteness of the thing itself. For historical materialists, phenomena cannot be known outside of the web of social relations through which they are produced and reproduced. For example, Chapter Six of this book discusses the organic crisis of Heisei Japan (1990–2012), attempting to analyze the critical context and conditions of the crisis. However, isolating discrete "causes" and "consequences" is easier said than done. Are the rise of poverty and insecurity since the 1990s causes of the crisis, or consequences? On one hand, poverty and insecurity might be seen as consequences of the crisis, given that they are clearly negative phenomena that resulted from preceding policy and structural changes. On the other hand, they could equally be understood as causes of the crisis, insofar as they directly impacted both the deflationary spiral (due to chronically low consumer demand) and the drastically low fertility rate that has prompted a major crisis of aging and population decline. Thus, rather than speaking in simplistic terms of cause and effect, this book tends to focus more on *conditions* and *dynamics* of both Japan's hegemonic order and organic crisis. The term conditions here refers both to a state, or the way things are, and a requirement, or something that is necessary. Dynamics implies change and causal force.

While an important methodological anchor to the approach developed here, historical materialism on its own is too general a paradigm to serve as a theoretical framework on its own. Within this overall historical materialist methodological context, then, I want to engage more specifically with the insights of Italian social theorist Antonio Gramsci.

2 Hegemony

Since the 1971 English translation of *Selections from the Prison Notebooks*, Antonio Gramsci's thought has become widely influential within critical political economy in general, and international political economy in particular. Originally from Sardinia, Gramsci moved to Turin when he was a young man where he observed at first hand the power struggle between capital and labour. Gramsci became a leading figure of the Italian left, even rising to leader of the Italian Communist Party, before he was imprisoned under Benito Mussolini. However, as an Italian growing up in the era following national unification, democratization and industrialization, Gramsci was also acutely aware of the ways in which the superstructural context of Italy differed from that of Russia before the Bolshevik Revolution. Not only that, he was also aware of the political and social impacts of this difference for revolutionary struggle. His socialist political philosophy thus differed in many important ways from that of the leaders of Russian Revolution.

Why is this neo-Gramscian approach able to serve as the starting point for a theory of Japanese post-war political economy and social order? Gramsci built on the political and economic understanding of capitalist exploitation and class struggle found in Marx and Lenin by adding a cultural dimension to the understanding of how political order is made and maintained under capitalism, particularly in popular democratic countries. Thus, while capitalist society is clearly dependent on economic growth and accumulation to be successful, it is also dependent on political legitimation, or consent to ruling relations, by a significant majority of people, including the working class. Moreover, this cultural dimension of hegemony is mediated – and given teeth – through various political, economic and social institutions that regularize relations of domination in ways that are seen as culturally acceptable (though never wholly uncontested) within civil society. While this consensual dimension of capitalist class-based rule is always inevitably combined with the threat of the use of coercive force, or violence, in order to maintain existing power relations, coercion can never be enough to ensure political stability. It can therefore never be enough to ensure the viability of capitalist society more generally either.

Gramsci termed this understanding of consent married with the threat of coercion as hegemony. He used it as the basis for his explanation of why capitalism continued to function and garner political support even in societies where the working class was empowered electorally. Gramsci said much about the conditions under which consent – and hegemony – can be maintained. He also had much to say about what might be needed for a counter-hegemonic movement – what he termed the modern Prince and associated with the

Communist Party of Italy – to successfully carry out a revolution under conditions of capitalist hegemony. While these issues will be taken up in later chapters, for now it is enough to think more carefully about the concept of hegemony, in relation to Japan.

3 Hegemony and Hegemonic Order

In this book, then, hegemony, or what I term hegemonic order, refers to the condition of a stable political and social order rooted in a broad-based degree of consent and support from the majority of people, including various social classes, for existing conditions of political and economic ruling relations. As discussed above, hegemonic order requires a cultural and political dimension of consent from the majority of people to be possible. Without this consent, only violence and coercion can be used to stave off the threat of revolution, and violence and coercion are themselves incompatible with stable capital accumulation, since the latter requires willing workers and consumers as well as conditions for secure investment and guaranteed private property rights. However, in addition to this general degree of political legitimacy, hegemonic order, at least under capitalism, also requires conditions for stable capital accumulation. Without these, the material basis for the capitalist system and for capitalist class-based rule is absent. Moreover, many of the material conditions for political consent to that rule are also absent. These include as an economic basis for stable employment for the majority of people, or the tax revenue needed to fund social programs (see also O'Connor 2003).

Clearly, hegemony requires not only activities to secure consent, or what I will call political legitimation, to ruling relations, but also activities to ensure stable capital accumulation. Yet these two requirements of hegemonic order do not always go together, since fundamentally unjust and exploitative class relations sit at the very heart of capitalism. On the one hand, attempts to reduce class antagonisms and ensure broad-based working-class support for political order – such as full employment guarantees, workers' rights or publicly funded welfare – run the risk of undermining conditions for stable capital accumulation. On the other hand, attempts to shore up conditions for stable capital accumulation – such as through the enclosure of common lands or more recent policies of deregulation, privatization and corporate tax cuts – run the risk of creating social dislocation and political discord. One of the key questions for our study, then, is how the tension between these two requirements of hegemonic order can be finessed.

This book posits that one of the keys to understanding Japan's post-war political order, and both the period of success – known as the Japanese miracle – up until the 1980s and subsequent period of crisis – known as the lost decades – since the 1990s can be understood by looking at attempts to maintain hegemonic order by pursuing conditions conducive to political legitimation and capital accumulation, as well as dealing with the contradictions and negative externalities that emanate from the inherent tension between these two dynamics. In this way, I borrow from James O'Connor (2003), who also drew on the importance of these two requirements of the capitalist state. As O'Connor (2003: 6) argued:

> the capitalist state must try to fulfill two basic and often mutually contradictory functions – *accumulation* and *legitimation* ... A capitalist state that openly uses its coercive forces to help one class accumulate capital at the expense of other classes loses its legitimacy and hence undermines the basis of its loyalty and support. But a state that ignores the necessity of assisting the process of capitalist accumulation risks drying up the source of its own power, the economy's surplus production capacity and the taxes drawn from this surplus.

However, while political legitimation and capital accumulation are important requirements of stable hegemonic order, I want to argue that there is a third requirement of equal importance that must be taken into account: social reproduction.

4   Social Reproduction

Marxist analyses of the capitalist system's dependence on and dialectical relationship with a system of social reproduction goes back as far as Marx and Engels, including sections of *Capital Volume 1* that deal with expanded reproduction as well as Engels' *Origin of the Family, Private Property and the State*. However, these ideas received relatively little attention within Marxist scholarship for nearly a century after *Capital's* publication. As a result, since the 1970s interventions of various feminist political economists, but most notably Michele Barrett (1988), Lise Vogel (1983) and Wally Seccombe (1974) have attempted to make up for lost time. Early feminist approaches to the analysis of social reproduction sought to bring questions of women's domestic labour into analyses of power and production within capitalism more generally (Bakker and Silvey 2008). Some, such as that of Michele Barrett (1988), were skeptical about whether feminist theory and gender-blind Marxism could every really be united theoretically and proposed a "dual systems" approach that sought to conceptually separate capitalism and class-based exploitation with patriarchy and gender-based oppression. In contrast, others such as Vogel (1983) saw the two as fundamentally interconnected. Indeed, Marxist scholars as far back as Wally Seccombe (1974) have pointed to the way the gendered division of labour in general, and women's unpaid domestic labour in particular, enabled men to work long hours outside of the home, and thus formed a key basis for the extraction of surplus value.[3]

In its most basic terms, the concept of social reproduction refers to the need to restore the vitality of human beings (and their labour power), both day to day and intergenerationally across society. As Bakker and Gill (2003b) have argued elsewhere, this includes various elements, including 1) biological reproduction of the species though childbirth and childrearing; 2) physical reproduction of individual labour power through the daily provision of meals, shelter, and the maintenance of health and hygiene; and 3) cultural reproduction of communities and societies through education, training, socialization, as well as caring for the young and the elderly.

Social reproduction and the gendered division of labour not only serves as a basic precondition for capital accumulation, as Seccombe argued. It also serves a more general basis in the reproduction and maintenance of the work force on a biological level, and of capitalist society more generally on a cultural level. Social reproduction, its gendered construction, and its complex relationship with capitalist production are thus necessary to understand both the reproduction of capitalist hegemony and, following Vogel, the reproduction of patriarchal social relations.[4]

---

3 While there is insufficient space here for a thorough treatment of debates from the 1970s and 1980s of the relationship between capitalism and patriarchy, suffice it to say that contemporary approaches generally recognize that the two are intrinsically interrelated, but that neither is wholly reducible as a function of the other.

4 Vogel (1983) argues that under capitalism, women's reproductive labor plays a contradictory role. On one hand, it serves as a barrier to capital accumulation, by inevitably taking women out of the workforce, at least immediately before and after childbirth and often for longer periods. The lack of a guarantee to stable access to women's productive labor leads capital to devalue women's labor. At the same time, reliance on an external source of income during this period of childbearing renders women dependent on others for their means of social reproduction (wages), usually men within the family. Women's contradictory relationship with the productive economy thus leads to their subordination to men, both within the workplace and at home. On the other hand, this biological reproductive labor that only women can provide is vital to the intergenerational reproduction of the workforce and thus of the capitalist system in general.

Moreover, "different forms of social reproduction can be associated with various social formations", as "patterns of social reproduction are shaped by and also shape socio-economic and political orders" (Bakker and Silvey 2008: 3). In this way Bakker and Silvey transcend the tendency apparent in Cox (1987) to see social reproduction, or "householding" as one more mode of production existing as an adjunct to the dominant capitalist system, but to see reproduction as a dialectically related to production, whatever its form, and situated "within a conceptualization of governance that involves both the public and the private processes and mechanisms that shape social and economic outcomes" (4).

Thus, feminist approaches such as those of Vogel, Seccombe and others enable us to see how social reproduction is intrinsically and dialectically interwoven with production. Moreover, social reproduction theory shows how the contradictory role of social reproduction, and its gendered effects, for capitalism plays a significant part in entrenching patriarchal relations within capitalism. Building on the work of earlier thinkers who attempted to bring together historical materialist theories of capitalism with feminist theories of patriarchy (Barrett 1988; Vogel 1983; Seccombe 1974), Isabella Bakker and Stephen Gill have recently attempted to incorporate feminist understandings of social reproduction with Gramscian understandings of hegemony. In so doing, they have explored how the contradictory relationship between production and social reproduction under capitalism – particularly in the context of post-Fordist neoliberal globalization since the 1980s – works to both reinforce and destabilize hegemonic ruling relations. At the same time, their analysis also examines the reciprocal implications for production, reproduction, and their relationship to one another in an era of profound political economic transformation.

5   Conditions for Hegemonic Order

For our purposes, it is important to recognize that social reproduction exists in dialectical tension with capital accumulation and with production more generally, while also being a precondition for the very existence of capital accumulation. Moreover, it is important to take a broad and inclusive view of social reproduction. Rather than equating it simply with domestic labour in the home, we must understand it as a web of institutions and practices. These institutions and practices exist both inside and outside of the home, in the formal and informal economy, provided by the market, the state, and volunteer community organizations as well as by private households, including activities such as education, health and welfare. We therefore refer to the mix of institutions and practices for fulfilling requirements of social reproduction that might exist at any one time as a regime of social reproduction. In the case of Japan, therefore, we must seek to understand 1) what practices and institutions constitute Japan's regime of social reproduction; 2) how they empower certain groups and identities while disempowering others; 3) how elements of the regime might complement or contradict other elements of Japan's overarching hegemonic order, including its regime of accumulation as well as practices of political legitimation; and finally 4) how the regime of reproduction is affected by changes, structural, institutional and political, to the conditions of political and social order. Building on the work of O'Connor (2003), then, I argue that we can provide a pithy evaluation of the degree to which hegemonic order is being maintained – in basic terms – by focusing on these three basic requirements of capital accumulation, political legitimation and social reproduction.

What conditions characterize or enable these three requirements for hegemonic order? With regard to capital accumulation, this includes conditions that ensure capitalist profitability and accumulation, as well as securing sites for profitable investment in the future. With regard to social reproduction, this refers to conditions that ensure that workers' labor power and society in general can be reproduced both day to day and generation to generation. Social reproductive functions can be provided either within the family, through the private sector, through volunteer programs or through public provisioning (i.e., the traditional welfare state). Finally, political legitimation involves the challenge of gaining and maintaining popular consent to ruling relations from the public, including subaltern classes. To what degree and through what means subaltern classes are coopted into the consensual framework of the ruling regime then becomes a key question in our study of the dynamics of hegemonic order.

While these three conditions are all necessary for stable hegemonic order on their own, we must also consider how they mutually reinforce each other. Capital accumulation is not only a direct requirement for the maintenance of the capitalist system and for the continuity of capitalist class rule. Insofar as the capitalist economy is the basis for the employment of the majority of people and for the provision of goods and services, it is also an indirect means of ensuring the basis for the other two requirements, social reproduction and political legitimation. Political legitimation is a direct requirement for ensuring that ruling relations can remain largely consensual rather than coercive. But it is also an indirect means of ensuring conditions necessary for stable capital accumulation. This includes what Gill (1998) has called "the three C's": consistency, credibility and confidence, all of which require conditions of consistent economic policies, general guarantees of private property rights and workplace stability (Bakker and Gill 2003a). Social reproduction, finally, is, as Bakker and Gill (2003a, 2003b) have shown, a requirement for the maintenance of conditions necessary for capital accumulation. This is especially the case if we consider that capital is dependent on the continuous supply of human labour of appropriate degrees of skill, something that is generated through public and family institutions largely external to the production process. Generally speaking, stable social reproduction is also necessary for the maintenance of political legitimation, since workers are unlikely to consent in the long term to a system that deprives them of even minimal conditions necessary for the reproduction of their labour.

These three questions are thus dialectically interwoven. While production cannot be sustained without reproduction, reproduction inherently requires a re-allocation of social labor away from production and towards reproduction. While redistribution is also often necessary in the long term to ensure political legitimation, it necessarily allocates resources away from capital and towards other social needs. In these ways, then, we must understand reproduction, accumulation and legitimation as operating in complex and contradictory ways, simultaneously preconditioning and undermining each other.

6 Historic Bloc

In the long term, the fulfillment of these three conditions – capital accumulation, political legitimation and social reproduction – is necessary to the maintenance of a hegemonic order. Yet aside from this proposition, we must also ask how a hegemonic order is formed, what social forces it represents, and what subaltern forces it excludes. Certain critical accounts of political order in capitalist societies have been characterized (perhaps inaccurately) as providing simplistic analyses of power relations, arguing that the capitalist class alone holds power, directly or indirectly, and their interests alone are reflected in political decision-making (see, for example, Marx and Engels 2008; Miliband 1969). In contrast, a Gramscian orientation of power and hegemonic ruling relations sees things differently. Following Gramsci, I want to understand the power relations inherent in any hegemonic order as being constituted through an historic bloc. An historic bloc can be understood as a coalition of different and even competing class and social forces that are brought together in history to form a coalition of rule. For example, in his own exploration of the concept, Gramsci saw how modern Italy of the *Risorgimento* brought together rural landowners, the urban bourgeoisie and the clergy into a ruling coalition, with each group compromising certain goals in order to maintain a ruling coalition with broad-based support.

However, while such an analysis recognizes how hegemony requires compromise among a broad range of social forces in order to maintain power in the long term, we must not mistake this recognition of the broad and cross-class nature of historic blocs for a total flattening of power relations. Within any historic bloc, certain social forces – generally the ruling economic class as well as core elements of the state with high degrees of institutional power – possess stronger bases of support, whether economic, military, political or cultural, and form the core element of the historic bloc.[5] Therefore, not only compromise and consent but also power and coercion are inherent in hegemonic ruling relations, and a hegemonic order wherein the power bloc is unable to impose its will on other, secondary social forces is just as unstable as one where the power bloc refuses compromise and cooperation. In the case of Japan, as I will develop further in Chapter Four, the post-war era saw the creation of an historic bloc that incorporated a broad range of social forces, including farmers, the *petit bourgeoisie*, middle-class *sararīman*, blue-collar workers and their families. Yet despite incorporating these groups to varying degrees, what was most significant was how this historic bloc was ultimately led by the tripartite leadership of the LDP, the bureaucracy, and corporations. Thus, while all these groups were incorporated into the historic bloc and had their interests represented to some degree, the degree of incorporation and the amount of power held by each social force was unequal.

Figure 1 presents a three-level hierarchy of the post-war Japanese historic bloc. The LDP, business and bureaucracy represent the top layer of the hierarchy, as the driving force behind post-war Japanese politics. In contrast, at the second level, groups including farmers, small businesses and doctors are represented. These groups generally enjoyed high degrees of political integration and were able to directly affect politics but were not fundamental agents of change and relied on the upper level of forces to advance their interests. Finally, the lowest level, which effectively included privileged and secure workers and their families, were incorporated as well, though much more tenuously. Indeed, their ability to influence policy and to enjoy policy benefits was highly mediated by capital, partially reflecting the corporatist nature of unionism that developed in post-war Japan. Moreover, in times where Japan faced challenges to the conditions of hegemonic order (such as an economic downturn),

---

5   This corresponds with what Jessop (2012) has called a power bloc.

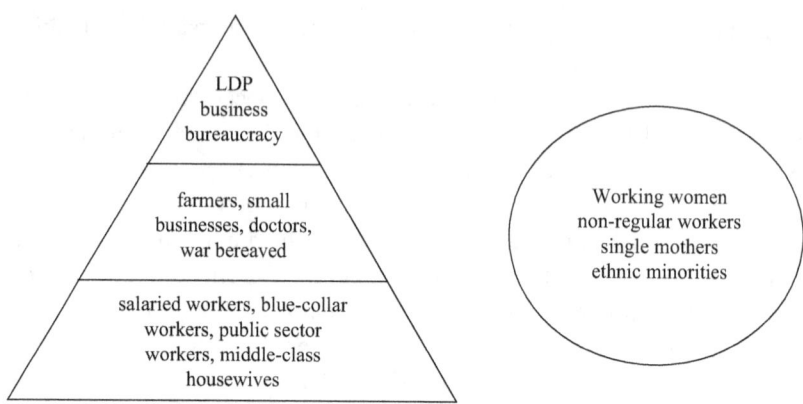

FIGURE 1   The post-war Japanese historic bloc (left triangle) and the groups excluded from it (right circle)

these groups were the first to feel the pinch. Their integration into the historic bloc is thus more ambiguous and shifting.

While this three-level hierarchy shows how Japan's post-war historic bloc was broad-based, it is important to note that however broad-based it was it was never universal. The circle on the right side of Figure 1 indicates all of the groups who were excluded from the historic bloc, and in many ways their omission and suppression are just as illuminating as the study of the constituent forces of the historic bloc itself.

7 Explaining Change: Conjunctural and Organic

While the above analysis shows how an historic bloc provides the political and social basis for hegemonic order, we must also ask what types of conditions are needed to ensure a balance between requirements for stable social reproduction, capital accumulation, and political legitimation? I argue that three types of conditions exist: structural conditions, political conditions, and institutional conditions. Structural conditions include conditions of world order and global political economy, as well as structural demographic conditions. Political conditions include more immediate conditions that result from political events, such as an election or a major policy enactment. Institutional conditions, such as relations among firms or between the bureaucracy and Cabinet, exist somewhere in the middle: they are neither as easily mutable as political conditions, nor are they as immutable as structural conditions.

These three types of conditions also signify three types of changes. Over time, structural, institutional and political changes impact the overarching conditions for hegemonic order. Though the categories employed here vary somewhat from those of a conventional Gramscian analysis, there is some overlap with Gramsci's understanding of the difference between the organic and conjunctural. Conjunctural changes occur relatively quickly and immediately, and thus closely resemble the notion of political changes developed here. In contrast, organic changes are much slower moving and gradual, and thus fit more closely with the notion of structural change (the category of institutional change falls somewhere in the middle). For Gramsci, the "organic" refers to relatively permanent, underlying structural conditions. Organic phenomena are deeply rooted, slow to evolve, but ultimately of greater significance than conjunctural phenomena. In contrast, the conjunctural refers to immediate and spontaneous events and phenomena. Conjunctural changes tend to be more superficial, but they can also signify an organic crisis, or a breakdown of organic structures due to the intensification of contradictions. While these different temporal orientations toward change are relevant to the analysis of post-war Japanese hegemonic order as a whole, they are particularly important to Chapter Five, which explores the transitional period of the 1970s and 1980s.

While this notion of different types of changes is central to historical materialist analysis, another way in which Gramsci develops the distinction between the organic and the conjunctural is in his orientation toward crisis. In particular, it is Gramsci's concept of organic crisis – and its dialectical relationship with hegemonic order – that is the focus of the next section.

8   Organic Crisis

Gramsci (1992) understood organic crisis as situations whereby "the old is dying and the new cannot be born" (276). The term thus refers to a deep, multifaceted, structural crisis manifest in various elements of society, with various morbid symptoms reflected in daily life. For Gramsci, an organic crisis constitutes a significant rupture to the basis for stable hegemonic order, prompting a transformation of the ruling historic bloc. Part of the question in understanding organic crisis, then, is not only to locate the various interrelated elements of the crisis (which may involve economic, political, demographic, cultural, ecological, or other elements), how they overlap and make easy solutions to the crisis difficult. Instead, it equally important to consider what implications various attempts to resolve the crisis might have for the political relations of force built into the ruling historic bloc.

The distinction between organic and conjunctural is equally important as a means of differentiating different types of crisis. A conjunctural crisis involves an immediate, short-term disruption of conditions needed for the stable reproduction of existing structures of hegemony (such as a stock market crash). In contrast, an organic crisis indicates a crisis rooted in deep-seated contradictions within the structures that constitute a hegemonic order, as with the Italy of the 1920s and '30s that Gramsci lived in or contemporary Japan. Unlike conjunctural crises, organic crises tend to evolve more slowly over time, emerging gradually. Moreover, because they take root deep within the structures of a hegemonic order, they cannot easily be solved or overcome without a reorientation of hegemonic order, enough to solve the contradictions at the root of the crisis. Given that such solutions often come at significant costs to the ruling forces of hegemonic order, it is unlikely that such radical change will be sought immediately: instead, attempts to solve the crisis merely by displacing its symptoms temporary will likely be pursued. However, this is not a long term or permanent solution, and the crisis cannot be solved until the structural contradictions underscoring it are alleviated, including through a reordering of ruling relations within the historic bloc.

9 World Order, Forms of State, Social Forces

While Antonio Gramsci's thinking of hegemony and organic crisis is of significant value to our understanding of post-war order in Japan, there are certain ways that his theory can be further enlivened to be more relevant to conditions in the contemporary world. For example, Robert Cox (1987) has developed a theoretical framework for exploring conditions of political economy since the 19th century from a perspective that draws on the insights of Gramsci, among others.

Gramsci's conception of politics emphasizes not only the state but also civil society as a realm wherein power relations are manifest and where the creation, maintenance and contestation of hegemony take place. Gramsci's concept of the integral state – the fusion of the narrowly defined state and the wider civil society that surrounds it – draws to our attention the need to see how struggles for power are manifest not only within the state – among parties, or between the government and the bureaucracy – but also between the state and civil society and within different segments of civil society, whether class-based or otherwise. Building on this insight of Gramsci, Cox seeks to expand the analysis further, but adding another level of analysis: world order. For Cox, world order acts as a structural constraint on both states and civil societies, though one that is malleable and in flux. It provides conditions of permissiveness to particular domestic regulatory regimes – state-society relations – and thus must be understood as a level of analysis that is ontologically separate from – though intrinsically interlinked with – the domestic level. Cox thus presents a formulation that suggests that there are three different though dialectically interrelated spheres wherein these power struggles take place: world order, the state, and civil society.

Cox draws our attention to the need to understand the state as a dynamic and heterogeneous entity and for this reason he uses the term "forms of state" to refer to it. Rather than observing one universal model of the state, Cox sees a multiplicity of forms of state, which vary over time and space, changing as the overarching conditions of world order and the underlying dynamics of civil society themselves change. As for civil society, Cox uses the term "social forces" to encapsulate all the entities in struggles over power that take place outside of (and inside) the formal realm of the state. This includes the productive economy, which Cox sees as taking many forms over time, depending on the presence or absence of four types of production relations, coercion, custom, clientelism and contract. For Cox, these social forces play a key role in developing certain constellations of state forces; he argues that forms of state are "largely a product of the configuration of social classes within a historic bloc on one hand and the permissiveness of world order on the other" (147–8). Together, the form of state and constellation of social forces struggling for power in the productive economy form a mode of social relations of production.

Cox emphasizes the importance of both social forces "below" the level of the state in the productive economy and "above" the state at the level of world order. In addition, recent contributions to global political economy have stressed the increased significance – particularly since the 1970s – of transnational actors to world political affairs (Gill 2008; van der Pijl 1998). For Gill and others, the transnational is a level of social order that is neither international (i.e., comprising the relationships "in between" various fully formed and autonomous national states) nor domestic (solely rooted within the fixed boundaries of a particular national state formation). Instead, it is manifest in a way that transcends the very notion that the international realm is populated merely by autonomous national states with their own hermetically sealed domestic societies. In other words, global politics can be directly impacted by sub-national actors (such as corporations, organizations or even individuals) that participate in global politics not merely indirectly through their respective states, but directly as well.

Within Cox's formation, therefore, states are too often assumed as the vehicles for transmitting the interests of domestic social forces into the domain of world order, and for instituting the prerogatives of world order as domestic policy in ways that subsequently affect domestic social forces. This approach, however, masks the way that otherwise domestic social forces can directly lobby and impact policy and politics both at the level of world order and within other states, such as the way the American toy retailer Toys"R"Us (through its partnership with McDonald's) successfully lobbied the Japanese government to relax restrictions on big-box retail stores in the late 1990s (Kay 1996). Such forces are clearly not direct features of world order themselves since they may be completely dissociated from both international institutions and the institutions of the states from which they emanate. Moreover, their actions may be merely bilateral, directing attention merely to one aspect of policy or political economic relations in one country, with little concern for "world order" as a whole. At the same time, they cannot simply be categorized as domestic social forces, insofar as they find themselves able to directly effect change in foreign countries, without even requiring the services of their home country government as a weigh-station. A transnational approach, which recognizes these transactions that cross borders without being crystalized within the narrow confines of "Foreign Policy" is therefore needed to understand these dynamics.

10   Relations of Force

While this distinction between the three levels of analysis – world order, the state, and society – can provide a degree of conceptual clarity in our analysis of the struggle over ruling relations, we must also ask what forces and factors drive that struggle and wider processes of social change? What forces manifest to transform history, either through the daily course of events or over the course of decades or centuries? For Gramsci, the relations of force within social formations shape processes of change and continuity. Gramsci sees the relations of force as the conditions of possibility for social transformation: instruments of power necessary though not sufficient for the realization of social change (or for the maintenance of status quo arrangements). For Gramsci, relations of force involve military, political and social components, and their united deployment is central to both the maintenance of and resistance to hegemonic rule. However, while relations of force may generally be dominated by the hegemonic or ruling regime, in moments of crisis, when the ideological or material foundations of hegemonic rule become destabilized, there exists the potential for social transformation. Importantly, this potential exists only insofar as counter-hegemonic social forces possess the capabilities to alter or transform the relations of force and to displace the existing hegemonic formation.

For Gramsci, then, the mobilization of relations of force is a necessary prerequisite to the prevention or realization of transformative social change.

In international relations theory, Gramsci's formulation of the relations of force has been adopted as a blueprint for many historical materialists to explain processes of continuity and change – the maintenance and contestation of existing power configurations – in the global political economy. Cox (1987) has reworked Gramsci's earlier formulation to explain the relations of force as the combination of material (including not only military but also political economic forms of power), institutional and ideational or ideological configurations of power central to the maintenance and contestation of hegemony in the global polity. Cox explores how this conceptual blueprint can help us understand relatively long and stable periods of hegemonic order under *pax britannica* and *pax americana* respectively, as well as the gradual erosion of the structural bases for their hegemony that led to crises and eventually (at least in the case of *pax britannica*) to their decline. Cox's model further challenges the one-dimensional understanding of power relations implicit in neorealism that focuses exclusively on horizontal power struggles between nation states by conceiving power as multidimensional and manifested on vertical (hierarchical) as well as horizontal axes. The hierarchical, imperialist relations inherent to *pax americana* and *pax britannica* are just as important as horizontal rivalries between states to the global political order. Moreover, such hierarchical relations extend beyond interstate conflicts and are increasingly manifest between states and non-state market actors in the global political economy.

This question of the relations of force and the ways various social forces struggle to maintain or overturn hegemonic ruling relations, depending on degrees of material, institutional and ideational relations of force is thus highly significant to our understanding of the drivers of social change overall. In that context, we will return to the concept of the relations of force in our discussion of the future direction of Japanese hegemonic order in Chapter Eight.

11   Caesarism, Passive Revolution and Trasformismo

If organic crisis results from inherent tensions and contradictions within an historic bloc, how might conditions of hegemonic order be restored in ways that entrench the power of prevailing ruling forces? Chapter Seven uses Gramscian concepts of Caesarism and passive revolution to explore Japan under the reign of Abe Shinzō between 2012 and 2020. Among all of Gramsci's concepts, Caesarism is one of the least well understood. Partially due to its extensive use outside of Gramsci (for a systematic history of Caesarism see

Baehr, 1999), Caesarism is often assumed to be the domain of authoritarian or fascist regimes. However, while Gramsci recognized Mussolini as an example of Caesarism, his understanding of the concept was not limited to authoritarian strongmen, including British Labour leader Ramsay MacDonald with Bismarck, Cromwell, Napoleon I and Napoleon III.[6] Following Gramsci, in the analysis of Caesarism under Abe developed below my own use of the term is not meant to be pejorative. Rather, it is meant to convey the Abe regime's attempt to cultivate an image of political boldness and vision capable of resolving the political stalemate of the past twenty years.

Key to Gramsci's understanding of Caesarism is therefore not its affiliation with fascist authoritarianism, but rather its ability to "break the deadlock" between rival class forces. Gramsci saw Caesarism as emerging under conditions where two opposing class forces, neither of which is preponderant, threaten to destroy each other if left unresolved. Under these conditions, it is through the intervention of a third force who is capable of "breaking the deadlock," restoring conditions for hegemony in a way that ultimately sides with one of the class forces but with sufficient concessions to the other side in order to obtain its (at least partial) consent, that the impasse can be overcome. Gramsci understood Caesarism as having both progressive and reactionary forms, depending on whether a Caesarist sought to "break the deadlock" under terms favorable to the restoration of class power for the old elite (reactionary) or to lead in the interests of the progressive class forces challenging the old order (progressive).[7]

Unlike Caesarism, passive revolution is a concept widely understood to originate with Gramsci, and much more often utilized in Gramscian political analysis. Gramsci sees passive revolution as a revolution from above, whereby a ruling elite tries to reorder power relations within an historic bloc in response to conditions of organic or conjunctural crisis without provoking any challenge to its own power. This sort of revolution differs significantly from the more active revolutions experienced in times of real counter-hegemonic upheaval, such as the Russian, French and Chinese revolutions. In contrast, Gramsci saw Italy of the *Risorgimento* as an example of a passive revolution, as

---

6 For a recent analysis of Caesarism in American President Donald Trump, see Heino (2020).
7 Gramsci cites Napoleon I, who broke the deadlock in favor of the bourgeoisie (over the royalists and aristocracy) as an example of progressive Caesarism. In contrast, Gramsci sees Bismarck, who sided with the Junkers – albeit with enough concessions to the bourgeoisie and working class to gain their consent to his unifying (in both class and national terms) hegemonic project – as an example of reactionary Caesarism.

the old, agrarian and ecclesiastical power structures largely retained their authority despite the transition to modernity and capitalism. Indeed, the same can be said for Germany, where the Junkers remained the dominant class force after German unification, and Japan of the Meiji Restoration, where a group of high-ranking *samurai* led the overthrow of the Tokugawa Shogunate and held oligarchical political power over the first six decades of modern Japan (beginning in the 1870s).

In the context of this book, Chapter Seven uses a Gramscian conception of passive revolution to explore the attempts of the government of Abe Shinzō to covertly pursue a conservative, nationalist and even soft-authoritarian agenda away from public view. Chapter Eight then considers the prospects for a passive revolution of this sort, where prevailing class power relations within the hegemonic order can be maintained through a recalibration of political order in response to the organic crisis facing contemporary Japan after Abe. However, while it sees a continuation of passive revolution in the neo-conservative vein that Abe himself pursued as leader as one scenario of passive revolution in the future, it also considers the prospects for a different kind of passive revolution through a more thoroughgoing neo-liberal reordering of the LDP's hegemonic project.

Similar to passive revolution, Gramsci's concept of transformism, or *trasformismo* is also of significance to the analysis developed in Chapters Seven and Eight. *Trasformismo* speaks to the tendency for hegemonic projects to co-opt efforts from within civil society that initially seek to oppose or challenge hegemonic order. In such moments, rather than forcefully repressing these agitations from within civil society, a ruling regime may instead seek to disarm them of their counter-hegemonic potential and repurpose them, thereby extending the degree of normative legitimacy enjoyed by the ruling regime. Thus in our discussion of the ways Japan's ruling regime has weathered challenges from subaltern groups and the political forces that represent them to pursue more progressive policies that enable greater inclusion within the historic bloc by these groups, we must consider how *trasformismo* has operated as a strategy by the ruling elite to coopt the forces behind these challenges without being forced to accept any shift in the relations of force among various elements of the ruling historic bloc.

12 Counter-hegemony and the (Post-) Modern Prince

In contrast to these expressions of the ruling elite's attempts to restore conditions for hegemonic rule under crisis conditions, we must also ask how subaltern classes might transform ruling relations and seize power themselves. Important in that regard is Gramsci's concept of the modern Prince, which Gill (2008) has updated into the post-modern Prince.[8] Gramsci drew his inspiration for the modern Prince from Machiavelli's *Prince*, which represented a political ruler interested in ruling based on what Gramsci termed the national popular collective will. For Gramsci, the modern equivalent of this prince was the Communist Party (which he led) and saw as the key vehicle for achieving a successful counterhegemonic revolution, first through a process of war of position (socio-cultural change and the intellectual and moral reform of society led by organic intellectuals of the left) and then through a war of movement (the swift seizure of political through a revolution, election, or coup). Chapter Eight thus partially considers how and whether any counter-hegemonic force, a "Japanese (post-)modern Prince", might form to seize power and push for a permanent resolution to the organic crisis that is progressive and democratic, while considering what social forces might coalesce to form such a movement.

13   Political Ecology

While social reproduction and gender have often been neglected in discussions of Japanese political economy, including both those of the period of rapid economic growth and that of political crisis, as I discussed in the previous chapter, recent approaches by Miura and others have sought to integrate gender and reproduction into analyses of Japan's overall political economic regime. In contrast, one issue that remains almost completely neglected is that of the environment. While it may have been something easily taken for granted in previous decades, in the wake of the alarming destruction of the biosphere and catastrophic effects of climate change that appear an almost inevitable consequence of capitalism as we know it, it is almost impossible to imagine how any sound and thorough critical analysis of political economy – whether that of Japan or elsewhere – can continue to ignore the environment, the way ecologies shape and constrain pathways of development and policymaking and conversely how environments are shaped (and so very often destroyed) as a result of political economic processes.

---

8   Focusing on transformative politics at the global level, Gill (2000) sees the post-modern Prince partly in embryo in the transnational network of progressive social movements that developed in the 1990s in opposition to neoliberal globalization, what has been referred to as the "alter-globalization movement" and was embodied by the World Social Forum held in Porto Alegre, Brazil (see also Gill 2012).

This book is not meant to be a "political ecology of post-war Japan" and the limited incorporation of a political ecological dimension is therefore sure to disappoint some. Nonetheless, it is imperative to at least engage on a basic level with some of the political ecological challenges posed by Japan's post-war hegemonic order and what the consequences of those have been. This includes not only issues of environmental destruction but also access to natural resources, including energy in particular, the varying availability of which has had major impacts on the trajectory of Japanese post-war development.

14 Towards a Gramscian Feminist Approach to the Japanese Post-war Order

Building on many of the foundational insights developed in the previous chapter, the rest of this book will argue based on the theoretical framework developed in this chapter that Japanese political economy, since at least the early 1970s, has been beset by a number of structural contradictions. These contradictions have deepened over the course of the past forty years and that can only be overcome through a significant restructuring of Japanese political economy and social relations. Moreover, these contradictions emerged out of changes in the conditions that underlay the post-war hegemonic order. Yet rather than having their root causes addressed, they were only addressed superficially. Policies that ensured the basic hegemonic order could remain intact were pursued instead of those that addressed the core contradictions. However, as overarching conditions amenable to the existing order were replaced with those that undermined it, it became increasingly difficult for the state maintain the existing hegemonic order in the face of these contradictions.

To understand the contemporary conjuncture of Japanese political economy, we must ask two questions: First, what characterizes the relations among various social forces and how did those relations secure and reproduce the hegemonic order during the post-war period? In other words, what conditions enabled and reinforced the hegemony of the ruling historic bloc? Second, in what way were those relations characterized by or dependent on contradictions, which eventually became destabilizing forces for the existing order? After exploring a basic blueprint for understanding the configuration of ruling relations among social forces integral to the maintenance of the hegemonic order, I will consider three basic contradictions that emerged over time as a result of these social relations and that ultimately served to undermine the stability of the hegemonic order.

Building on Okimoto's (1989) blueprint for post-war ruling relations in Japanese society, I argue that the post-war order was characterized by an historic bloc that centered on three core forces: the LDP, the *keiretsu* and the bureaucracy (and in particular MITI).[9] However, what was ingenious about this hegemonic project was how it could legitimately claim to represent a wide range of social forces, including white-collar workers, blue-collar workers, farmers, small businesses, large corporations, small firms and even housewives. Nonetheless, while each group enjoyed benefits and supports from the system, each also bore costs associated with its reproduction. For example, white-collar workers for large corporations benefited from steady pay raises, lifetime employment and relatively low income taxes (Steinmo 2010). However, they paid for this by providing total loyalty to the company and by refraining from organizing as a class politically (Pempel 1982). Similarly, blue-collar workers benefited from this system by having relatively stable employment as publicly funded infrastructure projects steadily provided jobs as part of what Miura has termed "welfare through work" (2012). Yet they lacked the same benefits of lifetime employment, and their labor was more flexible (Steinmo 2010). Farmers benefited through substantial price subsidies and small businesses received strong market protections and tax subsidies (Okimoto 1989; Katz 1998). However, in both cases, a lack of adequate publicly funded welfare provisions rendered them unstable even as they relied on the state's favor in other ways (Schoppa 2006).

Leading corporations benefited immensely from the support of the state, relying heavily on MITI and the MOF for access to financing, information, and technology but they were simultaneously expected to bear the costs of welfare for their workers and faced relatively high corporate taxes (Miura 2012; Schoppa 2006; Steinmo 2010). Similarly, their subsidiary firms benefited from the *keiretsu* system by having relatively secure access to markets and access to capital through preferential and long-term relationships with lead firms and banks. Conversely, they were expected to act as shock absorbers in times of economic downturn so that the lifetime employment provisions of lead firms could be maintained (Okimoto 1989). Finally, housewives benefited indirectly from a system designed to provide male breadwinners with a family wage under secure conditions over the course of a career. This saved them from

---

9 Among these three institutions (and especially the bureaucracy), there was an overwhelming concentration of graduates from Tokyo University, and the Faculty of Law in particular, creating a clique of elites across sectors with interpersonal connections dating back to their early twenties, what has been known as a *gakubatsu* (Johnson 1982; Kerbo and McKinstry 1995).

having to work long and hard hours as their husbands were doing. However, these women were not only highly dependent on their husbands but were also highly limited in their ability to pursue careers of their own. Moreover, housewives were forced to bear much of the burden of social reproduction and care work, not only for their husbands and own children but also for their parents and husbands' parents given the underdeveloped public eldercare system that existed until the late 1990s (Schoppa 2006).

Clearly, each group had to pay a price to keep this system afloat and not everyone benefited equally. Nonetheless, this LDP-led ruling regime appeared committed to consensually representing the interests of a broad swathe of social forces and played a significant role in ensuring conditions of systemic stability. Indeed, the hegemonic nature of this political order is reflected in the fact that during much of the post-war era, as many as ninety percent of Japanese people identified as members of the middle class. Ultimately, the pervasive hegemony and widespread legitimacy of this order played a significant role in promoting Japan's rapid economic rise. Thus, in addition to the favorable international conditions of the post-war era that Itoh (2000) outlines and the specific developmental strategies effectively developed by MITI that Johnson (1982) emphasizes, we must recognize how the broad popular base of support behind Japan's post-war hegemonic order was a major contributor to the success of Japanese capitalism. While this hegemonic order may have been rooted in the triad of the LDP, bureaucracy and *keiretsu* it relied on consent from virtually all segments of society, including farmers, small-business owners, salaried workers and housewives.

As the next chapter will show, this stable historic bloc provided, along with a number of other structural conditions, one basis for the robust hegemonic order that characterized the first two decades of the post-war. However, in the wake of structural demographic changes and changes to the conditions of world order as well as institutional changes, beginning in the 1970s this system encountered a number of contradictions. Moreover, these contradictions gradually deepened and eventually came to undermine the ability of the existing order to simultaneously elicit popular support and legitimacy from a wide range of social forces while maintaining conditions for profitable accumulation and stable social reproduction. In particular, I want to examine three contradictions at the heart of Japanese political economy and consider their implications, a discussion that will form the basis for Chapter Five.

First, there was a contradiction between the international political order that began to emerge in the early 1970s (what would ultimately come to be characterized as globalizing neoliberalism) and the regulatory regime of post-war Japanese capitalism. On one hand, Japanese capitalism had relied on a certain set of relationships between labour, the state and capital and between fractions of capital: relations that are often rooted in non-market norms and institutions that may be seen as antithetical to the neoliberal order that has become dominant at the global level. These measures included internal labour market protections, the lifetime employment system, and protectionist barriers to foreign competition in agriculture, construction, retail and other industries (Johnson 1995; Katz 1998), policies which all run contrary to the globalizing project of disciplinary neoliberalism (Gill 2008). On the other hand, Japan's economy has long relied on the international market for exports and thus is highly dependent on a liberal trading order at the same time as neoliberalism poses challenges to many elements of the existing regime. While the Keynesian era balanced a liberal international political economy with interventionist domestic political economies, this changed with the rise of neoliberalism. While Japan has had to deal with outside pressures to neoliberalize and become more competitive in the global economy, many of its firms have themselves been leaders in the project of economic globalization. However, insofar as firms such as Toyota have sought to evade domestic barriers to accumulation by moving operations overseas, it is no longer the case that what is good for Toyota is good for Japan, if it ever were so to begin with (Katz 1998).

Second, and building on the work of Bakker and Gill (2003a, 2003b) in theorizing the dialectical relationship between capitalist production and social reproduction, I argue that there is a contradiction between dynamics congruent with capital accumulation and the conditions necessary for social reproduction under Japanese capitalism. The system has relied on women, in particular, to reproduce men's labour power both on a daily basis (through the provisioning of meals and other domestic labour necessary for household maintenance) and from generation to generation (through childrearing and eldercare). However, while the capitalist system requires labor's perpetual reproduction for its own continuity, under the traditional family model it was largely assumed that women would naturally bear the burden of social reproduction without adequate support from the state. Moreover, as women have increasingly been forced to enter the workforce due to labour market shortages, the rise of precarious labour and the decline in jobs that can pay a family wage, it has only become more difficult for them to bear the full burden of reproducing society, reflected in a fertility rate that was among the lowest in the world in the 1990s and 2000s (Tanaka 2010; see also Miura 2012; Osawa 2013).

Thus, gender relations must be seen as one dimension of this contradiction between conditions conducive to stable social reproduction and those necessary for capital accumulation. At the same time, we must also recognize how changing demographics operate as another dimension and how the aging of society has exacerbated challenges relating to the maintenance of the existing regime of production and social reproduction and of the vitality of the hegemonic order more generally. Japan's lifetime employment model rewards workers' loyalty to the firm and willingness to accept low pay initially by providing them with permanent job security and regular pay raises over the course of a career. This system thus compensates for the relatively high salaries given to older workers by super-exploiting younger workers. During the high-growth era this system was highly effective because it furnished Japan with a young workforce invigorated by the guarantees of lifetime employment and progressive pay rises. In exchange for this security, workers were willing to work hard and work overtime even though their pay was relatively low, conditions which partly enabled a high rate of return for capital. However, the age balance of Japanese industry has radically shifted over the past fifty years, and it has gone from one of the youngest to the oldest industrial society in the world. Firms have responded to this by supplementing their aging permanent workforce with low-paid and insecure temporary and dispatch workers, but these measures have only increased the precariousness of the working class, further disrupting conditions for stable social reproduction.[10]

Finally, we must recognize class as a third contradiction that has increasingly posed problems for the existing order as the period of rapid economic expansion has given way to one of prolonged stagnation. During the era of expanded reproduction of capital, growth rates were high enough to ensure that labour and capital could both reap steady benefits from capital accumulation. Wages increased along with profits and the tax base and state budget could grow without undermining capitalist profitability. But after the post-war model started to disintegrate and GDP growth disappeared this has changed from a positive-sum into a zero-sum game and it has thus been increasingly impossible for the state to maintain this balance.[11] Policies designed in the interests of capital, such as labour market deregulation or consumption tax increases only increase labor's insecurity, leading to increased unemployment or dampened consumer spending.[12] Squeezed between the need to restore

---

10   Beyond the challenges that aging has caused for the lifetime employment system, it has also created budgetary pressures for the state. The growing costs of eldercare and healthcare have further posed challenges to the prospects of balancing social reproduction and capital accumulation (Itoh 2000).

11   In other words, to continue to distribute benefits of the system evenly so that hegemony can be maintained (all groups can be placated while conditions for capital accumulation are simultaneously maintained).

12   Indeed, every time the consumption tax rate has increased there has been a recession.

conditions for profitable capital accumulation and the need to maintain legitimacy in the eyes of the working class, the state has instead followed a course of tepid reform. Rather than pursuing bold reforms, it has tended to allow regulations and protections to gradually wither while inflating the national debt and without reaping any benefits in terms of economic recovery. Furthermore, while political legitimation for the LDP was long dependent on the clientelist relationship it enjoyed with various interest groups from the *petit bourgeoisie*, neoliberal structural and political pressures have led to a dismantling of many of these clientelist arrangements, in ways that have undermined the stability of the LDP's traditional electoral coalition.

Thus, by the 1990s these various contradictions that had developed out of changes to the structural and institutional conditions that undergirded the period of stable hegemonic order in the 1950s and 1960s had deepened. As a result, Japan fell into a deep, multifaceted, organic crisis, with particularly important political, economic and demographic dimensions. Not only were these various dimensions striking, they each reflected the declining capacity for the hegemonic order to maintain conditions for robust political legitimation, secure capital accumulation, and stable social reproduction. While the period since the 1990s has witnessed various attempts to resolve this crisis, these efforts have thus far proven insufficient. Indeed, unless they can fundamentally address the deep underlying contradictions between Japan's hegemonic order and regime of regulation on one hand and the structural conditions within which they are situated on the other – measures that would likely require a significant reordering of power relations within Japan's historic bloc – future attempts to solve the crisis are unlikely to be successful either.

15   Conclusion

This chapter has sought to provide an overview of the theoretical framework used in this book. It developed six aspects of this theoretical framework. First, it considered the basic philosophical point of departure of the book within historical materialism. Second, it clarified more specifically the core theoretical inspiration for the perspective developed here in the work of Antonio Gramsci (1992), providing an overview of many of his core concepts, including hegemony, historic bloc, passive revolution, *trasformismo*, and the modern prince, among others. Third, it posited a three-fold conception of the conditions necessary for hegemonic order as political legitimation, capital accumulation and social reproduction. Fourth, it used the work of Robert Cox to develop a modified version of Gramsci's original conception of the relations of force, considering their relevance for understanding conditions of political and class struggle in Japan. Fifth, it briefly considered the importance of using a political ecological lens to understand what is at stake in Japanese political economy of the post-war era. Finally, it provided a summary of the overall argument developed in this book. Building on the theoretical framework developed in this chapter, the rest of the book will sketch an analysis of Japan's postwar era from a Gramscian perspective. Starting with Chapter Four's take on Japanese political economy of the early post-war (1952–1972), the next four chapters will provide an analysis of the conditions of Japanese hegemonic order from the post-war to the present before Chapter Eight considers the implications of the analysis developed here for the future.

CHAPTER 4

The Post-war Hegemonic Order

This chapter explores the political economy of Japan in the early post-war era.[1] It thus corresponds with the period beginning with the return of Japanese sovereignty in 1952 and ending in the early 1970s with the first oil shock and the two "Nixon Shocks" internationally and the introduction of major welfare reforms under Prime Minister Tanaka Kakuei (1972–74) domestically. 1974 was the first year that Japan experienced a recession since the 1940s (World Bank 2019) and retrospectively came to be the end of the period of rapid GDP growth (around ten percent per annum) and the start of a period of medium growth (around four to five percent), while 1972 brought the end of the American occupation of Okinawa and the return to Japanese control, an event that Prime Minister Satō Eisaku (1964–72) saw as necessary for finally drawing closure to the post-war period. While the exact endpoint is academic, what is important is that this period saw the construction and entrenchment of the Japanese post-war hegemonic order, led by the tripartite rule of the LDP, the bureaucracy, and large corporations. These conditions were central to the rapid and yet egalitarian economic growth for which the era is known.

This chapter argues that key to Japan's post-war success was the establishment of a hegemonic order led by a historic bloc that represented a wide range of societal interests, including farmers, small businesses, the new urban middle class and blue-collar workers. Moreover, this historic bloc was able to successfully balance requirements of capital accumulation, political legitimation and social reproduction, conditions that underscored the much-lauded "Japanese miracle", and the chapter outlines eleven key conditions that enabled and maintained this period of relatively stable hegemonic order (at least domestically). Nonetheless, this order was dependent on a number of factors that ultimately proved difficult to maintain over time. In the long run, changing structural conditions, in particular the rise of neoliberal globalization and domestic demographic shifts combined with the high costs of placating such a broad coalition of social forces caused strains in the Japanese model to emerge, as the next chapter will show.

---

1 Parts of this chapter draw upon an earlier article, "From nationalist communitarianism to fragmentary neoliberalism: Japan's crisis of social reproduction", published in *Capital & Class* (2019).

1   The Post-war Hegemonic Order

The post-war era saw the development of a hegemonic order led by the three forces of the LDP, the bureaucracy and corporations. As I discussed in the previous chapter, the degree of stability and efficacy of a hegemonic order (at least under capitalism) can generally be considered by examining the degree to which it maintains three requirements: capital accumulation, political legitimation, and social reproduction. It is therefore worth considering exactly to what degree it was capable of fulfilling these three requirements. First, with regard to capital accumulation, the success of Japan's post-war economic development is obvious. Gross domestic product grew more than 35-fold from 14 billion dollars in 1951 to 498 billion in 1975, with an average rate of annual growth of more than 10 percent (Gordon 2003). Real wages in manufacturing tripled, growing by roughly 5.8 percent per year from 1955 to 1975 while nominal wages grew tenfold, increasing 12.2 percent a year over the same period (Itoh 1992, 1990). This was made possible by robust labour productivity growth, which averaged 8.5 percent from 1955 to 1975 and grew five-fold (Itoh 1990). The rate of investment was also extremely high, reaching 25 percent of GDP in 1973 (Itoh 2000). Finally, unemployment was low throughout the period, never rising above 2.5 percent (Nenji Toukei 2014), while industrial employment grew, and agricultural employment fell steadily over the entire period. Overall, these metrics indicate unambiguously the success of capital accumulation in post-war Japan.

With regard to political legitimation, it is less clear how to measure "success," but several metrics can be used to help us evaluate the effectiveness of the post-war hegemonic order in this regard. For example, the 1950s saw very animated student and labour movements that opposed the LDP and its foreign policy positions in particular. Yet despite this lively opposition, the LDP did very well in elections, successively winning a majority of the vote from its formation in 1955 until the 1972 election.[2] This occurred under an electoral system that was far more open and democratic than what had existed before the war, with the franchise having been extended to women in 1945. Moreover, compared to in recent decades, voter turnout was high, averaging 73 percent of the electorate.

Indeed, Japan's post-war constitution, created by the occupying forces, was developed with the express goals of liberalization, democratization, and a permanent commitment to peace. The last of these goals was particularly resonant with Japanese society in the aftermath of the horrors of the war and helped to

---

2   While LDP vote totals were slightly below 50 percent after 1967, when LDP-supporting Independents (most of whom join the LDP after winning) are included the number rises to 50 percent.

enhance the legitimacy of the new political order. As this legitimacy grew, the radical fervor of the immediate post-war receded. Through the 1960s, the labour movement, and to a lesser extent the student movement as well, became less militant, willing to engage with the state and capital and form compromises.

Yet while important political defeats, such as the 1960 renewal of the US-Japan Security Treaty and the defeat of the Miike mine strike, partly explain this decline of student and labor radicalism, these do not tell the whole story. Another contributory factor towards the decline of radical politics as well as to the high level of political legitimacy was the high degree of income and wealth equality that developed in post-war Japanese capitalism. Statistics show that Japan's income inequality decreased from the 1950s through the 1970s even as GDP grew more than tenfold (Minami 2008). While uneven and combined development – including rapid industrialization of particular regions – is a central feature of capitalism (ever apparent in contemporary China) the combination of rapid growth with *increasing* equality is a horse of a different color.[3] While conditions of relative equality are neither necessary nor sufficient for political legitimation overall, there is certainly good reason to assume that – in the case of Japan and elsewhere – they can mitigate or even temporarily resolve the negative political and social consequences of class struggle that capitalist hegemonic projects always face. Overall, these various measures provide sufficient empirical evidence to the assertion that that the LDP-led post-war order received a high degree of political legitimation.

Finally, with regard to social reproduction, there are clear measures with which we can deem whether any existing social order is successful or not at ensuring the reproduction of human labour, both from day to day and from generation to generation, in socio-cultural as well as biological terms (see also Bakker and Gill 2003b). At the biological level, the fertility rate is the most straightforward measure of intergenerational social reproduction, while other indicators – particularly health indicators[4] – provide a measure of the degree to which requirements for social reproduction are being met at a biological level on a daily basis.[5] At the socio-cultural level, it may be more difficult to "measure" degrees

---

3   And cannot be explained by an understanding of capitalist development alone, which – as the case of contemporary China shows – is structurally oriented towards increasing rather than decreasing inequality.
4   For example, the recent rapid growth of lifestyle-related diseases, including type-2 diabetes and obesity in many parts of the world are indicative of a great many people no longer having the time, money, or nutritional education to procure healthy meals and therefore points to a failure of institutions of social reproduction, with serious social and economic consequences.
5   The relevance and explanatory power of fertility rates in relation to social reproduction must be qualified and understood as limited to advanced capitalist societies. Within agrarian

to which social reproduction is maintained, but we can consider whether households are able to maintain time and space for the provision of care for dependent populations (especially babies and children) as an indicator of social reproduction on a daily basis and rates of educational attainment as an indicator for socio-cultural elements of social reproduction intergenerationally.

In all these measures, Japan scores well: its fertility rate fell from the very high levels immediately after the war to a stable level at around the replacement rate of 2.1 by 1956, where it remained until the mid-1970s (CAO 2018), while life expectancy grew from 59.7 (58.0 for men and 61.5 for women) in 1950 to 72.0 (69.3 for men and 74.7 for women) in 1970 (CAO 2012). Meanwhile, educational attainment rates grew steadily: while less than half of Japanese students attended high school in 1950, by the 1970s more than 90 percent did so, with female and male rates nearly equal (MEXT 2006). Moreover, admission to top universities was highly egalitarian (though overwhelmingly male), with 40 percent of students admitted to national universities coming from households in the bottom two quintiles in 1961 (and still 31% in 1971) (Gordon 2003; Kerbo and McKinstry 1995). While the stabilizing of fertility rates at 2.1 ensured intergenerational replacement of the workforce, the increase in life expectancy expanded the working lifespan of the average person. Moreover, the increase in educational opportunities, especially for those from the bottom two quintiles, ensured that each new cohort of workers possessed adequate skills and knowledge to contribute to Japan's economic development.

Overall, we can see how this period was clearly one where the hegemonic order was relatively capable of balancing requirements of capital accumulation, political legitimation and social reproduction. The next section will

---

societies where large families are the norm, families face structural economic incentives to have many children, while the penetration of capitalist relations of production may be limited. In contrast, within industrial capitalist societies, workers do not face economic incentives to maximize their number of children, and the ability of families to have their desired number of children can be understood as a reflection of the adequacy of social reproductive functions and institutions. In addition, the focus on fertility rates may appear for some to naturalize or essentialize reproduction, as if women's childbearing is not a product of their own agency but simply caused by external structural factors that they passively submit to. From the perspective of working-class families – and especially women – it would indeed be better to examine to what extent women are able to have their designed number of children – a number which is itself determined by women's (and men's) agency within the context of shifting socio-cultural norms. However, viewed from the perspective of capital, what is of significance is the long-term, inter-generational reproduction of the workforce. This is determined not by women's ideal number of children but by the actual fertility rate, which (barring immigration) must reach 2.1 in the long run, to replace the working population with each generation.

consider in detail what conditions enabled and maintained this hegemonic order during the post-war period.

2   Conditions of Post-war Hegemonic Order

The above discussion indicates just how successful Japan's ruling historic bloc was in maintaining conditions for hegemonic order in the post-war period. What factors account for this success? Eleven conditions were primarily responsible for the success of Japan's post-war hegemonic order. In general, they relate to four core areas: 1) conditions of world order; 2) dynamics of the Japanese state; 3) political-economic and class relations; and 4) Japan's regime of social reproduction. While this chapter shows how the eleven conditions developed in ways to maintain Japan's hegemonic order in the post-war period, Chapter Six will show how in many ways changes to these same eleven conditions paved the way to Japan's prolonged and systemic organic crisis since the 1990s. Understanding the causes and conditions of the organic crisis that has characterized Japanese society since the 1990s, therefore, requires an understanding of the period of hegemonic vitality that preceded it, and the contingent conditions that maintained that social order.

2.1   *Geopolitics: The Yoshida Doctrine and the US-Japan Security Treaty (Anpo)*

The first condition of the post-war hegemonic order was the high degree of stability provided by Japan's location within Cold War geopolitics as a staunch US ally in the Pacific. During allied occupation after World War II, Japan's military was fully disbanded, while the 1947 post-war Constitution explicitly forbade remilitarization. Instead, Japan's security was fully covered by the United States, which maintained a substantial military presence on Japanese soil (and even more so on Okinawa, which was not reverted until 1972) even after the return of Japanese sovereignty in 1952. In the aftermath of a devastating war, where approximately three million lives were lost, this security was understandably of utmost concern, particularly considering that by 1949 Japan was surrounded by three communist states (the USSR, the People's Republic of China and North Korea) and two other authoritarian former colonies (the Republic of China in Taiwan and South Korea).

On August 15th, 1945, Japan declared its unconditional surrender to the Allied powers, marking the conclusion of the Pacific War. Japan was subsequently occupied, ostensibly by the Allied Powers but in practice by the United States, led by General Douglas McArthur, Supreme Commander of the

Allied Powers (SCAP). After Japan gained full independence with the 1951 San Francisco Treaty, a debate ensued over post-independence foreign policy. The JSP and JCP, which had opposed the terms of the treaty, fought vehemently to avoid a military alliance with the US, instead favoring a foreign policy rooted in pacifism and neutrality. In contrast, the LDP sought to push through the US-Japan Security Treaty (known as *Anpo* in Japanese), due to pragmatic concerns more than ideological ones. Indeed, according to Rosenbluth and Thies (2010), Prime Minister Yoshida Shigeru (1946–47, 1948–54) was not particularly concerned about the communist threat and would have made peace with China and Mao but saw the Security Treaty as a cheaper foreign policy than rearmament. This pragmatism formed the underlying basis for Japan's security policy in the post-war era, known, after Yoshida, as the Yoshida Doctrine.

The Yoshida Doctrine was essentially characterized by a pragmatic decision to take a passive and pacifist orientation to domestic security and defense concerns. Instead of devoting resources to military armament and self-defense, the state could focus attention on national reconstruction, industrialization and international trade (Saltzman 2015; Dian 2015). Under the Yoshida Doctrine, constitutional bans on militarization imposed by the United States served as the basis for excusing Japan from playing an activist and interventionist role in geopolitical security in the Cold War. This not only spared Japan of a heavy defense budget but also saved it from problematic altercations with its postcolonial neighbors. Instead, Japanese security was guaranteed through a wide-ranging security alliance with the United States that was first renewed in 1960 (against much protest from left wing forces) and again in 1970 (with little ordeal) (Ikeda 2011; Nakajima 2011). This security alliance involved the direct deployment of American troops in Japan in exchange for guarantees of Japanese security. Under the terms of the Anpo, the US stationed troops indefinitely at a range of military bases throughout Japan (including in the Greater Tokyo Area), as well as in Okinawa.

As Dian (2015) has shown, the Yoshida doctrine amounted to a compromise between the aims of progressives animated by pacifist values and conservatives driven by concerns over the spread of communism. Thus although Yoshida himself was by no means a progressive, and never saw Japan's renouncement of war or militarization as permanent, he shrewdly forged a foreign policy doctrine that could unite all political forces in post-war Japanese society.[6] By combining official pacifism on one hand with a commitment to alliance with

---

6 According to Saltzman (2015), Prime Ministers Shidehara and Yoshida both claimed that it was their choice to include Article 9 as a way of proving to the world that Japan was not militaristic.

the US and an unambiguous position for Japan under conditions of Cold War bipolarity, the Yoshida Doctrine did enough to appease both sides of what was unquestionably the fieriest political flashpoint of the early post war era. This is not to argue that the terms of the Yoshida Doctrine went uncontested. As a compromise position between progressives and conservatives, it left neither side fully satisfied. While left wing political parties and labour unions engaged in some of the most militant protests of the post-war era in the run-up to the renewal of the Security Treaty in 1960 (protesting alliance with the US instead of a fully neutral foreign policy), some conservatives within the LDP remained frustrated by Japan's foreign policy "impotence" and yearned for the day when constitutional amendment would bring remilitarization. Nonetheless, shortly after the 1960 flashpoint over the Anpo's renewal, progressive militancy abated, while conservative voices remained relatively quiet for several decades, and a high degree of stability and hegemonic consensus emerged over Japanese foreign policy under the Yoshida Doctrine (Hook et al. 2011).[7]

What impacts did Anpo and the Yoshida Doctrine have on Japan-US relations? To be sure, the security alliance served as the bedrock for US-Japan relations and secured Japan as a bastion of American hegemony in the Asia-Pacific. At the same time, Anpo guaranteed for Japan a high standing as an irreplaceable American ally and did much to ensure an amicable trading relationship between the two countries. Moreover, relations with the US served as a conduit for re-establishing diplomatic and trading relations with other Asian countries, in particular, Korea, the ASEAN nations, and, after 1972, the People's Republic of China.

What other impacts did Anpo have on Japanese hegemonic order domestically? The geopolitical context of Anpo also helped shore up hegemony for the LDP by guaranteeing US support for the LDP (and economic concessions), since the US did not want to risk losing Japan as a close ally in Asia through the election of a JSP or JCP government. Moreover, Anpo was crucial to Japanese capitalism insofar as it provided not only relations for secure accumulation but also access to the US market; it locked Japan in, both politically and economically, to its relationship to the US, which was very important to Japanese capital.

---

7 The Japanese Communist Party and the Japanese Socialist Party remained opposed to Anpo throughout the post-war era, while other centre-left parties (Kōmeitō and the Democratic Socialist Party (DSP)) adopted a stance more in line with the LDP. Thus, a clear minority of a quarter to a third of voters consistently voted for parties that vehemently opposed the Anpo until the 1990s.

Finally, Anpo and the Yoshida Doctrine allowed the state to focus much more on economic development, such as with Ikeda's Income Doubling Plan, the hallmark policy of the LDP in the early 1960s that sought to double the GDP by the end of the decade and achieve the living standards of western countries, rather than on foreign policy (LDP n.d.a). Indeed, for conservatives, the low posture on foreign policy issues and the loss of autonomy on defense issues under the Anpo was a price worth paying for post-war growth and prosperity (Dian 2015).

Overall, we can see how Japanese foreign policy in the early post-war era was characterized by a high degree of deference to American foreign policy and security interests, in keeping with the Yoshida doctrine. Moreover, this posture was maintained in order to a) keep Japan out of Cold War proxy wars like the Korean and Vietnam Wars; b) ensure that Japan could continue to enjoy strong and preferential access to the American market for trade; and c) keep the spread of communism and socialism in check, both domestically and internationally.[8] The Anpo and Japan's relationship with the US were central to this, and the bedrock for Japan's revival as a major economic power in East Asia.

2.2 Global Political Economy: The Bretton Woods System

The second condition for Japan's post-war hegemonic order was the liberal trading order set up under the Bretton Woods system. As Cox (1992) has shown, such a system allowed for a relatively liberal regime of free trade between countries whilst also permitting a high degree of state intervention in domestic political economies, reflecting what Ruggie (1982) has referred to as "embedded liberalism". This system perfectly matched with Japan's economic policy, which, as Johnson (1982) has shown, was actively interventionist in industrial policy but nonetheless dependent on exports for economic growth. An international political economic order that accommodated both these elements of Japanese domestic political economy was thus tremendously beneficial to Japan's post-war economic boom. Indeed, it facilitated not only rapid economic growth but also a high degree of economic stability, a requirement for Japan's egalitarian lifetime employment system and thus for labour peace more generally.

---

8 The threat posed by the JSP was both a negotiating chip used by Satō in Okinawa negotiations (arguing that a bad deal for Japan would mean a JSP victory) and a reason for the LDP to favor a structural dependency on the US for trade and security purposes (since only the LDP could ensure amicable relations with the US, Japan had much to lose from a JSP victory insofar as it remained dependent on the US) (Ikeda 2011).

Prior to and during World War II, global trading relations had been anything but liberal, and largely dominated by intra-imperial trade, with major imperial powers trading with their colonies or quasi-colonies, such as Latin America's relationship with the US. For Japan, this dynamic had served as part of the impetus for empire building, and Japan's relatively backward position, and in particular its lack of access to natural resources, had left it vulnerable to shortages in the factors of production necessary to drive economic growth. Indeed, this vulnerability had been one force prompting Japanese imperialism in Korea and Manchuria, and later was partly responsible for the Japanese entry into the Second World War, in part as a response to blocked access to crucial fossil fuel resources located in Euro-American colonies and imperial spheres of influence. Needless to say, the results of this political economic order were disastrous, not only for the Japanese but also for the victims of Japanese imperialism in Asia.

In the aftermath of inter-war fascism, American, British and other world leaders sought to remake international political economic relations along liberal lines but in a way that granted states a high degree of latitude in managing domestic political economies (Ruggie 1982). The architecture of this system was first laid out at the Bretton Woods conference in 1944. The Bretton Woods System (BWS) was composed of the IMF, the World Bank and later GATT. Overall, what were the impacts of the BWS for Japanese hegemonic order? In general, it reinforced the stability of LDP-led rule by producing a stable trading order while also allowing a strong degree of permissiveness towards the high degree of state intervention, both through supports to export industries and barriers to imports, for Japanese industrial development. In particular, hard quotas on foreign exchange for imports and investment respectively existed after 1950, severely limiting the degree to which Japanese capital had to compete with American and other foreign capital domestically (Weiss 1986). Moreover, under the embedded liberal paradigm, the Japanese state had the freedom to import American technologies while also maintaining the authority to determine *which* technologies could be imported, so as to influence the trajectory of domestic industrialization in ways that advanced the developmentalist agenda of MITI and other sectors of the bureaucracy (Weiss 1986).

A further way in which the embedded liberal paradigm benefitted Japanese industrialization can be observed in the trading relationship that developed with the US. While Japan's proportion of imports from the US fell from 44 percent in 1950 to 29 percent by 1970, Japan's proportion of exports to the US grew from 22 percent in 1950 to 31 percent by 1970 (Hook et al. 2011). Japan's overall exports grew in value from 298 billion yen in 1950 to 8.8 trillion yen in 1972, a 30-fold increase, while imports grew from 348 billion to 7.2 trillion. Moreover, while Japan had an overall trade deficit for most years until the mid-1960s, starting in 1965 exports surpassed imports, leading to a 1.6 trillion yen trade surplus in 1972, driven by growth in exports of textiles and steel initially, and later, electronics, ships and automobiles (EPA 1981; MOF n.d.).[9] While Japan's entry into GATT in 1955 forced it to abandon quotas in favor of tariffs on most of its imports, it retained tariff rates at close to 20 percent on average until the 1970s, while rigid barriers to inward foreign investment remained intact (Flath 2000; Weiss 1986). In various ways, then, the embedded liberalism of the Bretton Woods System and the trading relationship with the US that developed under that system served as a major condition for Japan's post-war boom.

2.3 The Electoral and Party System: The Rise of LDP Dominance

The third condition of Japan's post-war hegemonic order was its electoral and party system. In particular, its electoral system did two things for LDP-led political order. First, it promoted LDP party hegemony by splitting the opposition vote and ensuring that no single opposition party could ever rationally choose to run enough candidates so as to actually threaten to win an election overall. Second, it promoted intraparty competition and a highly decentralized LDP (though this emerged historically) that encouraged a highly localized politics that helped ensure a distribution of political goods (pork-barrel spending) throughout the country in order to combat uneven development while also further entrenching LDP dominance. In these ways, the electoral and party system served as a key basis for ensuring stable LDP dominance without sacrificing the democratic legitimacy of the system overall.

What characterized Japan's post-war electoral system? While much changed in the immediate post-war to Japan's political institutions, such as the granting of suffrage to women and the transformation of the House of Councilors (Upper House) from a hereditary to an elected institution, one thing that did not change was the retention of the pre-war multi-member non-transferrable voting system. Within this system, voters each cast ballots for individual candidates in their electoral district, and between two and five candidates were elected depending on the size of the district. This meant that in most districts, parties seeking to win a majority of seats overall had to run multiple candidates who directly competed with each other. The implications of this intraparty competition were significant for the development of Japanese politics.

---

9 The share of steel consumed in the US that was imported from Japan grew from less one percent all the way to 7 percent over the course of the 1960s (Flath 2000).

While the first few post-war elections saw a range of parties enter government, by the mid-1950s Japanese party politics had settled into a relatively stable pattern after mergers brought about the formation of two major parties: the JSP on the left, and the LDP on the right. However, while the various centrist and conservative elements that constituted the LDP managed to maintain party unity over the ensuing decades, this was not true for the JSP, which split in two in 1960 with the formation of the Democratic Socialist Party (DSP).[10] Moreover, in 1964, Kōmeitō, a new, centrist party affiliated with the Buddhist organization Sōka Gakkai, formed. For three decades until 1993, then, Japanese politics was characterized by a relatively stable dynamic: on the right, the LDP would win roughly half of the votes (and seats); on the left, the four opposition parties (the JCP, JSP, DSP and Kōmeitō) would share the other half. In no election did any single party even come close to surpassing the LDP in votes. However, this should not be surprising: in no election did any other party run anywhere near enough candidates to challenge the LDP.

Readers familiar with first-past-the-post electoral systems will be aware of the tendency for parties that once held a majority of seats to suddenly see a significant decline in their seat count, or else see a party that previously held few seats suddenly make a major breakthrough. In Canada, the Progressive Conservative Party's 1993 defeat, where it was reduced to 2 seats, down from a majority of 156 before the election, or the New Democratic Party's 2011 breakthrough that saw it win 58 out of 78 seats in Quebec, up from one, each demonstrate the potential for a groundbreaking transformation in fortunes. In post-war Japan, this was not the case. Because each district elected multiple members and each party was allowed to run multiple candidates, the number of candidates each party nominated depended on their pre-election expectations. In this context, the strategy of a party audaciously running more candidates than they were likely to win seats could backfire and see the candidates split the party's overall vote in such a way that led it to fail to win any seats at all. Afraid of this scenario, the four minor parties rarely ran more than one candidate per district, while the LDP often ran three or more.[11] Thus, in most

---

10   The DSP was formed from members who had formerly been part of the pre-merger Rightist Socialist Party (remaining JSP members were mostly from the old Leftist Socialist Party). The DSP's split was mainly driven by disagreements over the JSP's opposition to Anpo (Ikeda 2011).

11   Moreover, in many cases even one candidate was too many for the JCP, DSP and Kōmeitō, and their candidates often finished just outside of the electoral cutoff.

cases, the LDP as a party was almost guaranteed to win at least an overwhelming plurality of seats even before elections took place.[12] Even if they were to suffer a significant loss of support, the electoral effects of this would likely be minimized unless voters somehow arranged to evenly distribute their votes among the opposition parties instead of, for example, mainly voting for the JSP and thus allowing their (single) candidates to run up massive vote totals in each district without ultimately leading to much of an impact on the overall seat distribution.

Clearly, this electoral system brought significant benefits for the LDP and virtually guaranteed their stable rule, while the opposition parties remained marginal.[13] However, it was not as if the opposition parties could have easily bridged their ideological differences: though all generally sided against the LDP (at least until the 1990s), this did not mean that they sided together. The ideological gap between the DSP and the JCP, for example, was significantly wider than the gap between the DSP and the LDP. Moreover, the LDP's policy fluidity and lack of a core ideology meant that in many cases, the LDP adopted (or rather co-opted) policies that opposition parties supported, while opportunities to join parliamentary committees, as well as the consensus-based decision making that characterized Diet (legislative) deliberations, ensured that being in opposition did not render these parties voiceless (see also Curtis 1988).

Thus, we see how Japan's multi-member district electoral system contributed significantly to LDP-led hegemony by creating major structural barriers to other parties' abilities to contest power. The LDP benefited doubly from maintaining a veneer of democratic legitimacy (and actual sustained electoral success) while in practice never facing any realistic threat of losing power, and consistently playing with a loaded dice.[14]

---

12   However, while this was true for the LDP overall, individual candidates often faced intra-party competition, as slightly more LDP candidates ran in each district than were likely to win. To avoid being the unlucky loser, then, LDP candidates were forced to engage in rigorous electioneering, as the next section will show.

13   Though not marginal enough to prompt their merger into a unified, non-LDP party: by each winning enough seats to stay relevant, opposition parties opted to stay small and divided.

14   Many have emphasized the degree to which the LDP benefited from mal-apportionment of districts in favor of rural voters as a key basis to their electoral success. While this was certainly part of the reason for their success, it is often over-emphasized. From 1960 until the 1990s, the LDP never received less than 42 percent of the vote, and only received less than 45 percent once, while the second best JSP never received more than 29 percent. Under these electoral imbalances, even a more evenly distributed electoral system would likely result in relatively stable LDP governments, while a pure first-past-the-post system would have resulted in consistent landslide electoral victories. Therefore, it was the

However, while the LDP as a whole rarely faced threats of losing office, the same cannot be said for individual LDP candidates. Individual candidates had to fight hard to guarantee that enough of the moderate and conservative vote went to them as opposed to their fellow LDP candidates from the same districts. This ensured that supporters and lawmakers alike always remained mobilized and engaged. Indeed, as Stockwin (2006) has argued, given the relatively set party preferences of the electorate, it was intraparty competition among LDP candidates, rather than interparty competition with candidates of the left parties, that provided the strongest motivation for active election campaigning. Within the LDP, then, this electoral system played a role in facilitating the development of three key institutions: factions, *kōenkai* and the PARC (Krauss and Pekkanen 2010).

Kōenkai are political support organizations formed by individual candidates – and not parties – as means of securing both votes and fundraising in their constituencies. They emerged after 1952, as a means of evading campaign-financing and electoral campaign restrictions (Krauss and Pekkanen 2010). *Kōenkai* drew membership – often in the tens of thousands – from a wide swathe of groups within constituencies. These included youth, women, farmers, salaried workers, and small business owners. *Kōenkai* also organized a wide range of social clubs, professional and hobby associations, including music, arts (such as the tea ceremony), and outdoor and indoor sports for members (Krauss and Pekkanen 2010). *Kōenkai* thus provided a setting for community engagement and participation structured around the personality of a single electoral candidate. Candidates usually spent significant amounts of time and money on their *kōenkai*, not only on the myriad club activities and excursions but also in attending numerous weddings, funerals and other major events for members, all in the name of building their personal appeal within the community. In exchange, *kōenkai* provided candidates with a major source of fundraising as well as a stable bloc of loyal voters, even including members who were supporters of other parties (Krauss and Pekkanen 2010).[15] In the context of intraparty competition, candidate-centric *kōenkai* ensured that votes would not all coalesce behind one LDP candidate and instead divide between two or three, so as to ensure they each won election.

---

electoral disincentives of running enough candidates to seriously challenges for power that minority parties faced that was the actual reason behind the LDP's unrelenting electoral success, rather than a rural electoral bias.

15   Sources of *kōenkai* fundraising came from both membership and from the wider business community that was often affiliated with *kōenkai*.

What were the consequences of *kōenkai*? First, they promoted a highly clientelist, personalized brand of politics. Voters would support candidates based on their personal appeal, as well as potential government spending that they could bring to the community, rather than the programmatic agenda of their party. Second, *kōenkai* prevented the centralization of the LDP's party organization. While LDP leaders tried to increase the power of the party relative to *kōenkai*, and even abolish them on several occasions, these efforts were unsuccessful. Due to the great size of *kōenkai* spending, and the importance of *kōenkai* support over party support for candidates' electoral success, *kōenkai* remained powerful and the LDP remained decentralized (Krauss and Pekkanen 2010). Third, and unlike the support groups of the JSP, JCP and Kōmeitō, which were much more clearly defined along class-based (and in the case of Kōmeitō, religious) lines, LDP *kōenkai* were built in ways that were highly personal and largely apolitical, drawing membership from a range of social classes. Overall, the *kōenkai* played a major role in ensuring stable and consistent electoral and financial support for LDP candidates in a way that promoted their re-election under the multi-member system. More importantly, it also helped maintain an orientation of Japanese politics that was personal and transactional rather than ideological. Such a model of retail politics was able to appeal at a personal level to voters from a wide range of class positions and thus weaken the appeal of the class-based rhetoric of the JSP and JCP.[16]

Along with the *kōenkai*, a second major institution that developed in this era, particularly in the LDP, were party factions. If *kōenkai* served as the basis through which candidates for office had built support and shored up votes, factions were the means through which powerful lawmakers built stable coalitions of supporters within the Diet to ensure their power and influence over major party and governmental bodies. As with *kōenkai*, factions were largely apolitical, with members joining and recruiting for personal and strategic rather than ideological reasons. Lead factions would recruit promising candidates and provide them with nominations and funding, highly valuable goods in the context of intraparty electoral competition. Once elected, faction

---

16 Candidates from other parties, especially the JCP and Kōmeitō, also had *kōenkai* that functioned in largely non-ideological ways similar to the LDP (Krauss and Pekkanen 2010). However, while this likely brought some electoral success (the JCP's *kōenkai* membership far exceeded party membership), it was never able to win over elites or bring in significant financing (aside from what the JCP obtained from subscriptions to its newspaper, *Akahata*). Emphasizing personality while downplaying ideology thus worked well for the party of the capitalist status quo (the LDP) but was an ineffective political strategy for the transformative left.

membership served as a means of gaining access to positions on both legislative and party policy committees, enabling officials to gain experience and gradually rise in status. At the top, factional membership provided the basis for the distribution of key cabinet and party leadership posts. Party presidents would usually allocate these posts in relation to the relative strength of each faction, while ensuring that factions that backed their leadership bids were especially rewarded (Krauss and Pekkanen 2010). In exchange, faction members would be expected to provide loyal votes for their leaders in party leadership contests. As Okimoto (1989) has shown, this orientation of LDP party politics around non-ideological yet powerful factions ensured that major ideological differences never led to party cleavages. In contrast, other parties saw the development of ideological factions that significantly undermined party unity. In particular, conflict between the left-wing and right-wing factions of the JSP led to the breakup of the JSP and the creation of the DSP in 1960 (only five years after the JSP's formation). Thus, while factions did nothing to undermine and may have even augmented LDP unity, they provided a major barrier to unity and cooperation among and within the left opposition parties.

A third and final institution central to the internal workings of the LDP was the Policy Affairs Research Council (PARC). PARC served as the LDP's key policymaking body and given the continuity of LDP majorities in both Houses until 1990, this effectively made it more important to the policymaking process than the Diet itself. For any piece of legislation to gain party approval (and thus be presented in the Diet), it needed to pass the scrutiny of the PARC, even before it went to Cabinet. The PARC was comprised of many dozens of divisions and within each, committees and subcommittees (Krauss and Pekkanen 2010). Each LDP lawmaker held positions on multiple PARC committees, while PARC committee assignments were often divided based on factional allegiance. As lawmakers gained experience, their roles within PARC committees increased. With enough terms in the Diet, anyone could position themselves for top leadership positions within PARC.

While PARC's influence over the policymaking process is notable on its own, PARC is even more important as the institutional basis for Japan's clientelist politics and as the institution responsible for cultivating *zoku* lawmakers.[17] *Zoku* lawmakers tended to be concentrated in the Construction, Transport, and Agriculture ministries, all areas with high amounts of discretionary spending. They were influential in generating close relationships with bureaucrats

---

17   The term *zoku* literally translates as "tribe" and refers to LDP lawmakers – usually backbenchers – with a strong background in a particular policy domain and with strong ties to bureaucrats in the corresponding ministry or department.

that enabled them to be the LDP's key means of collaborating with bureaucrats in the detailed process of policy formation (Krauss and Pekkanen 2010). Similarly, by forging amicable links with *zoku* lawmakers, bureaucrats were able to obtain budgetary increases for their ministry or department from the LDP. *Zoku* lawmakers then used their influence as a bridge linking bureaucrats with the LDP party mechanism to help craft policies that included government spending in their own constituencies, what has generally been referred to as "pork-barrel" spending. The PARC thus served as a vehicle for forging ties between bureaucrats and low-ranking party officials *outside* of the cabinet. This served to empower backbench *zoku* lawmakers in relation to the cabinet and even Prime Minister, giving the former significant control over policymaking (Krauss and Pekkanen 2010). More than anything, however, its significance lay in the way it helped foster a highly collusive, clientelist form of politics rooted in the LDP-bureaucracy power nexus.

2.4 The State Form: The Rise of Bureaucracy-driven Governance

The fourth condition of Japan's post-war hegemonic order is the strong role played by the bureaucracy and the synergistic relationship that developed between bureaucrats and elected officials. Bureaucrats had a preponderant role in policy creation in the post-war era. This was partly due to the high degree of decentralization of the LDP's power structures and the weakness of cabinet. It also had to do with the degree to which bureaucrats were empowered in the 1940s after many of the wartime lawmakers were purged. In a way, a division of labour developed between the bureaucrats and lawmakers. Bureaucrats, isolated from electoral pressures, could be left to deal with long-term national policy, in particular industrial and economic as well as welfare and fiscal policy. In contrast, lawmakers sought to influence the direction of funds for construction, public works and other targeted expenses towards their own local constituencies so as to maintain electability. The rational planning of a bureaucracy capable of looking beyond the two- or three-year window of an election cycle thus corresponded effectively with the long-term orientation of Japanese capital. Conversely, the more targeted pork-barrel politics of elected officials was more effective in maintaining democratic political legitimacy for the system while also balancing against the effects of an industrial policy oriented around the interests of big business.

Given the endurance of LDP domination,[18] it is tempting to equate the Japanese state with the LDP, and to see its other administrative organs and

---

18   While the period of LDP dominance officially began in 1955 with the formation of the party, it could just as easily be dated back to 1949, when the Liberal Party of Yoshida

the bureaucracy as mere vehicles through which the LDP's will was transmitted. However, the reality was much more complex. Chalmers Johnson (1982) famously said that in Japan, "the politicians reign and the bureaucrats rule" (154). While such an assertion is no doubt hyperbolic, there is no question that the bureaucracy played a significant role in the shaping and implementation of policy, often in ways that escaped the discretion the LDP.

Overall, the bureaucracy, and in particular the fractions of it related to the construction state or developmental state had a significant degree of autonomy in both the creation and implementation of policy, more so than in most other industrialized countries.[19] However, it would be a mistake to therefore suggest that the bureaucracy had more power than the elected (LDP) government, or that LDP governments were required to bend their wills to the bureaucracy. The LDP and the bureaucracy had a close, symbiotic relationship because the LDP was concerned mostly with 1) winning elections; and 2) broad, long-term policy goals, such as economic growth and the maintenance of social order. Beyond these general goals, the LDP was relatively flexible and not deeply concerned with ideology or the minutiae of policy. The bureaucracy in no way sought to negate or undermine either of the LDP's prerogatives. On the contrary, it worked effectively to implement them at the micro-level. Nonetheless, in cases where the will of bureaucrats fundamentally contradicted with the interests of the LDP, it was clearly the LDP who had the final say. This is evinced by the refusal by both the Cabinet and industry to follow MITI directives to concentrate the auto industry into two firms (Nissan and Toyota) (Okimoto 1989).

Along with the LDP, the bureaucracy also developed a symbiotic relationship with private capital, and in particular the *keiretsu*. There were two elements to these connections. The first was the transfer of personnel between the bureaucracy and the private sector through *amakudari*, discussed below. The second was bureaucratic organization and supervision of advisory committees, or *shingikai*, which incorporated business leaders, including those from the Japanese Business Federation (Keidanren), as well as other stakeholders including labour unions into negotiations over policy formulation.

Shigeru won the first of two majority governments prior to LDP unification. While Yoshida's Liberal Party exchanged power with the slightly more conservative Democratic Party of Hatoyama Ichirō before the two parties united as the LDP in 1955, given the ideological similarity of the two parties it makes sense to understand the period of (proto) LDP dominance as beginning in 1949.

19 While the construction state was associated with the Construction, Transport, Postal and Agriculture ministries, the developmental state was associated with MITI and the Ministry of Finance.

Overall, what role did the bureaucracy play in entrenching the hegemonic order of the post-war era? It clearly played a significant role, not only through effective policy creation and execution, but also by effectively depoliticizing much of what went on in the Diet. The system of bureaucratic rule meant that the direction of policy was less dependent on the partisan directives of the LDP and more directed by professional bureaucrats who were removed from the partisan world of electoral politics. As a result, not only was the ideological nature of policy reduced, but the understanding of it as ideological was also quelled.[20] The overwhelming transpartisan support that much legislation received is testament to this: Diet sessions were rarely characterized by the LDP forcing its agenda upon the JSP and JCP and were usually much more consensual. This, in turn, facilitated a wider societal appreciation of the work of the bureaucracy as in the common interest. The bureaucracy was thus a fundamental part of what made the post-war order hegemonic.

Another key element was the relationship between big business and the bureaucracy, characterized by the dynamic of *amakudari*. *Amakudari*, which literally means "descent from heaven," refers to the tendency for senior bureaucrats to "retire" from their positions and gain appointment on the boards or in advisory roles of private corporations or special public corporations, usually in the fields of the bureaucratic department that formerly employed them. Unlike in many countries, where personnel may flow informally between the public and private sectors, *amakudari* appointments were directly arranged by the bureaucracy as a deliberate and open means of maintaining linkages between the bureaucracy and the entities under their jurisdiction (Mizoguchi and Ngyuen 2012). *Amakudari* appointments not only brought insider knowledge of the bureaucracy to corporate boards, but also enabled the bureaucracy to disseminate its values and orthodoxy into the corporate sector, ensuring a harmony of interests between the two. Moreover, the *amakudari* system influenced bureaucrats' policymaking to be in the interests of the corporations they may serve on the boards of in the future.

According to Mizoguchi and Nguyen (2012), *amakudari*, which dates all the way back to the Meiji era, expanded during the period of high-speed growth in the 1960s, and developed partly due to the structural constraints of the bureaucracy. Japan's bureaucracy relied on a rigid internal labor market, characterized by seniority-based promotion that saw bureaucrats amass decades of service within the same ministry where they first started before being promoted

---

20   However, as the vociferous debate over the promulgation and later renewal of Anpo showed, security policy was a notable exception to this.

to executive ranks. Given that only a select number of bureaucrats could be promoted to top positions, *amakudari* developed partly to guarantee nearly all bureaucrats that they would enjoy job security even if they were not the beneficiaries of internal promotion. The system thus helped to guarantee that top talent continued to flow into the bureaucracy. Moreover, it ensured continued commitment to the ministry, even by those bureaucrats who know they were unlikely to be promoted (Mishima 2017).

Amakudari thus played a crucial role in cementing the link between the bureaucracy and the private sector. It did this not only by providing a safety valve for the career stability of bureaucrats, who generally received only modest salaries at the beginning of their careers, but also by ensuring that bureaucratic influence could extend to the corporations over which a bureaucratic department had jurisdiction. Moreover, it helped to ensure, from the perspective of firms, that firms had direct communicative channels with the bureaucrats that regulated them, thus enabling them access to bureaucratic favor in many cases. Thus, while it served as the basis for a close and cooperative relationship between the bureaucracy and private (as well as semi-public) enterprises, it also served as the basis for widespread and institutionalized corruption. This included the recurrent problem of *kansei dangō*, or bureaucratic bid-rigging (Mishima 2017). Nonetheless, in the early post-war era, *amakudari* was important as a means of maintaining the highly collaborative relationship between the bureaucracy and private capital that ensured general acceptance of the bureaucracy's key leadership role within developmentalism.

2.5 Production and Capital: Japanese Developmentalism and the Keiretsu

The fifth condition of the post-war hegemonic order was the role played by big business and the high degree of coordination and cooperation that developed among firms and between firms and the state. This high degree of coordination resulted in a high degree of hegemonic support across all sectors for Japan's economic model, and it also contributed to the stability of the overall economic system. The key elements of the system are as follows: 1) relationships between firms of the same *keiretsu*, especially with banks, and 2) relationships between firms and the bureaucracy, through MITI and the Ministry of Finance in particular. Japan's highly stable post-war growth was partially rooted in these two sets of complementary relationships.

Before the Second World War, Japan's economy was dominated by a small number of oligarchical, family-owned conglomerates called *zaibatsu*. The *zaibatsu* – some of which dated back to the 17th century – exercised extensive control over the Japanese economy, with each conglomerate holding major interests in numerous economic sectors, including mining, shipbuilding, trading, banking, and construction. The *zaibatsu* also exercised extensive political influence, as the primary vehicles for campaign financing. Moreover, *zaibatsu* relationships with the imperial family, the military, and politicians from Japan's two main pre-war political parties (Rikken Seiyūkai and Rikken Minseitō) were extremely close. Furthermore, they had a major influence on Japanese imperialism in Korea, Taiwan and Manchuria. In the context of the *zaibatsu* dominated economy, Japanese society was extremely unequal and polarized, with a small elite of extremely wealthy capitalists and nobility juxtaposed to a mass of desperately poor peasants and workers. Indeed, *zaibatsu* control over the economy, politics and society was seen as a major reason why Japan's brief period of liberal democracy during the 1920s and early 1930s, known as Taishō democracy, failed to consolidate, and ultimately led to extreme militarism and fascism. In the aftermath of war defeat, the occupying forces thus blamed the *zaibatsu*, and their unchecked power, for the failure of Japanese democracy, and consequently elected to break them up. The *zaibatsu* were thus disbanded, and their various component parts were turned into independent companies. Moreover, *zaibatsu* families were dispossessed of their ownership rights, and the resulting companies were largely self-owned. However, in the early years following the return of independence, the various companies that had previously formed *zaibatsu* conglomerates had come back together into new interlocking business networks called *keiretsu* (see also Gordon 2003).

These *keiretsu* networks were characterized by cross-shareholding and financing, usually centered on a major bank that provided secure, long-term financing to member companies. In many ways, the post-war *keiretsu* were copies of the pre-war *zaibatsu*, with Mitsubishi, Mitsui, Sumitomo and Fuji (formerly Yasuda) each holding interests in a full range of fields, including banking, insurance, trading, steel, shipping, mining and chemicals. However, in both their ownership structures and the relationship between member firms, there were also important changes compared to the pre-war *zaibatsu*, particularly due to the end of family ownership patterns.

What types of relations exist among firms in a *keiretsu*? Japanese *keiretsu* can be largely grouped into two categories: vertical *keiretsu* and horizontal *keiretsu* (Murakami 1996). According to Murakami (1996), vertical *keiretsu* are defined by an upstream-downstream network of relations, often known as subcontracting or distribution *keiretsu* (supply or value chain *keiretsu*). On the other hand, horizontal *keiretsu* are cross-sector networks. Horizontal or bank *keiretsu* are primarily bound together over the issue of financing, yet few firms obtain all their financing from their *keiretsu* bank. Moreover, the debt guarantee is a key part of financial *keiretsu* relationships, ensuring financial stability for member firms. Vertical *keiretsu* have generally emerged spontaneously at the will of firms, and not at the bequest or facilitation of the bureaucracy. Cultivating *Keiretsu* linkages takes time, and exit is also difficult (due to barriers and disincentives). As a result, firms have an incentive to endure difficult economic times and stay involved with *keiretsu*, a dynamic that further aided long-term economic stability (Murakami 1996).

The term *keiretsu* is usually used in a narrow sense to refer to the group of companies directly linked through cross-shareholding and direct financing from a major bank. Yet we can also conceive of the Japanese economy as a whole involving a more general structure of linkages. Indeed, each major firm within a *keiretsu* itself is linked to a range of smaller firms, both distributors and suppliers, with which it has a semi-stable relationship. Given the extent to which small and medium-sized enterprises dominate the Japanese economy, the role of these linkages with small firms should not be overlooked. Daniel Okimoto has shown how this relationship between lead firms and smaller firms settled into a symbiotic pattern. Access to large firms ensure small firms a high degree of stability, while small firms nonetheless exist as shock-absorbers in the system for large firms during times of economic contraction (Okimoto 1989). We can also think of Gary Gereffi's work on value chains (see, for example, Gereffi, Humphrey and Sturgeon 2005) and see how *keiretsu* networks represent neither the market pattern of business relations characteristic of North America nor the hierarchical model of the pre-war *zaibatsu*. Instead, *keiretsu* can be categorized as captive or relational networks, depending on the balance of power among members. While relations among large firms in a horizontal *keiretsu* might be characterized as relational networks, those between lead firms and subordinate firms in a vertical *keiretsu* fit the category of captive networks.

What were the benefits of *keiretsu* relationships for Japanese capitalism? How did *keiretsu* organization complement the role of the bureaucracy in driving economic development? Keiretsu networks served as a major basis for stability in the Japanese economy. In particular, this was achieved in three ways. First, the special relationship between keiretsu member firms and their core bank ensured that businesses could always rely on stable access to credit, even during times of economic downturn or when market signals alone might deter creditors (Anchordoguy 2005). This prevented bankruptcies and is the strongest reason why Japan experienced less than half as many bankruptcies in the post-war period as the US. Second, the practice of cross-shareholding, or *mochiai* among keiretsu firms, which accounted for as much as 75 percent of all stock, ensured that firms were generally protected from hostile takeovers (Estevez-Abe 2008). Moreover, the high proportion of stable shareholders corresponded well with the orientation of post-war Japanese capitalism that prioritized long-term growth and market share expansion over American-style quarterly profits and shareholder value. This enabled firms to largely ignore the interests of their shareholders (Anchordoguy 2005). Fourth, *keiretsu* linkages, as well as the wider linkages that took place at the level of industry and in the Japanese economy as a whole among firms through organizations like the Japanese Business Federation (Keidanren) promoted cooperation and restrained competition among firms, even among rival *keiretsu* (Anchordoguy 2005). This ability to control "excessive competition" is often seen as a major factor behind the high degree of stability (Murakami 1984). Finally, as the next section will show, *keiretsu* networks enjoyed an institutional complementarity with both the lifetime employment system and subcontracting, by facilitating labour market security and stable networks with smaller producing firms (Lechevalier 2014). In all these ways, we can see how the *keiretsu* system was a major factor behind the stable growth of the post-war era, promoting trust relationships among Japanese firms and between firms and the bureaucracy. Moreover, the stability that this system ensured was a precondition for the highly stable employment system that will be discussed below. In other words, the highly coordinated form of Japanese capitalism that emerged in the postwar not only provided important preconditions for stable capital accumulation within the Fordist-Keynesian world system. It also enjoyed strong institutional complementarities with other labour, welfare and political institutions, thereby promoting political legitimation and stable social reproduction as well.

2.6 *Production and Labour: Enterprise Unionism and Lifetime Employment*

The sixth condition for Japan's post-war hegemonic order was the role of the working class and the core relationship that developed between capital and labour. In particular, it was a relationship characterized by a high degree of economic empowerment for workers combined with a very low degree of political empowerment. Workers' economic empowerment was maintained through high wages, an egalitarian distribution of wealth, generous benefits and strong job security. In contrast, their low political empowerment was characterized by the perennial opposition status of the left parties that represented the interests of workers. Japan was thus able to simultaneously maintain a lean welfare state and small tax burden while ensuring a high degree of equality and nearly full male employment (see also Chiavacci and Lechevalier 2017). This meant that while politically it was invariably capital that exercised control, socio-economic outcomes more closely resembled social democratic countries, and partly for this reason political legitimation remained high.[21]

Japan's post-war employment regime has often been characterized by the concept of lifetime employment (Okimoto 1989). Though some firms developed lifetime employment provisions beginning in the 1930s for their core workforce, the concept became especially dominant during the period of economic boom beginning in the mid-1950s. Unlike in North America, where workers routinely make mid-career job changes, whether voluntarily or not, such a phenomenon has been relatively unusual in post-war Japan. Owing in part to paternalistic traditions and in part to labour laws that granted strong protections to workers against dismissal,[22] corporations often took on the role of an extended family for their workers under relationships characterized by loyalty on both sides. Consequently, when workers were hired – usually directly out of high school or university – they were expected to work for that company for their entire career. In return, they could expect that the company would continue to keep them employed until they retire. While workers were expected to work long hours,[23] accept job relocation and reassignment, companies were expected to provide full job security, fringe benefits and stable pay raises. While starting pay was generally low (ensuring firms could benefit from a young workforce early on), this was compensated by the guarantee of steady growth in wages (Okimoto 1989). Moreover, in cases of labour market contractions, dismissals were avoided at all costs, with job relocation, transfer to an affiliate firm or in some cases early retirement for senior workers the preferred options (Boyer 2014; Okimoto 1989). However, while lifetime employment ensured far-reaching job security – at the cost of total loyalty to the firm – it was not the only means through which Japan's employment regime was maintained.

Along with the lifetime employment system, we must consider a second element of Japan's post-war labour regime: the role of enterprise unions, their relationship with firms and their relationship with the state. Japan's pattern of

---

21 Nonetheless, as a result of the control wielded by capital over labor in relation to the state, the types of welfare and other benefits granted to workers was only available indirectly through employment in capitalist enterprises rather than directly available through government programs as in social democratic countries (see also Estevez-Abe 2008).
22 Unlike in the United States and elsewhere, employers were not allowed to dismiss workers simply to increase profits; dismissals were only allowed in cases where an employee violated the terms of employment or in cases where layoffs were proven to be the only means of avoiding bankruptcy or insolvency.
23 In some cases, beyond the point of physical and mental exhaustion, resulting in health problems and sometimes leading to death through suicide or illness, a phenomenon known as *karōshi*, or death from overwork.

labour organization in the post-war era has been characterized as "enterprise unionism" (Jeong and Aguilera 2008). Indeed, enterprise unions historically constituted up 95 percent of all unions (Chalmers 1995), while over 90 percent of unionized workers belonged to them (Jeong and Aguilera 2008). Enterprise unionism differs from craft industry-wide unionism in that the locus of labour organization is confined to the firm. While Japan has, throughout the post-war era, had a number of national labour federations,[24] along with industrial unions within each national federation, these federations were weak and decentralized. Little more than an aggregation of the enterprise unions that comprised them, they thus had little institutional power of their own other than the ability to push for wage negotiations in the annual Spring Offensive of bargaining (Jeong and Aguilera 2008).

Enterprise unionism emerged as the dominant model of unionism in post-war Japan as a result of class struggle and the role of the state in repressing industrial and national unions. During the pre-war and wartime period, unionism was heavily repressed by the state and capital. While labour activists tried to develop national or sector-level unions, the lack of a history of cross-sector unionization, combined with the high degree of repression of industry-wide organizing proved major barriers. In contrast, many firms accepted, and even encouraged, intra-firm labour organization, particularly under terms that emphasized collaboration or corporate paternalism rather than class struggle and confrontation with management (Jeong and Aguilera 2008). While labour unions were completely eradicated during the first half of the 1940s under the wartime totalitarian government, the US occupation saw the introduction of guarantees for workers' rights to organize, collectively bargain and strike. This period saw an unprecedented surge in unionization: the number of unionized workers grew from zero in 1944 to a peak of 6.8 million in 1948 (Jeong and Aguilera 2008).[25] These unions built on the pre-war institutional model of enterprise unionism but in a much more militant fashion, given their newfound freedoms and the economic and social upheaval of the immediate post-war. However, as with the pre-war period, the period beginning in 1948 saw a return to repression, as the SCAP and the Yoshida government both took action to break up the most militant unions through purges. Corporations, for

---

24   These nationwide labour federations have usually aligned with one of the major left wing political parties. For example, among the four major labour federations, the public sector Sōhyō aligned with the JSP, while private sector Dōmei aligned with the more conservative DSP. The JCP enjoyed the support of the much smaller Sanbetsu, while Chūritsu Rōren remained neutral.

25   Pre-war levels of roughly 380,000 were already reached by 1945 (Jeong and Aguilera 2008).

their part, tried to disarm unions by setting up alternative and management-sanctioned "second unions," which were successful in coopting white-collar workers, a strategy of divide and conquer (Jeong and Aguilera 2008). In this context, "Japanese labour lost the hope and energy needed to keep up the struggle to institutionalize a system of horizontal unions beyond the enterprise by the early 1960s" (Jeong and Aguilera 2008: 119).

Enterprise unionism thus came to be the dominant form of labour organization in post-war Japan. As far as its significance for the post-war hegemonic order, three things are of note. First, the corporatist and inward-looking nature of enterprise unionism meant that workers generally prioritized the interests of the firm over class struggle. Ideologically, this served as an important basis for the very low level of labour unrest from the 1960s on, in contrast to the highly turbulent late 1940s and 1950s. Second, given the full incorporation of the union within the firm, enterprise unions enjoyed a significant collaborative role with management. Indeed, managers themselves often came with significant experience in union leadership (Sakoh 1990). The division between management and labour was thus institutionally, as well as ideologically, minimized. Third, enterprise unionism did not mean that workers were completely powerless. Workers generally expected – and received – a significant share of profits, believing that their compensation ought to be reflective of the firm's profitability and competitiveness (Sakoh 1990). Fourth, enterprise unions generally limited membership to regular workers, withholding membership from the auxiliary workforce of part time and casual employees (many of whom were women) and subcontractor firms. This policy reflected management's concern for business-cycle flexibility and the union membership's concern with their own security and received tacit support from the state (Jeong and Aguilera 2008). Overall, we can see how the labour management regime enhanced the hegemonic order.

2.7 *Production and the Petit Bourgeoisie: Clientelism and the Old Middle Class*

The seventh condition of the post-war hegemonic order was the way the old middle class, including both farmers and *petit bourgeoisie*, particularly in the countryside, were incorporated into the processes of post-war modernization and industrialization. According to Sugimoto (2010), although Japan is often seen as a country of large corporations with their *sararīmen*, it is more accurately characterized as a country of small business. Emanating from the Edo period (1603–1868) class model, with artisans, farmers and merchants as the three main classes under the samurai class, the *petit bourgeoisie*, whether in agriculture, small-scale retail, or small-scale industry, was the overwhelmingly largest source of employment in post-war Japan. Indeed, even today more Japanese are employed in small business than in many other industrialized countries (Sugimoto 2010; see also Hashimoto 2001). What characterized the *petit bourgeoisie*, and this shift in its composition, in the early post-war era? What were the implications of this changing middle class for the post-war hegemonic order?

While the majority of Japanese worked in agriculture until the post-war period, they were by no means "middle class," and indeed functioned more as a peasant class until the post-war era. During the first half of the twentieth century, Japan was characterized by tremendous class inequality in both cities and the countryside. However, after World War II, the occupying forces understood that one reason for the rise of Japanese fascism was the weakness of the Japanese peasants as a class, both politically and economically. Predicting that the success of Japanese liberal democracy in the post-war era depended on relatively high levels of economic equality, they instituted a radical land reform policy that divided all rural land parcels above ten hectares and granted property rights to the cultivators. With the swoop of a pen, Japanese cultivators went from de-facto peasants to *petit bourgeoisie*. Between March 1947 and October 1948, the proportion of tenant farmers fell from 43.5% to 7.5% while 4.5 million acres were transferred (Babb 2005). This great land redistribution in rural Japan was a foundational step in the post-war development model, and ensured that, according to Murakami (1996) "the farming class did not feel left out of Japan's economic success" (198).

In this context, Japan's large and newly empowered *petit bourgeoisie* of farmers and small businesspeople developed a high degree of political organization and used it to cultivate a highly clientelist relationship with the state. Primarily, there were four main organizations that served as vehicles for organizing *petit bourgeois* interests politically: The Association of Japan Agriculture Cooperatives (hereafter Nōkyō), the National Federation of Small Business Associations, the Japan Medical Association, and the National Association of Special Postmasters. All four of these organizations (as well as others such as the Japan Nurses Association) developed close relationships with bureaucrats and with *zoku* lawmakers of the LDP, ensuring that their interests were represented in policies. For farmers, this included generous production and tax subsidies, protections against import competition, generous publicly subsidized pensions and publicly funded employment (often in construction) during the agricultural off-season. For small businesses, this involved tax subsidies, protection against competition and for small businesses associated with construction related industries, access to public works funding. Similarly, doctors received tax subsidies and LDP backing in medical fee negotiations with the bureaucracy, while special postmasters received access to funds for local infrastructure investment and privileged rights to sell insurance through their post offices (Estevez-Abe 2008). In exchange, these organizations all remained strong supporters of the LDP, providing a stable bloc of votes from their members.

However, while these interest groups that generally represented the *petit bourgeoisie*, and farmers in particular, ultimately came to be the most reliable source of the LDP's electoral coalition, this was not initially true. For example, in the immediate post-war era, the JSP was more popular with farmers, riding on their support to finish first in the 1947 election. However, after conservative parties gained control in 1949, they moved to shore up support from farmers by establishing and funding agricultural cooperatives under conservative leadership (Babb 2005). In the context of the economic boom that followed, these institutional path dependencies became settled, and farmers increasingly were identified as *petit bourgeois* rather than as workers. This orientation further entrenched their support as part of the conservative electoral condition led by the LDP after 1955. The clientelist relationship between the LDP and farmers, as well as small business owners, was further strengthened in the late 1950s when the Kishi government instituted special pension benefits for farmers and small business owners (Estevez-Abe 2008).

By the 1960s, these early institutional measures to shore up electoral support from farmers and small business owners had been institutionalized into a clientelistic relationship developed between these groups and the LDP and that also included key sectors of the bureaucracy, including the Transport, Agriculture, and Construction ministries. On one hand, this involved highly protectionist barriers to competition (including from large fractions of domestic capital as well as foreign firms and imports) and tax loopholes. On the other hand, it included generous subsidies including rice subsidies as well as extensive public works spending that mobilized local small businesses during times of economic downturn. As Estevez-Abe (2008) has shown, such policies served as proxies for direct welfare spending. They also had the effect of mobilizing strong political support for the LDP from the *petit bourgeoisie* by directly appealing to small and medium-sized businesses, rather than to the workers of those businesses. These policies thus served as the basis for mobilizing a relatively large segment of the population, one which often possessed a high degree of social standing within local communities and whose interests were aligned more with the capitalist class than with the working class, to be a major and active political constituency. What followed was a strong degree of support by local small businesses for local LDP politicians, often supporting their *kōenkai* and encouraging regular workers within their firms to join LDP politicians' *kōenkai*. In each case, the personal touch that can only be achieved through micro-level human interactions, both between small and medium enterprise (SME) owners and their workers and between SME owners and local politicians, buttressed the political incorporation of those employed by SMEs into *kōenkai*.

2.8 Gender and the Family: Extended Families and the Gendered Division of Labor

The first two characteristics of Japan's post-war welfare-employment regime have centered on male workers. This is true of both the system of lifetime employment that protected the core workforce of large firms through corporate welfare and the somewhat more precarious system of employment maintenance through infrastructure spending that protected the auxiliary workforce in construction and other sectors. Yet these two pieces of the puzzle cannot be understood without a recognition of how they relate to a third element, a rigid gendered division of labour (Miura 2012). While the above measures applied primarily to men, for women the conditions were very different. Though granted legal and political equality with the post-war constitution, women maintained a traditional social role primarily as domestic caregivers in the post-war era. While most women worked after finishing high school or university, they were expected to retire after marriage, or at least after their first pregnancy, which was often only a few years into adulthood. Women were then expected to serve primarily as caregivers, taking on nearly 100 percent of the burden of social reproduction. This included childbearing and childrearing, cooking, cleaning, shopping, and in cases where there were elderly or disabled relatives to care for, care work as well.[26]

Moreover, Miura (2012) shows how women filled a secondary, flexibilized labour market on the side of the core, protected labour market where their husbands worked. During times of economic downturn, these jobs were generally the first to be cut. While a small minority of women worked in the secure, career-track sectors of the economy, they faced tremendous structural barriers to employment in this field. Firms usually avoided hiring women to career-track positions. This was partly due to sexist attitudes about women's role in society. But it also emanated from the reality of the significant amount

---

26 In addition, women often had control over household financial decision-making (Sugimoto 2014) and were often responsible for making small-scale investments of household savings in the stock market (Kerbo and McKinstry 1995), a tendency that further buoyed Japan's rapid economic growth in the post-war period and points to the early financialization of social reproduction.

of in-house training required to develop career-track workers, conditions that conflicted with firms' expectations that women would retire when they got married. Moreover, labour laws designed to protect women, in particular, from harsh overtime work deemed "too strenuous" for women informally served as a disincentive to hire female workers (Miura 2012). Finally, income tax incentives were set up that ensured that families where only one income earner made more than 1,030,000 yen received a special tax deduction. This seriously penalized households with two full-time working parents while incentivizing women to work part-time only.[27]

In addition to this rigid gendered division of labour, another element of Japan's post-war regime of social reproduction was the extended family household and the persistence of extended family networks for caring activities. Unlike in European countries where nuclear families increasingly became the dominant family model after the war, the extended family, with three generations living under one roof, persisted in Japan for the first few decades of the post-war era (Tanaka 2010). This had several important implications. First, it meant that rather than the state assuming the burden for eldercare, this was usually taken care of by families (and usually by women). Second, it meant that less emphasis was needed on old age security programs, since cohabitation with adult children reduced the costs of supporting seniors. Third, it meant that unlike in countries with public supports for seniors where the costs of *not* having children are socialized, in Japan those costs were individualized. As a result, having one's own children continued to be an important measure for ensuring one's security in old age. As such, the fertility rate remained relatively high during this era – at least until the 1970s – and the Japanese labour force remained relatively young by international standards.

Overall, although it was premised on a rigid (and heteronormative) gendered division of labour that highly constrained the scope of autonomy and freedom for women (as well as men), the post-war Japanese regime of social reproduction served as a structural precondition for the highly stable patterns of social reproduction that occurred during the 1950s and 1960s. This system included several components, including the gender dual system, welfare through work,

---

27   Under the law, households with two incomes over 1.03 million yen ($10,000) receive a 380,000 yen tax deduction for each income, while those with only one income allow the two 380,000 yen deductions to both be applied to the sole breadwinner income. However, when the secondary earner is working for less than 1.03 million yen, in addition to the double deduction (760,000 yen total) applied to the main income, an additional deduction of 380,000 yen is applied to the sub-1.03 million yen income, a tax policy that incentivizes part time work only for secondary incomes known as the "triple dip" (Sudo 2014).

and extended family households. At the same time, this regime of social reproduction also provided a high degree of institutional complementarity with the lifetime employment model and thus indirectly buttressing Japan's highly stable, long-termist and coordinated model of capitalism overall.

2.9 Demography and Welfare: Young Society, Small Welfare State

The ninth condition of postwar hegemonic order was the favorable demographic situation. In particular, this included a relatively young workforce as well as a relatively small proportion of elderly people. These two factors contributed significantly to stable social reproduction and profitable capital accumulation. First, the structure of the lifetime employment system and its emphasis on progressive wage increases meant that while older workers tended to be paid wages that exceeded their productive output, young workers' wages tended to undervalue their labour. Thus, while a young workforce may generally be beneficial to capital accumulation, this was especially true in post-war Japan, and thus helped to further improve Japanese capital's competitiveness.

Second, the proportion of elderly people was significantly lower than in other industrial countries, comprising roughly five percent of the population in the 1950s and 1960s and still only seven percent by 1970.[28] This relatively small population of seniors, coupled with the persistence of extended family households, meant that welfare costs remained significantly lower than in other countries. Indeed, while Japan was one of the first countries to establish universal pensions and health insurance in 1958, the actual amount of compensation paid to seniors was small, amounting to little more than pocket money to give to their grandchildren (Estevez-Abe 2008).

This lack of a fiscal drain on the state from welfare spending afforded the Japanese state more revenue to spend elsewhere, particularly on public works spending as well as industrial subsidies, while keeping the tax burden low. The low degree of demand for welfare, driven by a young population and the persistence of extended family households thus provided an important condition of possibility for class compromise.[29] Without being tasked with the burden of funding universal welfare provisions (through taxes, both direct and indirect), firms had the means to maintain and strengthen corporate welfare provisioning, further entrenching company loyalty from their workers.

---

28 By comparison, the percentage of people age 65 and older in 1970 for the G7 as a whole was 10.3, while the number for the EU 28 was 11.5 (OECD 2019).

29 As discussed above, as well as the availability of women's unpaid domestic labour that was guaranteed by their role as housewives within stable breadwinner households also contributed to the low societal needs for public welfare.

While Japan went through a period of rapid urbanization in the post-war period, this change – unlike in many developing countries today – led neither to the hollowing out of the countryside nor to the development of pervasive urban slums. Instead, Japan was able to evade the problem of significant urban-rural uneven development even under conditions of rapid urbanization and industrialization. According to Murakami (1984), this was due to the high demand on the part of private capital for young workers who could be paid low wages in exchange for long-term employment security combined with state-led infrastructure spending to maintain high employment in the countryside. While this had much to do with other factors of Japanese labour management and the role of the construction state, ultimately it was these favorable demographic conditions that made this dynamic possible.

Nonetheless, far from being an era of stasis and stability, the 1950s and 1960s was one of unprecedented social change. Japan's population grew very rapidly in this period, from 84 million in 1950 to 105 million by 1970, a 25 percent jump (Statistics Japan n.d.). The population was relatively young, certainly by today's standards: in 1950, 35 percent of people were under 14, 60 percent were between 15 and 64 and only 5 percent were over 65. By 1970, the population was still young, though a higher percentage of people were of working age: 24 percent were under 14, 69 percent were 15 to 65 and 7 percent were over 65 (Statistics Japan n.d.). During the post-war period Japan continued a process of rapid urbanization and industrialization that had been going on since the Meiji Restoration.[30] While 53 percent of people lived in cities in 1950, by 1970 it was 72 percent (Ritchie and Roser 2018). This was particularly punctuated immediately after the war, where the fertility rate jumped above 4.0 for the last few years of the 1940s, before falling to just over 2.0 by the mid-1950s and remaining at that level for the rest of this period (Tanaka 2010; Statistics Japan n.d.). While urbanization played a transformative role in the Japanese economy, it played an equally significant role in relation to family life, culture and reproduction. While Japan's rapid urbanization in the post-war era was perhaps more successful than that of any other country, neither creating an underclass of slum-dwellers on the edge of cities nor leaving in its wake a backward and decaying rural society, it nonetheless had major social consequences. Perhaps the most significant of these was the decline of the extended family. In

---

30   Incidentally, Japan was arguably the most urbanized pre-industrial society in the world; pre-industrial Edo (Tokyo) was the biggest city in the world in the 18th century, with over a million residents (and over 90% rates of literacy), while Osaka and Kyoto were both home to more than 100,000 people. Castle towns such as Wakayama, Hiroshima, Nagoya, Kanazawa and Okayama were each home to 10,000s of people.

1955, approximately 35 percent of Japanese lived in extended families; by 1975, the number was only 22 percent (partly because elderly family members often stayed behind in rural towns and villages) (CAO 2006).

These social changes, including the slow aging of the population, rapid urbanization and the transition from the extended family to the nuclear family as the dominant household form all brought with them important consequences for Japan's regime of social reproduction, as the next chapter will show.

2.10 Nation and Ideology: The Pacifist Nationalism of the Post-war Era

The tenth condition of Japan's post-war hegemonic order was what I call pacifist nationalism, or the sort of nationalism that emerged after World War II in opposition to the militaristic, quasi-fascistic nationalism that had pervaded the pre-war era. This new nationalism was different from the old nationalism in important ways. For one, it was pacifist rather than militarist, seeking to position Japan and the Japanese people as peace seeking, driven by goals of demilitarization and denuclearization and to peaceful and amicable relations between sovereign and equal countries. Moreover, it was no longer characterized by a valorization of social stratification. While pre-war nationalism had held the emperor as the God-like top of the social order and Father of the Japanese ethno-nation, whilst also providing legitimation for a nobility class that occupied a position between the emperor and the ordinary people, the post-war nationalism spoke to an egalitarian social structure. The emperor was now seen as merely human and nothing more than a symbol of the nation and the nobility class was legally erased.

In this context of social transformation, the liquidation of the nobility class and the end of emperor worship, how were new identities based on class, race and nation narrated within socializing practices and what were the effects of this for entrenching the commonsensical nature of the post-war order? In this context, three powerful ideological tropes, each with long lineages in Japanese history characterized Japanese social order: *mura* (village), *ie* (household), and *tan'itsu minzoku* (ethnic homogeneity) are of note (see also Murakami 1984; 1996). The trope of the *mura* claims that all Japanese people today (regardless of class) are the descendants of the peasant class, who worked side-by-side in small village communities. These communities were self-sufficient yet internally co-dependent, and characterized by largely horizontal relations, other than age- and gender-based hierarchies. The effect of this is to posit that the old class society of the Edo period (1603–1868) has given way: with the erasure of the *samurai* class with the Meiji Restoration (1868) and nobility in the post-war era, modern Japan was no longer a class society. This ideology thus seeks to frame the Japanese *mura*, or nation, as an eternal construct with the descendants of peasants going back to time immemorial. Yet at the same time, *mura* is also specific to the contemporary world in its contrast with the previous feudal era of social hierarchy.

Moreover, the ideology of the *mura* was enlivened through Japan's wartime defeat and the impact that it had on post-war class society. As Kerbo and McKinstry (1995) argue, "in Japan, the suffering shared by elites, future elites, and the masses was a leveling experience which had profound effects on attitudes for many years" (13). Before the Second World War, four families in Japan controlled 25 percent of corporate assets and ten families controlled 75 percent (Kerbo and McKinstry 1995). The income gap between corporate elites and workers was one hundred to one. But that all changed with the wartime defeat and served as a major basis for Japan's post-war emphasis on equality.

However, while the erasure of class difference ideologically and its replacement with national homogeneity was clearly a major part of the postwar hegemonic project, this was not universally successful. Labour unions remained important forces, and the militancy of the student movement in the 1960s can attest to the fact that there was staunch resistance to this attempt to naturalize some hierarchies while erasing others. Nonetheless, the ethos of enterprise unionism, and of belonging to a (hierarchically ordered) company before belonging to the working class came to be entrenched. Part of this was the way the notion of *ie* (household or kinship group) existed to reconstruct hierarchies as a natural part of Japanese social order: as an almost innate cultural characteristic of the Japanese ethno-nation (Murakami 1984, 1996). Unlike *mura*, *ie* posits the samurai hierarchical social order as the foundation of Japanese social order. Under this system, people are linked hierarchically yet each hold the opportunity to ascend hierarchies over time through dedication. Murakami argues that this hierarchical structure serves as the basis for the Japanese corporation, and relations within the firm.

Clearly these two ideological constructs, *mura* and *ie*, are powerful regulatory ideals for Japanese national identity. Through *mura* we get a transhistorical explanation for the (mythical) notion of Japanese social equality and homogeneity. At the same time, *ie* generates a discourse of certain social hierarchies, including the family and the workplace, as essentially Japanese. Needless to say, both narratives are highly potent ways of naturalizing and justifying capitalist social relations. On one hand, class differences are erased through the *mura* discourse. On the other hand, they are justified, even celebrated, through the *ie* discourse. It would be wrong to make a culturally determinist argument that this cultural nationalism and an uncritical ideological commitment to traditional social structures served as the basis for Japanese ruling relations in post-war Japan. Nonetheless, it is clear that they served an important role in socialization at all life stages and provided part of the normative justification for hegemonic social relations.

While this appeal to the essential nature of indigenous social structures and their basis as the mediators of social relations was one effect of post-war nationalism, a further element was the degree to which it required the reproduction of a myth of ethnic homogeneity. Japan almost immediately lost touch with its former colonies after World War II and was fully exempt from having to deal with the post-colonial fallout. This clean break from the colonial half-century (1895–1945) allowed Japan to return to a myth of national homogeneity and isolation (the "island country" trope) that served as a major basis for claims to its uniqueness and separation from the rest of the world.[31] Yet it also prevented Japanese people from being able to adequately accept their role as an imperial aggressor in the first half of the twentieth century.[32]

Overall, the post-war era thus saw the development of a new kind of nationalism that rejected the militarism, authoritarianism, feudal hierarchies and emperor worship, replacing them with commitments to pacifism, grassroots democracy (*mura*), corporate hierarchies (*ie*), and egalitarianism based on shared ethnic community. This new nationalism served as the basis for a new collective ethos that played a major role culturally in anchoring Japan's post-war rebuilding under conditions of domestic stability. At the same time, it helped strengthen Japanese democracy and ensured that capitalist development proceeded in an egalitarian fashion, unlike in the pre-war era. Nonetheless, this pacifist nationalism was rooted in myths, not only about Japan's ethnic homogeneity (that denied the existence of internal Others) but also about Japanese people's roles in the Pacific War. This led to the erasure from memory of the complicity of society as a whole in Japan's wartime aggression and instead presenting the Japanese people as mere victims of the war, while excluding from both historical memory and from future society the presence of immigrants.

2.11 Environment and National Resources: Cheap Oil

The eleventh and final condition of post-war hegemonic order was the availability of cheap oil and other natural resources. Access to oil had been a major challenge for Japan in the pre-war era. Indeed, it is the lack of access to oil in the wake of American and European sanctions for Japan's invasion of China in

---

31 Importantly, this often made it difficult for Japanese people to identify with people of other countries, including those in similar class positions to themselves.

32 Moreover, as Dian (2015) has argued, this played into efforts by both parties to portray the Japanese as only victims of the war.

1937 that is often cited as the ultimate reason for Japan's entry into World War II with the US. Prior to Pearl Harbor, Japan's oil supply was reaching critically low levels, and war with the US (as well as the UK and the Netherlands), who held access to oil in the Middle East and Indonesia, was seen as the only way of getting that oil by certain elements of the military.

Unsurprisingly then, given Japan's complete lack of oil and gas and relative lack of other mineral resources (including coal), stable and cheap access to these resources was fundamentally necessary for Japanese industrialization. The immediate post-war era witnessed a flood of cheap oil onto the market. This easy access to natural resources was enabled by two things. First, technological breakthroughs in oil drilling and other extractive technologies reduced costs and increased the ease with which vital natural resources – and oil in particular – could be produced. Second, post-war American hegemony at the level of the world system, and the security that this brought to the global trading system, enabled a high degree of stability and openness in access to these crucial resources. Third, as Hall (2009) has shown, Japanese industry developed – with the facilitation of the bureaucracy – a strategy of exporting heavily polluting industrial production in particular to neighboring developing countries, especially in Southeast Asia. Through this process Japanese industry was able to partially displace the negative environmental effects of Japan's rapid industrial development, which included several public health crises caused by industrial pollution, including Minamata disease (caused by mercury poisoning), and Yokkaichi asthma (caused by sulfur dioxide).

Thus, under the conditions of the post-war liberal order, Japan was able to import vital natural resources – including energy resources – and export unwanted and dangerous polluting industries. As we will see in the next chapter, challenges to world order in the 1970s disrupted these conditions of stability, upsetting the ease of access to natural resources that Japan enjoyed until then, beginning with the first oil crisis in 1973.

3   The Post-war Japanese Historic Bloc

Through all these favorable conditions, Japan in the post-war era saw the development of a historic bloc, which was led by the triumvirate of the LDP, bureaucracy, and large corporations, what has been called *seikangyō* (politics, bureaucracy and industry) in Japanese (Ikeda 2011). While the exact degree of influence of each of the three constituents of this power bloc is the subject to significant debate, with Weberian thinkers such as Johnson (1982) privileging the role of the bureaucracy, policy-oriented thinkers such as Ramseyer and

Rosenbluth (1993) locating the LDP at the centre of analysis, and Marxists such as Itoh (1990, 1992, 2000) giving more influence to the capitalist class, such debates are beside the point. What is significant is that each of the three forces played its own role in the maintenance of hegemonic ruling relations through a division of labour.

The LDP was predominantly driven by its needs of maintaining political legitimacy, both at the aggregate level through general policy determined by the Cabinet and at the micro-level of individual lawmakers. These lawmakers were structurally required to seek maximal degrees of public funds for their districts as means of ensuring electoral survival under conditions of intraparty (as well as interparty) competition. Moreover, the electoral system of mixed member districts with intraparty competition meant that the LDP simultaneously enjoyed conditions of virtual guarantees of continued party rule with structural pressures for intense mobilization on the part of individual candidates. This had the crucial effect of forcing candidates to stay motivated to appeal to constituents.

The bureaucracy, on the other hand, was driven by economic and social questions. The more dominant economic ministries – MITI and the Ministry of Finance in particular – fashioned macro-economic and industrial policy aimed at generating and maintaining rapid economic growth. In contrast, other ministries such as Transport, Postal and Construction were more driven by the need for infrastructure and development in peripheral regions. Still others, such as the Ministry of Health and Welfare and the Ministry of Education were concerned with the development of Japan's social reproductive needs: health, education and welfare. The more long-term and general aims of the bureaucracy – and the economic ministries in particular – existed in dynamic tension with the more particularistic and short-term interests of individual LDP lawmakers.

Finally, the third member of the power bloc, Japanese corporations, played an important role in cooperating with the LDP and bureaucracy. These firms had a largely cooperative relationship with the bureaucracy, often accepting bureaucratic guidance and oversight at the cost of firm autonomy. In other ways, they participated in major policy deliberations through *shingikai* where they sought to achieve consensus in negotiations that included other stakeholders, including representatives from organized labour and the various *petit bourgeois* organizations. Overall, through both their structural and instrumental power, Japanese capital played a significant role in shaping the trajectory of post-war Japanese development, ensuring rapid growth and robust capital accumulation until the 1980s. At the same time, through multilateral negotiations that included the Japanese Business Federation as well as bilateral relations between firms and their workers or between lead firms and their subordinate firms, Japanese capital rarely sought to unilaterally dictate the direction of decisions. Instead, it sought dialogue and consensus in the interests of long-term stability and hegemony.

However, while this historic bloc clearly enjoyed coordinated leadership on the part of this three-pronged power bloc, it also incorporated, and generally represented the interests of a wide range of social and class forces. In this sense, we might, following Jessop (1983) understand Japan's post-war hegemonic order as an example of "expansive hegemony" that actively included a range of subaltern social and class forces, or as a "one nation hegemony" that tried to unite virtually all major social forces within the overarching hegemonic project.

Chief among the forces included within this coalition was most notably the *petit bourgeoisie*, which enjoyed a plethora of protections and supports maintained through Japan's political system in return for their active role in supporting the LDP. Partly due to their exorbitant electoral influence – which the LDP maintained by design – and partly due to the high degree of political organization and social visibility of their leading organizations, the *petit bourgeoisie* wielded a substantial degree of influence.

A second group that was also incorporated into the historic bloc, though on less favorable terms, was the privileged workforce of major corporations, who enjoyed the strong benefits of the lifetime employment model. However, as Estevez-Abe (2008) has shown, the benefits these workers enjoyed were, unlike in social democratic countries of Europe, mediated through employer firms rather than provided directly to workers. These workers were thus incorporated into the historic bloc as appendages of firms rather than as agents wielding effective power in their own right. Though they worked for the state rather than private capital, in general terms Japan's (comparatively small) public sector workforce can also be included in this category.

A third element of the historic bloc, further subordinated, was a group of other workers, often in blue-collar sectors of the economy, employed by relatively inefficient and uncompetitive small and medium enterprises, primarily in construction but also in a range of manufacturing and trade industries indirectly related to construction. These workers enjoyed the benefits of Japan's infrastructure-driven model of public provisioning, through state-funded employment maintenance systems. However, as with the white-collar workers discussed above, this was also indirect, as the SMEs who employed these workers, rather than the workers themselves, were the recipients of public works spending.

A fourth and final group that was incorporated into the post-war historic bloc was women, or more specifically, women who enjoyed the financial security of a breadwinning husband and either worked as housewives or took flexible part time jobs to supplement their husbands' incomes. Though Japan's post-war constitution, imposed under conditions of occupation, formally granted women equal rights to men, and instituted universal suffrage, post-war Japanese society remained strongly patriarchal and characterized by a rigid gendered division of labour. Women's freedom to pursue careers of their choosing outside of the home was thus severely limited, while their domestic obligations were significant and highly restrictive. Nonetheless, within the context of a dominant gender ideology rooted in the notion of *ryōsai kenbo* (good wife, wise mother), and the popular resonance of the ideological justification for the gendered division of labour in Japanese society, women enjoyed certain benefits – and even a degree of empowerment – within the post-war historic bloc.

As with the previous three subordinate groups, these benefits were largely indirectly attained through the economic security granted to men through the lifetime employment system. Women's economic security was thus largely contingent on marriage, and conditions for those who did not marry were often grim (Hashimoto 2001). Nonetheless, given the ideological normativity enjoyed by marriage and the equation of a woman's role with wifehood and motherhood, it is easy to see how such conditions could be seen as liberating rather than restrictive. Freed from having to work long hours as their husbands, many women enjoyed autonomy as the managers of their households. As housewives, they could closely oversee their children's development and exert control over the direction of household spending, even determining how much *kozukai*, or allowance, their husbands got after necessary household expenditures were deducted. Outside of the home, many women played active roles in community organizations, including their children's schools' parent-teacher organizations.

However, along with these various social forces that were integrated to varying degrees into the post-war historic bloc, it is also important to recognize the groups who were excluded from any form of social or political power. These marginalized groups included ethnic and cultural minorities, including ethnic Koreans, Ainu, and *burakumin*, as well as insecure workers, and many women who lacked the financial support of a male breadwinner, including unmarried women, divorcees, and single mothers. As Osawa (2013) has shown, many of these groups experienced high rates of poverty, and received virtually no supports from the state. All these groups lacked means for effective political organization and existed on the fringes of Japanese society, largely voiceless.

Their exclusion from the post-war historic bloc thus did little to upset the high degree of political legitimacy it enjoyed from the various groups who were incorporated into it.

4 Conclusion

Overall, we can see that the post-war period was clearly one of relative hegemonic order that effectively carried out requirements of accumulation, reproduction and legitimation. It did so by maintaining conditions of robust economic growth, low unemployment, strong growth in wages, high levels of inequality, steady and stable population growth, while promoting progressively improving outcomes in education and public health, high levels of popular participation in politics and support for the LDP in particular.

This hegemonic order was formed and maintained by eleven conditions that highlight the significance of world order, forms of state, domestic social forces and social reproduction. Hegemonic order was also rooted in the post-war global political economy and geopolitical order, constitutional and political reforms and the rise of a pacifist nationalist ideology. It was maintained by an historic bloc that was led by a ruling elite of the bureaucracy, the LDP and leading firms. Yet this historic bloc also incorporated various social groups, including protected white-collar workers, blue-collar workers, farmers, small business owners, and middle-class housewives, drawing on the support of each of these groups through a range of policies and institutions. While this approach to maintaining political order succeeded for several decades, in the long run, structural conditions (e.g., contradictions at level of world order and demographics) and the challenge of maintaining this historic bloc undermined hegemonic order, as following chapters will show.

CHAPTER 5

Contradictions and Transitions of the Late Shōwa Era

This chapter explores the period from the early 1970s until the late 1980s, a time that began and ended with crisis and transition.[1] The beginning of the period saw several significant changes in world order. These included the partial breakdown of the old Bretton Woods System, the end of the Dollar-Gold Standard and the First Oil Crisis, conditions that shook the Japanese economy and pointed to renewed uncertainty. The end of the period saw the rise of the bubble economy and ultimately the beginning of a long period of economic stagnation that persists to this day. More symbolically, this period also ended with the 1989 death of the Shōwa Emperor, who had reigned since 1926 and became an object of criticism both within and outside of Japan after World War II for his role in Japanese military aggression and imperialism.

This chapter argues that beginning in the 1970s, Japan's post-war hegemonic order began to slowly encounter changes to the underlying conditions that supported it. These changes gradually accumulated, and ultimately led to contradictions both between the roles actually performed by Japan's social, political and economic institutions versus the roles they were supposed to perform as well as among institutions that had previously functioned complementarily, and which increasingly functioned in contradictory ways. The chapter is divided into two parts. The first part of the chapter outlines the changes to conditions of hegemonic order and considers three types of change that are significant in this period. First, structural changes include not only changes to the structural conditions of global political economy but also changing demographic conditions. Second, political changes refer to significant policy changes, either in response to changing structural conditions or as a backlash against politically contested conditions of Japan's original post-war order.

Third, what I call institutional changes but also referred to as path-dependencies or institutional drift, represent a slow shift in the function or nature of an institution to the point that it no longer performs its original role. Under such circumstances, an institution may go from a complementary to

---

1 Parts of this chapter draw upon an earlier article, "From nationalist communitarianism to fragmentary neoliberalism: Japan's crisis of social reproduction", published in *Capital & Class* (2019).

a contradictory relationship with other institutions and with the hegemonic order as a whole. The second part of the chapter outlines the overall implications of these transformations for Japan's hegemonic order. In particular, it considers implications from the perspective of political legitimation, capital accumulation and social reproduction, and for the relations of force within Japan's historic bloc.

While the period in the 1950s and 1960s saw the development of a cohesive hegemonic order, the period beginning in the 1970s saw a host of changes. These included both abrupt and gradual changes. Moreover, these changes occurred within not only Japan's political and economic institutions but also with regard to structural demographic conditions and dynamics at the level of world order. This first part of the chapter considers three types of change during this period. After first considering six key structural changes to the conditions of Japanese political order that were manifest in the 1970s and 1980s, it turns to seven core political changes. Finally, it examines six major institutional changes. The second part of the chapter considers the implications of these changes for Japan's hegemonic order.

1 Structural Changes to World Order

Three major changes to the structural conditions of world order characterize the period of the 1970s and 1980s. These include the restructuring of the world economy under economic globalization beginning with the end of the Dollar-Gold Standard in 1971; the two oil crises of 1973 and 1979; and the growing frictions between Japan and the US that culminated in the Plaza Accord of 1985. It is important to note that each of the three structural changes had their origins in key political decisions, and thus might not be thought of as structural. Yet in each case, the decisions made had impacts on the structural conditions of world order, while further impacting Japanese political economy indirectly. In other words, from the perspective of the Japanese hegemonic order, these changes occurred largely outside the scope of the Japanese state's agency.

1.1 *The Nixon Shocks*

Beginning in the 1970s, the fundamental ordering framework of global political economy underwent a transformation that ultimately came to be known as economic globalization. This transformation was partially triggered by the end of the Dollar-Gold Standard, and later further advanced through technological innovation as well as a host of legal political transformations both within individual states and to the core institutions of global trade and commerce.² It resulted in an increase in not only global trade but more importantly, global financial flows and foreign direct investment as well as the rise of transnational corporations and increasingly deterritorialized production networks. In other words, it meant an end to the Keynesian-Fordist trading regime that had bolstered Japanese export-oriented developmentalism since the 1950s.

In Japan, this broader transformation was punctuated by two tumultuous events of the summer of 1971 that are referred to as the "Nixon shocks." First, in July 1971, American Secretary of State Henry Kissinger met with Chinese Premier Zhou Enlai for the first time, and President Nixon subsequently announced he would be visiting China himself (Nakajima 2011). The Japanese government was unaware of, and shocked by this sudden development, which also prompted Prime Minister Satō to visit China himself (Nakajima 2011). Overall, this first "Nixon shock" had critical geopolitical implications, as it marked the death knell of the Sino-Soviet alliance, while also marking the beginning of the integration of China into the capitalist world economy.

Second, in August 1971, Nixon unpegged the dollar from gold in a move to revive sagging economic fortunes and the growing trade deficit that the US had developed with Japan and Europe in particular. According to Hook (2005), "Nixon's abandonment of the gold standard and the move to a floating exchange rate system led to a rapid rise in the value of the yen" (41). While the yen had been pegged to the dollar at a rate of 360:1 since 1949, it was revalued up to 308:1 in 1971 after a meeting of ten finance ministers from major economies (Nakajima 2011). Its value grew further, up to 272:1 in 1973 and 210:1 in 1978 (Hook 2005). While the strong yen did not lead to an end to the American trade deficit, it did have a negative effect on Japanese exports in the 1970s. Moreover, it provided one of the first stimuli for the offshoring of Japanese industrial production, as we will explore below.³

Third, in the aftermath of the decision to abandon fixed exchange rates, conditions emerged that facilitated the development of financial capitalism, particularly in the US. These were extended in the 1980s as many countries removed another hallmark of the Bretton Woods System, capital controls,

---

2 These include the three Bretton Woods Institutions of the General Agreement on Trade and Tariffs, the World Bank and the International Monetary Fund.
3 Nixon's attempts to play hard-ball with Japan over its trade policy grew even more forceful in 1973, when he placed an embargo on American soybean exports to Japan, which accounted for 92 percent of Japan's soybean consumption and thus threatened Japan with the near total loss of one of its most important sources of protein (though the export embargo was overturned only a week later) (Du Bois 2019; New York Times 1973).

further enabling the free flow of capital across borders (Germann 2014). In the case of Japan, this ultimately led to the financialization of the Japanese economy beginning in the mid-1980s in the wake of neoliberal financial deregulation that took place under Nakasone and prompted the rise of stock market and real estate asset boom known as the bubble economy (Lechevalier 2014).[4]

1.2 The Oil Shocks

Along with these changes to the economic structures of world order, the two oil crises of the 1970s proved a major shock to the Japanese economy. In the 1970s oil accounted for nearly half of the value of all imports (Dore 1986). In 1973, decisions by OPEC to limit the supply of oil on the world market led to a sudden spike in oil prices in the Middle East, which provided 88 percent of Japan's oil (Wakatsuki 2011). While this caused the first post-war recession in Japan, it also led to a growing political awareness of the power of oil-rich countries in the Middle East especially and a recognition of the vulnerability of the Japanese economy to energy and natural resource shortages and price fluctuations. In other words, it meant an end to cheap oil, and the lack of concern over energy consumption and efficiency that had gone with it. Politically, the Oil Crisis forced Japan to forge a more nuanced foreign policy line in the Middle East, taking a more neutral stance in the Israel-Palestine dispute than the US (Wakatsuki 2011). Then, in 1979, the second oil shock occurred. This time, Prime Minister Ōhira Masayoshi (1978–80) took a more hardline position in relation to the Middle East, siding with the US. This ultimately paid off, as Carter backed Ōhira's proposal for oil import quotas, rather than that of France, which would have required Japan to reduce its imports by 75 percent in relation to estimates by 1985 (Wakatsuki 2011).

The first oil shock led to decline in GDP in 1974 for the first time in the post-war era. It (along with the shift to floating exchange rates) also brought Japan back into a trade deficit of 373 billion yen in 1973 and 1.9 trillion in 1974, which continued until 1981 (MOF n.d.). While Japan's economy as a whole recovered faster from the first oil shock than those of the US and UK, this marked the end of the high growth era and the start of a new era of moderate but stable GDP growth (Nakakita 2017). Moreover, recovery from the shock varied by industry, and some industries, such as shipbuilding and textiles in particular, began to decline as a result of the shock (Berggren 1995).[5] In addition, the recession

---

4 It also led to the development of high rates of Japanese purchases of American treasury bills, as the Reagan administration raised interest rates.
5 Steel, petrochemicals and aluminum also faced increased competitive disadvantages after the shock (Katz 1998).

caused by the shock prompted an increase in public spending, particularly public works, in order to revive flagging industries, including in construction (Nakakita 2017). The oil shock also served as a point of transition for the orientation of MITI, which moved away from its role in facilitating Japanese heavy industries and began to shift focus towards the knowledge industry, including semiconductors and computers (Berggren 1995). As a result, by the early 1980s, Japan was the largest producer in the world of semiconductors. In addition to prompting the development of high-tech sectors, Japan's economy also successfully adapted to the increased price of oil: by 1989, the volume of oil consumed per unit of GNP had fallen by more than half, while the value of oil consumed per GNP had also declined.[6] In contrast, in the US the volume of oil consumed per GNP only fell slightly and the value of oil consumed per GNP increased (Hutchison 1993). Thus, while Japan effectively weathered the storm caused by the oil shocks, they nonetheless had profound implications for Japanese capitalism.

1.3   American Trade Frictions and the Plaza Accord

Third, beginning with trade tensions over Japanese exports of synthetic fibers to the United States that emerged in the early 1970s, an increasingly complicated trading relationship with the United States developed. This was characterized by growing animosity directed to Japan on the part of the United States over protectionism and the substantial trade surplus that Japan enjoyed. In the late 1970s, pressures continued to grow, with American demands that Japan increase imports of lumber, beef and oranges, among other things (Wakatsuki 2011). These tensions reached a point of climax with the signing of the Plaza Accord in 1985 that forced Japan to revalue the yen and accept voluntary export restraints over a range of products in an effort to rebalance trade between the two countries. In other words, it meant an end to the highly favorable trading conditions that had characterized the Japanese-US relationship since the 1950s and served as the counterweight to Japan's role as a compliant but passive geopolitical ally of the US and host of major US military bases under the Anpo.

What course of events characterized the development of the Plaza Accord, and what were its consequences for Japanese American relations and for Japanese political economy more generally? According to Lucarelli (2015), "Japan's current economic malaise has its roots in the chain of events that led to the expansionary monetary policies enacted after the September 1985 Plaza

---

[6] This was partly due to the adoption of more efficient technologies by businesses (Kameyama 2017).

Accords" (312). The Plaza Accord was pursued by the US as a solution to contradictions that had emerged out of Reagan's monetary policy. In the aftermath of the Second Oil Shock (1979), the US Federal Reserve under Paul Volcker instituted major interest rate hikes in order to curb inflation and restore conditions for profitable accumulation domestically. This led to a high US dollar, which consequently led the American trade deficit to grow even bigger. While it was already 27 billion in the late 1970s, by 1984 it had reached 148 billion dollars. This, coupled with other Reagan-era policies such as massive tax cuts for the wealthy and substantial increases in defense spending, also led to the ballooning of the US deficit, from just 4 billion during 1978–80 to 128 billion by 1985.

Then, in the context of a pronounced global economic downturn at the start of the 1980s, the US government encouraged Japan and other countries to invest in stimulus policies designed to boost domestic consumption, thus boosting the yen and reducing the trade deficit. These policies were also reiterated by the Japanese government's own Maekawa Report. However, while the Japanese government was initially leery of the inflationary effects such moves might have, Central Bankers from the G5 countries instead intervened and coordinated a series of measures that led to the depreciation of the dollar compared to the yen. As a result, the value of the yen fell, from 260 in 1985 to 175 in 1986. Ultimately in the face of mounting US pressure, the Bank of Japan engaged in a series of interest rate hikes designed to increase the value of the yen. As a result, the yen's value soared, all the way to a high of 80 yen per dollar by 1995. The soaring yen led to a surge in speculative investment in the stock market and real estate, both from abroad and domestically, in what became known as the bubble economy (Lechevalier 2014).[7]

However, paradoxically, the main aim of the policy was not achieved: the US trade deficit did not go away despite the high yen. While Lechevalier (2014) argues that this was evidence that it was not an artificially weak yen that was responsible for the trade imbalance, this is not the whole picture. As Lucarelli (2015) shows, many Japanese firms made up for the higher costs of their exports to the United States by moving production to other parts of Asia. This led to the acceleration of the transnationalization of Japanese capital, a dynamic that would ultimately become a hallmark of the transformation of Japanese capitalism in the Heisei era. In response to the high yen, the Bank of Japan made efforts to rein in interest rates. But this only served to increase the flow of speculative financial capital, exacerbating the economic bubble and

---

7   Other factors were also responsible for the bubble, including the early 1980s' financial deregulation and the increase in surplus cash held by banks as a result of the decreased need for main-bank financing by their affiliate industrial firms (Lucarelli 2015).

the relentless asset price spiral that saw the Nikkei Tokyo stock exchange treble its value in only four years. By the time the Nikkei peaked on December 29th, 1989, at just under 39,000 points, the land value of the Imperial Palace in Tokyo exceeded that of the entire state of California (Haeber 2007).

While the effects of the bubble economy will be part of the focus of the next chapter, overall, we can see how these structural changes in the conditions of world order and of Japan's economic relationship with the United States had major implications for the nature of Japan's hegemonic order. The rise of financialization, globalization, neoliberal monetary policy and the transnationalization of production, all phenomena that are highlighted by the events discussed above, were developments in which the Japanese state was an active player. Nonetheless, they led to changing structural conditions in global political economy that were not easily reversible but that had major implications for domestic political economy and ruling relations alike, ultimately undermining the stable political economic order that had hitherto developed.

2   Structural Demographic Changes

In addition to these three structural changes to conditions of world order, three further changes characterized this era in relation to demographic conditions. These include 1) the onset of population aging; 2) the decline of extended family households and the growth of nuclear family households; and 3) the slow increase of women in the workforce.

2.1   *The Beginning of an Aging Society*

First, in the period from the 1970s to the 1990s the Japanese population transitioned from being markedly young in comparison to Western European and North American countries to being the oldest of major OECD countries. The population of young people fell both proportionately and, beginning in 1980, in absolute terms as well. While the proportion of elderly people (65+) had remained between 5 and 6 percent of the total population from the 1930s through the 1960s, reaching 7 percent in 1970 (Tanaka 2010), it subsequently started to grow rapidly, reaching 12 percent already by 1990. The median age grew very rapidly, and the proportion of the population of working age peaked by 1990. Given that seniors' welfare costs are invariably higher than those of children, this meant a growing budget for social expenditures.

Part of the reason for this population aging was the declining fertility rate, which had fallen from just above 2.0 from the mid-1950s until the early 1970s to between 1.8 and 1.6 from the late 1970s to 1989. Despite this change, the number of babies born to married couples stayed constant from the 1970s to the 1990s, as did the number of desired children, at 2.2 and 2.6 respectively (MHLW 1996). The change, therefore, occurred in the proportion of women who married, as increasing numbers of women opted to forego marriage and childbearing.[8]

2.2 The Decline of Extended Families

Second, this period saw a decline in extended family households and a rise in not only nuclear family households but also non-extended, non-nuclear family households, including single person households. While the proportion of extended family households fell from 36 percent in 1955 to 30 percent in 1965 to 23 percent in 1970 to just 17 percent in 1990, the proportion of nuclear family households stayed roughly the same during this period, at around 60 percent of all households (CAO 2006). Conversely, the proportion of single person households grew from 3 percent in 1955 to 20 percent in 1975 and to 23 percent by 1990 (CAO 2006). This meant a steady decline in the number of households where seniors lived with their children – practically a fall of 50 percent – from the mid-1960s to 1990, while the proportion of seniors doubled over the same period, and the population of seniors grew from roughly 6 million to 15 million. In other words, even though the total number of seniors more than doubled – implying that the maximum number of extended family households possible increased substantially – the actual number of extended family households shrank. Thus, while 79% of seniors lived with their children in 1968, by 1995 it was just 54%, and while approximately 1.7 million seniors lived apart from their children in 1970, by 1995 this number had quintupled to 8.4 million. This was due to the increase in the sheer number of elderly people, the continued movement of young people to cities, and the more general cultural trend of nuclear familialization (Kaneshiro 1998). With so many more seniors and so few extended family households this inevitably shifted the burden of care onto the state, while also necessitating a greater outlay on pensions.

2.3 Rise of Women in the Workforce

The third structural demographic change from this period, albeit a slow-moving one, was the gradual increase in women working outside of the home. Women grew from 33 percent of the total workforce in 1970 to

---

8   In the case of Japan, where the legal and social barriers to having children outside of marriage have remained significant, reduced fertility rates necessarily went hand in hand with reduced rates of marriage.

39 percent by 1994 (MHLW 1996). Moreover, the type of work women engaged in changed significantly. Two thirds of working women in 1955 and a majority of working women in 1965 were employed by a family business or self-employed, therefore representing the old *petit bourgeoisie*. Yet by 1995 78 percent of working women were employed by a company as wage laborers and only a fifth worked as *petit bourgeoisie* (GEB 2016). Among women who were married to salaried employee husbands, the proportion that worked grew from 25 percent in 1955 to 38 percent in 1970 to 53 percent in 1990. At the same time, the proportion who worked as employees (not as *petit bourgeoisie*) grew from 10 percent in 1955 to 25 percent in 1970 to 44 percent by 1990 (Kaneshiro 1998). Overall, the growing proportion of women in the workforce, and the changing social role of women in general, was another structural change that posed challenges to the male breadwinner, female housewife model.

During this period, attitudes about women's role outside of the home also changed. while 58 percent of men and 39 percent of women in 1972 thought that women should either never work or retire after marriage or their first child, 31 percent of men and 52 percent of women thought that they should keep working, either with or without a break from work while their children are young. In contrast, by 1995, only 29 percent of men and 22 percent of women thought women should never work or retire young while 64 percent of men and 73 percent of women thought women ought to keep working. In other words, between 1972 and 1995, support for working mothers (including those who return to work after a break during preschool years) went from a minority opinion to that of nearly 70 percent of Japanese (MHLW 1996).[9]

Overall, we can see how beginning in the 1970s, Japanese society was characterized by significant demographic changes, including population aging, changing household patterns, and a rise of women in the workforce. While the full effects of these changes would not be felt or understood for decades to come, beginning in the early 1970s a number of forward-thinking bureaucrats and politicians began to consider their implications for Japanese society. The policy changes that were pursued, both successfully and unsuccessfully, in the wake of these demographic changes will be part of the focus of the next section.

---

9 The reasons for this shift are not fully clear, but the growing rates of post-secondary educational attainment for women as well as the growing economic push towards dual-income-earning households are likely among the reasons for this attitudinal shift.

3   Political Changes

In addition to the above structural global political economy and demographic changes, a number of political changes, or new policy directions taken partly in response to the structural changes, were pursued in the 1970s and 1980s. These include both economic and social policies, aimed at addressing the challenges caused by economic globalization and population aging in particular. This section will examine seven of these changes in detail.

The 1972 election of Tanaka Kakuei as LDP leader represented in many ways a sea change in Japanese politics. Tanaka was young and from a humble background, having only received an elementary education, and connected very effectively with people, both in his district and at the national level (Wakatsuki 2011). During his two-year tenure as Prime Minister, Tanaka pursued two notable policies: public works spending to counter uneven development in the countryside and welfare expansion. Although Japan's post-war welfare state was often noted as being small by international standards,[10] Japan was actually one of the first countries to institute both universal health insurance and social insurance in 1961. It did this through a patchwork system that includes separate programs for private sector salaried workers, public employees, and for those not covered by the other two programs, thus reflecting the conservative corporatist variety of welfare provisioning more than the universalist vision of social democratic countries (Estevez-Abe 2008; see also Esping-Andersen 1990). In the 1958 election, the first contested between the unified JSP and LDP, both parties ran on the expansion of health insurance and social insurance. Unlike in Europe, there was not a partisan ideological split over the issue of social welfare. Instead, the LDP saw it as part of a sort of developmentalist nationalism, where reducing inequality was part of its overall economic growth strategy (Miyamoto 2008).

Moreover, the groups at the greatest risk of being left out of rapid growth, farmers and small businesses, were the LDP's core electoral bases, and welfare expansion was identified as much with the interests of the *petit bourgeois* as those of the working class. Nonetheless, throughout the 1960s, welfare budgets remained small, as the government focused on economic growth and the pursuit of full (male) employment through public works spending. However, beginning in the 1970s period of global turbulence brought on by the First Oil Shock and the end of the Bretton Woods System, the government of Tanaka

---

10   For example, in 1960, Japan spent only 4.9 percent of national income on social expenditures (in particular, healthcare, pensions and unemployment insurance), while West Germany spent 18.5 percent (Miyamoto 2008).

Kakuei turned to welfare expansion as well as policies to dramatically reduce uneven regional economic development, due to both changing structural demographic and global economic pressures.

Between 1973, known as the "year of welfare," and 1974, the LDP government passed legislation that expanded welfare and included massive income tax cuts for the working and middle classes coupled with spending increases in welfare of over 75 percent in total (LDP n.d.b). Much of this money was directed towards pensions, which more than doubled over the course of two years, while pensions were further indexed to the rate of inflation (LDP n.d.b). The LDP under Tanaka was forced to respond to growing electoral and demographic strength of the left and centre-left opposition parties, particularly in urban areas and including at the local level (Miyamoto 2008). But Tanaka was also forced to respond to the increasing strains the economy was bearing due to rapid economic growth and demographic change. Indeed, while Japan was increasingly urban, it was also increasingly middle aged. Population aging led to a ballooning of the welfare state. According to Estevez-Abe (2008), given the provisioning of free healthcare for seniors that had existed since the 1960s, the cost of seniors' health care grew from 400 billion in 1973 to 800 billion in 1975 to 1.8 trillion in 1979.

However, while the Tanaka government introduced stronger welfare provisions, it did not create corresponding means of paying for these new programs, instead opting to lower taxes even further while incurring the first deficit budget in 1974 (Sadoh 2012). This was compounded by problems with the financing estimates for Tanaka's plan for significant public works spending aimed at countering underdevelopment and depopulation in the countryside. Tanaka's now famous "Plan to Remodel the Japanese Archipelago" had been his signature policy at the 1972 LDP convention. But its estimates were based on the assumption that the 1970s would see a continuation of the double-digit GDP growth that characterized the 1960s, something that did not occur (Wakatsuki 2011). Even after Tanaka left office in 1974, public works spending continued to grow: for example, the 1978 budget called for a 20 percent spending increase over 1977, mostly from public works (Wakatsuki 2011).

The early 1970s thus brought recognition of the negative externalities of Japan's breakneck development, including both environmental problems and rural underdevelopment. It also saw increasing recognition of the effects of population aging and urbanization, and thus the need for stronger welfare programs. Yet these realizations proved to be a double-edged sword, upsetting the balance behind the low-spending, low-tax regime that had characterized Japan's welfare-through-work system, where the costs of social reproduction were largely borne by corporations and households rather than the state. Indeed, by

1979, public debt had already grown to 40 percent of GDP (Wakatsuki 2011). In the wake of the budgetary deficit that resulted from these policy changes, the LDP pursued fiscal retrenchment, beginning in 1979.

At first, under Ōhira Masayoshi the government sought to follow the model established in other Western countries of expanding general taxation and proposed the first ever consumption tax, which he intended to run on in the 1979 election. Yet Ōhira faced backlash from the public and within the LDP, and withdrew the tax proposal during the 1979 election, which resulted in a poor showing for the LDP. More than anything it was the *petit bourgeoisie* who opposed the tax hikes, even though these groups had been among the biggest beneficiaries of the LDP's free spending ways in the 1970s (Wakatsuki 2011). In the context of this backlash against the consumption tax (both within and outside of the party), the LDP under Suzuki Zenkō, who succeeded Ōhira after his sudden death ahead of the 1980 election, pursued a policy of "fiscal reconstruction without tax increases" (*zōzei naki zaisei saiken*). Though this promise was politically successful in the immediate term, it proved to be a watershed in Japanese political economy, and the beginning of what Lechevalier (2014) has called Japan's neoliberal transformation.

In the aftermath, the program for fiscal reconstruction in the early 1980s was developed under the Second Provisional Commission on Administrative Reform *shingikai*, or deliberation council, known as Rinchō II, from 1981 to 1983 (Jun and Muto 1998; Masujima 2005). Rinchō II called for spending cuts, deregulation, and privatization among other measures. At the behest of Nakasone Yasuhiro, chair of the Economic Planning Agency, Rinchō II was chaired by Dokō Toshio, president of Keidanren and former CEO of Toyota. It saw the privatization of Japan Salt and Tobacco, Japanese National Railways, Japan Telegraph and Telephone and Japan Airlines. Overall, Rinchō II had three aims: 1) administrative reform and reduction of the size of government; 2) rationalization and simplification of the administrative system; 3) privatization of state-owned-enterprises (Wakatsuki 2011). Along with these policies of administrative reform, deregulation and privatization, in its pursuit of fiscal reconstruction the Suzuki government adopted policies of welfare spending cuts. These included reductions to public pensions and child allowances; the introduction of co-payment in seniors' health care; increases to the copayment burden for national health insurance; increases to university tuition; and reductions to private school subsidies (Wakatsuki 2011). All of these measures together meant that the 1981 budget was kept at the same level as in 1980.

In addition to Rinchō II, the 1986 report of the Maekawa Commission, another panel organized under Prime Minister Nakasone (who succeeded Suzuki in 1982) on economic issues, this time on the issue of trade tensions, also led to a range of neoliberal recommendations. The Maekawa report called for economic reforms and harmonization with international society in order to promote trade, calling for reforms to elements of the distribution system that stifled growth in domestic demand. Yet with regard to public works spending meant to support employment in the regions, it called for proactive spending to encourage domestic demand growth, much as under the traditional construction state regime (Miyamoto 2008). The Maekawa report's call for investments to promote domestic demand over the continuation of Japan's export-based growth model thus differed in important ways from the neoliberal orthodoxy of Rinchō II. Nonetheless, Nakasone used it, and its emphasis on trade liberalization in particular, as a basis for promoting a neoliberal agenda (Miyamoto 2008).

Along with policies of retrenchment, privatization, and liberalization, Rinchō II also led to the first major policy of labour market deregulation with the extension of Japan's dualized labour market regime under the 1985 Worker Dispatch Law. In retrospect, this reform can be understood to represent one of the first shifts away from the lifetime employment system. The Worker Dispatch Law was the first major piece of legislation relating to labour market deregulation and was among the policy recommendations of Rinchō II. While labour market deregulation was touted as a measure to ensure Japanese competitiveness in a globalizing world economy, there were tremendous barriers to the removal of protections for workers included in the lifetime employment system. Instead, Japanese labour market reform targeted fringe sectors of the economy, or irregular work outside of the category of *seishain* (regular worker), creating a new category of *haken* (dispatch worker). Under the law, dispatch workers are not employed by the actual firm where they work, but rather by temp agencies that indirectly mediate between the worker and the workplace, often on a temporary, flexible and ad hoc basis. Because they do not technically work for the host company, they do not enjoy any of the legal protections and benefits guaranteed to workers of the host company, while employment in the temp agency itself provides no guarantee of stable access to work and is at the discretion of the company.

The *haken* system thus created a new category of flexibilized worker that firms in applicable industries could draw on in times of need and easily discard whenever their labour was no longer needed. Under the 1985 Worker Dispatch Law, the number of job categories where temp agencies could operate was limited to thirteen "white listed" job categories, expanding to sixteen in 1986 (Hamaguchi 2015).[11]

---

11 These included 1) software development, 2) operation of business equipment, 3) interpretation, translation and stenography; 4) secretarial work; 5) filing; 6) market research;

Clearly, many of these job categories are highly specialized, and thus do not appear to apply to low-skilled workers, those normally at greatest risk of seeing an increase in precariousness under labour market deregulation policies. Indeed, due to pressure from workers protected by the lifetime employment system, the law was formulated in such a way as to only include job categories usually seen as outside the scope of lifetime employment positions, to ensure protected workers that they would not have to compete with dispatch workers (Hamaguchi 2015). However, in practice, some of these job categories, such as "filing" and "operation of business equipment" were interpreted so broadly as to cover a significant proportion of tasks required in office work. As Hamaguchi (2015) has argued, this also had a disproportionate effect on women, who were still largely expected to retire in their late 20s or early 30s and were seen as easily replaceable by *haken* workers, compared to men, whose protected status as *sararīman* was much more difficult for companies to challenge politically.

Thus, the Worker Dispatch Law saw the first major extension of what came to be Japan's dualized labour market, divided between protected, mostly male, lifetime employment workers on one hand and precarious, mostly female, workers on the other (see also Thelen 2012). Yet in other ways the entrenched institutional power of enterprise unionism and the lifetime employment system was largely retained, despite the growing costs of lifetime employment due to the rapid aging of the workforce.

Along with these various neoliberal economic policies as outlined by Rinchō II, the Nakasone administration also sought to bring a renewed nationalist militarism to Japan. This included his commitment to the Anpo, referring to Japan as the US's "unsinkable aircraft carrier" in an era of renewed Cold War tensions under Reagan, while also breaking the unofficial limit on military spending at one percent of GDP. This symbolic act must be understood as a reflection of the staunch nationalism and militarism of Nakasone, who was the only post-war Prime Minister to fight in the Second World War. Moreover, in 1985, on the 40th anniversary of the end of World War II, Nakasone made an official state visit to the Yasukuni Shrine, which provoked widespread condemnation from China (Wakatsuki 2011).[12] The Yasukuni Shrine had been relatively uncontroversial

---

7) financial processing; 8) business document preparation; 9) demonstration of machinery; 10) tour conducting work; 11) reception and guide services and parking management; 12) building cleaning work; and 13) operation, checking and maintenance of building equipment. In 1986 it was expanded to include 14) machinery design; 15) operation of broadcasting equipment; and 16) production of broadcast programs (Hamaguchi 2015).

12 The Yasukuni Shrine is a war memorial shrine in Tokyo that houses the spirits of all Japanese people, including both soldiers and civilians, who have died in wars since the

until the late 1970s, and visited by various leaders, including Miki Takeo. Yet the 1978 decision by the new shrine chief to enshrine a number of war criminals immediately transformed the shrine into a highly political and controversial site. As a result, even the emperor announced that he would never again visit (Mochizuki and Porter 2013). In this context, Nakasone's official visit marked a strong departure from the past, and one of the first examples of right wing LDP leaders attempting to normalize revisionist accounts of wartime history.

Along with these conservative and neoliberal policies, however, from other quarters there was a push in the 1980s to further the project of welfare expansion and modernization that had begun under Tanaka and to prepare Japan adequately for the demographic changes ahead (Estevez-Abe 2008). Most importantly, this involved the Angel Plan for public daycare and other proposals by the Ministry of Health and Welfare to expand welfare. However, these proposals were ultimately shelved due to opposition within the increasingly neoliberal Ministry of Finance, thus postponing a solution to the emerging demographic crisis facing Japan (Osawa 2013).

Finally, in 1988, Prime Minister Takeshita Noboru, who succeeded Nakasone and brought the clientelist approach to politics back to the *kantei*, was able to successfully institute the consumption tax that Ōhira had failed to introduce back in 1979. In the decade since the LDP had first backtracked on the consumption tax, the deficit had grown significantly, and the strategy of fiscal consolidation without tax increases had failed. While this proved to be an important measure in bringing fiscal balance back to the Japanese state (and occurred on the eve of Japan's stock market crash), it proved to be electorally and politically costly, as the next chapter will show. Overall, we can see how various policy changes of the 1970s and 1980s attempted to rectify many of the challenges and contradictions facing Japanese society, including those that were occurring due to globalization and demographic transitions. Some of these were successful in responding to immediate challenges, such as the need for greater welfare provisions for seniors and the need to adjust to the competitive market pressures of globalization in order for Japanese firms to remain profitable through deregulation policies. Yet these solutions themselves created new contradictions, such as the budgetary deficit and growing social problems caused by labour market deregulation.

Meiji Restoration. It is controversial because it has, since the 1970s, housed the spirits of convicted Class-A war criminals. As such, visits by public figures are seen across East Asia as efforts to downplay or even celebrate Japan's role in the Pacific war, despite the enormous brutality unleashed upon other Asian peoples during and before the war.

4   Institutional Changes

In addition to these structural and political changes, the period from the 1970s to the early 1990s was characterized by a range of institutional changes. These changes were manifest in both the structure and order of the Japanese state and the nature of relations within the Japanese economy. Moreover, they included not only relations between firms and the state but also relations among firms, between capital and labour, and between the state and *petit bourgeois* producers, including farmers. The changes implied here were usually slow moving and occurred according to institutional path dependencies rather than as the result of immediate and deliberate policy prerogatives. In this sense, they fit more with Gramsci's notion of organic change rather that conjunctural change, the latter a dynamic more closely characterized by the political changes discussed above.

4.1   *The Heyday of the* Kōenkai

First among the political institutional changes were the growing cost of elections, the increased power of the *kōenkai* and how these were linked with corruption and growing criticism of the overall electoral system. For example, in the 1974 Upper House election, Prime Minister Tanaka travelled 40,000 kilometres by helicopter to every prefecture making campaign speeches, nominating businesspeople and celebrities as candidates and all the while generating enormous fundraising, in what came to be known as the "rule of money election" (*kinken senkyo*) (Wakatsuki 2011). In the aftermath, news of corrupt campaign activities by Tanaka's *kōenkai*, the Etsuzankai, forced him to resign with an approval rating of just 12 percent (Wakatsuki 2011). As a result, the party chose Miki Takeo as a clean option to succeed Tanaka. Yet this did little to alter the growing role of *kōenkai* as massive get-out-the-vote machines, the enormous amount of money required to finance *kōenkai*, and the staggering levels of corruption required to maintain sources of financing. While Miki introduced legislation targeted at curtailing corruption by reducing the influence of money in elections, his efforts were rejected by more powerful and entrenched interests within the party (Wakatsuki 2011). The depth of LDP corruption was soon further revealed: in 1976, the Lockheed corruption scandal broke,[13] implicating Tanaka Kakuei, among others, and tarnishing the image of the LDP further.

---

13   The Lockheed scandal occurred in October 1972, when Prime Minister Tanaka, along with officials from All Nippon Airlines (ANA) received bribes from American aerospace manufacturer Lockheed to give Lockheed a contract to manufacture ANA airplanes. The scandal broke in 1976 after an American congressional hearing, and Tanaka was later

In addition, this era also saw massive increases in the costs of elections, driven by the increasing power of factions and the growing effectiveness of *kōenkai* as fundraising machines. According to Shinoda (2013), while the total cost of political financing in 1976 was 110 billion yen, by 1988 it had nearly tripled to 307 billion yen. However, this does not include a significant amount of non-reported expenses (including bribes). Indeed, some suspect the total cost could have been three times as high.

What enabled the rise of *kōenkai*? Part of it was loopholes in campaign financing laws: while political parties were required to report all donations above 10,000 yen, political organizations such as *kōenkai* only had to report sums over one million yen. While individual politicians could only receive 150,000 yen a year, there was no limit on the amount received by political organizations (Shinoda 2013). In this context, *kōenkai* expanded rapidly: while Tanaka Kakuei's Etsuzankai had only 80 members when it was launched in the 1950s, it had nearly 100,000 members by the early 1970s (Krauss and Pekkanen 2010). Tanaka's *kōenkai* famously once spent 1.4 million dollars on *onsen* (hot springs) visits for 11,000 people. Moreover, during this time the number of people belonging to *kōenkai* also grew markedly. While only 8 percent of LDP supporters belonged to *kōenkai* in 1967, by 1979 the number was 25%, and by 1993 it was 31 percent (Krauss and Pekkanen 2010).

4.2 The Rise of Factions and the PARC

The third major institutional political change of this period was the rise of factions within the LDP as major power brokers and the implications this had for internal party democracy and accountability, as well as the growing influence of the PARC and *zoku* lawmakers. According to Shinoda (2013), the PARC took on importance after the 1970s' oil shock, as the government no longer faced a fiscal situation of ever-growing budgets. Under those conditions the question had simply been where to allot the new revenue on top of existing spending. In contrast, after the Oil Shock, the state now faced much more difficult questions, such as which programs – and which social and class interests – to advance, and which to postpone or even cut.

Parallel to the rise of *kōenkai* was the growing power of factions. According to Krauss and Pekkanen (2010), beginning with Tanaka Kakuei, "factions also began to help Diet members perform constituency services. Tanaka referred once to his faction as a 'general hospital'" (115). Factions' role increased with the turn to a membership vote in leadership elections because faction

---

arrested for accepting bribes from Lockheed. Then Defense Minster Nakasone was also implicated, though never arrested (Tokumoto 2016; Chapman 1978).

members (and their *kōenkai* voters) became the surest way for would-be LDP Presidents to get votes. This strongly benefited Ōhira in the 1978 election: "the mobilization of *kōenkai* members in the 1978 party presidential primary was the culmination of the institutionalizing of the extension of the factions into the electoral districts" (Krauss and Pekkanen 2010: 117). Moreover, this period saw a growing tendency for intraparty competition within mixed member districts to occur along factional lies. While in 1958 over 40 percent of districts had multiple candidates from the same *faction*, by 1980 just 10 percent did, and by 1993 just five percent did (Krauss and Pekkanen 2010). Furthermore, the relative importance of factions over the party's central organization for fundraising grew markedly. While political parties raised 43 billion yen in 1976, only 26 billion was raised and spent by factions. In contrast, by 1988, 88 billion was raised by factions, more than what was raised by parties (Shinoda 2013).

4.3 *Growing Bureaucratic Influence:* Zoku *and* Amakudari

In addition to the growing roles of factions, *kōenkai* and the PARC, this period also witnessed the hardening of relations between the bureaucracy and elected officials. These included the so-called *zoku* lawmakers of the LDP, and the LDP's PARC, as well as officials from other parties. Main faction leaders, and Tanaka Kakuei in particular, actively sought to cultivate *zoku* lawmakers from among their factions to maximize their own faction's ability to control the direction of discretionary spending for their benefit, and thus the faction's overall power (Krauss and Pekkanen 2010). Indeed, by the 1980s, Japanese bureaucrats located *zoku* lawmakers as the most influential forces on their decision-making, ahead of the cabinet and other interest groups (Krauss and Pekkanen 2010). This dynamic of a close relationship between *zoku* lawmakers and bureaucrats functioning with a high degree of autonomy from the Cabinet and Prime Minister not only served as the basis for the increase in public works spending during the 1970s; it also undermined the development of a strong executive (Estevez-Abe 2008).

In addition to the growing importance of this relationship between bureaucrats and LDP lawmakers, a collusive relationship between the bureaucracy and major corporations developed through the *amakudari* system, which became institutionalized in the 1970s (Mizoguchi and Nguyen 2012). Indeed, the number of *amakudari* appointments to private companies doubled between 1967 and 1981 and peaked in 1985 (Usui and Colignon 1995). Similarly, the number of semi-public *tokushu hōjin* corporations such as the Japan Foundation and the Society for Prevention of Pollution grew from 38 in 1967 to 81 in 1981 (Blumenthal 1985; Krauss and Pekkanen 2010; Usui and Colignon 1995). Importantly, these institutions were often set up by ministries in order provide venues for *amakudari* appointments easily within ministry control.

Amakudari appointments during this period were dominated by bureaucrats from the Ministries of Finance, Construction, Agriculture, Transport, and MITI, reflecting the economic policy areas where bureaucrats held the greatest influence overall. Even more tellingly, the Ministry of Posts and Telecommunications increased its *amakudari* appointments from just two in 1965 to 29 in 1985, reflecting the power of that Ministry to direct pork barrel spending through its control of the postal savings system (Usui and Colignon 1995). In various ways, then, the 1970s saw an extension of bureaucratic influence through *amakudari* appointments as well as an entrenchment of collusive relations not only between bureaucrats and *zoku* lawmakers but also between bureaucrats and private corporations.

4.4 Institutional Changes and Continuities in Japanese Business Relations

Two major changes affected Japanese capitalism, and relationships between Japanese firms, during the 1970s and 1980s that ultimately had major ramifications in the 1990s and 2000s: 1) the globalization of production and investment and 2) changing financial conditions, including the rise of financial capitalism and the fragmentation of financing relations.

The globalization of Japanese capitalism began in the 1970s. According to Komiya and Wakasugi (1991), Japanese foreign direct investment (FDI) until the 1970s had been concentrated mainly in mining and had amounted to less than a billion dollars. Following a change in policy by the Japan Import-Export Bank in 1969 to lower interest rates, Japanese capital shifted outward FDI into manufacturing, and total outward FDI surged from 1 billion dollars in 1970 to 53 billion in 1988. The US was a particularly large recipient of Japanese FDI, increasing its share from 10 percent in 1970 to 46 percent in 1990 (Hook et al. 2011). While the liberalization of FDI regulations was one factor behind this (Cowling and Tomlinson 2011), equally important was the increasing costs of domestic production, as well as the emerging trade tensions with the US. However, according to Schoppa (2006), there was a difficulty in determining whether outward FDI was a sign of an internal hollowing out or merely a normal expansion of Japan's export strategy. As a result, the outward flow of FDI was not initially seen as a sign of domestic regulatory problems.

The 1970s and 1980s thus saw the rise of leading Japanese firms as transnational corporations. Beginning with the apparel and aluminum sectors, Japanese firms moved production overseas in order to reduce labour costs (Schoppa 2006). Thus, rather than pushing for deregulation domestically, firms sought already deregulated markets for overseas production. This led them to build plants in right-to-work US states, including Kentucky and Tennessee, as well as developing Southeast Asian countries, where they did not treat workers with the same protections as their core workforces in Japan. Increasingly, then, these firms came to be bifurcated between a relatively uncompetitive and protected domestic workforce and a super-competitive workforce in Asia or the Southern US (Schoppa 2006). The transnationalization of Japanese capital soon spread to other industries: beginning in the 1970s, in response to American pressure, both politically and structurally from increased tariffs and export restrictions, Japanese electronics firms Matsushita, Sony and Sharp all built factories in the US. Then, beginning in the late 1970s, auto firms, including Mitsubishi, Honda, Nissan and Toyota followed suit. Moreover, the subsidiary firms that were set up abroad did not simply mimic their domestic Japanese counterparts. They took on their own independent business identities in response to the competitive pressures of their new markets, no longer "Japanese" in any meaningful sense (Hook et al. 2011).

In addition to the globalization of capital through the offshoring of production, changing patterns of financing also developed in this period. Several tendencies characterized Japanese corporations' financing relations and activity in the 1970s and 1980s. First, on average turnover fell markedly compared to the preceding period (Lucarelli 2015). Second, firms increasingly sought to globalize and establish offshore production. However, in general the key *keiretsu* relationships, including domestic ownership and main bank functions, were largely retained until the late 1980s. Beginning in the 1980s, then, financial deregulation led to the asset boom, combined with a shift away from main bank financing. Globalization and neoliberal reforms also had a major impact on *keiretsu*, dissolving the previous bonds that had tied them together. According to Lucarelli (2015), "by the late 1980s, most of the large keiretsu began to generate internal funds for investment and curtailed their traditional reliance on the [Bank of Japan] and the big banks" (314). While leading *keiretsu* had previously obtained roughly 40 percent of their loans from major banks, in the context of financial deregulation in the 1980s, this number was down to just six percent by the late 1980s. In this context, major banks could no longer secure investment fixes through the stable relationships with affiliated firms, and instead pursued reckless speculative activity in the stock market and real estate, injecting as many as 220 billion dollars of loans into the real estate sector in the late 1980s (Lucarelli 2015).

In other ways, Japanese capitalism of this era was marked by continuities. State support for unprofitable industries and corporate preference for market share over profit continued (Katz 1998). The same can be said for MITI financing, although it moved into new sectors, particularly information technology (Okimoto 1989). In this way, the hegemonic, consensus-based model of Japanese capitalism continued through the 1980s. Japanese firms adapted to new structural conditions of economic globalization and financialization, while in depressed industrial sectors, MITI-led recession cartels that provided financing, market coordination and protections, ensuring the effects of industrial hollowing out were muted (Katz 1998).

Overall, these changes to the dynamics of Japanese capitalism suggest that globalization, financial deregulation, and increased pressure, both from the US and from export competitors led to a transformation of the financial relationship among firms within *keiretsu* and the transnationalization of production through offshoring. While MITI continued to play a major role in coordination and in softening the effects of market forces for Japanese firms, the 1970s and 1980s marked the beginning of an era of significant adjustment that challenged the stable relationship between Japanese capital, workers, and the state.

4.5   Lifetime Employment and the Dual System

The second major institutional economic change of this era was in the changing conditions of Japan's post-war system of labour management and organization. As discussed in the previous chapter, this system was characterized by commitments from firms to lifetime employment and seniority-based wages in exchange for workers' total commitment to firms. Importantly, this commitment on the part of workers included norms that limited labour movement organizing to the firm level through enterprise unions. This system served as a basis for Japan's low levels of labour unrest since the 1960s, its high levels of productivity growth, as well as the willingness by many workers to work long hours and accept job transfers. While this system remained more or less intact during the period of the 1970s and 1980s, a number of important institutional changes placed pressure on this system that ultimately undermined its ability to contribute to capital accumulation in the 1990s.

While the turn towards neoliberal deregulation and austerity in the 1980s saw attacks on Japanese unions and welfare programs, the corporate welfare provisions and labour security associated with lifetime employment received little overt criticism, either from policy makers or from corporations (Anchordoguy 2005; Schoppa 2006). Indeed, by the late 1980s, the lifetime employment system appeared no less intact than it had been two decades earlier. Nonetheless, beneath the surface a number of changes were emerging that ultimately served to undermine lifetime employment both politically and economically, beginning in the 1990s.

First, as discussed above, the aging of Japan's workforce, combined with wage growth that outpaced profits due to the declining number of rural migrants to major urban centres led to a growing wage bill for firms (Itoh 2000). This was especially pronounced given how the seniority wage system tended to underpay young workers while overpaying older workers. Second, and partially in response to this, dynamics of globalization and liberalization of foreign direct investment laws led a number of leading Japanese firms to begin outsourcing production in the 1970s in order to remain competitive in export markets.

Third, and also in response to growing pressures on profitability, manufacturing firms, and Toyota in particular, drove innovation in labour management techniques through the creation of Just in Time production, or Toyotism. This production technique relied on highly flexibilized and rationalized practices and the constant drive for further improvements at the micro-level of production (a principle known as *kaizen*). It corresponded well with the structural transition towards flexible and fragmented production in the global economy. It also enabled Japanese firms to benefit from the early stage of neoliberal globalization, helping to make Japanese auto makers, in particular, competitive on world markets and spur the boom in auto exports beginning in the late 1970s (Johnson 1995; Lechevalier 2014; Flath 2000). Japanese workers and capital alike were active participants in the development of Toyotism (Sakoh 1990). Yet ultimately, the development of Toyotism, and the rise of Just in Time production more generally, led to a shift away from the stable and long-term orientation of Fordist production, which had corresponded more closely with the requirements of the lifetime employment system. Thus, while Toyotism is not a direct cause of the rise of precarious work, and certainly benefited the workforces of the firms who adopted it successfully in the immediate term, the long-term effects of its popularization may have undermined the basis for the lifetime employment system.

Fourth, a number of measures taken by the government in the 1980s had the effect of transforming Japanese labour organization away from the prevailing post-war model. These included the 1985 Worker Dispatch Law, discussed above, which served as a harbinger for the rise of precarious employment, and the 1985 Equal Employment Opportunity Law. The Equal Employment Opportunity Law was a victory for women insofar as it banned gender discrimination in the workforce. At the same time, it did nothing to protect workers from harsh conditions of overwork. It thereby further extended the norm of harsh working conditions and long hours to all full-time, career-track workers, women and men alike. Additional neoliberalizing measures of this era included the efforts under Nakasone to destroy militant public sector unions through the privatization of Japanese National Railways. This was aimed as much at reducing the state's debt burden and promoting capital accumulation as it was at crushing the power of public sector unions hostile to the government, and thereby hurting the left-wing parties (JSP and JCP) affiliated with the unions (Tiberghien 2014). Importantly, this defeat severely weakened the JSP-affiliated Sōhyō union, which merged with other unions in 1987 to form the Japanese Trade Union Federation (Rengō). While Rengō represented a much larger proportion of the labour movement than Sōhyō, it has proven to be both more timid and submissive in the face of anti-worker policies since the 1990s (Tiberghien 2014).

Overall, then, we can see how the period of the 1970s and 1980s did not bring an overt challenge to Japan's post-war employment regime centered on lifetime employment, the seniority wage system and enterprise unionism. Nonetheless, it did witness a number of changes – structural, political and institutional – that collectively undermined the basis for Japan's labour regime and the complementary relationship it held with Japanese post-war capitalism.

4.6 Clientelism and the Construction State

The third process of institutional change in the Japanese economy is the continuation and deepening of clientelist pork-barrel infrastructure spending. Indeed, the period of the 1970s saw the largest increase in the scope of the so-called Construction State. This was encouraged by four factors: 1) the *kōenkai* of local politicians, particularly those of the Tanaka faction. 2) the increasing institutional power of *zoku* lawmakers, particularly in the Postal, Construction, and Transport policy areas; 3) major elements of the bureaucracy, particularly the Postal Ministry, the Construction Ministry and the Transport Ministry, who worked with *zoku* lawmakers and the PARC to have their institutional interests advanced; and 4) the LDP's PARC, which in many ways served as the institutional conduit for *zoku* politicians' networking and engagement with bureaucrats (Krauss and Pekkanen 2010).

According to Miyamoto (2008), rather than focusing on economic transition (away from outdated industries), LDP governments of the 1970s focused on propping up businesses in the countryside. Following the parameters of Tanaka's Plan to Remodel the Japanese Archipelago, in the 1970s, the support system for SMEs was expanded. This included measures in 1973 to create a new small business financing system that could provide stronger financing for SMEs in exchange for further integrating them into the LDP's electoral coalition (Miyamoto 2008). This program expanded rapidly: while the 1973 financing budget was 30 billion yen, by 1975 it had grown to 240 billion yen. Other financing programs also grew, and overall the financing for SMEs tripled between 1970 and 1975 (Miyamoto 2008). In other ways, protectionist legislation was strengthened: in 1973 the LDP strongly opposed a bill that would have allowed department stores to build supermarket expansions through a simple notification to government (rather than requiring an application for permission). This further led to the Large-Scale Retail Store Law that granted governments the authority to block large retailers from establishing businesses, thereby protecting SMEs from competition with more profitable large firms. In 1979, the category "large retailer" was further broadened by including stores of 500 to

1500 square meters in area (rather than only those above 1500), while regulations were further strengthened in 1982 (Miyamoto 2008). These protectionist measures had the effect of strongly buttressing employment at SMEs. Between 1972 and 1981, the number of people who worked for a large company increased by 120,000, while the number of people hired by a nonagricultural SME grew by 6.8 million (Miyamoto 2008).

Thus, the 1970s and early 1980s saw the continuation of Japan's highly clientelist politics that distributed significant political goods to key electoral groups, particularly the farmers and small business owners of the *petit bourgeoisie* in exchange for electoral support. Notably, this tendency continued despite countervailing forces, including the steadily declining number of farmers, increasing political and structural pressure due to the ballooning budgetary deficit, the changing dynamics of economic globalization and the pressure from the US and its corporations. According to Katz (1998: 83), "by the 1980s, more than 75 percent of all farm income came from subsidies and price support programs." In general, the period of the 1970s saw an increase in public works spending from 2 trillion to more than 7 trillion yen. Moreover, total public fixed capital investment grew from 6 to 24 trillion and rice subsidies grew from 137 percent above production value in 1970 to 287 percent above production value by 1985, while rigid barriers to imports were strengthened (Honma and Hayami 1988; MLIT 2010). Furthermore, while the number of people employed in agriculture full time fell precipitously, the state indirectly provided new employment opportunities for these now part-time farmers through construction jobs, which outnumbered agricultural jobs by the 1970s (Nakakita 2017).

However, if there was any reminding of just how important these groups were to the LDP's political fortunes, the 1989 Upper House election was proof (Stockwin 2006). In response to American pressure, the LDP broke with tradition and ran on a platform of agricultural trade liberalization. While the 1989 election saw the LDP lose half its seats and control of the Upper House to the JSP, this was primarily driven by rural communities abandoning the LDP *en masse*. The LDP's control of Japan's 26 least populous (mostly rural) single-member prefecture-wide constituencies fell from 24 to only two out of 26, while the JSP and its labour union affiliate organization increased their share of rural seats from one to 23. Overall, then, we can see how strong the political impetus remained for the LDP to shore up support from stable voting blocs of farmers and small business owners, groups that remained core LDP clientele through the 1980s despite their declining proportion of the electorate. While the extension of this support benefited the LDP politically and the *petit bourgeoisie* economically, these policies ultimately created pressures on Japan's regime of capital accumulation, as the next chapter will show.

5 Implications of these Changes for Hegemonic Order

Thus, we can see how the period of the 1970s and 1980s brought a number of changes to the conditions of hegemonic order in Japan. These included slow-moving and organic structural economic and demographic changes, conjunctural political changes, and path-dependent changes to political and economic institutional configurations. However, we must consider what the implications of these changes were for Japanese hegemonic order, including for the ability of the ruling regime to fulfill the three key requirements of capital accumulation, political legitimation and social reproduction. The next section will consider this question in detail.

5.1 Economic Implications

What implications did the above collection of structural, institutional and policy changes have for the Japanese ruling regime's ability to meet requirements for capital accumulation? Overall, three major implications can be observed. First, neoliberalization and globalization may have contributed to an economic boom and bubble that enabled the Japanese economy to continue to grow at a relatively robust pace through to the end of the 1980s. Yet alterations to the structure of Japan's economy placed it in a precarious position, as the ensuing crisis has shown. As Lechevalier (2014) has argued, Japan was in many respects an early winner of globalization. Its robust economic growth in the 1970s and 1980s, combined with the transformation of many Japanese firms in the automobile, electronics, and semiconductor industries from followers to leaders, and growing Western interest in Japanese management practices are demonstrative of this. At the same time, the aggressive ways in which the Japanese state and firms helped drive neoliberal globalization in the 1980s ultimately proved to be a double-edged sword, as the bubble economy and subsequent banking crisis of the early Heisei era proved. In other words, the resolution to the short-term economic crisis of the mid-1970s may have restored conditions for capital accumulation in the short term, but it brought about its own set of contradictions that became apparent by the late 1980s.

Second, the economic system continued to distribute benefits to all groups concerned and continued to do so against the logic of market efficiency. This included the way subsidies were continuously recycled to inefficient small businesses and farmers, as well as the significant corporate welfare packages and generous pay (irrespective of productivity) that were distributed to aging protected workers. Firms financed these practices by earning super-profits from exports or by selling goods at high prices domestically, and, beginning in the 1980s, even by moving export-oriented production itself overseas. Yet this led, as the next chapter will show, to a growing disconnect between the conditions required for profitable accumulation for increasingly footloose Japanese firms on one hand, and those conductive to the overall growth and health of the Japanese economy domestically on the other.

Third, the power of capital, including what Gill and Law (1989) have termed both the structural and instrumental power of capital, as well as the political (instrumental) power of the *petit bourgeoisie*, negated the possibility of restoring fiscal balance through tax increases. Indeed, the instrumental power of the *petit bourgeoisie* also proved a barrier to cuts to infrastructure spending. Thus, with GDP growth falling to modest levels, deficit spending was the only way to meet budgetary demands without cutting programs. While Japan came through the period of stagflation and economic restructuring in the 1970s and early 1980s stronger than many other countries, this was partially conditioned by a turn to the disequilibrium of a structural deficit.

5.2   *Political Implications*

In addition to the above economic implications of these changes to the conditions of hegemonic order, three key political implications are also manifest. First, the period beginning in the 1980s saw growing corruption and scandals as well as dissatisfaction with the electoral system and the clientelist politics that it entailed. This was partially due to the path dependencies inherent in Japan's multi-member electoral system. But it was also due to the increasingly entrenched policy-making institutions within the LDP and networks between bureaucrats and *zoku* lawmakers. While the voices of opposition to these dynamics – strong in the 1970s – were partially muted during the LDP's 1980s revival, these dynamics ultimately led to a major push for electoral and administrative reform in the 1990s, as the next chapter will show.

Second, while this period saw a virtual stasis in the seat count for all of the major parties, this apparent electoral stability masked a growing ambivalence among the public over the LDP. Indeed, the LDP's inability to introduce a consumption tax in 1979, and the degree to which the party was punished for finally doing so in 1989 with the 1989 Upper House election loss to the JSP, demonstrate that public consent to the conditions of LDP rule was weaker than it appeared on the surface. This growing public ambivalence over the legitimacy of LDP rule reached a boiling point in the 1990s and 2000s, but it was already beginning to emerge in the 1970s. After the 1972 election the LDP retained a narrow majority only through a careful and unsustainable balancing act of social and economic policies designed to please everyone coupled with its ability to outspend other parties at election time – both legally and illegally – through their well-organized *kōenkai* and privileged access to corporate donors.

Finally, we must consider the implications of attempts to revive Japanese nationalism through remilitarization and the forging of closer ties with the US under Nakasone's neoconservative program. Though this, along with Rinchō II was part of a bold and partially successful move to restore conditions for LDP hegemony on more hardline conservative and nationalist terms, it was ultimately short lived. Indeed, the party moved back towards the communitarian model under Prime Minister Takeshita after 1987. The LDP's electoral defeat in 1989 showed that ultimately Nakasone's nationalist drive was unsuccessful in restoring political hegemony in neo-conservative terms, foreshadowing an increasingly ideologically rudderless and anchorless LDP in the 1990s.

5.3   Social Implications

Finally, three key implications for conditions of social reproduction emerged from all of these changes in the 1970s and 1980s. First, the delay of improved revenue generation and the failure to develop welfare institutions capable of meeting the social and demographic challenges of the coming generation brought increasingly tough fiscal conditions even before an economic crisis emerged in the 1990s. As discussed above, this was partially due to the government's aversion to taxation and commitment to clientelist infrastructure spending. While the 1970s saw this revenue shortfall problem met through increased deficit spending, in part riding the global wave of neoliberalism the 1980s saw the emergence of a commitment to fiscal consolidation through spending retrenchment alone. This in turn negated much of the gains in welfare provisioning that had been made in the 1970s and weakened Japan's capacity to deal with the growing challenges of demographic transformation.

Therefore, and second, in the context of labor market deregulation, the rapidly growing elderly population, the decline of extended family households and woefully insufficient welfare institutions, Japan's welfare regime was poised to suffer challenges in its ability to sustain social reproduction. The negative effects of this growing disconnect between the institutions – both formal and informal – that existed to deal with social reproduction on one hand, and the changing realities of society on the other, did not become apparent until the 1990s. Yet we can say, in hindsight, that the Japanese state missed a chance to adequately recalibrate its regime of social reproduction in anticipation of the changes that were already occurring – population aging, household diversification and fragmentation, women's participation in the workforce, and the falling birth rate – before it was too late.

Finally, while the drop in GDP growth from the high levels of the 1950s and 1960s (around ten percent) to the moderate levels of the 1970s and 1980s (around five percent) should not in itself be seen as a negative, or a sign of declining hegemony, Japan's fiscal policy since the 1960s had left little room to adapt to a slower-growth economy without either instituting major spending cuts or budget deficits. As Park and Ide (2014) have shown, Japan's state has long displayed a weak extractive capacity, partly because LDP governments – as well as the left opposition parties – consistently campaigned on tax cuts. In Europe and North America, governments enjoyed a steady rise in tax revenues even without raising taxes as wage growth lifted people into higher tax brackets. In contrast, Japanese policy negated this natural increase in public revenue, leaving zero room for error when the period of rapid growth had ended and the welfare needs of society suddenly expanded (Park and Ide 2014). In this way, we must recognize that the basis for social reproduction in Japan, including the fiscal basis for its regime of social reproduction and welfare, was fundamentally unsustainable from the beginning.

6 Conclusion

Overall, the 1970s and 1980s was a period characterized by a high degree of superficial continuity with the previous era contrasted with a number of significant changes below the surface that ultimately came to have far reaching implications for Japanese political economy and hegemonic order. First, beginning with the 1971 "Nixon Shocks" of the United States' adoption of floating exchange rates and the subsequent transformation of the Bretton Woods System and continuing with the oil shocks and the later rise of neoliberal globalization, the 1970s and 1980s witnessed a number of significant changes to the structural conditions of global political economy. These ultimately led to the unraveling of the system of embedded liberalism that had aided Japan's rapid economic development in the early post-war period. Second, a number of key structural demographic changes to Japanese society occurred. These included the steady aging of society and the decline of extended family households, as well as the steady increase of women in the workforce. These changes brought about new contradictions between core elements of Japan's regime of social reproduction, such as the extended family household and the minimalist welfare state, and the needs of a changing society.

In addition to these structural changes, a number of key policy changes also characterized the 1970s and 1980s, particularly in response to these structural changes. In response to the changing demographics, the LDP under Tanaka tried to expand Japan's welfare state, and public provisions for seniors in particular, through a major enlargement of pensions and other social programs. Then, in response to the growing budgetary deficit, as well as prevailing global norms of economic deregulation, the 1980s saw a shift towards spending cuts, financial and labour market deregulation and privatization. These moves ultimately contributed to the bubble economy and banking crisis of the 1990s.

While the LDP and bureaucracy pursued these policy directions, institutionally this period saw the entrenchment of a number of elements of the electoral and political system. These included the high degree of collusion between bureaucrats and *zoku* lawmakers, the growing influence of the PARC, factions and *kōenkai*, and the growing costs of Japan's clientelist political system, where huge sums of money used to fund election campaigns would be cycled back through equally huge distributions of pork-barrel spending. While this system only strengthened the structural and institutional advantages of the LDP (as the party of both large corporations and small businesses), it also served as a breeding ground for corruption, undermining the system's political legitimacy.

Finally, a number of key institutional changes to Japanese political economy also had significant impacts on the conditions of hegemonic order. The pressures of global competition, foreign trade pressures and the liberalization of investment beginning in the 1970s enabled the transnationalization of Japanese capital, beginning with the auto and electronics sectors. At the same time, financial deregulation led to a shift away from the main bank system of financing for firms beginning in the 1980s. With regard to workers, the 1970s brought about the entrenchment of the enterprise union system and robust growth in real wages (which outpaced GDP growth). In contrast, the 1980s saw growing labour market deregulation and the beginning of a slow decline in labour activism, partly driven by the union-busting privatization of JNR under Nakasone.

Thus, while the structural demographic and political economic changes created new contradictions to the postwar hegemonic order, the above institutional and policy changes pursued largely enabled it to adjust to the new conditions for the time being. The period of the 1970s and 1980s thus saw Japan's ruling hegemonic order emerge from the early 1970s' global crisis in an even stronger position than before the crisis. Economic growth continued to be robust after the first post-war recession in 1973. The LDP restored its electoral dominance in the late 1970s after coming close to losing its majority in 1974. The expansion of pensions and seniors' medical care appeared to help Japan's regime of social reproduction adjust to changing social and demographic conditions. Nonetheless, while these measures provided temporary solutions to immediate challenges, many of these policy changes themselves brought about new contradictions that ultimately served to undermine the conditions necessary for stable hegemonic order, as the next chapter will show.

CHAPTER 6

The Organic Crisis of the Heisei Era

This chapter deals with the period beginning in 1990 in the aftermath of the NIKKEI stock market crash until the 2012 return to power of Prime Minister Abe Shinzō. During this era Japan went through a period of crisis and transformation that remains unresolved. Economically, the crash of the stock market exposed deep problems within the finance system as trillions of dollars' worth of non-performing loans were exposed. This caused the Hokkaido Takushoku Bank and other financial institutions to become insolvent, something unprecedented in the post-war context of continued financial stability under the *keiretsu* system. Politically, various corruption scandals led to further public distrust and outrage with the LDP, pushing it into opposition in 1993 for the first time since its formation. The coalition that replaced the LDP was unstable and the LDP's time in opposition was brief (only eleven months). Yet this short period saw the reform of the electoral system in the Lower House, ending the multi-member district system that had served as a basis for the LDP's intra-party factional competition as well as its clientelist electioneering strategies. Socially, this era saw the rise in earnest of a demographic crisis, as the fertility rate fell to historically low levels, while the proportion of elderly people increased rapidly. This led to a rapid expansion of Japan's welfare system, with escalating public costs that had to be funded through borrowing. This led Japan's national debt to steadily escalate, producing a structural deficit that even income and consumption tax hikes could do little to quell.

These three elements of the Heisei Era crisis all have their origins, as we have seen, in the previous two eras of the Japanese post-war order. The failure to adequately address the changing social and demographic context – in other words, the structural conditions of social reproduction – led to a crisis of social reproduction. The failure to reform a political system that was increasingly corrupt led to further popular dissatisfaction with the system and ultimately to the LDP's electoral defeat. Moreover, the consequences of Japan's largely neoliberal response to changing conditions in the global and domestic economy led to a quarter century of economic stagnation whereby the state has only been able to keep the economy treading water, and at the cost of a structural budget deficit of almost 8 percent of GDP. All these problems were partially the result of decisions, discussed in the previous chapter, to privilege the short-term maintenance of political order over the restoration of conditions for its long-term sustainability. The question for this chapter is how we should understand these transformations and crisis conditions of the Heisei Period in the context of the Shōwa Period of relatively stable hegemony. How did dynamics of the hegemonic order beget these crisis conditions, and what have the crisis conditions meant for Japan's post-war political order under the LDP-bureaucracy-*keiretsu* led historic bloc?

In its analysis of Japan's organic crisis, this chapter starts by providing a historical overview of key events of the Heisei Period from the vantage point of Japanese political economy and hegemonic order. This section considers key political, economic, social and foreign policies and reforms of the period, in the context of the changing structural, institutional and political conditions under which they take place (and in particular those discussed in Chapter Five). Next, taking these developments of the Heisei Era as its point of departure, it seeks to analyze the implications of these dynamics from the vantage point of the conditions for Japanese hegemonic order outlined in Chapter Four. It thus asks in what ways these conditions were manifest differently in the 1990s and 2000s and what consequences this holds for Japan's hegemonic order. Finally, after finding that in many cases, conditions once favorable to hegemonic order had now become the basis for contradictions in the structure of Japanese hegemonic order, it characterizes Japan's Heisei Era as a period of organic crisis. It seeks to theorize Japan's organic crisis, focusing on its implications for key hegemonic requirements of political legitimation, social reproduction and capital accumulation. Taking organic crisis as the moment at which "the old is dying but the new cannot be born" (Gramsci 1992: 276), it explores how the organic crisis of the Heisei Era brought about various attempts to reconstruct Japan's ruling historic bloc. It sees Ozawa Ichirō, Hashimoto Ryūtarō, Koizumi Jun'ichirō and the DPJ each in their own way attempting to do so, though in each case, unsuccessfully. This chapter ends where the next chapter begins, with the return to power of Abe Shinzō in 2012.

1   Historical Background to the Crisis

1.1   *1989–1993: Two Electoral Shocks*

On January 7th, 1989, the Shōwa emperor Hirohito died and was succeeded by his son, the Heisei emperor Akihito.[1] Akihito's enthronement ceremony the following year – the first since the 1920s – was watched by a television audience

---

1   This section draws heavily on Sadoh's (2012) detailed historical account of political events of the 1990s and 2000s, based on my own original translated interpretation of passages from the Japanese language text.

of 30 percent of the public (Sadoh 2012).[2] Yet just as the Heisei era was beginning, a new period of crisis and instability was emerging. Very quickly, the signs of strain, political, economic, and social, began to rear their heads. In February 1989, facing public backlash over both the Recruit-Cosmos scandal[3] that had directly implicated him and the unpopular consumption tax, with an approval rating of just 4.4 percent, Prime Minister Takeshita resigned (Sadoh 2012). Rather than holding a leadership election, Takeshita handpicked his successor as Uno Sōsuke, an experienced yet relatively unknown figure chosen for his distance from the Recruit scandal. Yet shortly before the election, Uno himself was hit by a sex scandal. With public trust in the LDP at an all-time low, the party suffered a major defeat in the Upper House election to the JSP led by its dynamic (and first female) leader Doi Takako, losing its double majority, and thus unfettered political control.

In the aftermath of the LDP's electoral defeat in 1989, the party chose yet another new leader in August, Kaifu Toshiki of the Miki faction. Like Miki, Kaifu had the clean image desperately needed by the LDP at the time. While Kaifu helped restore some public trust and weather the storm of the scandals, in the summer of 1990, Kaifu was caught off guard by the start of the Gulf War. While backing American sanctions against Iraq, Kaifu hesitated over demands from Bush to send troops to the conflict. For the first time, powerful voices within the LDP called for direct involvement of the Self-Defense Forces (SDF). However, these calls were rejected by the bureaucracy and by Kaifu himself, as well as by the opposition (Sadoh 2012). In the end Japan spent 13 billion dollars on the Gulf War but had little to show for it in terms of international recognition. Japan's foreign policy was characterized by American critics as "pacifism in one country," refusing to sacrifice blood and sweat, while trying to solve everything with money alone (Sadoh 2012).

Along with this political turbulence, the end of 1989 had brought economic turbulence in the context of the bubble economy that had bloated asset values to the point of the land value of the Imperial Palace in central Tokyo exceeding that of the entire state of California by 1989. Yet while the Nikkei stock market peaked at just under 40,000 points on December 29th, it began to fall the next day, a moment that served as a harbinger for the economic crisis to come

---

2   This number should not be seen as particularly high: by comparison, the 1987 and 1988 seasons of the popular *Taiga Dramas* that run every week on Sundays each had average viewership of nearly 40 percent, while nearly two thirds of Japanese watched the 2002 FIFA World Cup match between Japan and Russia (Biglobe 2019; Matome Naver 2013).

3   Under the Recruit-Cosmos scandal, numerous lawmakers (from various parties) were implicated or found guilty in a scheme of being offered (and accepting) shares by Cosmos (owned by Recruit) before the company went public (and share value increased) (Shiratori 1995).

(Komine 2018). While the Kaifu government took measures to abate the stock market plunge, which had fallen below 30,000 by March 1990, these proved ineffective, and the stock market fell below 20,000 yen by October 1990 (Sadoh 2012). The stock market crash was followed by a real estate market crash, partially engineered by the government, which tried to deflate the speculative bubble by instituting control measures over real estate loans for banks (Komine 2018), as well as through hikes in interest rates to over 8 percent in 1990 (Lucarelli 2015). While this had the effect of controlling the real estate boom that was making housing unaffordable for many people, the sudden decline in asset values led to a credit crunch among major financial institutions, as their debts were no longer leveraged by their assets. This led GDP growth to fall to 0.8 percent in 1991 and -0.5 percent in 1992 (Berggren 1995). By the early 1990s, Japan's economy had fallen into a state of debt deflation (Komine 2018).

In addition to the economic challenges posed by the sinking stock market and the foreign policy challenges of the Gulf War fiasco, growing public anger over LDP corruption – highlighted by the 1989 electoral defeat – emboldened the voices of electoral reform, both inside and outside of the party. As with foreign policy and (neoliberal) economic reform, one of the leading voices for electoral reform was LDP general secretary and rising star Ozawa Ichirō. While unions and business groups had been calling for electoral reform since the late 1980s, the LDP itself had formed a Political Reform Committee that advocated a switch to a full first-past-the-post electoral system, alongside other measures, such as campaign financing reform (Sadoh 2012). Yet this sort of change threatened the power of *kōenkai*, and thus received little outright support from lawmakers.

These debates over electoral reform – which Kaifu supported – divided the party, and ultimately weakened his support within the party. He resigned in October 1991 and was replaced with veteran lawmaker Miyazawa Kiichi. Miyazawa was credited with improving Japan's image abroad by sending SDF troops to participate in minesweeping operations in the Persian Gulf and in peacekeeping operations in Cambodia in 1992 and because of his prominent leadership role in the high-level Trilateral Commission. Yet at the same time he faced domestic political adversity. First, in 1992, news of yet another scandal, the Sagawa Kyūbin scandal, broke. The scandal implicated LDP general secretary Kanemaru Shin, who was found to have taken a 500 million yen (3.6 million US dollars) bribe to save Sagawa from bankruptcy (Sadoh 2012). Second, there were growing divisions and debates both within the LDP and among parties over electoral reform in early 1993. While the LDP was split between those pushing for a first-past-the-post system and those opposed to reform altogether, much of the opposition favored a proportional representative electoral system. Within this context, Ozawa, the boldest advocate for reform among the

LDP, called for a compromise system that combined first-past-the-post with proportional representation. Miyazawa, meanwhile, promised on national TV pass electoral reform legislation before the summer election (Sadoh 2012).

At a caucus meeting on June 15th, however, it was determined that this promise could not be kept. When the opposition tabled a motion of non-confidence on June 17th, the pro-reform Ozawa led his faction to vote in favor of the motion, which passed. Within a week, 54 LDP members had mutinied from the party, with 43 following Ozawa as he formed the conservative but reformist Japan Renewal Party (JRP) and ten others forming another, slightly more left-leaning party, Sakigake. Despite this upheaval, the result of the election that followed saw both the LDP and JRP maintain their seats. Indeed, it was the JSP that saw a major decline, going from 134 to 70 seats, while the newly formed centrist and reformist Japan New Party (JNP), led by Hosokawa Morihiro, won 35 seats. The result thus saw the LDP slightly improve its post-defection seat count from 222 to 223 seats, though still fall short of a majority. However, rather than resulting in an LDP-led minority or coalition government, the government formation that followed saw Ozawa orchestrate an unthinkable seven-party coalition.[4] In the end, it was Ozawa's shrewd decision to offer Hosokawa the position of Prime Minister that led the JNP to join the seven-party coalition rather than form a coalition with the LDP (Sadoh 2012). This unforeseen set of events led to the most significant upheaval of Japanese post-war political history and brought an end to the LDP's uninterrupted 38-year reign of office.

1.2   1993–1996: Coalition Governments, Political Reform

The coalition cabinet was sworn in with a seventy percent approval rating, hinting at a fresh start for Japanese democracy after more than a decade of LDP corruption. Yet the honeymoon did not last long, as interparty infighting and scandals led the coalition government to fall apart after less than a year. Nonetheless, the brief spell of coalition government brought one major policy achievement: political reform, including electoral and campaign finance reform. This was achieved through a compromise bill that stipulated an electoral system that combined first-past-the-post with proportional representation and won support from the LDP, which was needed to secure passage in the Upper House. However, while reform had been what brought the seven-party coalition together, its achievement marked the beginning of the coalition's unraveling. In February, Hosokawa held a press conference at 1 AM saying that he

---

4   This coalition included the JSP (70 seats), Ozawa's own JRP (55 seats), Kōmeitō (51 seats), JNP (35 seats), DSP (15 seats), Sakigake (13 seats) and the Socialist Democratic Federation (4 seats).

wanted to change the consumption tax to a social welfare tax and raise it from 3 to 7 percent. Uninformed of this, the JSP and Sakigake were irate and while Hosokawa quickly backtracked one day later, it severely damaged him (Sadoh 2012). With allegations of Hosokawa's implication in the Sagawa Kyūbin scandal emerging shortly thereafter, he was forced to resign in April.

While Ozawa next tried to orchestrate a new coalition, with the JRP's Hata Tsutomu as Prime Minister, the JSP refused to join, frustrated with Ozawa for not giving the JSP a strong voice in the coalition despite their leading seat total. The Hata-led coalition thus took over the reins with just 33 percent of seats in the Diet and lasted all of nine weeks. After the LDP tabled a motion of non-confidence, the cabinet was forced to resign. This time, however, the LDP offered JSP leader Murayama Tomiichi the position of Prime Minister in a new, LDP-JSP-Sakigake coalition government. However, the JSP faced a major problem regarding fundamental policy differences with the LDP, particularly over defense. As an opposition party, the JSP had never renounced its opposition to the Anpo nor its claim that the Self-Defense Forces (SDF) was unconstitutional. Suddenly, the realities of government forced it to confront this question. Perhaps predictably, the SDP bowed to pressure to accept the existence of the SDF and the Anpo, along with Japan's national anthem, *kimigayo* and flag, *hinomaru* (Sadoh 2012). Ultimately this cooptation proved costly for the JSP: Seen by the general public as having abandoned their principles for power, they fell even further in the 1996 election, and gradually declined into virtual non-existence over the next two decades.[5]

While the Murayama-led coalition government was successful in developing a number of social programs, its 18 months in power were widely seen as ineffective. On one hand, Murayama faced bad luck: 1995 brought two major challenges, first with the Hanshin Earthquake in January near Kobe, then with the Tokyo sarin gas attack in March.[6] On the other hand, Murayama was criticized for indecisiveness and an absence of leadership in both cases, criticism that he himself accepted (Sadoh 2012). These problems only further hurt the JSP, which lost half its seats in the 1995 Upper House election. Murayama

---

5   However, despite generally renouncing the SDP's critical stances on major foreign policy issues, there was one major exception to this under Murayama's tenure: the 1995 Apology on the 50th anniversary of the war's end, where Murayama apologized to Japan's Asian neighbours for Japan's wartime actions, recognizing the state's complicity in the comfort women issue, and identifying the war as an "imperialist war of aggression" (Sadoh 2012).
6   The Tokyo Sarin gas attacks were a terrorist plot that killed 13 Tokyo subway passengers using sarin gas during the morning commute on March 20, 1995, carried out by new-age religious cult Aum Shinrikyō. The Hanshin earthquake occurred near Kobe in the early morning of January 17th, 1995, killing over 6,400 people.

resigned in January 1996 and was replaced as Prime Minister with the LDP's new leader, Hashimoto Ryūtarō.

1.3   1996–2001: LDP's Return to Power, Administrative and Financial Reform

Thus, in January 1996, the LDP returned to the *kantei* (Prime Minister's Office), just 30 months after vacating it. While it remained in coalition with the JSP and Sakigake, after winning the June 1996 Lower House election – the first under the new system – the LDP could still more or less govern on its own. The LDP did well in the 1996 election, winning a majority of seats despite experiencing a decline in its popular vote, largely due to vote-splitting between the newly formed New Frontier Party (NFP)[7] and the Democratic Party (DPJ), a new party formed at the start of the year by Sakigake and JSP members unhappy over the coalition with the LDP. The new electoral system thus quickly proved to be more punitive to small parties – and rewarding of large parties – than the old system. It thus paradoxically enabled the LDP to regain majority control of the Diet with a vote total that would have proven insufficient to maintain power under the old system.

After the 1996 election, Hashimoto unveiled a program for reform, focusing on six areas: education, finance, administration, fiscal policy, social security and structural economic policy. Hashimoto's reform agenda was driven by the aging crisis in Japan, as well as by the growing weight of arguments for neoliberal structural reform, including from opposition forces such as Ozawa Ichirō (Sadoh 2012). Hashimoto had worked as the LDP's representative at the Rinchō II and overseen the privatization of JR as Transport Minister. To adjust Japan's political economic system to the needs of an aging society and rein in the mounting public debt, he felt that Japan must move away from clientelist infrastructure spending and instead pursue economic deregulation, welfare reform and greater investment in science and technology (Sadoh 2012).

In 1997 Hashimoto deemed that the after-effects of the bubble had abated and decided to introduce his reforms. Part of Hashimoto's plan was to cut public works spending by seven percent while raising the sales tax from three to five per cent in order to cut the deficit to within three percent of GDP by 2003 (Sadoh 2012). However, the tax hike led to the first decline in consumer spending in postwar history. In addition, Hashimoto's administrative reforms involved shrinking the number of government ministries from 21 to 12, while bolstering

---

7 The New Frontier Party was formed in December 1994 through a merger of the Japan Renewal Party, the Japan New Party, the Democratic Socialist Party and Kōmeitō.

the power of the PM in order to increase executive authority and responsibility in Japan's political system. This administrative reform received backlash from entrenched interests in the Postal, Construction and MITI ministries principally from both bureaucrats and *zoku* lawmakers. At the same time, it was seen by many as a necessary step in reducing corruption and increasing accountability in Japan's political system.

However, in the fall of 1997, economic crisis struck yet again, this time in the form of the Asian Financial Crisis. The crisis brought a market downturn, including the bankruptcies of Hokkaido Takushoku Bank and Yamaichi Shōken, pushing the Japanese economy back into recession (Sadoh 2012). In response, Hashimoto introduced a financial liberalization policy designed to ensure that the yen would not decline as a major currency in world markets.[8] Yet the Asian Financial Crisis proved that the Japanese financial sector was still vulnerable. The Treasury had discovered that the bad debt of the financial industry was worth not 30 trillion but 70 trillion yen (Sadoh 2012). News that the GDP had fallen 0.7 percent came before the 1998 Upper House election, where the LDP lost 22 seats, forcing Hashimoto to resign.

Though Hashimoto only served for two years, he has since come to be seen as an important figure in Japanese politics (Estevez-Abe 2008), primarily for the measures of administrative reform that he instituted. These included streamlining the number of ministries and introducing measures to strengthen the role of the Prime Minister (in relation to both the party and the bureaucracy), including by giving Prime Ministers the power to directly appointment the three top positions of each ministry (Sadoh 2012). These changes took effect beginning in 2001 and were responsible for the new leadership style and increased authority enjoyed by future leaders. In other ways, Hashimoto (and his successor Obuchi) made serious efforts to roll back Japan's clientelist state and pork-barrel spending in the wake of growing budget deficits and economic stagnation. In 1998 Hashimoto repealed the Large-Scale Retail Store Law of 1974, while Obuchi ended wage subsidies for declining industries (Estevez-Abe 2008).

The years that followed (1998–2001) under Obuchi, and his successor, the gaffe prone and unpopular Mori, saw a continuation of the policies introduced under Hashimoto. One major accomplishment for the LDP in this time was the 1999 negotiation of a coalition agreement with Kōmeitō, who had left the NFP and re-founded itself as an independent party in 1998. While Kōmeitō had

---

8   Over two occasions in 1998 the Hashimoto government and its successor Obuchi government injected a combined 40 trillion yen of stimulus into the financial sector (Katada 2013).

long been an opponent of the LDP and little cross-party dialogue had existed, in 1999 the LDP's Chief Party Secretary Nonaka Hiromu made a shrewd observation that a coalition with Kōmeitō could help ensure political stability and keep the LDP in power (Sadoh 2012). For their part, Kōmeitō was intrigued by the possibility of controlling cabinet positions and gaining policy concessions from the LDP, and thus the LDP-Kōmeitō coalition was born, and has remained to this day.

While the 1990s saw a focus on electoral reform, economic crisis management and neoliberal deregulation, these years also saw the development of at least four major social policies. First, in the aftermath of the 1989 Upper House election defeat to the JSP, the LDP introduced the Gold Plan, which greatly expanded public elder care (Estevez-Abe 2008). Second, in 1991, JSP lawmakers who controlled the Upper House pushed the government to pass a Childcare Leave Act that mandated a year of unpaid leave for new mothers, a compromise policy that emerged out of *shingikai* negotiations between business and labour groups (Estevez-Abe 2008). Third, following the end of LDP rule and the rise of the proto-DPJ coalition in 1993, the Ministry of Health and Welfare crafted a wide-ranging pro-natal policy called the Angel Plan, which called for expanded public daycare, expanded child benefit payments, extended daycare flexibility, and the introduction of lump-sum baby bonuses.[9] Fourth, in 1999 the Child Care and Family Care Leave Law was created, which added to existing unpaid childcare leave protections similar measures for those who need to care for sick (non-infant) family members (Estevez-Abe 2008; MHLW 2010). Thus, despite the enduring economic stagnation and political upheaval caused by electoral and administrative reform, the period of the 1990s saw a significant expansion of social programs designed to target two elements of Japan's emergent demographic crisis: population aging and the low birth rate.

1.4   *2001–2006: Rise of Koizumi, Postal Privatization*

In 2001, Koizumi Jun'ichirō, a third-generation lawmaker who was not from any faction but was known as a maverick and reformer, faced off against Hashimoto to succeeded Mori as LDP leader. Koizumi had little support from within the party but appealed to the wider party membership and public at large, framing himself as someone who could get rid of the old-style, clientelist and collusive LDP politics from within through a far-reaching agenda of liberalization. This,

---

9 According to Osawa (2013), the Angel Plan of 1994 predicted that 70 percent of childbearing age women would be working by the 21st century and advised provided daycare services that could cover the working hours for children from babies to age 6, located at workplaces or on the way to workplaces.

along with his cool and suave image, made him popular with the masses (Sadoh 2012). Koizumi ran for the LDP presidency as if he was running for president of Japan, making speeches all over the country. Supported by Tanaka Makiko (daughter of Tanaka Kakuei), he appealed strongly to women. Electoral rule changes that tripled the votes of prefectures enabled Koizumi to target party membership rather than try to cultivate factional support. The strategy paid off: he won 123 to 15 over Hashimoto on regional ballots. This then impacted the voting of LDP lawmakers, who elected Koizumi 175 to 140 (Sadoh 2012).

Koizumi, who began his term with a 92 percent approval rating, paid little attention to factions when selecting his cabinet, choosing five women as well as a non-politician, Takenaka Heizō. Koizumi was bullish in advancing his neoliberal agenda to cope with globalization, while also advancing a more militarist foreign policy. In August 2001 he visited the controversial Yasukuni Shrine, angering China and Korea. Then, after 9/11, Koizumi announced support for the US in the War on Terror, angering pacifists by sending SDF troops into non-combat duty in Afghanistan, their first non-PKO mission. Economically, Koizumi announced a Basic Plan for Economic and Financial Activities' Management and Reform that included privatization and regulatory reform, fiscal retrenchment, social insurance reform and stronger intellectual property rights. His program also sought to resolve the bad debt problem of the banking sector within three years and proposed to bring the national debt down to 30 trillion yen (Sadoh 2012).

While Koizumi and his economic policy minister Takenaka Heizō received praise for successfully addressing the bad debt problem at the beginning of his tenure, most of Koizumi's time was dominated by his pursuit of postal privatization.[10] Koizumi had been obsessed with postal privatization since he first worked as an undersecretary for the Treasury during the Ōhira administration. In that role Koizumi noticed the immense amount of capital held by the Postal Savings and Postal Life Insurance public entities that was being used as to finance spending in very inefficient ways. This led Koizumi to see privatization as necessary for getting rid of inefficient, pork-barrel spending that ran counter to the neoliberal economic system that he thought Japan needed. Koizumi also supported postal privatization for personal reasons, seeing it as the fiscal basis for the clientelist politics that had underscored the power of Tanaka Kakuei, whom Koizumi deeply resented (Sadoh 2012).

---

10   Koizumi also privatized the Public Highway Corporation in 2004, a policy that drew much criticism for his lack of leadership as well as the backlash it caused among both *zoku* lawmakers from the MLIT and rural voters (Sadoh 2012).

Despite initial public enthusiasm, support for Koizumi waned in 2004, resulting in a defeat in the Upper House election to the DPJ, while opposition within the LDP to postal privatization left his signature reform measure in jeopardy. In response, Koizumi tightened his resolve in the drive for postal privatization. In 2005, Koizumi was able to force postal privatization despite lacking an Upper House majority by dissolving the Lower House and winning a landslide election in what became known as the postal election. During this election, Koizumi famously delisted anti-privatization "rebels" from the party nomination and ran "assassin" candidates – many of whom were younger or female – against them. The landslide win gave Koizumi the political capital he needed to get the Upper House to agree to the bill. Overall, Koizumi was brilliant in the way he used appeals to the public and public opinion as a basis for his power. Part of this was because Koizumi lacked his own faction within the party. More importantly, though, was the way he used the emerging forms of popular media to his advantage. In the 1990s and 2000s TV was becoming a more important medium than newspapers, and Koizumi exploited TV media very effectively. In an era of image politics, Koizumi was the master of the sound bite (Sadoh 2012).

1.5   2006–2009: LDP *Impasse*

Koizumi was barred from running for a third term in 2006 and was instead succeeded by Abe Shinzō, a young conservative who had served as Koizumi's Chief Cabinet Secretary. Though he would later make a spectacular political comeback, Abe's first year in office was one of failure. First, he was accused of cronyism by forming a "cabinet of friends," many of which became engulfed in scandals. Abe himself faced a major scandal involving the loss of personal data relating to the pensions of 50 million people (Sadoh 2012). Second, his obsession with right wing causes suggested that he was out of touch with the needs of the majority of Japanese, who were increasingly concerned with continued economic stagnation and rising inequality.[11] Abe's popularity fell over the course of his term, and in the fall of 2007, he resigned after losing the Upper House election to the DPJ.

Fukuda Yasuo, son of former Prime Minister Fukuda Takeo, and a senior figure within the conservative faction that his father once led, succeeded Abe. While Fukuda brought a more measured approach to Japanese politics, he was hampered institutionally by lacking a majority in the Upper

---

11   As Chapter Seven will discuss, these causes included the introduction of a "patriotic" moral curriculum in schools and remilitarization through constitutional revision.

House, and thus had trouble passing legislation. With slumping approval ratings, Fukuda was pushed out by the LDP, who feared that he was not the right "face" to contest the upcoming 2009 election against an insurgent DPJ (Sadoh 2012). Fukuda's term thus lasted just one year and he was replaced in September 2008 with Asō Tarō. While Asō hoped to call an early election, he was very quickly forced to deal with the Global Financial Crisis, as American investment bank Lehman Brothers filed for bankruptcy just a week before Asō's inauguration.

As with the Asian Financial Crisis ten years earlier, the subprime mortgage and financial crisis in the US quickly spread to Japan: in 2008 Japanese GDP contracted by 6.3 percent, while the Nikkei fell below 7000 points – the lowest since the early 1980s – and unemployment also grew from 3.8 to 5 percent (Katada 2013). In the context of the crisis, the Fukuda and Asō governments took measures to stimulate the economy, cutting interest rates and introducing four financial stimulus packages in August, October and December of 2008 and April 2009. These stimulus packages totaled 91 trillion yen, while the April 2009 stimulus also included an additional 42 trillion yen aimed at boosting consumer spending, making it the largest stimulus package in history (Katada 2013). However, despite these measures, with the sharpened crisis conditions of the 2008–09 recession adding to the long run of LDP scandals as well as image problems facing Asō (Sadoh 2012), the LDP began to prepare for electoral defeat in 2009.

1.6   2009–2012: Rise and Fall of the DPJ

In August 2009, the DPJ led by Hatoyama Yukio won a landslide election, winning 308 seats to the LDP's 119. The DPJ had been formed in 1996 by a group of Sakigake and JSP lawmakers unhappy with the coalition with the LDP, expanding in 1998 when a large number of NFP lawmakers joined.[12] The party expanded further when Ozawa Ichirō joined the party along with most of his Liberal Party lawmakers in 2003. Overall, the DPJ might be seen as a catchall party to the left of the LDP with both social democratic (former JSP) and neoliberal (former NFP) factions that had its lineages in the 1993 coalition government. The DPJ's electoral breakthrough – thirteen years after the party's founding – occurred due to a number of reasons, including both the public's frustration with the post-Koizumi LDP's poor leadership,

---

12   Many of the New Frontier Party members who joined the DPJ in 1998 had previously been part of the Democratic Socialist Party and Japan New Party (rather than from Kōmeitō and the Japan Renewal Party).

growing concern over issues such as inequality (which the DPJ campaigned on) and an appeal to rural voters through promises of clientelist supports (Sasada 2015).

Upon assuming office, the DPJ was steadfast in the pursuit of a reformist agenda. On foreign policy, Hatoyama led Japan to sign the 2009 Copenhagen Accord, calling for 25 percent cuts to CO_2 emissions by 2020, while also signaling a major foreign policy pivot away from the US and towards Asia through a political summit with Chinese leader Hu Jintao. At the summit he called into question the long-term status of the US-Japan security alliance, a move that drew immense criticism from both the LDP opposition and the US. In other ways, Hatoyama failed to fulfill foreign policy promises, and his inability to reach an agreement with the US over the relocation of the Pentagon's Futenma base in Okinawa brought about his resignation in 2010.

With regard to domestic politics, Hatoyama pursued a further strengthening of the administrative reforms that began under Hashimoto, further strengthening Cabinet control over the selection of top bureaucrats. Additionally, Hatoyama got rid of the weekly deputy ministers' meeting, where top bureaucrats from each ministry gathered in advance of cabinet meetings to determine the agenda of those meetings (Shinoda 2013). These meetings had existed for decades as a leading example of the bureaucratic "tail" wagging the "dog" of the cabinet by setting the agenda of discussion, which meant that cabinet meetings were often little more than a rubber stamp for previously agreed-upon bureaucratic prerogatives. By getting rid of these meetings, Hatoyama had challenged the power-knowledge-institutional complex of the bureaucracy. A hostile relationship with the bureaucracy, which the DPJ blamed for many of Japan's problems, characterized much of the DPJ tenure (see also Kamikawa 2016).

Partially due to their lack of experience in governing and partly due to the hostility incurred from the bureaucracy and media, the DPJ's term was dogged by major campaign financing scandals implicating prominent cabinet ministers. While Hatoyama's resignation and replacement with Kan Naoto brought an uptick in approval ratings, these problems continued to linger. Indeed, Kan's immediate task of maintaining DPJ control of the Upper House after the 2010 election proved to be too much to ask. To the DPJ's chagrin, the campaign was framed around Kan's plan for sales tax increases, a proposal for which Kan could never find a consistent explanation to justify. Defeat to the LDP not only led to the end of DPJ control of both chambers but also forced Kan to whether a leadership challenge from Ozawa, hurting party unity.

Along with this electoral setback, the DPJ faced renewed foreign policy challenges. While Kan had worked hard to restore bonds with the United States, an incursion into Japanese territorial waters by a Chinese fishing boat led to a major diplomatic row with China, erasing the good will that Hatoyama had established just one year earlier. Mismanagement of the issue as well as public perceptions of Japanese weakness in the face of Chinese aggression seriously hurt Kan (Sadoh 2012).

All these challenges paled in comparison to that posed by the triple disaster of March 11th, 2011: A Magnitude 9 earthquake off the coast of Miyagi prefecture and a tsunami that killed nearly twenty thousand people and led to a nuclear meltdown at the Fukushima Daiichi nuclear power plant. Together these amounted to the costliest disaster in human history. Though a disaster of this scope would stretch the limits of any government, the DPJ proved particularly ineffective in dealing with it. It was widely perceived that Kan interfered too much with the emergency response and in ways that were not helpful and misemployed resources (Sadoh 2012). Part of this was because of the degree of mistrust that had developed between the bureaucracy and the DPJ cabinet. As a result, the flow of information between the government, bureaucracy and business was interrupted, often leaving Chief Cabinet Secretary Edano Yukio with nothing to report, and further presenting an image of incompetence to the public (Sadoh 2012).

After five months of trying to resolve the nuclear emergency, Kan finally resigned in August 2011, replaced by Noda Yoshihiko. In a bid to switch tracks in the face of ailing polling numbers, Noda tried to advance a more neoliberal agenda, pushing trade liberalization through the Trans-Pacific Partnership as well as fiscal reconstruction through sales tax increases. Ultimately, however, neither measure could reverse the trends of crumbling party support and party unity. Thus, in the December 2012 election, the DPJ suffered an emphatic defeat, seeing its share of the vote fall from 42 to 15 percent and losing 20 million votes as the LDP was revived under one-time political failure Abe Shinzō.

Ultimately, the DPJ's three years in power were nothing short of disastrous politically and damaged the image of the party so seriously that it has failed to win more than 21 percent of the vote in any of the five elections since 2012,[13] in stark contrast the 42 percent it received in 2009. Nonetheless, the DPJ – particularly in its first nine months of double legislative control under

---

13   The DPJ received 15 percent in the 2012 Lower House (LH) election; 13 percent in the 2013 Upper House (UH) election; 18 percent in the 2014 LH election; 21 percent in the 2016 UH election (after merging with the Restoration Party); and 20 percent in the 2017 LH election (as the Constitutional Democratic Party).

Hatoyama – passed a number of important economic and social policies. This included policies designed to target both Japan's terminally slow growth and its growing social and demographic crisis of rising inequality and population aging. These included an expansion of the child allowance and the elimination of high school fees as well as anti-poverty welfare programs, subsidies for farmers, increases to the minimum wage and other protections for workers (Osawa 2013). However, while the DPJ had initially claimed that such programs would be financed by the elimination of wasteful LDP spending, this ultimately proved naïve. It was only through the increase of the deeply unpopular consumption tax that their social policies could be rendered affordable, a move that in the process all but ended the party's chances of re-election.

2   Conditions of the Crisis

What accounts for the dynamics of political instability and upheaval, combined with economic stagnation and stasis, outlined in the previous section? Following Gramsci, I want to conceptualize the period beginning in the early 1990s as one of organic crisis. This crisis is wide-ranging, and thus incorporates social, economic and political elements. In what follows, I consider eleven different elements in the crisis, each corresponding to one of the eleven conditions of hegemonic rule developed in Chapter Four. While all these conditions helped buttress the hegemonic order in the early post-war period, due in part to the structural, institutional and political changes discussed in Chapter Five, things had dramatically changed by the 1990s.

2.1   *Geopolitics: Security Alliance in a Post-Cold War World*

Changing geopolitical conditions beginning in the 1990s brought new challenges for Japan's domestic hegemonic order. While it would be wrong to suggest that these changing conditions are directly at fault for Japan's prolonged crisis, in various ways they have disrupted the stable basis for hegemony domestically.

First, the end of the Cold War brought new challenges as Japan's relationship with the US was increasingly called into question, with some American leaders seeing Japan's economic threat as the biggest challenge to US hegemony in the 1990s. Yet Japan lacked the political leadership to chart a different course than that of the alliance with the US. Japan was therefore criticized for being a political and foreign policy lightweight, not contributing with blood and steel to the Gulf War. This led to efforts to re-forge Japan's foreign policy identity under Kaifu and public concern over Japan's global role and image.

At the same time, increasingly powerful voices, such as that of Ozawa Ichirō, called for Japan to reformulate its role in world politics as a "normal country" – in other words, a country with a normal military that engages in its "fair share" of international policing.

Second, the period of the 1990s and 2000s saw the rise of new threats beyond the purview of the nation state, particularly that of terrorism, challenged the sense of domestic security that had previously existed in Japan.[14] Indeed, the loss of civilian life at the hands of terrorist groups, both in the US – the supposed protector of Japan – and in Japan itself, were politically and existentially destabilizing. Moreover, despite the end of the Cold War East-West antagonism, new threats emerged in the 1990s from Japan's neighbours in China and especially North Korea. This included the launch of North Korean missiles over the Sea of Japan in 1993 and the development of the North Korean nuclear program a decade later, as well as 2003 revelations of North Korean abductions of Japanese nationals from the late 1970s and early 1980s.

Third, the rise of China was another factor generating ambivalence over the future direction of Japanese regional foreign policy and overall increasing doubts over what Japan's role in the world ought to be. This ambivalence about the role of China in regional geopolitics and the prospects for a more peaceful and amicable Sino-Japanese relationship is reflected in the perception among some Japanese politicians, including Abe Shinzō, that China has two faces. One is a friendly face regarding mutually beneficial trade, while the other is a more ominous face in relation to security policy.

Overall, these three foreign policy challenges all had destabilizing effects on the fabric of Japanese post-war security policy and raised new concerns over the validity of the post-war regime rooted in Anpo and the Pacifist Constitution, challenging the old order in ways that have brought about difficult political challenges for LDP and DPJ governments alike.

2.2 *Global Political Economy: Japan in a Global Neoliberal Era*

As noted, the period of the 1990s and 2000s was characterized by consistent economic crises. Three dynamics in the global political economy were transformed into underlying elements of these crises.

First, Japan's project of neoliberal deregulation in the 1980s was a key source of the problems that Japanese financial institutions faced until the early 2000s, including the bubble economy of the late 1980s and early 1990s and

---

14   This included both international terrorist groups such as Al-Qaeda and domestic terrorists such as Aum Shinrikyō.

the non-performing loan problem that led to costly bank bailouts and failures and was only resolved in the early 2000s (Lechevalier 2014). As the previous chapter showed, the neoliberalization of Japan's economy in the 1980s was primarily characterized by the privatization and financial deregulation that emerged out of Rinchō II. Moreover, it was as much a product of indigenous neoliberal organic intellectuals as it was a result of pressure from forces within the American government and capital who wanted easier access to Japanese capital (Tiberghien 2014). Though far from systematic or complete, it served as a principal driver for both the speculative boom of the late 1980s bubble economy and the transformation in corporate relations that followed in response to the stock market crash.

By the late 1990s, the system of coordination and support between banks, firms and the state had broken down, as the main bank system of corporate financing had been replaced by shareholder supremacism, and the state was no longer willing to bail out ailing banks (Takahashi and Mizuno 2013). The speculative bubble and subsequent bust led to a decline in trust relations among both public and private actors (Komine 2018). Indeed, this loss of trust is one factor behind why took over a decade until the bad debt problem was finally resolved in 2002. This lack of trust was responsible not only for delaying the end of the banking crisis; it also brought about a vicious cycle of market pessimism followed by a structural dynamic of debt deflation (Boyer 2014). This led commodity prices and real wages to fall in the late 1990s, while in 2002 the unemployment rate surpassed five percent for the first time in the post-war era (Komine 2018). The bursting of the speculative bubble also brought about a fiscal crisis, as revenues fell, and stimulus packages necessitated more spending. While Japan's budget had been in surplus as late as 1992, by 1997 it had the largest deficit among industrialized countries (Komine 2018).

In addition to the emergence of financialization and the rise of shareholder supremacy, a second factor behind the enduring economic crisis was the high degree of integration into world markets, and the negative effects of that dependency. Japan's bubble economy was itself an early cause of the Asian Financial Crisis of 1997–8, and in turn the effects Asian Financial Crisis itself came full circle to Japan, as a credit crunch brought the economy back into recession in 1998. The 2008 Global Financial Crisis was even more serious, prompting the biggest single year contraction of GDP in postwar history and leading to 790,000 job losses and the highest unemployment rate of the postwar era despite having its US origins (Shibata 2017). Indeed, according to Katada (2013) the historic contraction in GDP experienced as a result of the 2008 Global Financial Crisis had little to do with the activities of Japanese banks. Instead, it was caused by a sudden and sharp withdrawal of foreign investment from the Japanese stock market. Foreign ownership of stock had grown dramatically since the 1990s, totaling 28 percent of stock and 65 percent of the volume of traded stock in 2007.

A third factor behind Japan's lost two decades is the rise of China since the 1990s. While Japan had four times as much trade with the US compared to China until the 1990s, by 2005 trade with China passed the US (Lechevalier 2014). This gave Japanese capital an abundant supply of cheap labour close by that helped ensure conditions of profitability for Japanese firms, particularly in manufacturing industries. However, it led to an outflow of Japanese capital to China, undermining domestic growth and playing a role in entrenching conditions of domestic deflation (Jayasuriya 2018).

Overall, the integration of Japan into the global framework of disciplinary neoliberalism destroyed the social fabric of Japanese-style capitalism. At the same time, it also deepened contradictions between conditions conducive to capital accumulation (i.e., neoliberal deregulation) and those conducive to stable social reproduction (i.e., social welfare provisioning and employment maintenance).

2.3 The Electoral and Party System: Crisis, Reform, and the End of LDP Rule

In what way did conditions relating to Japan's electoral and party system contribute to the crisis? As noted above, Japan's post-war electoral system had a significant impact on post-war political order, helping to maintain conditions for stable LDP-led one party rule. LDP hegemony was beset by a number of high-profile scandals, beginning in the 1970s and extending into the 1980s and 1990s, laying bare the dark side of Japan's political system.

The beginning of the 1990s thus saw a mounting political crisis, with high levels of public distrust with politicians and bureaucrats alike and calls for reform. The political crisis of the 1990s was famously characterized by the 1992 arrest of Kanemaru Shin, the party's deputy president and former chief secretary and one of the most powerful figures in the LDP, in relation to the Sagawa Kyūbin scandal.[15] Indeed, the fallout of the crisis was significant. Within months the LDP was out of power, and a broad coalition government that included socialists, Kōmeitō, and LDP rebels stayed together just long enough to pass far-reaching electoral and campaign finance reform. To be sure, the electoral reform had far-reaching implications on Japan's political system. Since reform, there have been no major corruption scandals involving large private firms to parallel the Lockheed, Sagawa and Recruit scandals.

---

15 When police later raided his home, they found gold bars weighing hundreds of pounds as well as cash and bearer bonds worth fifty million US dollars (Pollack 1996).

At the same time, reform has brought with it new challenges for Japan's hegemonic order, while failing to resolve old ones. As Krauss and Pekkanen (2010) have shown, it did not have the expected effects of removing the influence of factions and *kōenkai*. Except for Koizumi, the LDP leadership continued to be determined based on factional politics. Nor did it have any impact on the formation of political dynasties. While only seventeen percent of lawmakers had inherited their districts from family members in 1958, by 2003 this number was forty percent, and especially pronounced in rural districts (Krauss and Pekkanen 2010). Indeed, while their membership has declined somewhat, little changed in the function of *kōenkai* compared to before the electoral reform, nor in their basic activities (Krauss and Pekkanen 2010).

Second, and linked with the continued relevance of *kōenkai*, electoral reform only went so far in creating party-centered politics. Candidates continued to be important, and neither the LDP nor the newly formed DPJ were characterized by ideological coherence. While the LDP used its lack of ideological coherence as a means of being all things to all people, for the DPJ a lack of ideological coherence simply led to party infighting and a scattergun approach to policymaking.

Part of the cause of this, as noted, was an ironic consequence of the new model for electoral reform that was chosen – a compromise position between the mixed-member proportional system (MMP) favored by the small progressive parties and the first-past-the-post (FPTP) system favored by the LDP. In hindsight, either MMP or FPTP would likely have posed challenges to the LDP. While MMP would have given small parties a number of seats proportionate to their vote share, FPTP would have forced all opposition parties to unite behind the DPJ. Unlike with FPTP, the mixed system that was chosen gave small parties just enough incentive to avoid joining the DPJ, since they could still win seats through the proportional representation element of the system. Yet compared to MMP, it was still heavily favorable to the LDP overall, since over two thirds of seats were awarded on a winner-take-all basis and thus dominated by the LDP.

Moreover, the electoral reform did not extend to the House of Councilors, nor to the 47 prefectural assemblies, all of which retained the old multi-member system. In the Upper House, this system allows the LDP to win nearly all of the single-member, winner-take-all races in small prefectures while still winning a handful of seats in the multi-member urban prefectures where the second or third-place LDP candidates are still able to win seats despite finishing behind the DPJ.[16] Thus despite electoral reform of the Lower House,

---

16 For example, the 2010 Upper House election brought a major electoral defeat to the DPJ and ended their majority in both houses, effectively creating legislative gridlock only

the largely unreformed Upper House and (regional governments) continue to heavily favor the LDP while encouraging the old-style clientelist politics that electoral reform was supposed to replace. Moreover, even the Lower House reform did not bring with it a thoroughgoing transformation of Japanese democracy as many had hoped.

A final consequence of the events of the 1990s was the elimination of Japan's two nominally socialist parties, the JSP and DSP. While the DSP was officially merged into the New Frontier Party that eventually joined the DPJ, the JSP suffered a gradual but in the end near-total decline, partly due to its disastrous two years in government. In coalition with the LDP, the JSP was seen to have simultaneously abandoned long-time supporters by selling out to the LDP on security issues while poorly managing other issues and thus convincing moderate voters that it was incapable of governing. While the DSP and JSP had never previously been in government, their presence as active opposition parties on the left and centre-left played an important role in situating political debates in Japan and pulling the LDP to the centre. Without these two parties, opposition to the LDP since the 1990s has taken the form of the ideologically incoherent DPJ on one hand and the JCP – largely ignored as far-left radicals – on the other. Overall, we can see how the early 1990s witnessed a political crisis that prompted widespread reform. The reforms were successful in solving some elements of the crisis but not others, while new problems emerged instead.

2.4 The State Form: Institutional Decay and Administrative Reform

In the early 1990s, it was widely acknowledged that Japan's system of bureaucrat-led rule was no longer a driver of Japanese political and economic success but rather a hindrance and cause of the wider political and economic

---

10 months into their term. Yet while the DPJ actually won 39 percent of the vote to the LDP's 33 percent in the MMD portion of the electoral system, it only won 28 seats to the LDP's 39, due to the extreme imbalance of the system in favor of small, rural prefectures. Osaka and Kanazawa, each with a population of 9 million, elected only 3 councilors each. While the DPJ placed first in both prefectures, the sole candidates of second and third-placed parties (including the LDP in both cases) did better than the DPJ's second candidate, leading the DPJ to only win one seat in each prefecture. In contrast, Tokushima, Tottori, Shimane and Fukui, each with 800,000 people or less, each elected LDP candidates with a similar share of the vote. Overall, in eight large prefectures amounting to nearly half of the Japanese population the DPJ beat the LDP 38 percent to 23 yet only won 10 seats to the LDP's 8, while 24 small prefectures amounting to less than a quarter of Japan's population voted 49 percent for the LDP to 40 for the DPJ and saw 18 LDP members elected to the DPJ's 6.

problems that were emerging. As a result, the revamped LDP government pursued an agenda of administrative reform in the 1990s under Hashimoto.

However, while these reforms were somewhat successful in empowering cabinet-based leadership (as demonstrated by Koizumi's five-year term), the return of a series of weak leaders is evidence that this administrative reform was not wholly effective.[17] Indeed, under Hatoyama, the DPJ argued that administrative reforms had not been successful in overcoming the collusive relationship between bureaucrats and the LDP and sought to end once and for all unaccountable bureaucratic-led politics. However, this proved impossible. The bureaucracy resisted the DPJ's attempts at reform, while the DPJ was already highly disadvantaged by its lack of party unity and experience in government. After the failure of Hatoyama's attempts to curtail bureaucratic power by allowing cabinet ministers to appoint the top three ranking staff of their departments, Prime Ministers Kan, and especially Noda returned to the old system of cabinet deference to bureaucrats. Noda even brought back the vice ministers' meetings (Shinoda 2013). For a beleaguered DPJ eager to turn the page on two years of ineffective policymaking, this return to "bureaucratic rule" may have been politically expedient. Yet the underlying problems of democratic accountability in a system where bureaucrats who are neither elected nor directly appointed by elected officials have the authority to craft policy in ways that conflict with the aspirations of the elected government were only exacerbated.

The other problem with the bureaucracy-led system was the way it encouraged clientelism. Although this system was successful both politically and economically during an era of ever-growing budgets, various structural and institutional changes in the 1970s and 1980s meant that by the 1990s it was extremely costly and wasteful.

In this context Koizumi emerged looking to get rid of these clientelist networks and wasteful spending through his postal privatization drive. However, it was not entirely successful: public works spending went back up after Koizumi left office (CAO 2015). Moreover, Koizumi's neoliberalism, including his rejection of public infrastructure spending, led to major social problems, including heightened poverty and inequality. These problems in turn necessitated further government spending, including through a return to pork-barrel infrastructure spending, after the 2008 financial crisis and 2011 earthquake.

---

17   This occurred both under the LDP (Abe, Fukuda and Asō) and more importantly under the DPJ.

2.5 Production and Capital: The Americanization of Japanese Capitalism?

In what ways have changes to the underlying conditions of Japanese capitalism and Japanese business networks underscored Japan's organic crisis since the 1990s? Three changes to the sociology of Japanese business played a role in the crisis. First, as Lechevalier (2014) has argued, changes to corporate financing and the withering of *keiretsu* relations led to a growing lack of complementarity between Japan's economic institutions. For example, while the labour management and financing patterns had both previously prioritized long-term stability over short-term profits, neoliberalism brought about a liberalization of financing arrangements even though in other ways corporate reforms did not take place to the same degree. In this way, a business culture that prioritized stability and long-term growth has been replaced with an incoherent model that combines short term, quarterly profit-oriented financing and shareholder-centrism with residual elements of the old system that still prioritize stability and consensus-based decision-making. In this context, barring further neoliberal deregulation, Japanese firms are unable to provide the short-term rewards for innovation of American-style firms, nor the long-term, cumulative gains of the old, stable domestic model.

Second, we must consider the growing neoliberal orientation of major corporations and business networks, which in many ways meant a decline in their support for the inclusion of other key forces (SMEs, workers) within the historic bloc. Both the growing neoliberal orientation of Keidanren and the shift to a more American style model of corporate management oriented around lucrative executive pay with generous stock options are indicative of this trend. And though there are many such cases, Nissan under the leadership of CEO Carlos Gohsn, which fired over 20,000 workers while paying Mr. Gohsn ten million dollars a year, is perhaps the best example of this (Anchordoguy 2005; Bloomberg 2014). While the president of Toyota, Toyoda Shōichirō made only 690,000 dollars without stock options in 1991, by 2013 his son, Akio, who succeeded him as president, was earning 1.8 million dollars with 7.5 million dollars in stock options (Bloomberg 2014). Though still significantly less than in the US, overall executive pay has increased from 378,000 dollars in 1991 – with no stock options, which were banned until 2006 – to more than one million dollars in 2014 (Kerbo and McKinstry 1995; Nikkei 2015). Under the 2006 Companies Act, firms are now allowed to freely issue stocks to any party, a legal change that prompted a rise in stock options to CEOs based on the American model (Hasegawa, Kim and Yasuda 2017). Along with this shift towards an American style, "greed is good" orientation towards executive pay that was strongly encouraged under Koizumi, the consensus-based hegemonic orientation of major firms and business organizations declined. In a break from the past, these groups no longer called for policies in the broad interests of society (including workers), instead focused narrowly on their own immediate interests of capital accumulation and neoliberal deregulation (Jayasuriya 2018). In the context of this Americanization of Japanese business culture, the shared cultural ethos that united the interests of large firms, the bureaucracy, and the privileged core workforce began to fragment.

Third, there has been a general decline in the close links that bound *keiretsu* members through main bank financing. This is also true for the practice of subcontracting, wherein SMEs benefited from high levels of security through long-term relations with the large enterprises that they engaged in business with. Moreover, these trends have been accompanied by a decline in industrial policy and other means of economic coordination between firms and the state through MITI (Lechevalier 2014). While long-term subcontracting arrangements fell precipitously in the late 1990s and early 2000s, replaced with more fluid and short-term market-based transactions, MITI's influence has declined markedly in the face of neoliberal opposition to industrial policy.[18] *Keiretsu* linkages, meanwhile, have weakened due to the declining centrifugal power of the main bank system, which has been replaced by stock market-based financing. Similarly, reciprocal and main bank shareholding – the stable "institutional investors" that enabled firms to make long-term decisions without worrying about a sudden drop in their share price – has declined from nearly half to less than a quarter of all shares, and largely replaced with foreign shareholders (Lechevalier 2014).

Overall, we can see how the period of the 1990s and 2000s saw a reordering of Japanese economic relations, both among fractions of capital and between capital and the state.[19] These reforms were only partially successful, as certain elements of the old, highly integrated, long-termist and consensus-based

---

18 MITI was renamed as METI (Ministry of Economy, Trade and Industry) in 2001 under the Hashimoto administrative reforms.

19 In addition to all of these dynamics that collectively amount to a neoliberal shift in the orientation of Japanese business networks, another important dynamic that characterized *keiretsu* relations in the 1990s and 2000s was the concentration of *keiretsu* due to a number of bank mergers. While six main *keiretsu* (Mitsubishi, Mitsui, Sumitomo, Fuyō (Fuji-Yasuda), Sanwa, and Dai-ichi Kangyo) existed until 2000, since the 1997 reform of the Anti-Monopoly Act series of bank mergers between 2000 and 2006 has produced only three: Mitsubishi UFJ (formed by the merger of the Bank of Tokyo, Mitsubishi, Tokai and Sanwa banks); Sumitomo-Mitsui (formed by Sumitomo, Mitsui, and Taiyō-Kobe banks); and Mizuho (formed by Industrial Bank of Japan, Fuji and Dai-ichi Kangyo banks) (Grbic 2007).

system, remained. Moreover, these reforms did little to restore conditions for profitable accumulation, while creating new problems, in particular inequality and the decline of political consensus between core elements of the historic bloc that had hitherto been maintained.

2.6 Production and Labour: Deregulation and the Rise of the Working Poor

The Heisei era also saw a transformation in the fortunes of the working class. In particular, two major changes are of note. The first change is the growing dualization of the workforce. Here, dualization refers to the maintenance of the lifetime employment system for a gradually shrinking cohort of protected workers while allowing a parallel labour pool of unprotected *haken*, part time and contract workers (see also Thelen 2012). According to Jayasuriya (2018), "the dualistic labour market is reflected in the slow erosion of the institutions of lifetime employment. ... the share of non-regular workers which was below 20% in the early 1990s reached 35% by the early 2010s" (597). Faced with shrinking profits due to the growing labour costs of an aging workforce, many firms tried to restore profitability by reducing the size of their core, protected workforce, mainly through attrition and early retirement and only rarely through layoffs (Boyer 2014). Instead, they focused on expanding the scope of their non-protected (mostly female) workforce hired under part time or *haken* categories, without the benefits, protections or higher pay of the protected core (see also Noda and Hirano 2013).

The second change is the absolute expansion of flexibilized labour, especially in the service sector, and the corresponding decline of the *petit bourgeoisie*. While this had been going on for decades, the 1990s saw a major expansion of it, as fast food chains, fast fashion retail outlets and convenience stores became ubiquitous (see Table 1 below), particularly after the repeal of the Large Scale Retailers Law in 2000.[20] This second change reflects a transformation at the macroeconomic level characterized by two dynamics: 1) the decline in employment in manufacturing, which was less pronounced in Japan than in the US and UK but still significant, falling from 24 percent to only 16 percent of total employment between 1992 and 2014 (JIL 2016); and 2) the declining proportion of employment in traditional *petit bourgeois* job categories, whether self-employment,

---

20 For example, looking at Japan's two largest convenience store chains, Lawson opened its first store in 1975, its 100th store by 1977 its 1000th store by 1982 and number 10,000 by 2011; Seven Eleven's first store opened in 1974; its 100th store in 1976; its 1000th store in 1980 and its 10,000th store in 2003 (HighCharts 2019).

TABLE 1   Types of labour categories in Japan

Job category	Definition
Regular (*seishain*)	Full time, directly employed, permanent workers with job security and benefits
Part time (*pāto*)	Technically part time, though often working 35 hours per week; can be either temporary or permanent but often without job security or benefits
Dispatch (*haken*)	Workers employed by dispatch agencies who are given limited term postings at workplaces without becoming employees of those workplaces; can be full or part time
Arubaito	Part time, casual work without job security or benefits, often associated with students; not an official category (officially considered "part time")
Contract (*keiyaku*)	Limited term employees, usually full time and directly employed (very short-term workers are called "temporary workers," while longer term contract workers are called "contract workers")

SOURCE: DEFINITIONS DRAWN FROM ASAO 2011.

family businesses or small businesses, and their replacement with big box retailers and chains since the 1970s.[21]

What were the underlying causes of these changing conditions? First, labour market deregulation may have kept unemployment relatively low, but it led to a massive increase in poverty and inequality, while disrupting the old lifetime employment system (Osawa 2013). Second, population aging, which sped up markedly in the 1990s as the baby boom cohort started to reach middle age, led to increasing fiscal strains on firms due to seniority-based pay provisions. In other words, the system that had once been an advantage to Japanese firms when its workforce was young had slowly turned into a drain on profits.

Third, Japan's enterprise unions were unable to resist the deterioration of working conditions, including wage stagnation and deflation, the decline in

---

21   For example, the percentage of workers in the categories "self-employed" or "family business" fell from 33 percent of women and 21 percent of men in 1985 to 15 percent of both women and men in 2005 and 10 percent of women and 12 percent of men in 2014 (GEB 2016).

lifetime employment protections, and more importantly the dualization of the workforce (see also Noda and Hirano 2013). Part of this was due to the long-term strategy of the Japanese labour movement of prioritizing job security over remuneration. During a period of economic downturn, then, it made sense to forego the annual *shuntō* coordinated wage negotiations, sacrificing deterioration in working conditions or reduced pay in order to minimize layoffs. While unemployment more than doubled to more than five percent during this period, it remained below the level of most OECD countries. At the same time, unions possessed institutional weakness due to their decline since the 1970s, where union density fell from 35 percent in 1975 (largely unchanged since the 1950s) to less than 20 percent by the 2000s (Noda and Hirano 2013). Even during a period of robust economic growth, labor unions could do little to rebuff the neoliberal onslaught, characterized by Nakasone's privatization drive and the breaking of the National Railway Workers' union. While the 1988 formation of Rengō united three of the main trade federations, its formation was driven by the decline of the more assertive JSP-affiliated Sōhyō trade federation. Rengō thus served to function as a weak and passive federation, despite its broad representation (Tiberghien 2014).[22] As a result, even during the recovery, when GDP grew continuously from February 2002 to February 2008 (and corporate executive compensation grew significantly), wages remained stagnant (Osawa 2013).

Another way in which Japanese labour organizations did little to challenge the growth of working-class insecurity and inequality during this period was the insular nature of enterprise unions, which usually only included the protected core (and male) workforce. These unions were usually deeply integrated into the ethos of management and identified more with the interests of the firm than with the labour movement in general. Workers thus felt little solidarity even with the non-regular workers in their own company, let alone the growing numbers of precarious workers in other firms and sectors. If the precarious and flexible status of those workers could boost corporate profitability without undermining the own job security of the core workers themselves, protected core workers were more likely to support than oppose such changes (see also Shibata 2017). Deregulation and dualization of the workforce were thus effectively executed as a strategy of divide and rule, co-opting the well-organized but conservative core unionized workforce while marginalizing the

---

22   This weakening has also been exacerbated by the rise of service sector jobs, which are only very rarely unionized. While Rengō has since 1997 focused more on promoting unionization and workers' rights for service sector and irregular workers, unionization rates remain at around 2–3 percent (Royle and Urano 2012).

rest. As a result, since the 1990s there has been an increase in wage inequality both within and across sectors, including among unionized workers (Lechevalier 2014).

2.7   *Production and the Petit Bourgeoisie: End of the Pork-barrel System?*
As for the *petit bourgeoisie*, long an integral piece of the LDP's electoral coalition, how did the crisis of the Heisei manifest itself in relation to its role within Japan's historic bloc? While the government had previously used pork barrel spending, protections for SMEs and supports for blue-collar workers in rural areas to combat uneven development and to shore up *petit bourgeois* electoral support, this regime encountered problems in the 1980s due to its high costs. While public infrastructure spending as a percentage of GDP already stood at 4.8 percent – more than double the US, UK and Germany – in 1989, by 1995 it had grown to 6.4 percent, despite declining public revenues (CAO 2015). Then, while neoliberal reforms under Hashimoto and Koizumi successfully cut it to 3 percent of GDP by 2007, after Koizumi left office it rose again, up to 3.5 percent of GDP by 2009 (CAO 2015). These decades thus saw a shift back and forth between neoliberal austerity aimed at fiscal consolidation and returns to pork barrel spending aimed at fighting the negative economic and political consequences of that austerity.

In addition to reductions in public works spending, the LDP of the late 1990s and early 2000s also displayed a willingness to abandon protections for small businesses. In 2000, under pressure from the US government and large-scale American retail firms, the LDP pushed through a repeal of the Large-Scale Retail Store Law (Shimotsu 2014). The law was replaced with significantly weakened piece of legislation that greatly opened the scope of big-box store development in Japan. This move only sped up the decline of small businesses in retail.

Then, with Koizumi's postal privatization, things reached a watershed and one of the key means for pork barrel spending was substantially reformed with the privatization and breakup of the postal savings system (Estevez-Abe 2008; Sadoh 2012). Koizumi also pushed for agricultural liberalization and other neoliberal policies, in addition to defunding the construction state. However, while popular at the time, and successful in combating the deficit, these policies lead to greater insecurity in the countryside. As a result, rural voters began to feel abandoned by the LDP, and instead voted for the DPJ in the 2007 and 2009 elections, as the DPJ made a major pivot to favor agricultural subsidies, something that had gone against its hitherto neoliberal position (Sadoh 2012).

In other ways, the hollowing out of Japanese agriculture, with severe labour shortages and the average age of a farmer over 65 emerged as a growing problem for Japan's future food security. This is despite costly agricultural subsidies that contradict the trade deals that both the LDP and DPJ have supported, including the TPP. Moreover, as we have seen, in other ways the *petit bourgeoisie* has declined in numbers steadily since the Second World War and has been replaced by precarious service sector workers. Many of the voters that remain are elderly farmers and shopkeepers that rely on protections and supports to remain economically viable against increasingly transnationalized and concentrated competition.

Overall, we can thus see a contradiction with the programs aimed at supporting the *petit bourgeoisie* and policies pursued to restore conditions for profitable accumulation. The latter have included reduced agricultural subsidies, commercial deregulation and cuts to public works spending, which have both politically and economically undermined small businesses and farmers. In the context of drastically suppressed tax revenues, the wild spending of the FILP (Fiscal Investment and Loan Program)-funded public works programs led to a massive deficit by the mid-1990s, which prompted spending cuts and deregulation. However, efforts since then to rein in the debt by defunding pork-barrel spending led to a political backlash against the LDP, which forced the party to backtrack under Koizumi's successors. Moreover, the DPJ, understanding the implications of this, made a successful play for *petit bourgeois* votes, promising greater financial supports and protections to farmers just as they tried to cut wasteful spending (Krauss and Pekkanen 2010). However, once in power, the DPJ was unable to find sufficient revenue to fund many of its promises and quickly lost the support of the *petit bourgeoisie*. Thus, while the LDP was mostly effective in scaling back the scope of protection and spending to prop up inefficient small businesses (and, to a lesser extent, farmers), it paid a heavy political cost for abandoning these core constituencies with the end of LDP electoral hegemony in 2009.

2.8 *Gender and the Family: The End of the Male Breadwinner Model and Shōshika*

What about gender and the family and its relation to social reproduction? The post-war era saw the development and entrenchment of the gender-dual system and a rigid gendered division of labour characterized by male breadwinners and female housewives. This model was highly patriarchal and placed rigid social boundaries around male and female roles. It not only deprived women of the option of pursuing a meaningful career but also obligated the majority of men to work long, hard hours with only limited opportunities to participate in family life. Nonetheless, this model was successful in providing conditions for a stable basis for social reproduction: rates of marriage were high, and the fertility rate remained relatively high until the 1980s. The proportion of households where one parent (almost always the husband) earned enough money to support the family on his own was also high.

Since the 1990s, many of these things have changed. First, the proportion of jobs falling into the category of lifetime employment has declined, while the proportion of precarious jobs has grown rapidly. Importantly, the majority of people working in this field are women, and indeed a majority of women work in precarious jobs (see also Miura 2012).

Second, due to growing insecurity, poverty and inequality, as well as changing norms about gender, marriage and the family, the fertility rate fell rapidly to a low of 1.26 in 2010, far below the replacement rate of 2.1. As increasing numbers of women have sought to pursue careers outside of the home, they have been forced to choose between a career and family, and many have chosen the former (Schoppa 2006). At the same time, growing inequality and poverty, which have largely resulted from neoliberal reforms coupled with two decades of stagnation, have meant that increasing numbers of people feel that they cannot afford to get married and have children. This is further reflected in the decline of nuclear families and the rise of single person households. Moreover, this dynamic can be seen in a range of other social problems, including the rise of *hikikomori*, so-called parasite singles, freeters and NEET, and elderly people who die alone.[23]

The decline of this system in the 1990s is one key reason why the crisis has been so prolonged. Moreover, it is the reason why what began as an economic crisis has gradually mutated into a wider social and demographic crisis. Both the economic crisis itself and attempts to rectifying it (particularly through neoliberal deregulation) upset the basis for stable social reproduction in Japan.

2.9   *Demography and Welfare: The Rise of the 'Pension State'*

While Japan's young population was a major condition of the post-war period of rapid economic growth, the Heisei era saw the rapid aging of Japanese society. Indeed, over the course of thirty years, Japan went from being the youngest industrialized country to the oldest. The 1990s saw Japan's ruling regime scramble to fill in the gaps of a porous and insufficient welfare regime. A number

---

23 "Parasite singles" refers to young adults in their 20s and 30s, generally from middle class backgrounds, who live with their parents and off of their parents' incomes (or pensions). "NEET" stands for "not in employment, education or training" and tends to refer to young people who are neither in school nor working (nor actively looking for work). "Freeters" refers to young people who shift between low-wage, casual jobs (such as at fast food restaurants) without looking for a permanent job or career.

of major programs were constructed or expanded, particularly regarding pensions, subsidized eldercare provisioning and paid eldercare leave for family members (see Estevez-Abe 2008). However, these led to major increases in welfare costs, which more than doubled between 1990 and 2010 even while revenue stagnated (CAO 2016). Indeed, by the beginning of the 2010s, Japan's welfare costs were in line with other industrialized countries, even though its tax base was substantially smaller, leading to a massive budget deficit and growing government debts.

Moreover, the Heisei era saw a rapid hollowing out of the countryside. While the effects of this have been most strongly felt in villages and towns that have seen extreme population decline, in the coming decades whole prefectures are expected to witness rapid population decline. While overall government estimates project the population to fall from a high of 128 million in 2010 to 107 million by 2040, the degree of this decline varies widely by region. While Tokyo is expected to maintain 94 percent of its 2010 population, rural prefectures such as Akita and Aomori in the north of Japan are expected fall to only 64 and 68 percent respectively of 2010 levels by 2040 (Kantei 2013).[24]

Thus, while in the context of the demographic crisis of the Heisei era, coming decades are expected to witness varied outcomes of demographic change. In some cases (such as Akita), population aging will be combined with rapid population decline. In other cases (such as Tokyo), even if population decline is slower, the rise in the absolute number of seniors will be much more substantial. The effects of this demographic crisis had only begun to be felt in the 2010s, as Japan's population has entered a period of absolute decline after many years of low birth rates. Yet these trends show that it will continue for decades to come, and that the real consequences of the demographic crisis still await.

---

24 Overall, nearly a third of Japan's 47 prefectures are expected to lose at least a quarter of their population by 2050. This population aging is even more apparent when the working age population alone is considered: by 2050, Akita, Aomori, Iwate and Kōchi prefectures will all have working age populations at least forty percent smaller than in 2010, while Tokyo, Aichi, Okinawa and Shiga are expected to have roughly 80 percent of their 2010 working population, compared to 71 percent for the country as a whole. In contrast, all but three of Japan's prefectures are expected to have more seniors in 2050 than in 2010, while Tokyo, Kanagawa, and Okinawa are all forecasted to have at least 1.5 times as many seniors as in 2010, and the national total of seniors is expected to grow 1.3 times. Among those 75 and older – those most likely to need costly medical care – the total population is expected to grow 1.6 fold, while Kanagawa and Saitama expect to see more than twice as many people aged 75 and over by 2040 (Kantei 2013). In Kagoshima, the population of people over 75 will be the same as the population under 35, while Shimane will have as many people over 90 as under 10; Akita will have more people over 75 than under 40, and more people over 60 than under 60 (Kantei 2013).

Necessarily, this will require even greater expenditures in pensions, eldercare and health care to add to the already unsustainable levels of spending.

2.10   Nation and Ideology: 'Normal Country' or Tan'itsu Minzoku?

In addition to these questions of social reproduction of the labour force, we must also ask what challenges the organic crisis has brought in relation to the socio-cultural aspect of social reproduction. As discussed in Chapter Four, post-war Japan's pacifist nationalism was long a source of nationalist solidarity, promoting a peaceful harmony among society anchored in a widespread commitment to democracy, human rights, peace and multilateralism. Yet the myth of ethnic homogeneity that was a part of this cultural framework also served as a barrier to any attempts to cultivate a more pluralist and multicultural society.

The organic crisis has thus brought two implications for Japan's cultural nationalism. First, globalization, demographic crisis and changing geopolitical relations have forced a rethink on Japan's ideology of *tan'itsu minzoku* and pacifist nationalism. While some leaders have pursued a more open and assertive Japan, such as Ozawa in his "normal country" doctrine, others within the LDP have called for a return to a more conservative society that is less "masochistic about the past". In both cases changing conditions have disrupted the post-war cultural consensus.

Second, labour shortages have led to growing calls for foreign workers since the 1990s. In response, the state has pursued several programs, each of which has important implications for our understanding of Japanese identity, its relationship with non-Japanese others, and the consequences for Japanese hegemony. Indeed, as Akashi (2014) has shown, in the wake of increasing labour shortages and projected population decline, Japan since the 1990s has seen the development of a disparate collection of policies aimed at foreign nationals in Japan that collectively amount to something akin to an immigration policy (see also Koike 1996; Hosono 2011). These include programs to take in ethnic Japanese *nikkei* from South America and foreign trainees since 1989, as well as care workers from the Philippines and Indonesia since 2008. Within this context, while business groups have generally pushed hard for more migrant workers, labour groups, including their representatives in the bureaucracy (the MHLW) have generally been opposed, citing concerns of the effects of competition with foreign workers for Japanese workers.

A small number of voices, within the bureaucracy, LDP and civil society, have spoken of the need for Japan to become a more open, pluralist society, accepting of immigrants, in order to solve its demographic crisis (many of which are based on neoliberal arguments). However, generally speaking a more conservative and inward policy that rejected immigrants and only begrudgingly accepted a limited number of temporary foreign workers through a patchwork of disparate programs that became the *de facto* policy during the Heisei era. While this meant that Japan has thus far avoided any serious backlash to immigration as in Europe, needless to say the low levels of immigration did very little to solve the demographic and labour market challenges.

Overall, then, by the Heisei era, the underlying basis for Japan's pacifist nationalism was called into question from all sides. Conservatives called for a re-militarization and return to a more conservative, patriarchal and traditional social order. Neoliberals called for greater pluralism and diversity in the name of global competitiveness along with a more assertive role for Japan within international society. Those on the left called for a more serious commitment to peace along with a stronger commitment to solidarity and support for all minority groups, coupled with a greater degree of pluralism and a more thoroughgoing escape from the remnants of pre-war nationalism. Yet in practice meaningful changes on immigration policy were relatively tepid and a wider discussion of the meaning of Japaneseness in the twenty-first century largely did not occur.

2.11 *Political Ecology: Climate Change, the Nuclear Turn and 3/11*

The final factor behind the success of Japan's postwar hegemonic order was the easy, cheap access to national resources, including energy resources that it enjoyed. By the end of the Heisei era, this was characterized by a vastly different set of conditions. To understand these conditions, we must ask, how did the state react to growing energy and environmental challenges caused both by the growing concerns over climate change and by the rising cost of oil? And what did the 3/11 disaster and nuclear meltdown tell us about the double-edged sword of forging a viable energy future for Japan?

First, the nuclear meltdown showed the problems of nuclear energy and created significant opposition to it. While nuclear energy was initially pursued beginning in the 1970s to allow Japan to overcome its dependence on foreign oil, the period post-3/11 saw a major backlash against nuclear energy, which already accounted for close to 30 percent of electricity generated by then (WNA 2019). With various political parties and activist groups calling for a full denuclearization, the LDP has been in a tough situation: risk public backlash by defending nuclear power or shut down generators and increase Japan's reliance on foreign gas and coal. The path chosen has generally been somewhat in between these two extremes.

The second question, linked to the first, relates to climate change. If Japan is to abandon nuclear energy, then the task of reducing greenhouse gas emissions caused by oil, gas and coal, which comprise the vast majority of its energy sources will be even greater. While Japan has made relatively strong progress in the adoption of solar power since the 2000s, the concomitant reduction of nuclear power generation has meant that efforts to curb the consumption of fossil fuels and thus meet greenhouse gas reductions targets will be insufficient (see also Kameyama 2017).

3 Implications of the Crisis

On what basis do we therefore argue that Japan of this period experienced an organic crisis? We suggest that it is important to consider the capacity of the ruling regime to fulfill its three main requirements: capital accumulation, political legitimation and social reproduction.

3.1 Summary of the Economic Accumulation Crisis

With regard to capital accumulation, the period from 1989 to 2012 was generally one of recession and stagnation punctuated by periods of slow growth. The stock market also fell very sharply over the course of 1990 and 1991, and stayed low throughout the rest of the period, never recovering. Domestic investment stalled, as firms preferred either to invest in production overseas or to horde their cash due to the lack of profitable sites for investment domestically. Along with a reduction in private capital investment, domestic consumption fell due to the overall depressed economic conditions. Moreover, unemployment grew, if ever so slightly, compared to historic levels, despite the declining size of the labor market after 1995. In sharp contrast with conditions even a decade earlier, wages remained relatively stagnant across the period. In many cases workers voluntarily accepted wage restraints (implicitly as an alternative to layoffs), but even this could do little to boost investment. As a result of these dynamics, GDP growth slowed, averaging only one percent over the course of the 1990s and 2000s. Overall, these conditions amounted to a dynamic of economic deflation, which proved very difficult to escape. Indeed, despite various diverse attempts to reverse trend through deficit financing Japanese economy continued to be frail, sensitive to international turbulence and unable to revive domestic consumption or investment. It had entered a deep-seated economic crisis.

One of the major causes of this crisis of depressed demand was the deregulation of the labour market and the ensuing rise in precarious labor. While deregulation was expected to restore conditions for profitable accumulation by giving capital access to a growing pool of cheap, flexible labour, this proved to be a double-edged sword by creating an inescapable trap for domestic consumption. The neoliberal reforms taken may have benefited Japanese domestic capital in certain ways (and they certainly benefited foreign capital in Japan), and political support for the LDP among the Japanese capitalist class remained unwavering throughout the crisis. Yet it is hard to see the political economic dynamics of the 1990s and 2000s as anything other than a crisis of capital accumulation, and to consider the ensemble of policies taken to alleviate the crisis as anything other than a failure.

3.2   Summary of the Political Legitimation Crisis

Politically, after four decades of unbroken centre-right majority rule, Japan's ruling regime – led by the LDP – started to crumble. Indeed, the period of the 1990s and 2000s saw constant swings back and forth between the LDP and both centre-left and new, centre-right reformist parties (particularly with the Upper House elections). Even when the LDP did win, it was under leaders who ran on promises of bold reform. Due to both economic stagnation and public backlash over a plethora of LDP corruption cases, political legitimacy of the hegemonic order reached a crisis point, as voters turned away from the LDP, and more precisely, the clientelist corporatism of the LDP-led order.

However, the alternatives to that order, whether social democratic or neoliberal, were never well defined or wholeheartedly embraced, even by the politicians who espoused them. While bold reformist rhetoric was central to Japanese political discourse for nearly two decades, the reforms that ultimately passed were often tepid, as reformers stopped short of taking bold measures that risked alienating important interest groups. Thus, while in many ways the acute crisis of political legitimation was solved more adequately than the other elements of the crisis, as the next chapter will show, many elements of the old, corrupt system remained intact. Moreover, aside from the backlash against government corruption and anxiety over the future of the economy, this era saw a massive increase in income and wealth inequality. While such inequality does not inherently negate the political legitimacy of the ruling regime, it does provide one more condition that complicates it.

3.3   Summary of the Social Reproduction Crisis

Finally, how did the ruling regime of Heisei Japan fulfill the requirement of providing stable and legitimate conditions for social reproduction? In the wake of economic stagnation and neoliberal deregulation, the 1990s and 2000s saw a cratering of Japan's fertility rate, falling to as low as 1.26 in 2009. In this context, and with the door virtually closed to immigration aside from a relatively small number of ethnic Japanese migrants from South America, population aging sped up, and became an increasingly profound social problem.

While major welfare policies were created to solve the aging crisis, these led Japan's previously lean welfare state to very quickly approach levels of spending similar to other developed countries without any clear means of paying for it (see also Estevez-Abe 2008). The result was a massive budgetary deficit that quickly ballooned into the largest public debt in the world. While the government tried several times to introduce a consumption tax at the behest of industry to pay for this spending, public backlash and economic frailty let to repeated postponement of such tax hikes, starving the government of much needed revenue.

Thus, overall, we can see how social reproduction provisions and conditions became increasingly non-functional, with the birth rate cratering, the population beginning to shrink, and welfare institutions unable to meet growing demand, in addition to problems of mounting public debt. Moreover, other social problems, including the rise of *hikikomori*, *karōshi*, freeters, NEET, parasite singles and seniors dying alone, point to a deep and systemic crisis of social reproduction. They show how growing numbers of people feel isolated and alienated from society, unable to bear the pressures of a deregulated, insecure and exploitative work environment. Therefore, while the economic and political crises of the Heisei era received the most attention in conventional portrayals of Japan's organic crisis, this crisis of social reproduction is equally important to our understanding of the overall collapse of Japan's post-war hegemonic order.

4   Conclusion

Overall, we can see in this era how the conditions for stable hegemonic order were lost as dynamics of crisis emerged instead. Politically, the early 1990s saw Japan's post-war political system reach its logical conclusion. This period thus saw increasing tensions among all the major forces within Japan's historic bloc. Unmoored from the project of developmentalism, businesses became increasingly self-interested and oriented towards immediate accumulation. The bureaucracy meanwhile became an object of scorn, and efforts from both the LDP and DPJ to rein it in had mixed results, increasing dysfunctionality without increasing accountability.

Economically, as a result of changing conditions of world order, economic globalization and the neoliberalization of Japanese firms, there appeared a number of contradictions within Japan's economic system that proved impossible to reconcile and led to first the bubble economy, then the period of deflation until the 2000s. While Koizumi's tenure briefly saw a return to continuous growth, this was only due to favorable global conditions. As a result, the period since 2007 saw a reversion to conditions of stagnation and recession. Moreover, while Koizumi's neoliberal reforms may have benefited capital in the short term, they led to an increase in inequality and precariousness, and foreshadowed the LDP's electoral defeats in 2007 and 2009.

Socially, the period saw a dramatic decline in the birth rates, as large numbers of young people no longer experienced the economic security needed to raise families, while social norms about the role of women in society changed, even as the system rooted in the male breadwinner, female housewife model did not change so quickly. Furthermore, bound by the shackles of its insular ideology of *tan'itsu minzoku*, the government found itself unable to propose immigration as a solution to the falling birth rate and shrinking population problem. While social programs were expanded in an *ad hoc* fashion at various stages, there was no cohesive and comprehensive plan to refashion the Japanese welfare state for the 21st century, nor any reasoned means of paying for these new programs under stagnant economic conditions.

While many of these changes had been building over time quantitatively since the 1970s, by the 1990s many of them reached a breaking point and brought qualitative changes to the conditions of Japanese political order. So many of the factors that had once collectively facilitated and maintained conditions amenable to capital accumulation, social reproduction and political legitimation now collectively worked to undermine the capacity of the ruling regime to achieve these three ends. As a result, the crisis became entrenched and seemingly unmovable, at least under the status quo. Even the 2009 landslide electoral victory of the DPJ ultimately proved ineffective in facilitating any meaningful change.

Overall, then, this chapter has argued that the above crisis conditions that have characterized Japan since the 1990s together amount to what Gramsci referred to as an "organic crisis." The crisis is deep-seated, complex and multifaceted. Moreover, following Gramsci, we must understand organic crises as crises that prompt or necessitate attempts to reorder ruling relations and that fundamentally disrupt the careful power balance within an historic bloc. In attempts to resolve an organic crisis and restore conditions for hegemonic order, new coalitions are forged among powerful social forces and weaker or subordinate social groups are disempowered in the process. We can see how attempts to resolve various elements of Japan's organic crisis involved struggles over the relations of force within the hegemonic order that the LDP attempted to restore.

Ultimately, however, each of these attempts at reform provoked reactions, and few of them became institutionalized. The DPJ's landslide election win in 2009 represented a widespread rejection of the LDP. Yet the DPJ itself was unable to deal with the contradictions inherent in its own attempts to reorder relations within the historic bloc and was demolished in the subsequent election.

CHAPTER 7

Caesarism, Passive Revolution and the Return of the LDP under Abe

This chapter considers developments over the past eight years, during the second tenure of Abe Shinzō from 2012 to 2020.[1] It argues that during this period, the LDP-led hegemonic order reasserted itself, largely breaking the political impasse that had existed for the preceding two decades. Initially at least, Abe's return brought not only renewed LDP dominance but also a renewed optimism over the future for many Japanese. These conditions enabled Abe to become Japan's longest serving Prime Minister in history before resigning due to health issues in August 2020, in stark contrast to the revolving door of Prime Ministers that served during the 1990s and 2000s.

This chapter asks what accounts for Abe's longevity, and whether, in the historical context of Japanese post-war order, his regime can be understood to have restored conditions for hegemonic order. It argues that the key to Abe's return to power and longevity was a strategy that combined what Gramsci (1992) termed "Caesarism" with what he called "passive revolution." In basic terms, Abe's "Caesarism" involved various efforts to "break the deadlock" of the past twenty years through rhetorically effective and seemingly bold economic and social policies that appealed to the interests of a wide range of class and social forces. At the same time, Abe's "passive revolution" can be understood as the covert imposition of a range of militarist, conservative and even soft authoritarian defense, security and administrative reforms that often went unnoticed but that hold profound consequences for Japanese society. Primarily through its exploration of these two concepts and how they relate to the Abe administration this chapter provides a Gramscian analysis of Abe's tenure and its implications for our understanding of the Heisei era organic crisis and its potential resolution.

In section 1 the chapter provides a biographical background to Abe, reviewing the significance of his early life and failed first term as Prime Minister. Section 2 discusses Caesarism under Abe, analyzing a number of key policies through which his regime tried (but ultimately failed) to "break the deadlock"

---

1 This chapter is a revised version of "Passive revolution in Japan: The restoration of hegemony under Abe?", published in *Critical Sociology* (2021).

of post-bubble Japanese political economy and the implications of these policies for the restoration of conditions of hegemonic order. Section 3 then argues that Abe's Caesarism was augmented by the advancement of a very different set of political goals – through covert and even coercive measures – which I offer as an example of "passive revolution." Though diametrically opposed in an ethico-political sense to the hegemonic (consent-based) orientation of Abe's economic and social policies, the passive revolution that Abe engineered was nonetheless central to his success. After considering the ways Abe cultivated and maintained power through this combination of Caesarism and passive revolution, the chapter concludes by assessing the overall implications of Abe's tenure for Japanese hegemonic order and the extent to which he was successful in restoring its conditions of possibility.

1   Abe's Political Comeback

Born in 1954, Abe Shinzō comes from one of the most powerful political families in post-war Japan. Hailing from Yamaguchi Prefecture in the south of Honshu Island, Abe's family has been a dominant force among Yamaguchi's elected Diet members since the pre-war days. Both of Abe's grandfathers, Abe Kan and Kishi Nobusuke, served in the Diet. The latter, who was convicted of war crimes for his role as the *de facto* political head in wartime Manchuria, went on to serve as Prime Minister (1957–1960) and remained an influential lawmaker and elder statesman until the late 1970s. Abe's great uncle and Kishi's brother Satō Eisaku served as Japan's longest serving post-war Prime Minister (until Abe himself broke the record) from 1964 to 1972, while Abe's father, Abe Shintarō was elected to the Diet eleven times between 1958 and 1991. His father served as leader of the Kishi faction and in four different cabinet posts and was poised to become party leader (and thus Prime Minister) himself before his sudden and untimely death at age 67. Indeed, it was his father's sudden death that brought Abe Shinzō, then 36 and working as his father's secretary, into politics, as he ran in his father's old district in the first post-reform election in 1993.

Abe spent the first decade of his political career as a rising star and the voice of a new, more hardline conservative wing of the LDP. Under the Koizumi administration, he served in two prominent positions, first as the Chief Party Secretary from 2003 to 2004 and then as the Chief Cabinet Secretary from 2005 to 2006. During his early years as a lawmaker, Abe developed a reputation as a foreign policy *zoku* and a defense hawk, more in the image of his grandfather Kishi Nobusuke than his father (Sadoh 2012). Indeed, Abe was part of a new generation of conservative lawmakers enamored by constitutional revision and critical of the LDP's soft foreign policy positions, including the 1994 Kōno statement that recognized Japanese responsibility for wartime aggression (Envall 2011). During these years, Abe was heavily involved in efforts to repatriate Japanese nationals who had been abducted by the North Korean government. Perceived by many during his time in the Koizumi administration as diligent and deferential, while also young and from a powerful family, he was seen as Koizumi's chosen successor and tipped to lead the party after Koizumi (Burrett 2017; Pugliese 2017).

Abe contested and won the 2006 LDP leadership election to succeed Koizumi. However, as discussed in the previous chapter, his yearlong tenure as Prime Minister was largely unsuccessful. He was plagued by various scandals, while seen as a weak, and ineffective, leader, unable to challenge the party's old guard despite being leader himself, while surrounding himself with an inner circle of cronies and political friends ill-equipped at running a government (Burrett 2017; Envall 2011). Moreover, Abe provided little in the way of a compelling vision for Japan, failing to present a cohesive economic vision for the country. Instead, he was overly consumed by the pursuit of constitutional revision, a policy direction of very little interest to the general public, who were increasingly concerned with the growing inequality of Japanese society (Burrett 2017). After initially making promising gains in negotiations with China, Abe tarnished his image in the eyes of neighboring countries by calling into question the validity of the comfort women issue,[2] while also associating with historical revisionists hoping to overturn the Kōno statement (Envall 2011). All of this led to a hefty defeat in the July 2007 Upper House election that caused the LDP to lose its double majority. Abe abruptly resigned exactly one year after taking office in September 2007, officially for health reasons.

However, Abe made a sudden and emphatic comeback five years later in 2012, first winning the September 2012 LDP leadership election over Ishiba Shigeru and then winning the December 2012 general election in a landslide. Though Ishiba was more popular with the party membership, and won a plurality of membership votes, Abe won a majority of LDP lawmakers' votes on the second ballot, and thus rode to victory on the basis of the strong personal

---

2 "Comfort women" refer to women, mostly from Korea, who were forced by the Japanese military to work as sex slaves for Japanese soldiers during World War II. Despite widespread consensus among historians, the degree of complicity of the Japanese government in organizing the comfort women program and the issue of whether comfort women worked consensually have long been questioned by conservative and nationalist forces in Japan, including Abe Shinzō.

networks he had cultivated with his fellow lawmakers. In particular, he owed much of his success to a group of young and conservative lawmakers who had grown in significance following the party's 2009 electoral defeat, where many older members from moderate factions had been voted out (Burrett 2017).

2   Breaking the Deadlock: The Caesarism of "Abenomics"

Abe swept to power in 2012 on his bold economic agenda, a bundle of policies referred to collectively as Abenomics. This focus on economic policy differed sharply from his previous attachment to militaristic defense policy. Instead, Abenomics was presented as a novel program of heterodox economic policy. On one hand it proposed policies designed to increase demand through Keynesian spending and reflationary monetary policies designed to promote domestic consumption and wage increases. On the other hand, it called for policies aimed at promoting supply through deregulatory measures targeted at increasing and stock market values and private investment. Abenomics thus appeared as an ambitious plan capable of simultaneously addressing Japan's chronic economic crisis from the perspective of both capital and labor, potentially even providing a long-awaited solution to the crisis. In this sense, it can be understood as a bold, even charismatic effort to "break the deadlock" of the Heisei era organic crisis, echoing Gramsci's understanding of Caesarism.

Before considering why it makes sense to see Abe's political project as Caesarist in a Gramscian sense we must first establish why Japan of the early 2000s was ripe for a Caesarist intervention. Indeed, while Gramsci understood Caesarism as emerging under conditions where two oppositional social forces are locked in a struggle that threatens to destroy them both, Japan of the past thirty years has witnessed no such struggle. Unlike with the Glorious Revolution, the French Revolution or in early 1920s Italy, post-1990s Japan has seen no direct confrontation of opposing class forces. In what sense then can we speak of conditions ripe for a Caesarist intervention in Japan?

First, even if Japan of the 2000s saw little outright confrontation between opposing class forces, as the previous chapter showed it did exhibit conditions of deep structural crisis. This included a two-decade long period of economic stagnation punctuated by recession; a mounting debt crisis, and a deep demographic crisis characterized by cratering birth rates, population aging and attendant increases in welfare and health care costs (Carroll 2018, 2019). In this sense, the old regime, as a concatenation of competing class and social interests, was no longer capable of fulfilling basic requirements for hegemonic order, including economic growth and stable social reproduction.

Second, following Schoppa's (2006) use of Alfred Hirschman's theory of voice and exit to understand conditions of political alienation in contemporary Japan, we might suggest that for various cultural and social reasons the organic crisis of the 1990s-2000s did not lead those dissatisfied with the existing order to express their opposition through "voice," direct confrontation with authorities. Instead, they did so through passive acts of resistance, or "exit," as discussed in Chapter Six. As Schoppa suggests, one example of this is that of large corporations making little attempt to criticize the state's pork-barrel spending and costly protections for inefficient small businesses directly and instead gradually moving production offshore in order to maintain international competitiveness. Another such case may be the tendency for young people facing economic insecurity and inadequate social provisioning choosing simply to passively forego career-track employment, marriage, and childrearing rather than actively protesting their insecure life conditions.

The third way we might see evidence of conditions necessary for Caesarism is in the actual, albeit restrained, political turmoil of the 1990s and 2000s. For the first time since its 1955 founding, the LDP lost elections and power on several occasions, indicating mounting public unhappiness about the LDP and a search for alternatives. This tendency, which started in the 1989 Upper House election defeat, came to fruition in the LDP's 2009 landslide defeat to the DPJ. Yet, as the previous chapter showed, the DPJ itself was found wholly incapable of managing the Japanese administrative state and suffered its own landslide defeat just three years later at the hands of Abe himself.

The above all indicates a deep political deadlock or crisis ripe for a Caesarist intervention that could somehow resolve the tension, both politically and structurally, between Japanese capital's needs for a restoration of conditions for profitable capital accumulation on one hand and the working and middle class's needs for renewed conditions for economic and social stability, on the other. While previous LDP governments, most notably Koizumi's (2001–2006), had governed solely in the interests of Japanese capital, allowing social problems of insecurity, poverty and inequality to exacerbate, the DPJ had, despite its promising social policies, failed to win confidence from Japanese capital and the administrative state. In this context, Abe re-emerged, promising to break the deadlock.

How did Abe employ Caesarism and what were its impacts, both as a strategy for expanding and maintaining his authority within the wider hegemonic project and as a means of resolving Japan's organic crisis? During his abortive yearlong stint as Prime Minister in 2006–7, where he unsuccessfully governed from the right, focusing on foreign policy and security. In contrast, in returning to power in 2012 Abe tried to restore his reputation by focusing attention on social and economic crises facing Japan – two of the most significant elements of its organic crisis – and claiming to hold the solution to them in a bold set of measures that even bore his name, Abenomics. A critical discourse analysis of Abenomics and its rhetorical impact in promoting a widespread popular image of a bold new economic program finally capable of resolving Japan's long-term economic crisis authored by Abe himself is beyond the scope of this chapter. Yet there is little doubt that such image politics proved important in generating public support and trust.

Yet however effective its branding may have been, Abenomics won the praise of a wide range of economic and social policy organic intellectuals from both the centre-left and centre-right, further lending it credibility. Understanding how Abenomics worked as a Caesarist political strategy therefore requires us to look more closely into its policy measures. These included: 1) Keynesian fiscal and monetary policies; 2) neoliberal regulatory reforms; and 3) social welfare policies. Yet while these policies may have appeared at first glance to be adequate to the task of "breaking the deadlock" of the Heisei era, in hindsight they have often proven inadequate and even internally contradictory, as we will see below.

2.1   *Breaking the Deadlock through Expansionary Keynesian Policy*

Initially included in Abe's campaign for a return to LDP party leadership in Fall 2012, Abenomics was designed to be seen as a savvy combination of the two schools of economic thought that had driven policymaking in Japan since the 1980s: neoliberal deregulation and expansive Keynesian spending. From a historical vantage point, Abenomics' novelty and promise was in its bold combination of these two seemingly conflicting policy paradigms. During the 2012 election, Abenomics was launched in the form of "three arrows:" 1) inflation targets of two percent annually; 2) flexible fiscal policy, including public works and infrastructure spending financed by a new government bond program (Tiberghien, 2014); and 3) a range of liberalization policies, including free trade, labor market deregulation and corporate governance policy. While the third arrow, referred to as "growth strategy" represented Abenomics' neoliberal side, the first two held its Keynesian elements.

Abe's Keynesian economic policies were rooted in the idea that a condition of chronic deflation was central to Japan's economic woes, whereby economic stagnation and deflation lead consumers and businesses to hoard rather than buy goods or invest in production. This hoarding then only leads to further deflation and stagnation, creating a deflationary spiral. From a Keynesian perspective, the only way to break out of this spiral is for the state to intervene, through fiscal and monetary policy, to alter macroeconomic conditions so as to induce inflation. This inflation thereby incentivizes spending rather than hoarding, as the value of savings steadily depreciate under conditions of inflation. This increase in consumer demand in turn leads businesses to increase investment, driving growth in employment and wages, promoting further demand and inflation as well as economic growth. However, while in theory central banks are at liberty to print money and reduce interest rates, this only causes inflation if the extra cash released into the economy actually circulates, through investment in production, employment and wage increases (which workers then spend rather than save).

How did Abe seek in practice to achieve these reflationary goals? Abe's Keynesian policies included quantitative and qualitative easing, ultra-low (even sub-zero) interest rates and numerous stimulus packages, both within and in addition to annual budgets (Wakatabe 2015). While these measures succeeded in temporarily inducing inflation, devaluing the yen (making exports more competitive) and generating a stock market boom, in the long run Abe's expansionary monetary and fiscal policy had trouble keeping the rate of inflation buoyant. This led the Japanese economy to fall back into recession already by 2015, while GDP growth never exceeded two percent per year during his tenure. It is therefore difficult to argue that Abenomics succeeded by its own standards in this area. Nonetheless, despite the difficulties of achieving inflation targeting in practice, the basic reflationist strategy continued to win support from economic organic intellectuals, if not from the general public more broadly.

2.2 Breaking the Deadlock through Neoliberal Economic Reform

While the first two arrows of Abenomics – monetary policy and fiscal policy – were launched immediately, Abenomics' third arrow, the so-called "growth strategy," remained ill-defined for many years. Finally, in 2015 the Cabinet Office outlined a set of ten goals that comprise its growth strategy (Shibata 2017). Seen together, they can be largely grouped in three areas: corporate reform, labor market reform and agriculture and trade reform.

Abe's corporate reform policies were aimed primarily at creating greater structural incentives for "risk-taking" behavior in Japanese corporate governance, incentivizing firms to make bold investment decisions rather than hoarding cash under the traditional "safety first" mentality (Lucarelli 2015). While Japanese corporate management had already been moving towards the American model, which prioritized short-term increases in shareholder value over the traditional Japanese model of long-term expansion of market share, this tendency only solidified under Abe's reforms (Shibata 2017).

However, despite these efforts at reviving accumulation through corporate reform, as Jayasuriya (2018) has argued, "the reorganisation of the corporate sector ... proved to be ... difficult to accomplish [...] far from a cohesive political project, the reform programme [was] inconsistent and contradictory and unable to build long-term coalitions" (597). Moreover, as Vogel (2018) has shown, the growing tendency for Japanese firms to pursue reforms to corporate governance that pay greater attention to shareholder concerns for short term profits "opens up the very real possibility that the Abe administration's corporate governance reforms could undermine its labor market reforms" (291). This is because the increased profits from reforms are quickly consumed by shareholder dividend payments and a declining proportion of profits actually make it to workers. Indeed, while the return on equity of Japanese corporations grew from six to eight percent between 2010 and 2016, the share of total income that went to labour fell from 66 to 61 percent between 2008 and 2015, undermining the goals of other policies to boost wages and thus consumer demand (Vogel 2018).

Along with these efforts at corporate reform, Abe's neoliberal reforms also included labor market reforms in three areas: 1) efforts to promote women's employment, particularly in positions of management; 2) efforts to promote more flexibilized labor among skilled workers; and 3) the piecemeal adoption of migrant worker policies that together amount to something akin to an immigration policy. "Womenomics" was styled as a key component of Abe's program in 2013, with the government setting targets of thirty percent female corporate leadership by 2020 (up from nine percent in the early 2010s) (Dalton 2017). The impetus behind womenomics, both for Matsui and later for Koizumi and Abe, was the economic benefits that would come from a higher participation rate for women. It was estimated by the IMF that bringing women's participation up from 63 percent to the G7 average of 70 percent would grow GDP by 4 percent (Dalton 2017). Ultimately, however, womenomics failed to deliver, particularly as the targets of raising women into leadership positions went wholly unmet.

Moreover, as Dalton (2017) has argued, womenomics focused primarily on the interests of women pursuing high ranking, career-track jobs, while largely ignoring the needs of the majority of women who work in more precarious jobs. While womenomics sought to encourage the promotion of women to upper-echelon executive jobs, it did nothing to challenge the underlying bases for Japan's enormous gender pay gap and the related gap between regular and (highly feminized) irregular employment (Chiang and Ohtake 2014). While only 22 percent of working men were employed in non-regular jobs in 2012, 58 percent of working women were (Dalton 2017). Indeed, as Dalton (2017) has shown, it is the enormous commitments that working men and women must make to regular jobs with long working hours that render these jobs unavailable to the vast majority of women who have to balance work with family commitments (see also Nemoto 2013).

Along with its efforts to promote a society where "women can shine," the Abe government also introduced a range of measures to allow foreign workers to come to Japan. This occurred first through a policy aimed at attracting highly skilled workers in 2015 (IBJ 2018) and then with legislation to create a new system for medium and low skilled workers in 14 blue-collar occupational sectors. While the former program failed to attract applicants, the latter policy was lambasted by various opposition parties critical of the lack of time given for reviewing the consequences of the legislation and for the lack of oversight measures included to ensure workers' safety, legal protections and social supports (Schwarcz 2018).

While these programs may have suggested a major shift in Japanese immigration policy, the government remained reluctant to refer to it as such. Instead, the government continued to use the term "foreign workers" and denying that these workers can be termed "immigrants," while retaining formal obstacles to foreign workers' ability to achieve Japanese permanent residency by imposing five-year limits on their visas (Osaki 2018). As I will consider in more detail below, this reticence to allow "foreign worker policy" to become "immigration policy" may have allowed LDP governments to postpone difficult questions about the status of Japanese national identity and *tan'itsu minzoku* ideology, but it also precluded a solution to the problem of population decline.

Additionally, Abe introduced a number of labor market deregulation measures aimed at shifting Japanese employment culture away from the "lifetime employment" model and towards a more fragmented and flexibilized model that is less costly for firms and less secure for workers. This has included the liberalization of dismissal laws and the institution of policies that legally permit skilled workers to work overtime without compensation (Vogel 2018).

The final element of Abe's neoliberal reforms included Abe's agriculture and trade reform measures. These included two main elements: 1) liberalization of agriculture through disempowering Nōkyō; and 2) promotion of free trade, particularly through participation in the TPP. After years of recalcitrance on the part of Nōkyō, Abe succeeded in forcing through administrative changes to the organization that weakened its centralized control, an important political victory for Abe given Nōkyō's steadfast opposition to agricultural trade liberalization (Sasada 2015; Feldhoff 2017; Mulgan 2015). This served as an important prerequisite for Japan's accession to the TPP agreement, which Abe enthusiastically led as a way of shoring up export markets for Japanese goods and counterbalancing Chinese influence in the Pacific region.[3]

2.3 Breaking the Deadlock through Welfare State Expansion

The above mix of Keynesian and neoliberal economic policies served as the initial thrust of Abenomics, enabling Abe to present it as a bold and novel approach that could resolve Japan's longstanding economic woes. Then, beginning in 2015 a third side to Abenomics was launched, styled "Abenomics stage two," rooted in a range of social policy targets designed to overcome Japan's mounting social and demographic crisis. These social policy targets included: 1) reaching a GDP of 600 trillion yen by 2020 (from 470 trillion in 2015); 2) increasing the total fertility rate to 1.8 (up from 1.4) by 2020; and 3) saving people from having to leave the labour force to care for aging parents (Nikkei 2015; Hayakawa 2015). The government proposed to reach the first target by promoting the hiring of women, the elderly and disabled people as well as by achieving a "productivity revolution." It expected to reach the second target by creating 500,000 new free childcare spaces by the end of 2017 (Japan Times 2015). Finally, it planned to achieve the third target by creating 500,000 new spaces in elderly care homes. Abe further augmented the social wing of Abenomics by promising in 2015 an increase of the minimum wage from 800 to 1000 yen by 2020 and later by calling for the elimination of tuition for all universities and high schools, including both public and private (Nikkei 2015).

The government ultimately failed to reach the first two targets. While the government's estimate of GDP growth to 600 trillion yen by 2020 was beyond reach even before the COVID 19 pandemic plunged the country into its worst ever recession, the fertility rate in 2019 was, at 1.39, even lower than before Abe had taken office. Conversely, the government succeeded in creating 500,000 new daycare spaces by 2018 (Asahi 2019), although increased demand meant that the waiting list for spaces remained largely unchanged (MHLW 2018a). Moreover, while Abe was unable to meet his minimum wage goal, the average national minimum wage went up every year of his term, rising from 749 yen in 2012 up to 901 yen in 2019, an increase of 20.2 percent that was much stronger than those of his predecessors (MHLW 2020).

---

3 While the TPP was temporarily shelved after US withdrawal from negotiations, a new agreement that did not include the US was reached in 2018 without the US, known as the Comprehensive and Progressive Agreement for Trans-Pacific Partnership.

2.4   Implications of Caesarism under Abe

What are the implications of Abenomics for Abe and the LDP's hegemonic project and how can it be understood as Caesarism? Abenomics won initial support from a wide range of social forces due to its claim to be able to resolve the long-term organic crisis facing Japanese society. It did this by proposing a combination of neoliberal deregulation measures aimed at promoting corporate profits with Keynesian policies aimed at boosting demand and social policies designed to reduce social insecurity. Upon its initial inception, Abenomics appeared as a promising strategy for finally pulling Japan's economy out of a state of chronic stagnation after twenty years, with robust stock market growth, moderate inflation, and GDP growth in 2012 and 2013.

Yet this optimism proved short-lived and overall the effects of Abenomics were largely underwhelming. The economy underperformed its GDP and inflation targets, with scarcely any improvement from the period of the lost two decades. The effects of "Abenomics stage two" were even more underwhelming, with the birth rate falling to record low levels, prompting the government to rapidly expand its foreign worker policy without much forethought. Nonetheless, while its actual policy achievements may be minimal, Abenomics succeeded as a political project in reviving the LDP and restoring public trust in its ability to manage the economy, at least initially. However, given its underwhelming effects, the success of Abenomics as a popular strategy to "break the deadlock" of the preceding twenty years must also understood as limited. Even by 2016, the public had already grown disillusioned with the effects of Abenomics, with 61 percent suggesting it ought to be rethought versus only 23 percent in support of it (Mainichi 2016). As a result, it is difficult to suggest that Abenomics succeeded in practice as a strategy to "break the deadlock." Yet while Abe's Caesarism may not have achieved its desired results in shoring up consent-based hegemony under a bold popular project to "break the deadlock," Abe was much more successful in the second of his two political projects: a conservative and even soft authoritarian passive revolution.

3   The Real Abe? Passive Revolution, Militarism and Soft Authoritarianism

While Caesarism was a major part of Abe's agenda, his success in restoring LDP hegemony and ultimately becoming Japan's longest serving Prime Minister cannot be attributed to Caesarism alone. Along with Caesarism, Abe employed a strategy of passive revolution to promote a range of defense, security and administrative reforms that might otherwise have been politically unviable but that were nonetheless important to his ability to shore up his own power and promote his conservative agenda.

However, while Abe's passive revolution involved the surreptitious advancement of policies to advance these ends, this is not to say that Abe did not try to frame these policies as in the interests of the public. While his defense policies, discussed below, could be framed as reflecting growing public concerns about an increasingly aggressive China and unpredictable North Korea, his security policies, likewise, were framed to reflect popular concerns about terrorism. Similarly, his administrative reforms dovetailed with longstanding public frustrations over the lack of executive control of the bureaucracy, a problem that had especially plagued his DPJ predecessors. Nonetheless, while framed in ways that responded to legitimate public concerns, under the surface the actual policies pursued in each of these areas served decidedly different ends. Indeed, these policies have helped to advanced Abe's conservative, militarist and soft authoritarian instincts while gradually whittling away at the foundations of Japanese post-war democracy.

Abe's economic and social policies attempted to appeal to the interests of a wide range of stakeholders and partially succeeded in framing his overarching agenda as representing the interests of the country as a whole. In stark contrast, these policies were combined with a range of strategies and techniques designed to advance a number of conservative, militaristic and soft authoritarian political prerogatives under the radar. Moreover, in some cases these policies had the effect of politically disarming and muzzling opponents, whether in the bureaucracy, the media or civil society. In this way, we can see how central to Abe's success was not only the image his social and economic policies created of a unifying approach to resolving the economic and social crisis in the interests of a broad range of social forces. It has also included a coercive, if covert, campaign to pursue otherwise controversial conservative policies and suppress would be oppositional forces. Insofar as these policies were advanced in a covert manner that obfuscated their true meaning and intent they can be understood as examples of passive revolution. After considering the three main elements of this passive revolution – foreign and defense policy, administrative reform and domestic security policy – I want to consider the overall implications of this strategy of passive revolution within the context of Abe's hegemonic project.

3.1   Asserting Control over the LDP

Insofar as Abe's conservative nationalist passive revolution would have been impossible without support from within the LDP, one of Abe's primary early accomplishments was his ability to shift the party to the right. In both his election as party president in 2012 and even more forcefully in his re-election in 2015, Abe relied on support from a cohort of younger conservative lawmakers much like himself. Moreover, according to Burrett (2017), Abe was further able to consolidate his power through the appointment to Chief Cabinet Secretary of (future Prime Minister) Suga Yoshihide, a shrewd and "self-made" politician who was highly respected throughout the party. This helped Abe remake the LDP in his own image while simultaneously winning support from formerly rival factions. Moreover, it secured him a mandate from within the party to advance his nationalist conservative passive revolution, described below.

3.2 Passive Revolution in Foreign and Defense Policy

Long recognized as a defense hawk who favored re-militarization and downplayed the extent of Japan's wartime aggression, the failure of Abe's first term was partly a result of his overzealous attachment to constitutional revision and historical revisionism, concerns that contrasted sharply with public opinion. After returning the power in 2012, Abe appeared to have learned from these mistakes, taking a more subtle approach to foreign and defense policy. Yet, as we will see, this does not mean that Abe had abandoned his commitment to conservative militarism altogether. On the contrary, important developments were made, albeit under the surface, reflecting the passive nature of his defense revolution.

While first term Abe proposed a revision of Japan's constitution that would have removed Article 9, and instead allowed the creation of a full-fledged military, after returning to power Abe's proposal for constitutional reform involved nothing more than an explicit recognition of the legality of Japan's already existing Self-Defense Forces without making any change to Article 9 (Murakami 2019). Although Abe was ultimately unable to achieve even this more modest revision while in office, its softer tone likely helped counter the image of himself as a strident hawk out of touch with the interests of the country and did nothing to undermine the image he created through his Abenomics program.

Looking deeper, however, we can see how this call for a modest approach to constitutional revision was accompanied by more aggressive defense policy changes below the surface. In addition to announcing a redefinition of the scope of SDF activity legally allowable within the constitutional limits of "self-defense" that went far beyond what had previously been imagined as constitutional, Abe also oversaw the construction of *Izumo* and *Kaga*, Japan's first postwar helicopter destroyers (Easley 2017). Moreover, he also sought to revive the export of arms for the first time in five decades (Khilji 2015). Abe also oversaw the *de facto* opening of a permanent base for the SDF in Djibouti from which to launch operations in the Persian Gulf and elsewhere, regions of extreme importance to Japan given its dependence on Middle East oil (Evron 2017).

In addition, looking beyond foreign policy narrowly defined and instead considering the way "foreign policy," the Japanese nation and its role in world history is defined and portrayed in schools, efforts to shift public discourse and popular understandings of Japan's wartime past must also be understood as part of militarist passive revolution. In particular, through education reforms passed in 2018–19 that mandate the teaching of "patriotism" (*aikokushin*) in schools, Abe sought to advance a revisionist interpretation of history under the radar (Bamkin 2018; Fukuoka 2018).

Along with the promotion of nationalist education policy, Abe also had an indirect role in conservative educational reform through his membership in Nippon Kaigi. According to Fukuoka (2018: 323):

> Nippon Kaigi is 'arguably… [the] most powerful nationalist lobby group' in Japan and this 'grass-roots conservative' organisation has approximately 40,000 fee-paying members; its local branches count about 250 nationwide … there are about 290 members of the Nippon Kaigi's parliamentary league in the Diet along with around 1,800 members at the local assemblies. Also important, PM Abe Shinzo … has been a 'special advisor' since the inception of the organisation in 1997.

Nippon Kaigi has been the leading advocate and pressure group for textbook reform, seeking to obtain MEXT recognition for revisionist historical textbooks that sanitize depictions of Japanese wartime aggression in Asia, particularly regarding the comfort women issue and the Nanking Massacre (Fukuoka 2018). Despite widespread opposition by the Japanese Teachers' Union (JTF), Nippon Kaigi succeeded in pressing for changes to the rules over textbook selection. In the process, it helped to empower local governments[4] instead of teachers themselves to hold primary authority over the selection of education board members and textbooks, and leading to a growing uptake of revisionist textbooks, particularly in Tokyo and Yokohama (Fukuoka 2018). In all these ways, in the context of continued public support for Article 9, Abe's militarist agenda operated within the scope of what was politically feasible, while passively engineering a rather profound transformation in Japanese foreign and defense policy and discourse.

---

4   In most cases, these local governments were controlled by centre-right mayors and assemblies sympathetic to the LDP and Abe.

3.3 Passive Revolution in Administrative Reform

A second element of Abe's passive revolution was his attempt to shore up control over the bureaucracy. In some ways, this was prompted by the chaotic relationship that the DPJ had with the bureaucracy during its brief three years in power from 2009 to 2012. After returning to power in 2012, the LDP under Abe had a relatively easy time reestablishing an amicable relationship with the bureaucracy. Despite three years out of power, the LDP still had all the connections with the bureaucracy that had been developed over its previous half century in power. Abe also benefited from assuming the premiership after three years of a highly dysfunctional and combative relationship between the DPJ government and the bureaucracy. In that context, bureaucrats were hopeful of a return to a more cooperative relationship with the government, and willing to compromise with Abe much more than they otherwise would have (Burrett 2017).

However, beginning in 2014 the government pursued key reforms that further altered the balance of power between the government and bureaucracy under revisions to the National Public Service Law (Mishima 2017). These reforms included measures to expand the Prime Minister's scope of authority over bureaucratic appointments, marking a decisive shift of power away from the bureaucracy and towards the Cabinet and PM in ways that previous governments could never achieve. Among the new institutions established through the reforms was the Cabinet Bureau of Personnel Affairs, a body designed to nominate candidates for roughly 600 top-ranking bureaucratic appointments at the behest of the Prime Minister. Without question, this further strengthened Abe's institutional leverage over the bureaucracy (Kato 2018). In a political system famously described by Chalmers Johnson as one where "the politicians reign and the bureaucrats rule" (1982: 316), these measures to strengthen cabinet and PMO control of the bureaucracy were often seen as necessary steps to increase accountability in Japan's political system and thus reflected widely held concerns about the problems with excessive bureaucratic power in Japan's political system. Indeed, given that such efforts at administrative reform had already begun under past LDP governments in the 1990s and 2000s and had been tried unsuccessfully by the DPJ, it is difficult to see efforts to empower the cabinet at the expense of the bureaucracy as anything out of the ordinary, let alone authoritarian.

However, despite the commonsense look of these administrative reforms, the 2017 unfolding of two scandals revealed a very different, darker purpose that can be understood as another element in Abe's passive revolution. First, with the Moritomo Gakuen scandal, it was revealed that top ranking bureaucrats had intervened to hide sensitive information regarding the involvement of Abe's wife in an 86 percent discounted sale of public land to a private and deeply conservative nationalist kindergarten in Osaka of which she was made honorary principal (Japan Times 2018). While the top-ranking bureaucrat in charge of the sale was forced to resign after a sworn testimony to the Diet, he consistently denied having received any pressure from the PMO or cabinet in relation to either the land sale or the document redaction.

Then, with the Kake Gakuen scandal it was revealed that bureaucrats had been pressured into licensing a new department of veterinary science at a college in Imabari, Ehime run by a close friend of Abe. Again, while the Prime Minister consistently denied involvement, internal Ministry of Education documents revealed language implying that the licensing was "the Prime Minister's intent" (Japan Times 2017).

While in neither of these cases was Abe's direct involvement in influencing bureaucratic decision-making for the benefit of friends proven, whether such direction took place is almost beside the point. In the aftermath of the National Public Service Law revision, the power to control top bureaucratic appointments has become remarkably concentrated in the Prime Minister's hands. As a result, rather than improving bureaucratic accountability through democratic (i.e., Cabinet-based) control of appointments, bureaucrats are increasingly pressured to curry favor with the Prime Minister, knowing that their future career opportunities depend as much on merit as on personal approval by the Prime Minister. In this context, bureaucrats have become increasingly afraid to make statements that could be incriminating towards the Prime Minister and have engaged in *sontaku*. This phenomenon can be translated in English as sycophancy or obsequiousness and understood to refer to self-censorship designed to please superiors (Kato 2018; Mulgan 2018). As Kato (2018) has argued, the concentration of control of the bureaucracy in the PMO's hands means that "political pressures are undermining whatever professional autonomy ... civil servants may have had, effectively turning them into the prime minister's errand boys." Overall, we can see just how effectively the government, through the Cabinet Bureau of Personnel Affairs, reordered the relationship between the cabinet and bureaucracy. Moreover, the two scandals, and the willingness of top bureaucrats to back Abe at all costs, demonstrate how this has occurred through something akin to a passive revolution designed less to give the Cabinet greater executive authority and more to turn the bureaucracy into a brigade of partisan sycophants.

3.4 *Passive Revolution in Domestic Security Policy*

A final element of Abe's passive revolution can be observed in the way he sought to alter relations between the government and the media. These attempts have amounted to a carrot and stick approach designed both to promote pro-government perspectives and silence opposition through a range of tactics, including policy changes and more subtle intimidation measures. The carrot of Abe's approach was reflected in the tendency to ingratiate journalists who cover the LDP favorably: according to Facker (2016), "Abe dined with top political journalists and media executives more than 40 times during his first two years in office alone." Abe sought to create allies in the press more forcefully as well, engineering an ideological makeover of the national broadcaster NHK in 2013 by appointing as the new chairman and three board members close personal friends who shared his conservative nationalist perspective (Japan Times 2013; Mulgan 2015).

At the same time, the government used a heavy-handed approach to stifle critics in the media and in academia on multiple occasions (see also Kingston 2019). In 2013, the government passed the Specially Designated Secrets Protection Law. This vague and sweeping law threatens to send journalists and whistleblowers in government to jail for leaking "state secrets," and a move that was heavily criticized as undermining journalists' abilities to investigate stories potentially damaging to the government (Jayasuriya 2018; Facker 2016). A further attempt to manipulate the media through legislation came in 2018, when the government proposed an amendment to Article 4 of the Broadcast Law that mandates political fairness. This amendment attempted to do away with regulations that nominally prevent increasingly pro-government TV news sources – and NHK in particular – from excluding opposition perspectives (Asahi 2018a, 2018b).

Along with these legal measures, the government also sought to silence opposition within the media through public admonishments. In 2014 Abe publicly lambasted the *Asahi Shimbun*, Japan's second widest circulating newspaper and the most important source of government criticism and scrutiny, for minor factual inaccuracies in stories it had printed in the early 1990s on the comfort women issue. Far from generating a backlash from other media companies, this led other media sources to display an open hostility towards the *Asahi*, harming its reputation (Facker 2016).

In all these ways, Abe sought to exert control over the media, rewarding allies and punishing opponents. As a result, Japanese journalism came to be characterized by a growing tendency for journalists and media to seek to placate politicians through favorable coverage, another example (as with the bureaucracy) of *sontaku* (Facker 2016). At the same time, journalists' commitment to the companies that employ them rather than to their profession precluded any willingness for media companies to resist government kowtowing, further enabling the government's divide and rule strategy. In the process, while open opposition to the LDP and its agenda became increasingly muted, Japan plummeted in the rankings for press freedom compiled by Reporters Without Borders, from 11th place in 2010 to 72nd place in 2017 (RSF 2018; Economist 2015).

3.5 Abe's Passive Revolution

What have been the overall implications of Abe's passive revolution in defense, security and administrative policy? First, with regard to defense policy, Abe's calls for limited revisions to the constitution that respect its original spirit combined with under the radar moves to push the actual practice of Japanese defense policy beyond recognition might be understood as an effective way to shore up support from among the party's nationalist conservative base without alienating the general public. Thus, while he left office having failed to achieve his longstanding goal of constitutional revision, his passive revolution in defense policy appears to have succeeded in pushing Japan in the direction he long hoped it would go, both within popular discourse and in practice.

Second, Abe's administrative reforms greatly increased his control of the bureaucracy, both formally through the ability to handpick top bureaucrats, and informally through the rise of *sontaku*. This made Abe further immune from pressure and criticism, with a deep bench of top-ranking bureaucrats loyal not to the ministry or even the LDP more generally but to Abe personally. Whether this passive revolution of bureaucratic reform will ultimately result in an entrenched bureaucracy of nationalist, conservative Abe acolytes or in a cadre of instrumentally driven yes-men willing to serve as sycophants to the Prime Minister of the day regardless of ideology is unclear, but in either case Abe's legacy will be profound.

Finally, under the guise of anti-terrorist policy, Abe used the Specially Designated Secrets Protection Law – originally designed as counter-terrorist security legislation – to pacify and silence critics in the media, while employing a range of other tactics to promote *sontaku* from other media sources. While these measures succeeded in promoting the advancement of journalists and media executives who share Abe's conservative agenda into positions of power, pushing Japanese public discourse further in line with Abe and the LDP's views, they potentially have grave implications for press freedom – and with it, liberal democracy more generally – in Japan.

4 Consequences of Abe's Reign for the Hegemonic Order?

Overall, this combined strategy of Caesarism and passive revolution clearly succeeded in restoring the LDP's political dominance while also enabling Abe and his allies to subtly push the country in a conservative direction in various ways. Yet aside from these narrow and short term achievements, what are the consequences of the Abe regime and its dual strategy of Caesarism and passive revolution for conditions of hegemonic order in Japan? How did the policies of the Abe regime fare in solving the multifaceted crisis facing Japan?

4.1   Capital Accumulation

From the perspective of capital accumulation, early signs were that conditions had been restored by the stock market boom, while many had thought that Abe's strategy possessed the right combination of neoliberal measures designed to boost investment and Keynesian measures designed to boost demand to help escape the crisis of deflation. While the NIKKEI stock market doubled over the course of 2013, the yen depreciated, GDP grew during 2013, and inflation reached target levels in 2014 (Wakatabe 2015). However, due to the persistence of deflationary pressures in the economy (such as population decline and stagnant wages) inflation targeting proved hard to sustain, remaining below one percent since 2015, despite effectively negative interest rates since 2016 (Trading Economics n.d.). Moreover, the virtuous cycle of growth that quantitative easing and deficit spending was supposed to bring has amounted to little: capital expenditure only grew by 2.6 percent, real wages by 0.3 percent and private consumption by 0.2 percent (Nikkei 2015). Overall, early success belied an overall story of failure, as the Japanese economy barely treaded water, falling into recession six times during Abe's tenure, in spring 2014, summer 2015, winter and summer of 2018, fall of 2019 and again in spring 2020.

While the overall economic picture ultimately proved to be underwhelming, Abe's economic policies failed, in particular, to reach the middle and working classes, with wage growth stagnant despite the stock market boom, thus preventing any meaningful escape from structural conditions of deflation. Indeed, as of September 2013, just 16 percent of people had felt an improvement in Japan's economic conditions, while 84 percent of people remained anxious about Japan's public financial conditions (Mochizuki and Porter 2013). Five years later, a September 2018 poll found that the number who had felt an improvement had fallen to 11 percent, while those who had not remained at 84 percent (TBS 2018). In this way, then, it is difficult to say that Abe has succeeded in restoring conditions for capital accumulation, and whatever benefits his programs brought to the Japanese economy are likely to be short-term only and confined to those who benefited from the stock market boom (Takahashi and Mizuno 2013; Lechevalier and Monfort 2018).

4.2 Political Legitimation

If Abe's politics ultimately proved ineffective in resolving the economic crisis facing Japan since the 1990s, how did his program fare from the perspective of political legitimation? At first glance, Abe appears to have succeeded both in asserting personal and factional dominance within his party and in asserting the LDP's dominance overall, winning three consecutive landslide elections in the Lower House and two more in the Upper House, consistently winning a two-thirds' majority of seats between the LDP and coalition partner Kōmeitō in the Lower House. Yet a deeper look shows that in the proportionate representation vote, only 27 to 33 percent of voters have chosen the LDP as a party, with 67 to 73 percent choosing other parties (including Kōmeitō). Moreover, beginning in 2012 the DPJ splintered into several parties and although some of these later reunited into the Constitutional Democratic Party (CDP), it remained fractured at every Lower House election. The 2019 Upper House election also saw the LDP lose nine seats and outright majority control of the chamber (though it maintained its majority through its coalition with Kōmeitō). The LDP's string of landslide election wins under Abe thus had much more to do with the strategic benefits of working with Kōmeitō, the disunity and chaos of the centre-left opposition, and overall distrust of potential alternatives (including the Japanese Communist Party) than with enthusiastic support for the Abe government (Burrett 2017).

In comparison to his success in consolidating power within the LDP and consistently winning elections – however favorable the circumstances – Abe's success in winning over other elements of the state and civil society, such as the media and bureaucracy, was more mixed. Whenever his policies failed to merit praise and support from these circles, he resorted to indirect and direct means to stifle opposition in the media and elsewhere. At the same time, due to his suspected personal involvement, various scandals, including the Moritomo Gakuen and Kake Gakuen scandals in particular, plagued his regime. This was partly a consequence of renewed contradictions that have emerged between the nominal function of the bureaucracy as a politically neutral and rational institution and the reality of greatly increased dependence of bureaucrats on the Cabinet, and Abe in particular, on a personal level, for their job security. The *sontaku* problem that plagued relations between the government, media and bureaucracy thus reflects the political contradictions that emerged out of Abe's attempts to disarm opposition to his political project in both the bureaucracy and the wider civil society. Finally, insofar as the defense, administrative and domestic security policies pursued as part of Abe's passive revolution were implemented in a covert manner away from the public view, they appear at odds with conditions necessary for hegemony in an open and democratic society.

Given the broad hegemonic appeal of the latter and the soft authoritarianism of the former, this forces us to ask how did these policies aimed at shoring up control over the state and civil society fit with Abe's Caesarist strategy of a broad based and conciliatory program of economic and social reform through Abenomics? While some have attempted to focus on the Abe of the second term as having learned from the mistakes of his first time. Compared to his first term, he succeeded in distancing himself from right wing causes, such as constitutional revision and to have instead realized the importance of showing leadership in the interests of the whole of society through his economic policies. Yet following Dobson (2017: 205), we must also recognize:

> Attempting to separate Abenomics from Abe's nationalist agenda represents something of a false dichotomy and, rather like Schrödinger's cat, Abe the pragmatist and Abe the nationalist exist together at the same time and are mutually reinforcing. In Abe's worldview, Japan cannot provide a strong regional and global presence unless it emerges from its long-running economic malaise ... Abenomics is as much about regional security, Japan's status in the world and the Meiji-period slogan of *fukoku kyohei* (rich country, strong army) as it is about economic growth.

Nonetheless while this narrative of economic growth fueling national – and with it nationalist – revitalization, in the process restoring the basis for a conservative hegemonic order is appealing, a closer look throws this narrative into doubt. Although the 2012 election resulted in a landslide win for the LDP and their highest ever seat percentage, the win came with only 28 percent of the vote,[5] only one percent higher than in their crushing defeat in 2009 (Kitaoka 2013). The 2014 and 2017 elections brought slightly higher numbers, (each 33 percent) but still very low numbers for the LDP (see Figure 2). These numbers challenge the idea that Abe's mix of bold economic policy and under the radar authoritarianism has succeeded in restoring widespread support for the LDP.[6]

---

5 Numbers relate to the proportional representation portion of the electoral system only. Unlike in the single-member districts, where vote-splitting deters small parties from running and where the LDP-Kōmeitō alliance enables much higher scores for both parties' candidates, in the PR section, all parties can compete equally without risks of vote-splitting, and vote distributions more accurately reflect partisan electoral support.
6 2000 was the only election besides the most recent four where the LDP received less than 33% of the vote.

4.3 Social Reproduction

With regard to social reproduction, the government also failed to address major challenges relating to Japan's crisis of social reproduction despite its bold rhetoric. Though the fertility rate recovered from a low of 1.26 in 2005 to 1.43 in 2015, by the time Abe left office in 2020 it had fallen to 1.39 (lower than when his term started), despite Abe promising to raise it to 1.8 by 2020. Moreover, Japan witnessed fewer births and more deaths every year under Abe, indicating the growing urgency of Japan's demographic challenges and his inability to resolve them. While the effects of this demographic crisis are already being felt, particularly in rural regions, in the long run these trends point to an unprecedented social crisis characterized by not only a labor shortage but a massive revenue shortfall in the face of rapidly escalating welfare costs (just to maintain existing standards of living for the majority of people).

Sensing the scope of the crisis, the government finally bent to the will of Keidanren in 2018, hastily pushing through (very worker-unfriendly) legislation that amounted to a major expansion of the intake of migrant workers to Japan. Yet the government has simultaneously included measures that guarantee that such workers will never meet requirements to obtain permanent residency and remained steadfast in calling these workers only temporary migrant workers instead of permanent immigrants. In the long run such a policy cannot possibly help assuage the long-term effects of population aging and decline without these workers to stay permanently, something that would be fundamentally at odds with Japanese ethnic nationalism and the ideology of *tan'itsu minzoku*.[7]

Thus overall, despite optimistic rhetoric, after years of unfulfilled promises of a return to robust fertility rates, the elimination of daycare waiting lists, and other measures that would lead to more stable conditions of social reproduction, it is difficult to deny that the Abe government's social policies ultimately proved to be insufficient to the task of resolving Japan's crisis of social reproduction. Indeed, it is ultimately unclear whether Abe's commitment to resolving

---

7 This is because guest workers that are only temporary do not in the long run lead to any net population (or workforce) gain. With Japan's population expected to shrink by at least 20 million by 2050, accepting 300,000 guest workers per year, with each allowed to stay a maximum of ten years, would lead to at an increase in only 3 million people by 2050 (and a net population decline of 17 million), while accepting the same number of people as permanent immigrants every year would lead to an increase of nine million (plus potential family members). Looking even further forward, by 2080 the first scenario would still have only brought an increase of 3 million people to Japan, while the latter would have then brought 18 million.

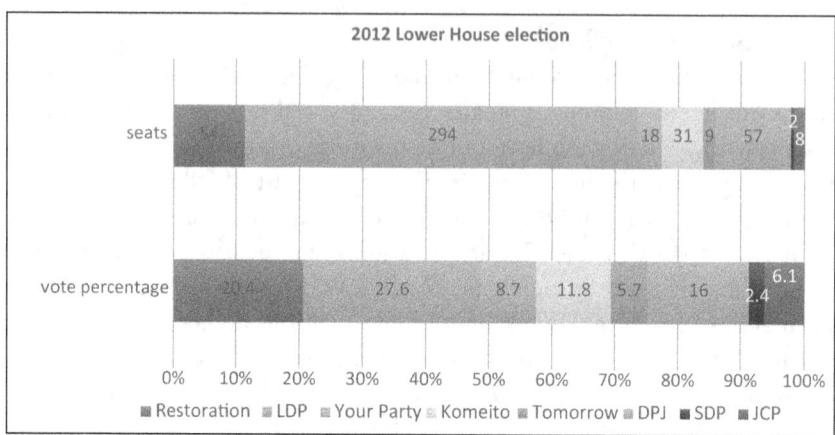

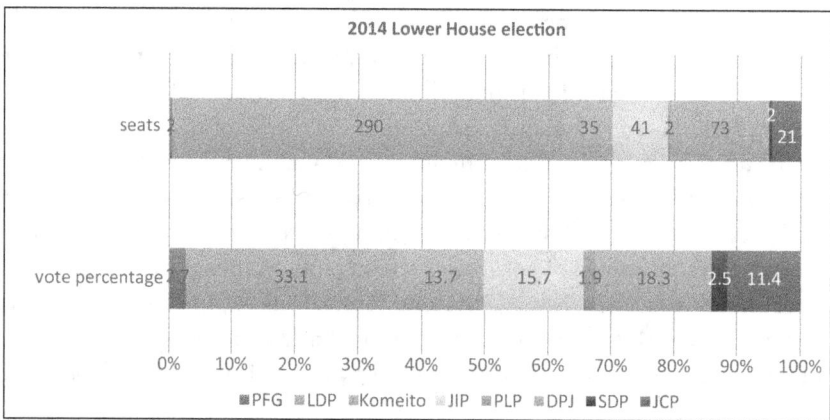

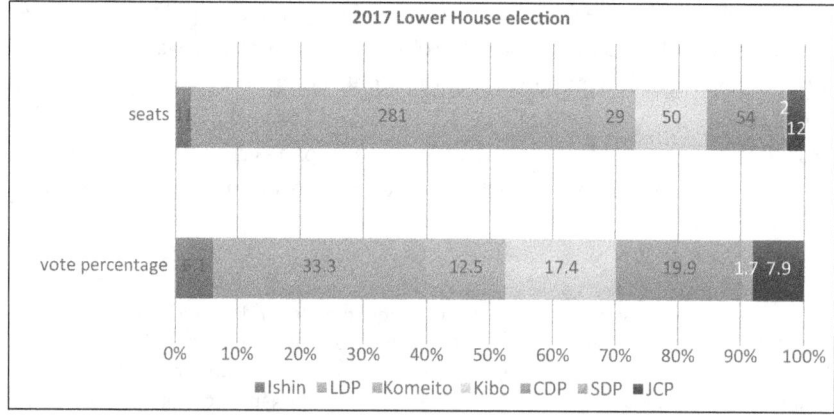

FIGURE 2   Results of the 2012, 2014 and 2017 Lower House elections. Parties are arranged based on political ideology, from right to left (reverse order to visual representation). Vote percentage is for the PR bloc vote only (author's original work).
SOURCE: MINISTRY OF INTERNAL AFFAIRS AND COMMUNICATIONS [MIC] (N.D.) SHIRYOSHU: SENKYO SEIJI SHIRYO. DATE ACCESSED: 10 AUGUST 2021. AVAILABLE AT: HTTPS://WWW.SOUMU.GO.JP/SENKYO/SENKYO_S/DATA/SHUGIIN/ICHIRAN.HTML.

the crisis of social reproduction and accepting the costs of such a program to the state and capital was genuine, or whether promises of increased welfare spending and bold social policy goals were little more than electioneering tactics. Regardless of the motive, these promises mean little if they do not amount to substantive improvement in the conditions of social reproduction, something that has yet to occur in any meaningful way.

5 Conclusion

As we consider the legacy of Abe's regime and its implications for the future, we can see that however much it may have succeeded in keeping him in power for eight years and restoring LDP electoral dominance, Abe's combined strategy of Caesarism and passive revolution is unlikely to provide the basis for a permanent solution to Japan's organic crisis post-Abe. Indeed, any possibility of serving this end is undermined by a number of contradictions that further demonstrate the deeply rooted intractability of Japan's organic crisis and the difficulty of resolving it within existing political economic structures going forward.

First, there is a contradiction between many of the more hardline neoconservative elements of Abe's political project and his attempts to resolve the chronic labour shortage that has become a major damper on economic growth through the liberalization of immigration. Attempts to strengthen the appeal of nationalist, militarist and *tan'itsu minzoku* ideology that stress the uniqueness and difference of a homogeneous Japanese race have historically been important to right-wing factions within the LDP. Yet these values appear entirely incompatible with a society that increasingly relies on the active participation in public life of people from a range of cultures and societies and whose exclusion from the dominant national discourse is only likely to further cause tensions if these policies are continued into the future.[8] The government has so far attempted to massage this contradiction on the side of nationalist conservatism by denying that these "foreign workers" are immigrants and instituting administrative hurdles to their ability to one day obtain permanent residence rights. But such a policy cannot ultimately be a solution to the problem of population decline and labour shortage.

Second, there is a contradiction between policies that the government pursued in its attempts to resolve the crisis of social reproduction and win over welfare-minded citizens on one hand, and other attempts to increase the

---

8 This is especially the case if key questions of welfare and security for migrants are not given enough attention.

competitiveness of Japanese capital through further labour market deregulation on the other. In devoting a large amount of attention to social welfare policies – many of which were taken from the DPJ's policy book – Abe followed a long-time LDP strategy of coopting popular policies of the left opposition. Yet rather than being implemented on their original terms, these policies have been transformed into bit-part elements of the LDP's overarching conservative political project, a political strategy that Gramsci referred to as *trasformismo*. While Abe might receive partial credit for pushing for moderate increases in the minimum wage, this was overshadowed by the complete stagnation in overall wages, despite a chronic shortage of labour.

As Takahashi and Mizuno (2013) argue, attempts to make Japanese capital more competitive without focusing more squarely on boosting value-added production and demand-driven growth are unlikely to work economically and only likely to be deleterious socially, exacerbating the social reproduction crisis. In this sense, Abenomics' promise of simultaneously restoring conditions for capital accumulation through deregulation while also boosting consumer demand through Keynesian fiscal spending appears less as a bold, "win-win" policy and more as a naïve incapacity to recognize the inherently class contradictory nature of capitalism.

Finally, there is a contradiction between the policies needed to win elections, including renewed spending on social programs, infrastructure and tax cuts on one hand versus those needed to create a fiscal balance on the other.[9] Abe postponed an increase of the consumption tax to ten percent on two occasions before finally implementing it in 2019, while the past 25 years in general have seen near constant budget deficits and led the state to amass a public debt that is 250% of GDP. Yet this continued borrowing is only possible under rates of ultra-low interest, and thus appears unsustainable in the long run (Lechevalier 2014).[10] Moreover, while Japan's demographic crisis is already having major impacts on economic accumulation and social reproduction, the worst is yet to come. Japan's population has only fallen by two million people over the past decade since it peaked in 2010. Yet absent major changes, it is expected to decline at a rate of nearly one million people per year by the 2030s.

---

9 These include both progressive policies such as tax increases on the wealthy and corporations and more conservative options such as consumption taxes and spending cuts.
10 While deficits are not necessarily problematic under conditions of expanded reproduction, robust demand and inflation (where the real value of debt steadily falls as GDP grows), this is not the case under conditions of chronic stagnation and deflation, dynamics that have plagued Japan since the 1990s and may become even worse as the demographic crisis worsens over the coming decades.

In this context, Japan faces the possibility of a rapidly declining overall population and workforce and a rapidly expanding elderly population. In other words, constantly declining revenue streams and constantly growing welfare costs. As Abe was ultimately able to do little to prepare Japan for this looming fiscal crisis, it is difficult to see how his overall project will ultimately prove to be a long term and permanent solution to the crisis.

CHAPTER 8

Whither Post-Abe Japan? Four Scenarios for the Future

In late August 2020, Abe Shinzō abruptly announced his resignation, weeks after becoming Japan's longest continuously serving Prime Minister and one year before his tenure was set to end in September 2021. Within days of the announcement, major power brokers within the party quickly consolidated around his chosen successor, the well-liked, mild-mannered and technocratic Chief Cabinet Secretary Suga Yoshihide, partly as an attempt to sideline long-time Abe rival and "maverick," Ishiba Shigeru, who had fought Abe for the leadership in both 2012 and 2018 and had announced his intention to run to succeed Abe just days after Abe's resignation.

Yet despite seemingly unified support within the LDP for Suga, Suga is unlikely to hold office for long or stray meaningfully from Abe ideologically, and thus appears as little more than a transitional figure. In the wake of Abe's 2020 resignation and the end of the longest Prime Minister tenure in Japanese history, this chapter examines a number of scenarios for the future of political order in Japan in the years and decades to come. It argues that, as a result of the inherent contradictions between Japan's regime of accumulation and its regime of social reproduction, Japan's organic crisis can only be resolved in the long term through a reformulation of ruling relations that places the interests of the working class at the centre and particularly that prioritizes a revitalization of conditions necessary for progressive and stable social reproduction. However, it recognizes that the barriers to this, in the context of the LDP's return to power and the enduring power of capital, are high.

This chapter therefore identifies a number of possible approaches to solving the crisis, considering the political, economic and social consequences of each of them. As the chapter considers what is at stake in each of these four potential pathways, it explores 1) the basic policy considerations of each scenario; 2) the relations of force, or political and social bases of support for each scenario; 3) how each scenario would fulfill requirements for social reproduction, political legitimation and economic accumulation; and 4) the problems, barriers and contradictions inherent in each scenario.

1 The Neo-conservative Option

In its simplest form, neo-conservatism combines a relatively free market approach to economic policy with social conservatism and nationalistic, hawkish foreign policy. This sort of political program most obviously has its antecedents in the pre-war model of Japanese society, dating all the way back to the Meiji Restoration, where the logic of *fukoku kyōhei* (rich nation, strong army) served as the underlying ideological basis of state formation and empire-building. More recently, neo-conservatism has been a powerful political current among the right of the LDP, and a relatively coherent neo-conservative program was articulated by the Nakasone administration, which balanced a shift towards neoliberal economic policies with an emphasis on militaristic nationalism. Though he projected a strikingly different image, the substance of Koizumi's politics had much in common with Nakasone, particularly in his combination of neoliberal economic policies and nationalistic militarism. Indeed, it was Koizumi that oversaw the actual participation of Japanese troops in semi-active conflict during the Afghan and Iraq Wars, while Koizumi's regular visits to Yasukuni Shrine drew the ire of Chinese and Koreans while pleasing nationalists at home.

However, the neo-conservative program has been embodied, more than anyone else, by Abe Shinzō. As such the neo-conservative scenario discussed below must therefore be situated within the elements of Abe's program that have long defined him as a figure, rather than his later attempts to latch on to Keynesian fiscal and welfare policies.[1] Given the way Abe has pushed these various elements of his worldview under the radar – through the passive revolution strategy outlined in the previous chapter – there is good reason to consider neo-conservatism as an ideology that is likely to remain influential and even dominant, at least within the LDP, if not within society more generally.

1.1 Overview

On economic policy, the neoconservative option mostly reflects neoliberal orthodoxy with some neo-communitarian elements (discussed below) insofar as it identifies the need to protect sectors of the economy deemed important to nationalistic interests. In contrast, on social policy, it is conservative, nationalistic, and patriarchal, emphasizing a return to traditional values, respect for authority, including the emperor, and a return to more traditional gender roles,

---

[1] Such views his militarism, nationalism, authoritarian impulses towards opposition forces in the media, support for generally pro-business economic policy and a general dislike of the left.

emphasizing women's roles in the home. It would also pursue a more conservative approach to education, including through controversial policies such as Abe's promotion of *aikokushin* (love of one's country) within official school curriculum and textbook revision. Moreover, a neo-conservative program would seek a stronger revision of the constitution than that proposed by Abe, perhaps returning to the proposal developed by the LDP under the first Abe administration in the 2000s that included a larger role for emperor, the elimination of the total separation of religion and state, a withering of individual rights, and the re-establishment of a full-fledged military.

Along with such constitutional reforms and remilitarization, under a neo-conservative program Japan would pursue much more hawkish foreign policy, likely characterized by a more antagonistic relationship with China, Russia and the two Koreas. This would likely be combined with a strong alliance with the US, but not necessarily, as critique of the US alliance, both overtly and covertly, has long been a feature of neo-conservative rhetoric. This perspective was most notably advanced by former Tokyo governor (1999–2012) Ishihara Shintarō, whose 1989 essay, *The Japan that can say no*, specifically took aim at a foreign policy of American subservience (Ishihara 1991).

Under the neo-conservative model, Japan's welfare policy would follow the direction taken by reforms under the Nakasone and Koizumi regimes to be workfare-centric, with piecemeal supports to ensure a modicum of stability for breadwinner-dominant families. Immigration levels would likely be kept low, but a neo-conservative regime might not rule out importing temporary low wage guest workers to ensure that conditions for accumulation could be restored, at least in the short term. In this way, it may begrudgingly accept the immigration reforms pursued by the Abe government in 2018 but remain vigilant in ensuring that "migrant worker policy" never turns into "immigration policy" that could lead to new rights claims among ethnic minorities, or other challenges to the ideology of *tan'itsu minzoku*. Finally, neo-conservative fiscal policy would rely on some tax increases – likely consumption tax – to pay for increased military spending, while the lean state model – what Abe has endorsed in the past as "small government" (*chiisana seifu*) – would otherwise be preserved, in order to reign in Japan's chronic deficit.

1.2 Relations of Force behind Neo-conservatism

What are the relations of force behind a neo-conservative program? What political constituencies and actors would give such a movement political support? In many ways, we can see a neo-conservative project drawing on many of the same groups that helped bring Abe to power. On one hand, it would involve conservative factions of the LDP, especially the Seiwa Seisaku Kenkyūkai, now by far the largest faction of the LDP and the base of Abe's support, as well as other conservative factions, such as the Shikōkai led by Asō Tarō. At the same time, it would include various conservative elements of the bureaucracy, including the Ministry of Justice, the Ministry of Defense and with it the Self-Defense Forces, as well as parts of the Ministry of Education, and the anti-China faction of Foreign Ministry (see also Hook and Gilson 2011). While many of these departments may have been sympathetic to conservative ideas before, it is likely that the growing control over the bureaucracy that Abe has achieved through the revision of the National Public Service Law in 2014 has only made bureaucrats more likely to display obedience to the ruling regime. Moreover, other elements of the bureaucracy, particularly the economic ministries, would generally be comfortable with such a scenario, given the pro-business economic policies a neo-conservative regime would pursue.

Outside of the LDP and bureaucracy, a neo-conservative coalition would rely on a high degree of grassroots support from a number of nationalist and militaristic social groups such as the War Bereaved Association and Nippon Kaigi, various Shintō organizations, as well as support from a more disparate but extensive group of nationalists, including anti-Chinese and anti-Koreans, with which mainstream conservatives retain a measured distance. Though small, a number of other parties to the right of the LDP, including the Osaka Restoration Party and Japan Innovation Party would also be important allies. Finally, a group of conservative organic intellectuals, primarily defense hawks from the fields of international relations and political science but also some neo-liberal economists, both at universities and in private research think tanks would provide a major ideological and normative anchor for the neo-conservative coalition. These organic intellectuals also have expression in the mainstream media, most notably the increasingly reactionary and Abe-aligned NHK and the far-right *Sankei Shimbun*, but also the centre-right *Yomiuri Shimbun*, Japan's largest newspaper, and generally a standard-bearer for the LDP's consensus position on key issues.

On the other hand, the neo-conservative movement would face opposition from various other groups, including labour groups, liberal or left groups in civil society and from the bureaucracy's Ministry of Health, Labour and Welfare, which has consistently pursued a more social democratic model for the welfare state since the 1970s. Corporations and major business organizations such as Keidanren would likely have a neutral attitude towards this type of hegemonic order, favoring generally pro-business economic policies while pushing for more liberal immigration policies in the face of labour shortages, just as they have until now.

Additionally, recent backlash against the sexist and patriarchal nature of Japanese politics and society – even from among otherwise conservative nationalist LDP politicians such as former Defense Minister Inada Tomomi – indicate the difficulties in coopting women – even conservative women – into a project that emphasizes traditional gender roles in a society where changing societal attitudes towards gender have moved considerably rapidly than political and economic institutions and policies. Whether the LDP could resolve this "women problem" simply by placing a Thatcher-like figure at the top, or whether doing so would require substantively tackling issues of women's equal representation and participation in society (from a nationalist conservative perspective) is unclear. But there are limits to how far such a program could go to substantially address questions of gender inequality without abandoning conservative principles altogether, given how central the traditional family is to conservatism in Japan.

1.3   The Neo-conservative Solution to Organic Crisis

It is easy to see how a neo-conservative political program could generate the relations of force necessary to construct a new historic bloc capable of seizing and maintaining power, considering the already great degree of institutional penetration of these forces within Japan's leading political institutions, particularly the LDP. Indeed, some may argue that under Abe, a neo-conservative seizure of power already occurred, even if parts of its program have remained controversial and advanced via passive revolution rather than openly. Yet regardless of its current ascendancy, any such program cannot achieve and maintain hegemonic status in the long term if it cannot solve the organic crisis that has plagued Japan since the 1990s, and restore conditions for political legitimation, social reproduction, and capital accumulation. Therefore, we must ask how the neo-conservative coalition could possibly succeed in solving the organic crisis facing Japan.

First, conditions for political legitimation could be restored through a return to militaristic nationalism, insofar as the public is persuaded into accepting a more conservative and hierarchical social order as necessary for preserving the "Japanese" way of life. Indeed, between attempts to turn the page on the postwar era through constitutional revision, efforts to challenge records of Japan's wartime atrocities and promoting a revisionist history, including through textbook reforms that reject the "masochism" of prevailing interpretations and by promoting "patriotism" (*aikokushin*) as a school subject, various measures pursued by the Abe administration that advance this agenda and "naturalize" a conservative and hierarchical social order have already been pursued in recent years.

Second, conditions for stable social reproduction could be restored through a return to traditional gender roles and a greater acceptance on the part of women of their responsibilities as wives and mothers to nurture children for the *kokutai* (national body), regardless of the heavy burden and stress such a role entails without proper support. However, while pressures against women's participation in public life remain (despite superficial pro-women rhetoric), it is unclear how and whether a return to a traditional gender division of labour would be compatible with the demands of the capitalist economy, given the chronic labour shortages facing Japanese society, not to mention the backlash such a move would receive from a women's movement that appears increasingly assertive (as discussed in the previous section). To this end, as Abe already sought to promote women's participation in the workforce, we can imagine neo-conservatism's viability may hinge on its proponents' ability to construct a new gender dichotomy that emphasizes women's roles as domestic caregivers *and* as (lowly paid and insecure) workers in service sector jobs, especially in the care economy, in contrast with men's more traditional jobs as breadwinners (and continued holders of social power).

Finally, under the neo-conservative model, conditions for capital accumulation could be restored through a combination of pro-business neoliberal economic policies that promote profits plus greater compliance from the public as diligent workers and consumers. Neoconservatives would hope that a renewed nationalist vigor would inspire Japanese people to work hard and make great personal sacrifices in order to improve Japan's flagging economy. Moreover, Japanese firms would be pressured to take more risks and return to the nationalist orientation (pursuing business strategies that balance the national interest with profitability rather than solely focusing on profits) that partially characterized Japanese development capitalism until the 1990s.

1.4 *Challenges and Contradictions of Neo-conservatism*

The above suggests not only a credible means for the neo-conservative coalition to achieve power (indeed, arguably it already has) but also a way to transition short-term power into long-term hegemonic leadership by solving the organic crisis by attending to its three most pronounced social, economic and political dimensions. Nonetheless, such a program would face social, economic and political challenges of its own, while its pursuit would likely generate new contradictions and problems.

First, a return to traditional gender roles and militarism is likely to – indeed it already has – elicit strong resistance from pacifists, progressives and women in general. Resistance from workers could be strong as well if neo-conservative leaders are not able to at least integrate privileged workers (including those still protected by lifetime employment) into the project. While the Japanese left has long been far removed from the echelons of power, many of the positions it has championed remain widely popular. While support for the pacifist constitution has remained strong throughout the postwar, public opinion on issues of gender equality, women's roles in public life and minorities have steadily become more progressive, despite the LDP's preponderant control of political power. Challenging these increasingly widespread progressive attitudes would thus require not only top-town legislation but also a deeper cultural change, or what Gramsci would term intellectual and moral reform, a process that cannot occur overnight but only through a long-term and organic war of position for the hearts and minds of civil society. As the previous chapter suggested, there is little evidence to suggest that such a cultural shift to the right has occurred.

Second, the role of immigrants – if immigrants are seen as necessary to fill labor shortages – would also likely become a flashpoint given the existential challenges minorities pose to discourses of national homogeneity. As argued in Chapter Seven, there is no way to use term-limited guest worker policy as a means of solving the problem of a chronically shrinking population and labour force. This is because by the time the first group of migrant workers have to return home, each new migrant worker who arrives afterwards only replaces one who leaves rather than replacing retiring Japanese nationals. Thus, permanent settlement and immigration is the only long-term solution to the labour shortage problem, but one that creates major complications for the legitimacy of Japanese cultural nationalism, either prompting a cultural shift towards a more multicultural and pluralist society or breeding marginalization of ethnic minorities and eventually ethnic tensions.

Third, given that this scenario would see heightened economic inequality and precariousness for the Japanese working class, it is easy to foresee the backlash such a project would receive from working class forces rendered more insecure by such policies, even from those sympathetic to its other conservative and nationalist elements. We have already seen this type of dynamic in the past, as the Nakasone and Koizumi governments faced backlashes to the oppressive effects of their austerity agendas in the early 1990s and late 2000s respectively. Thus, only by successfully leading a transition towards a social order more deeply rooted in nationalist and conservative values could these growing conditions of inequality and precariousness be naturalized or legitimized.

Finally, we must also consider the foreign policy barriers to this project. Scapegoating of minorities and enemies, both foreign and internal (including the left) was one of the ways conditions of oppression and inequality were mediated in the pre-war period, yet this only led to colonialism and war. Would such a scenario be needed to shore up hegemony under neo-conservative rule? In a world where China's growing military and economic power is already posing challenges to Japan, it is unclear what foreign policy implications such a scenario might have. Overall, the neo-conservative program clearly faces numerous challenges in becoming and staying a viable option for Japan in the long term. Given the impacts such a reactionary program would have on women and the working class in particular, it is difficult to see how it could succeed in garnering widespread consent even from these (and other) disempowered groups. As a result, its best prospects for success may be less in trying to restore the "one nation hegemony" of the post-war model by winning active support from these groups and instead in pursuing a "two nation hegemony" characterized by a clear distinction between those included (privileged workers and conservative women) and those excluded (most other workers and progressive women) (see also Jessop 1983).[2]

2   The Neo-liberal Path

A second option for Japan would be to pursue a more thoroughgoing neoliberal approach, extending the fragmentary neoliberal logic of the past 35 years into a more systematic and ideologically cohesive neoliberal program. Such a project would favor policies designed to promote immigration as well as women's full participation in public life as ways out of the labour shortage crisis and the wider crisis of social reproduction. While actually existing neoliberalism in Japan has never reached the systematic level of English-speaking countries, neoliberalism has powerful political antecedents in Japan and has long enjoyed a degree of ideological support from certain segments of the business community and from organic intellectuals.[3]

2.1   *Overview*
Under a neoliberal scenario, economic policy would see a push for even further deregulation, trade liberalization, labor market reform. It would also

---

2 Jessop (1983) has argued that a two nation hegemony characterized Thatcherite Britain, where the self-identifying (and Labour-supporting) working class was deliberately marginalized and excluded from the hegemonic project rather than incorporated through concessions.
3 Some examples include former UCLA scholar Ohmae Ken'ichi and economist and Koizumi confidante Takenaka Heizō.

include further measures aimed at corporate governance reform, including efforts to promote stock-market-based corporate financing, shareholder-driven decision-making, greater risk-taking at the corporate level and an end to subsidies and protections to the *petit bourgeoisie*. In general, it would involve a wholesale Americanization of the Japanese economy in ways that have thus far only been advanced in a limited and fragmentary fashion by the Koizumi and Abe governments, along the lines called for by neoliberal critics of Japan (see, for example, Anchordoguy 2005; Katz 1998).

In addition to economic policies designed to promote free markets and unrestrained capital accumulation, social policy would be minimal, but would emphasize individual rights and individual responsibility. Neoliberal social policies would likely promote women's participation in the workforce (without providing much in the way of protections for workers, male or female). The state would likely take a more negative view of traditional approaches to business-labour coordination that stress consensus-based decision-making, instead seeking to further disempower labour unions, while lifetime employment would encounter a further challenge as efforts to promote performance-based pay and flexible employment are strengthened. The government would likely also pursue devolution and localization, grafting new responsibilities for service delivery onto local governments, without granting them new means of accessing the funds needed to fulfill program mandates.

Somewhat in contrast to the neo-conservative approach, neoliberal foreign policy would likely be a continuation of current trends, with the SDF increasingly deployed in peacekeeping. Indirect support for US military endeavors, if carried out under a US president similar to Barack Obama or Bill Clinton, would continue, but Japan would also pursue strong economic ties with China, South Korea and other Asian neighbours. Reflecting the trajectory of the TPP as well as other efforts to forge closer ties with the rest of Asia, regional cooperation would likely increase, insofar as Chinese and Korean governments were equally keen on pursuing free trading relations with Japan, as increasingly open access to the mammoth Chinese economy would be a major boon to Japanese capital. While coaxing unfettered access to the Chinese market for Japanese firms out of the Chinese state may be easier said than done, such efforts would likely be central to a new, more transactional China policy emphasizing the strategic economic benefits of locating Japan as an interlocutor between China and the US over the security benefits of remaining unreservedly loyal to the US.

Due to both fiscal pressures already evident and the allure to neoliberals of personal responsibility, we might expect that social welfare policy would be heavily workfare-based, with very little public supports. Even more significantly, the skyrocketing costs of supporting an elderly population may drive major cutbacks in areas of public pensions and public health insurance and their replacement with a dualized private system. Given the lack of public supports, seniors would be expected to retire later, or rely on informal family supports, while well-off seniors may enjoy the benefits of financial deregulation for the private pension industry, a bifurcation in post-retirement livelihoods that would further deepen inequality. The education system would also likely be deregulated, granting more scope for profit-making activity than currently allowed under the current ostensibly non-profit education-corporation system. Public education would be increasingly defunded, with public universities expected to be "self-financing" through private sector partnerships and ever-growing tuition fees. Profit-making mandates would also be encouraged in hospitals and other institutions, and private insurance would be deregulated and promoted as an alternative to the increasingly underfunded public system, drawing inspiration from the American model.

In major contrast to the neo-conservative scenario, immigration policy would be much more open, allowing a blend of low wage and high skill workers from around the world to fill the gaping labor shortages in a wide range of economic sectors. This would be seen as the long-term or permanent solution to the falling population, as the domestic birth rate would likely not grow at all given the lack of public supports for families under a neoliberal scenario. As a result, a neoliberal Japan would likely also become a more pluralist and multicultural Japan, as "universal values" of industriousness and personal responsibility are emphasized above particularist cultural values.

Finally, fiscal policy would likely see an initial prioritization of measures to rein in Japan's massive public debt. This would involve fiscal consolidation and debt reduction through significant program cutbacks, including publicly funded healthcare, education and pensions. Once fiscal balance is restored, a turn to tax cuts for corporations and the wealthy would be expected to follow in order to further promote capital accumulation.

2.2   *Relations of Force behind Neo-liberalism*

What are the relations of force behind a neoliberal coalition in Japan? As with the neo-conservative program, a neo-liberal program could expect to enjoy support from a broad and powerful coalition of forces that could be decisive in forging a new historic bloc. As discussed above, the neo-conservative scenario is primarily rooted in the LDP's now-dominant conservative factions and the pressure groups from society that they are highly integrated with (such as Nippon Kaigi). In contrast, a neo-liberal historic bloc would be driven at its core by dominant economic forces, and primarily transnational corporations and their political representative organizations, including Keidanren. Importantly, this would include not only Japanese corporations but also increasingly active foreign corporations with operations in Japan, who have been successful in pushing for deregulation.[4] However, while free market policies obviously appeal to domestic corporations, we must also not overemphasize the affinity of established Japanese firms to neoliberalism. As Gotoh and Sinclair (2017) have shown, Keidanren has long sought to preserve many of the protectionist and clientelist elements of Japanese political economy, in contrast to more neoliberal groups such as the Dōyūkai and nouveau riche capitalists from Japan's IT startup firms.[5]

In addition to this core support base from among corporations, the neoliberal coalition would also be expected to draw support from a range of political actors, including various forces within the LDP. In particular, LDP factions led by former Foreign Minister and Chair of the PARC Kishida Fumio and former Secretary General Ishiba Shigeru, both of which have been characterized as more socially liberal than the now-dominant right-wing faction, could be more easily drawn to support a neoliberal program than a neoconservative one. Additionally, groups outside of the LDP, including the right of the former DPJ (now split between the CDP and Democratic Party for the People) represent a broadly neoliberal perspective reflected in former DPJ Prime Minister Noda's championing of the TPP and fiscal restraint and former DPJ leader Ozawa's longstanding advocacy of neoliberal deregulation (Sadoh 2012). A neoliberal coalition could also potentially have many allies in the bureaucracy as well. In particular, the economic ministries – the Ministry of Finance and the Ministry of Economy, Trade and Industry, as well as the Bank of Japan – increasingly represent neoliberal positions (rather than the developmentalist positions of the past) and could thus be a key institutional base of support within the state, something which the past ten years of conflicting political fortunes for the DPJ and the LDP under Abe respectively has shown to be central to effective governance and ultimately political legitimacy.

Within society more generally, we might expect a neoliberal program to appeal to a range of groups, particularly well educated, white-collar workers in cities, for whom traditional social values and nationalism have declining appeal, but for whom neoliberal norms of consumer choice, low taxes and personal responsibility resonate. Indeed, such voters were partially responsible for Koizumi's ability to push the LDP in a neoliberal direction against

---

4 Examples include the late 1990s' attempts of Toys 'R' Us and other American retailers to remove restrictions on big box retailer construction.
5 Examples include Rakuten CEO Mikitani Hiroshi and Softbank president Son Masayoshi, who have tended to be much more vocal advocates of neoliberalism.

strong pressure from within the party to preserve the status quo. A neoliberal program would also enjoy support from a range of organic intellectuals, particularly in business-related think tanks (many of which have been set up by corporations). Neoliberal intellectuals would also be represented in academic fields such as economics and political science, which are increasingly characterized by methodological individualist rational choice and pluralist approaches imported from American academia. Finally, within the mass media, the centre-right *Nihon Keizai Shimbun* broadly speaks on behalf of a neoliberal vision for Japan and would be an effective mouthpiece for a neoliberal coalition, given its reputation (much like the *Wall Street Journal* or the *Financial Times*) for delivering economic "common sense".

While a neoliberal hegemonic project clearly possesses an impressive array of allies and advocates, this is not to say that the relations of force behind a neoliberal project would necessarily be decisive. Indeed, there are good reasons why neoliberalism has thus far failed to gain hegemonic status in Japan, including entrenched resistance from across the political spectrum and from within the bureaucracy, certain factions of the LDP and still-influential *petit bourgeoisie* interest groups (especially *Nōkyō*). Though neoliberalism would receive strong tacit support from corporations and business federations, unlike in many countries it would likely not enjoy strong vocal support from these organizations. As Schoppa (2006) has argued, Japanese corporations tend to avoid making explicit demands that conflict with the interests of other social forces. This has historically led to only muted support for neoliberal reforms from corporations and would likely mean so again if there were important social forces opposed to it such as the *petit bourgeoisie* and anti-immigration conservatives (see also Brenner et al. 2010).

2.3 The Neo-liberal Solution to Organic Crisis

How would a neoliberal program seek to resolve contradictions relating to political legitimation, social reproduction, and capital accumulation? First, conditions for political legitimation would only be restored through a widespread ideological shift towards neoliberal understandings of the virtues of free markets, freedom of choice, individual initiative and responsibility, as well as respect for diversity and other liberal values. These values would have to be rendered strong enough to eschew not only nationalistic identities but also to justify inequality and economic insecurity for a great many people. While neoliberal rhetoric became hegemonic in the US and UK by the 1990s, with the Clinton and Blair governments both adopting it into their political programs despite nominally representing the left of centre choices in their respective countries, Japan has not experienced such a full-blooded neoliberal cultural revolution to date. Nonetheless, the 1990s and 2000s experienced a growing trend towards neoliberal ideology in public discourse, with notions of personal responsibility (*jiko sekinin*) gaining in popularity. However, these seem to have faded in the wake of the 2008 Financial Crisis and 2011 earthquake and tsunami, where the deleterious social effects of free market capitalism and the need for solidaristic ties in times of hardship were brought into renewed focus. The financial crisis brought increased attention to social inequality (*kakusa shakai*), ultimately leading to the DPJ's electoral win in 2009. Though not impossible, a more systematic return to neoliberalism would thus require a reversal of these more recent trends.

Second, conditions for social reproduction, however regressive, would only be restored through the adoption of a mass immigration policy similar to English speaking countries such as Canada, Australia, Britain and the US. Indeed, given that neoliberalism would necessitate the hollowing out of an already underfunded welfare state, it is difficult to imagine how families could find the resources needed to have more children, and thus how the labor shortage could be overcome, without a major turn to immigration policy. Fortunately for neoliberals, countries such as Canada enjoy robust population growth despite a birth rate only slightly higher than Japan, so this approach is not impossible in theory, regardless of the social consequences it would have for people's livelihoods.

Finally, conditions for capital accumulation could be restored through a comprehensive neoliberalization of the economy that opens up numerous spaces to capital accumulation and generally seeks to provide optimal conditions for short-term profit making for capital. Free trade, especially with Japan's Asian neighbors as well as further deregulation and privatization of the health and welfare sectors, among others, could provide a significant new scope for capital accumulation. Whether such a policy is likely to have much prospect of continuing for a long time in the wake of the other challenges likely to emerge is another question.

2.4 Challenges and Contradictions of Neo-liberalism

However, a neoliberal program would also face three challenges in its attempts to assert hegemony in Japanese society. First, a more systematic turn to deregulation and liberalization would invariably lead to heightened inequality and insecurity. Yet unlike in the neo-conservative scenario discussed above, this would occur without any capacity for the state to rally the public around a nationalist or militarist ideology. Such conditions could easily lead to a crisis of legitimacy and class conflict. The commitment to free market ideals and individual choice and responsibility would have to be very strong in order to overcome this problem, as it has proven to be in the US, Canada and elsewhere, where the ideology of personal responsibility has been powerful enough to shift blame for growing poverty and inequality away from the capitalist system and onto the backs of the poor themselves.

Second, growing economic inequality and precariousness combined with mass immigration could potentially bring a significant degree of anti-immigrant backlash, if immigrants (rather than capitalist systemic forces) are targeted as the cause of declining economic security and prospects for ethnic Japanese workers. Such a scenario could prompt a reactionary shift towards right-wing nationalist populism, as we have seen in Europe and the US in the rise of the British UK Independence Party, the French National Rally, the Alternative für Deutschland in Germany, the Italian Lega Nord and most prominently with the election of Donald Trump in the United States.

Third, full-blooded economic deregulation, coupled with decreasing real wages, is likely to cause the same sort of economic crisis that plagued Japan in the aftermath of the late bursting of the bubble economy, or in the United States and elsewhere with the 2008 financial and subprime mortgage crisis. Thus, even if such a scenario could restore conditions for profitable capital accumulation in the short term, it is even likely to cause long-term problems from the perspective of capital, not to mention the aforementioned challenges of political legitimacy and social reproduction. As Takahashi and Mizuno (2013) have argued, it is unlikely that any accumulation strategy that focuses predominantly on price competition and supply-side economics can bring long-term economic growth.

Overall, as we have seen over the past few years in Europe and North America, neoliberalism, and the social dislocation and insecurity it causes for a great many people, is highly at risk of facing challenges from both the left and the nationalist right. In Japan, it is easy to imagine such a scenario, and a subsequent turn towards neo-conservatism (or, though less likely, democratic socialism) in response to the new contradictions that would be opened under attempts to build a neoliberal hegemonic order.

3 Back to the Future: Neo-communitarianism?

While the neoliberal and neoconservative programs appear the most plausible scenarios for Japan in the near future, there remains some – though perhaps dwindling – support for a return to the previous model of developmentalism combined with the "welfare through work" construction state model of welfare (Miura 2012; Miyamoto 2008), what I have previously called "nationalist communitarianism" (Carroll 2019). This prospective model, what I will term "neo-communitarianism" to differentiate it from the model that existed from the 1950s to the 1990s, requires slightly more imagination to appear viable. Indeed, since the old communitarian model ultimately proved incompatible with conditions of globalization, and in particular population aging in the 1990s, it would appear that a return to that model would be even more unrealistic today, where both of those dynamics have only become more pronounced. Nonetheless, particularly in the context of a growing global backlash against globalization in many countries – driven by both the left and the right – it is not impossible to see a return to at least some of the conditions that were more conducive with this model in previous decades.

3.1   Overview

What policies would characterize a neo-communitarian program? To start with, harkening back to the construction state policies common until the 2000s (Miyamoto 2008), economic policy would involve a return to protectionism coupled with developmentalist industrial policy, as well as public infrastructure spending, particularly to counter depopulation in the countryside. Moreover, such a model would promote a return to the lifetime employment system and attempts to promote stable breadwinner wages for a privileged, largely male workforce while also including extensive supports for the *petit bourgeoisie* through tax subsidies, special financing arrangements and protectionist benefits for small businesses.

In contrast with the road taken under both neo-conservative and neoliberal projects, social policy under a neo-communitarian program would involve attempts to promote a pacifist soft nationalism and conservatism with traditional gender values. Moreover, unlike under both neo-conservative and neoliberal scenarios, egalitarianism would be a relatively important principle, which would be partially reflected in welfare policies.

Under the neo-communitarian model, therefore, welfare policy would see attempts to return to conditions of familialism and the welfare through work paradigm of the post-war era (Miura 2012). This would involve attempts to incentivize the return to household-based provisioning of many welfare functions and the curtailment of state-funded provisioning, even if such measures would be out of step with the continuing decline of extended and nuclear family households. Attempts would therefore be made to ensure that women and families are economically secure enough to take on these roles primarily within the household. Pro-natal policies such as child subsidies would also be strongly emphasized, though publicly funded daycare that disrupts the traditional gendered division of labour might not be supported as strongly.

Moreover, the state would seek to counter recent trends such as the decline in extended and nuclear families and falling rates of marriage through policies designed to incentivize and make possible a return to more traditional family patterns, including extended families.

Again, harkening back to the post-war era, neo-communitarian foreign policy might be characterized by a very low posture with support for the US, with as little development of military capabilities as possible. Cooperation with neighboring countries would be encouraged, including China and South Korea, but not at the expense of the US alliance. In some ways, this foreign policy thus reflects the status quo up until now and does not require any drastic change from the present context. However, insofar as the rise of China as not only an economic but also a military power prompts continued conflict between Beijing and Washington, the role played by Tokyo in such a scenario is unclear.

Unlike with the neoliberal program, immigration policy would be minimal, given that immigration undermines the ideology of ethnic homogeneity, or *tan'itsu minzoku* that characterizes part of the communitarian model, where ethnic community ties serve as the social basis for mutual aid and solidarity. The labour shortage facing Japan would therefore have to be solved through other means, primarily through strong neo-natal policies that encourage and enable parents to have children at levels seen in the 1970s and 1980s.

The neo-communitarian model clearly calls for a host of new public expenses, including through industrial policy, public works, and social welfare cash subsidies designed to encourage child rearing, along with existing (albeit limited) welfare programs. How would the state pay for all of these programs? If the post-war record were to serve as the basis for future fiscal policy, under the neo-communitarian model, fiscal policy would involve a low tax regime but would probably have to rely on corporate taxes and consumption taxes to sustain increased public works spending. However, such a model appears at face value to be fiscally unsustainable, particularly considering the divergent demographic conditions caused by population aging over the past forty years. Instead, a revenue shortfall would have to be compensated through increased income taxes, particularly on higher income earners. In addition, reductions to public welfare expenditures (especially pensions) that serve to encourage a return to extended family households by prompting the re-privatization (or familialization) of various social reproduction functions – in particular eldercare – might also be necessary.

3.2 Relations of Force behind Neo-communitarianism

Given that neo-communitarianism largely failed to respond to growing challenges of globalization and population aging in the 1990s and 2000s, it is unlikely that many of the actors within Japan's ruling historic bloc would support it as enthusiastically as before. Nonetheless, we can imagine a number of still powerful groups that may be tempted by the prospects of a return to the good old days. The moderate factions of the LDP that support traditional clientelist public infrastructure spending, would be a necessary support group. This includes those few remaining *zoku* lawmakers and the old Tanaka-Takeshita faction, which long served as the political basis for LDP clientelism from the 1970s to the 1990s. In addition, such neo-communitarianism would rely on elements of the bureaucracy that had previously supported it, including the now reorganized Ministry of Internal Affairs (formerly the Postal Ministry), and the major "construction state" ministries, the Ministry of Land, Infrastructure and Transport (MLIT) and the Ministry of Agriculture, Forests and Fisheries (MAFF).[6] Whether these ministries would be willing to take on a role of administrative leadership – or participate at all – in a return to the protectionist developmentalism of the construction state remains to be seen.

Outside of the main power blocs, such a coalition would require strong support from farmers and small businesses, groups that stand to lose from neoliberalization and have generally been its most vocal (and effective) critics. While these groups have declined numerically throughout the post-war era, they are still politically and culturally influential (Hayes and Kawaguchi 2015). Otherwise, a neo-communitarian project would seek to expand its historic bloc around a cross-class coalition that includes more conservative labour unions seeking to preserve the lifetime employment system and opposed to neoliberal deregulation yet also weary of a more dramatic left movement that challenges the power of capital. It may also court support from more inward fractions of capital who favor protected access to the home market over liberal access to foreign markets. Finally, support potentially rests with other parties, most notably Kōmeitō, which has long pushed for socially conservative yet economically egalitarian policies and courted the votes of the urban poor (without using class-based rhetoric). The now defunct People's New Party, a small breakaway group from the LDP that opposed Koizumi's postal privatization and existed from 2005 until 2013, also reflected this perspective.

---

6 Both created in 2001 under the Hashimoto administrative reforms, MLIT was formed out of the Ministry of Construction and the Ministry of Transport respectively, while MAFF was created out of the Ministry of Agriculture and the Ministry of Fisheries respectively.

While a return to the neo-communitarian model of the post-war era would no doubt draw support from the *petit bourgeoisie* who benefited most strongly from the old regime, it is unclear to what extend the Japanese capitalist class, and major business organizations such as Keidanren would support such a direction. On one hand, Japanese capital long accepted and even openly supported the communitarian and clientelist political model of post-war Japan, recognizing how it shored up a high degree of political legitimation across class lines without giving real power to the working class. Insofar as a return to such a model could restore conditions of political hegemony and social security for the Japanese working class without overtly politicizing issues of economic distribution, such a model may be in Japanese capital's strategic political interests. On the other hand, the growing drag that various elements of the old system posed to capital accumulation may signal that Japanese capital is no longer willing to throw its support behind this system.

3.3 The Neo-communitarian Solution to Organic Crisis

What characterizes the neo-communitarian solution to organic crisis? First, conditions of political legitimation might be restored through a return to the post-war model that brought significant growth and stability. At the same time, it would seek to return to the pacifist nationalism of the post-war era that was still rooted in ethnic homogeneity but that encouraged values of cooperation and solidarity (but not class struggle). In other ways, a return to more conservative ideological positions would be required, such as a traditional gender division of labour. The still influential *petit bourgeoisie* would have much to gain and would be a key source of political support, given that there would be little in the way of support from organic intellectuals, liberal or conservative, who have largely abandoned the policies of the post-war model since the 1990s. Given the "class compromise" nature of the neo-communitarian model, there would be much scope for it to maintain the political legitimacy required to become hegemonic, just as it was in previous decades.

Second, conditions of social reproduction would be restored through a return to the welfare through work system that brought livelihood security for the majority of households up until the 1990s. Measures that encourage women to return to their traditional role within the home through public supports, combined with a Keynesian style efforts to promote the (re)creation of breadwinner jobs would help restore a social balance, providing families with the economic and social security needed to have their desired number of children. At the same time conditions making it harder for women to have fulfilling careers would be a push factor towards marriage and childbearing, though these would no doubt draw staunch resistance from liberal and progressive forces, especially the women's movement.

Finally, conditions conducive to capital accumulation could be restored through activist industrial policy geared at export promotion as well as policies designed to maximize labour output. This includes through male breadwinner flexibility and informal overtime work, conditions that were supported by the female housewife system and played a major role in buttressing the post-war boom. The gender dual system could potentially provide enough cheap and flexible (female) labour to complement the needs of a large class of protected and well-paid (male) breadwinners. However, even if the corporatist-clientelist model of the developmentalist construction state was successful in securing conditions for stable capital accumulation in the post-war period, it seems that this is the hegemonic condition least likely to be maintained under a neo-communitarian model in the future, given the dramatically different structural conditions facing Japan today, including economic globalization and an elderly society.

3.4 Challenges and Contradictions of Neo-communitarianism

Despite its potentially broad appeal, neo-communitarianism also faces various challenges. Foremost among possible challenges are serious doubts as to whether this accumulation model can work in an era of globalization. Lechevalier (2014) has argued that the post-war model in and of itself was not characterized by systemic contradictions that led to the crisis of the 1990s, and that it was precisely the neoliberal turn away from that model beginning in the 1980s that was the root cause of the crisis. However, as this book has shown (particularly in Chapter Five) I am much less sanguine about the viability of this model under changing structural conditions, particularly considering the enormous fiscal costs to the state that this model already produced in an era of relatively smaller societal needs for welfare. Given the extent to which public debt has grown and population aging has progressed since the 1990s, fiscal and demographic conditions of the 2020s will be even worse than those of the 1990s and 2000s, and thus only sharpen the contradictions between the post-war model and the challenges facing contemporary society. Simply put, an already elderly society and workforce surely cannot support the lifetime employment model in the same way, while it is difficult to see how such a high number of seniors could be supported through extended family households instead of the now extensive yet highly costly public welfare supports, including pensions and eldercare services.

This therefore leads to serious doubts over how to pay for so much programming and keep all major groups satisfied, without challenging the power of capital, which remains the elephant in the room. Indeed, throughout the post-war, Japan's lean welfare model and weak extractive capacity existed less because prevailing social arrangements did not necessitate such institutions more because of capital's power relative to labour. Beyond the fiscal balance sheet, a return to the past would also entail potential for conflict over women's roles in society, and there would certainly be a strong backlash if women were encouraged to return to roles as wives and mothers, rather than offered new opportunities to pursue careers in public life. With women who work outside of the home – even those with young children – now the social norm, Japanese society has transformed significantly since the 1990s in this regard and is unlikely to go back.

4 Counter-hegemony and a Democratic Socialist Future

The final model for Japan in the 21st century is one that appears at face value to be the least likely in the immediate future, but perhaps one that could become increasingly likely as the social, political, economic and ecological contradictions of capitalism sharpen, both within Japan and globally. Occupying the lower left quadrant in Figure 3, and incorporating progressive social policies mixed with progressive economic policies, this is the social democratic, or democratic socialist future. However, while all four projects discussed in this chapter are characterized by internal variegation, I want to make a particular point of discussing two varieties of this model – first, social democracy and second, democratic socialism – and clarifying their differences. Both socialism and social democracy value economic equality and support active state intervention to promote equality. However, they differ in a very important way on the question of whether to directly challenge (and surmount) the power of capital, or whether to leave it intact and ameliorate its negative effects through policy. This distinction reflects how Nancy Fraser (1995, 1997) has theorized the distinction between transformative redistribution (democratic socialism) that seeks to transform power relations in the economy on one hand, and affirmative redistribution (social democracy), that tries to redistribute revenues from capitalist economies while affirming the power dynamics that underlie them on the other.

In the case of Japan, between one quarter and one third of the electorate voted for socialists from both the JSP and JCP from 1960 until 1990, while social democratic policies were advocated by the smaller DSP and arguably Kōmeitō. Yet since the JSP's decline that began in the 1990s, this number has fallen dramatically, to around 10 percent support for the JCP. In contrast, social democracy received greater policy penetration in the 1990s and

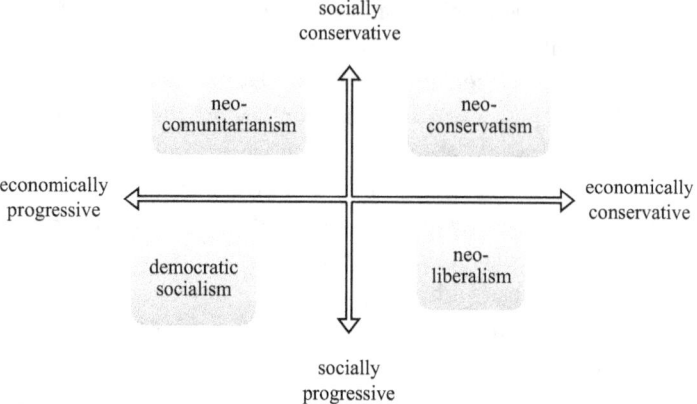

FIGURE 3   A political compass of the four ideal type future scenarios of Japanese ruling regimes

represented the position of the left wing of the DPJ (which was affiliated with the Japanese Federation of Trade Unions), a tendency that has been carried over into its more left-leaning successor party, the Constitutional Democratic Party (CDP) that formed out of the DPJ's implosion prior to the 2017 election. With even the more centrist DPJ (and CDP) a virtual electoral irrelevancy since 2012 (see Figure 2 above) it is clear that the electoral basis of support for democratic socialism, and even social democracy, has been in decline since the 1990s.

4.1   Overview

What policies would characterize a social democratic, or democratic socialist program? First, economic policy would be oriented towards activist intervention in the economy to promote equality, social stability, and environmental protection. Such a program would call for the strengthening of protections for workers, consumers and the environment, among other things. While a social democratic program would push for reregulation and an increase in the above protections, a democratic socialist program would also include bolder efforts to challenge the power of capital, including through the nationalization of industries, likely starting with the transport and energy sectors. However, more important than this would be efforts to encourage community economies, empowering democratic control and management at the local level, including through existing groups, such as the consumer cooperatives and *seikatsusha* networks that have formed an important part of progressive social movements since the 1990s (Avenell 2010).

Social policy would seek to promote equality and human rights for all people, including women, ethnic minorities, disabled people and the LGBTQ community. Social policy would thus be geared around principles of feminism, multiculturalism, and pacifism, while eschewing nationalism, militarism and traditional hierarchies. While all these characteristics are important, it is perhaps the explicit commitment to feminism and a reordering of society away from its current (and deeply entrenched) patriarchal structures that is of most significance. Not only because of the extent of women's disempowerment and exclusion from politics but also because of the depth of Japan's crisis of social reproduction, it is impossible to imagine a socialist project succeeding in Japan without being explicitly feminist. Based therefore on its commitment to social justice on a wide range of issues, a socialist program would also favor constitutional revision to guarantee strengthened rights for workers, women, sexual and ethnic minorities, as well as environmental and social rights. A mirror image of the militarist vision of constitutional revision proposed by neo-conservatives, socialists would seek to strengthen the constitutional commitment to pacifism and nuclear disarmament.

In contrast to the largely US-focused foreign policy of the other programs, socialist foreign policy would be geared around multilateralism, neutrality and pacifism, ending the alliance with the US while pursuing closer ties with all countries, including in Asia, Africa and Latin America. Under such a scenario, Japan would pursue socially just trading relations instead of free trade and look to play a much larger role in world affairs, albeit on completely different terms than until now. This foreign policy approach would involve a major pivot away from the Anpo. Yet in other ways it would retain Japan's strong post-war commitment to multilateralism and the UN, which Japan would likely try to support even more and reorient in a direction more closely concerned with global social and environmental justice. Rather than seeking alliance with other G7 countries, then, Japan would seek to engage in greater dialogue and cooperation among the developing and post-colonial countries that comprise the majority of members in the UN General Assembly. Such a foreign policy may include calls for a radical overhaul or repeal of the UN Security Council and the veto power enjoyed by the five nuclear powers. While Japan could strengthen its own monetary contributions to development through ODA, it might also seek to institute a broader global compact on development designed to enlist Northern countries (and their corporations) in a program of green, participatory democratic development in the Global South.

Borrowing from the welfare policies pursued in the post-war era in Scandinavian countries, welfare policy would likely involve a robust expansion of public welfare provisions, amounting to a cradle-to-the-grave set of universal programs, including paid parental leave, free daycare, free education from pre-school through to university, free health care and moves to strengthen public pensions. Employment protections for workers and an end to precarious work would also be pursued,[7] along with measures that further strengthen workers' rights regardless of gender, race, or sexual orientation. In addition, measures to reduce the *"petit bourgeois"* elements of Japan's health care system, by challenging the power of doctors and encouraging community and publicly controlled health and welfare provisioning, and more general efforts to curtail or outright end private education, either by nationalizing private providers or by regulating them to ensure that no functional qualitative difference exists between public and private programs, could also be pursued.

In contrast to the insular policies of neo-conservative and neo-communitarian programs, socialist immigration policy would involve a more open policy geared at welcoming people from around the world to Japan. However, unlike under the neoliberal model, immigrants would be accepted not solely based on their ability to contribute to capital accumulation in Japan but equally for their ability to enrich Japanese society and culture. A socialist or social democratic immigration policy would also seek to admit more refugees to Japan, particularly in the context of growing ecological crisis stemming from climate change around the world.

Finally, democratic socialist fiscal policy would involve greatly increased taxes for corporations and the wealthy in order to pay for robust welfare state expansions. Given the dire fiscal situation facing Japan already, it is unclear whether reductions in existing consumption taxes would be viable immediately, but their replacement with a full slate of progressive taxes would likely be a long-term fiscal goal.

4.2 Relations of Force behind Democratic Socialism

What social forces would support a democratic socialist or social democratic program? To begin, such a program is the only one of the three that enjoys zero support from the LDP. Within the bureaucracy, there is also relatively little basis for support for truly left-wing policies.[8] Yet while a social

---

7 In other words, mandating that all workers are treated as regular employees.
8 At the same time, the Ministry of Health, Labour and Welfare has often aligned itself with social democratic notions of welfare and sometimes developed proposals that more strongly reflected the interests of labour unions (such as Sōhyō, Dōmei and Rengō) than those of business (and the Keidanren in particular) at *shingikai* deliberative councils, suggesting that

democratic program is the only one of the four proposed here that would be comprehensively opposed by the LDP, two potential options exist for support among Japan's parties. On one hand, a social democratic model could enjoy support from the left wing of the former DPJ, which currently corresponds to the CDP, while also receiving passive support from the JCP and the tiny SDP. On the other hand, a more robust socialist program would be far too radical for the CDP but would cohere reasonably well with the program of the JCP. The JCP has consistently been one of Japan's four major political forces throughout the post-war era, generally obtaining around ten percent of the vote at elections and maintaining a committed and loyal membership (with a widely circulated party newspaper, *Akahata*). Yet under Japan's electoral system, this never translates into more than a handful of seats, and the JCP's national exposure is thus minimal (even if the degree of its support, in terms of intensity as much as extensity, is not far from the DPJ/CDP and Kōmeitō).

Outside of state and party institutions, a socialist program could potentially enjoy support from certain segments of organized labour, as well as more loosely from unorganized sectors of the working class, including working women and precarious workers. While mainstream unions would be more amenable to a social democratic option (if even that), more radical unions, including those affiliated with the JCP, would likely support a more radical socialist option. Other than the working class, however, a left project would have little traction – and would likely face hostility – from the *petit bourgeoisie* and – needless to say – from the capitalist class as well.

Beyond these class forces, academic intellectuals from political science, sociology, and other social sciences – at least those on the left – would serve as an important group of organic intellectuals to a left-wing movement, much as how foreign policy hawks from IR would serve as neo-conservative organic intellectuals, or mainstream economists might serve as neoliberal organic intellectuals. To these organic intellectuals we can add movement intellectuals from a myriad of non-governmental organizations and civil society groups, including environmental groups, women's groups, the peace movement, LGBTQ rights groups, and consumer cooperatives.

However, while all these forces would be instrumental in advancing a democratic socialist or social democratic project, by far the most significant – certainly from a numerical perspective – would be the support obtained from women. Even today, women continue to be virtually excluded from politics,

---

MHLW bureaucrats could be supportive of at least a moderately social democratic model (Estevez-Abe 2008).

largely absent from top leadership and cabinet positions within the LDP. Indeed, in the LDP leadership elections of 2018 and 2020, prominent female lawmakers were not able to run because they could not find enough male colleagues to nominate them. This has led to an increasing outspokenness of even conservative female lawmakers such as Inada Tomomi and Noda Seiko. This political exclusion, combined with women's economic exclusion and the enormous burden of undervalued domestic labor placed on women's shoulders, demonstrates the incompatibility between Japan's existing political order and conditions necessary for women's political, economic and social liberation, an incompatibility that is largely shared among the other three projects discussed here.[9] While gaining widespread support from women would be no easy task, given the systemic disempowerment they already face it is difficult to imagine a socialist project succeeding without placing women's leadership as a central facet and women's emancipation as a central goal.

Needless to say, socialism or social democracy would face staunch opposition from both capital and from nationalist conservatives, while likely facing resistance from other elements of the bureaucracy as well. Indeed, there are good reasons why it has received so little recognition or support and faced so much suppression until now. The political barriers to its popularization remain enormous and must not be discounted. However, we can nonetheless envision a scenario where a left project mobilized the relations of force necessary to seize power. To do so, a process of intellectual and moral reform, and what Gramsci called a war of position, would first be required. Organic intellectuals, left parties, unions and more than anything, left wing NGOs must be the starting point of this effort to build a Japanese post-modern prince, much as how Gill (2000) has theorized the role of social movement organizations as the starting point for a global post-modern Prince.

4.3 *The Democratic Socialist Solution to Organic Crisis*

Insofar as these barriers to success could be overcome and relations of force necessary for a successful counter-hegemonic socialist project

---

9   While the neo-conservative project relies on women's exclusion from political and economic life (without doing much to alleviate the burden of social reproduction) and is the most anti-feminist of the three, neoliberalism would also be problematic by abandoning public welfare functions and placing the burden of social reproduction fully on women's shoulders, despite equal demands for their paid labour. Neo-communitarianism, though in some ways resolving the problems relating to social reproduction evident in neo-conservatism and neoliberalism, would nonetheless imply a return to the gendered division of labor that relied on cultural and legal barriers to women's participation in politics and the paid economy.

established – admittedly a task of seismic proportions for the Japanese left – how would such a project seek to solve Japan's organic crisis? First, conditions for political legitimation – in order words, consent to ruling relations – would be restored both materially and ideationally. Materially, this would occur by bringing economic and social security to the working and middle classes, thus enabling the vast majority of people to live under conditions of freedom from want and insecurity. Ideationally, the creation of a new national ethos geared around solidarity, human rights, and principles of equality and justice would buttress conditions for the democratic legitimacy of Japan's newfound hegemonic order.

Second, conditions for social reproduction would be restored through the creation of robust welfare institutions that guarantee stability and security for all people. Such a program would seek to promote work-life balance while giving all people the time and financial ability to live freely and have the number of children that they desire (which would amount to around two per woman based on surveys). Labour shortages would also be filled through a more open immigration policy, though not one geared around a logic of economic calculability over the utility of immigrant labour. On the contrary, immigration policy would seek to welcome people from a range of backgrounds for the cultural and social enrichment they provide to Japanese society, as well as a commitment to social justice globally and concomitant willingness to welcome people seeking refuge in Japan.

Finally, under a social democratic scenario, conditions for capital accumulation could be restored only insofar as capital accepted the ethical basis for a social democratic Japan and identified it with their long-term interests, a notion that – however unlikely in the context of four decades of neoliberalism globally – could emerge from attempts to strike a renewed class compromise through some variety of green global Keynesianism. At the same time, social democracy could have benefits for capital, given that robust welfare institutions ensure a well-educated, secure and healthy workforce capable of dedicating attention and energy to work, though these benefits are less applicable to Japanese investments abroad than to Japanese and foreign capital that invest in Japan. Ultimately and in the long term, restoring conditions for social reproduction, while also encouraging women's full participation in the workforce, are in the interests of capital, and this is the only scenario that seeks to do both things.

4.4 *Challenges and Contradictions of Democratic Socialism*

However effective it might be in solving Japan's organic crisis, socialism faces significant questions relating to its viability, both in seizing power and in maintaining it. First, is it possible to directly challenge the power of capital and not pay a significant, or even prohibitive cost politically? Would Japan be immune from a capital strike or capital flight? While in past decades institutional barriers to the flow of capital across borders combined with the loyalty of Japanese capital and capitalists to the national economy may have provided a safeguard against these risks, in an era of neoliberal globalization it is hard to imagine that this would still be the case. Second, how would the bureaucracy support or at least allow such a program to be advanced? Even if a left movement was able to win elections, what would it take to transform a powerful and resistant bureaucracy without running into problems far worse than the DPJ did in 2009, when it tried to reform the bureaucracy in a fairly modest fashion? Third, how could the *petit bourgeoisie* possibly be brought onboard to such a project? Social democratic projects in the past, such as that of Sweden, have sometimes sought to forge a compromise between labour and capital that isolates the *petit bourgeoisie* from power (Steinmo 2010). However, while this might gain partial support from capital and purge the economy of inefficient sectors, it would be politically risky in the case of Japan, where small businesses and farmers continue to have a high degree of public legitimacy and political influence. Conversely, courting the *petit bourgeoisie* into a counter-hegemonic coalition while isolating capital would be economically dangerous, bringing a return to the fiscal problems of the communitarian model (through the lavish supports for the *petit bourgeoisie* that such a move would entail) while simultaneously requiring heavy welfare state spending, and without the support of capital.

More fundamentally, as many have pointed out, there are contradictions in social democratic attempts to pursue economic and social policies that undermine conditions for capital accumulation, even if only in the short term, and empower labour politically whilst at the same time shying away from outright class struggle and attempts to challenge the power of capital in a meaningful way. Social democratic policies are therefore likely to run into trouble this way, just as the post-war Keynesian class compromise ultimately ran into contradictions that brought about its own unraveling and the rise of neoliberalism in the 1980s. In contrast, democratic socialist policies that seek to explicitly challenge the power of capital do not face this contradiction, but face a far greater political challenge, given their radical nature, while also being forced to deal with the question of how economies will be reordered to meet social needs if not under capitalist relations of production. Indeed, the complicated legacy of actually existing socialisms forces us to ask how, without the power of capital, economic relations would otherwise be ordered to ensure that the social and economic benefits that capital accumulation itself provides for hegemonic order (and thus for consensual political relations) can be maintained under an alternative system.

Along with these domestic political obstacles, democratic socialism would face enormous global political obstacles. These include staunch opposition from other capitalist states (most notably the US) and global institutions of neoliberalism such as the World Bank and IMF, not to mention the risk of capital flight (by both foreign and domestic capital) and other barriers socialism faces from the structural power of capital (Gill and Law 1989). In all these ways, then the social democratic or democratic socialist vision faces monumental challenges politically, even if it potentially offers the most compelling vision of a long-term solution to the organic crisis, at least in theory.

5   Conclusion

Overall, based on the scenarios presented in this chapter, what conclusion can we draw about where Japan is headed? For one thing, all these scenarios face enormous challenges. While the neo-conservative option is the closest to the status quo, it is likely to face challenges and see its contradictions deepen. Neo-conservatism combines pro-business economic policy with conservative and nationalistic social policies, relying on nationalism to shore up ideological support. Yet it is hard to see how social reproductive requirements could be fulfilled without some migrant workers, which leads to further contradictions with the nationalist ideology, especially since growing insecurity and class tensions accompany this model. In contrast, the neo-liberal option might be the second most likely in the short term, given the support it enjoys from leading forces within the incumbent historic bloc, in particular Japanese (and foreign) capital and economic segments of the bureaucracy. Indeed, compared to the neo-conservative program, neoliberalism might have stronger prospects as a solution to the crisis of capital accumulation. Nonetheless, it faces even greater barriers to succeeding politically. Though the neoliberal scenario provides a clear pathway to restored accumulation while bringing in immigrants to fill labour shortages, it faces the risk of encountering class or ethnic tensions due to the conditions of insecurity it is likely to bring to many people. If these tensions are class-based, they could potentially lead to socialist transformation, while if they are ethnic-based, they could lead to neo-conservatism or nationalist populism.

The other two potential pathways are, for completely different reasons, clearly less likely in the immediate term. The neo-communitarian model invokes nostalgia for many but because it is unviable fiscally in the context of economic globalization and Japan's now elderly society it is likely impossible to return to now. Indeed, the model's post-war success was contingent on specific underlying structural conditions that are very different from those that exist in the present world. While the neo-communitarian model would provide greater security and could potentially restore social reproduction (especially if it is combined with modest increases of migrant workers or immigrants) it is hard to see how it could generate capital accumulation or be fiscally sustainable given recent dynamics of globalization and demographic transformation. For that reason, it remains the least likely scenario. In contrast, as a project that seeks to be truly participatory, democratic and represent the foundational interests of the majority of working-class Japanese, democratic socialism provides the greatest potential for restoring conditions for widespread democratic legitimacy and stable and progressive forms of social reproduction but faces tremendous political barriers from virtually all established sources of power within Japanese society. Moreover, such a movement faces key questions of strategy regarding whether it would be worthwhile to try to pursue this option as a reformist social democracy or as a revolutionary socialist approach that does not try to cooperate with capital.

Ultimately, we must remember that these four scenarios are ideal types. They may be advocated in their pure forms, or in hybrid forms that attempt to make up for the contradictions of one with elements of another. This type of hybridization has already been manifested before, including in how Koizumi tried to combine militarist and nationalist overtures to conservatives with a program of neoliberal economic policy, how the DPJ initially sought to marry neoliberal deregulation with social democratic welfare policies, and how the Abe government tried to combine neo-conservative security policies with a mix of neoliberal and Keynesian economic and social policies. Therefore, it is likely that in practice, further attempts to resolve the crisis will involve similar attempts to combine elements of these four programs, though it is unclear whether any such combination will provide a permanent solution to the crisis.

CHAPTER 9

Conclusion

This chapter seeks to do three things in providing a set of concluding remarks to the book as a whole. First, it examines a number of central and general themes and dynamics that span across multiple chapters. Thus, rather than returning to a summary of each chapter, it seeks to analyze the overarching themes explored over the scope of the entire book. To that end, it will consider the broad sweep of post-war Japanese political economy by contemplating in turn each of the three conditions for hegemonic order discussed in the third chapter: political legitimation, capital accumulation and social reproduction, observing how overarching conditions relating to each of these requirements for hegemonic order have shifted over the course of the post-war era. Second, and building on this analysis of the Japanese case, it considers a number of overarching theoretical implications of the argument as a whole, particularly focusing on the relationship between hegemony and crisis, and the contradictions between conditions conducive to capital accumulation, political legitimation and social reproduction under capitalism. Third, it presents some of wider theoretical implications of the Gramscian approach developed throughout the book, while calling for the development of a wider research program in Gramscian political economy.

1   Conditions for Hegemonic Order: Political Legitimation

Beginning with the first of three conditions for stable hegemonic order developed in Chapter Three, we can see how dynamics of political legitimation affected the hegemonic order overall in various ways. First, as Chapter Four showed, the post-war electoral and party system, which was characterized by a multi-member district electoral system and a party system anchored around competition between a unified conservative party (the LDP) and a divided left opposition, not only provided structural conditions that heavily favored continuous LDP rule but also enabled an overall veneer of democratic legitimacy for the LDP and the system as a whole. This legitimacy emanated not merely from the regular holding of free and fair elections with relatively high voter turnout; it was also emboldened by the highly localized and clientelist version of politics that developed, partly as a result of the candidate-centric electoral machinery of *kōenkai,* and that facilitated a high degree of clientelist incorporation of voters into the support networks of local lawmakers. Moreover, while all parties' candidates operated *kōenkai*, only the LDP's candidates had access to public monies, which enabled them alone to make credible promises of local infrastructure spending. In addition to the advantages borne to the LDP from the electoral and party system, we must also consider the synergistic relationship between the bureaucracy and LDP lawmakers, including *zoku* lawmakers, in policy creation. The division of labour between these two forces combined long-term national interest policies developed by the developmentalist section of the bureaucracy that served the interests of the capitalist economy as a whole with politically popular, locally-tailored infrastructure spending developed by individual lawmakers in concert with the Construction State sections of the bureaucracy that brought in LDP votes while also helping to ensure the continued vitality of the *petit bourgeoisie*, a vital LDP constituency.

However, these stable and favorable conditions ultimately proved to be temporary. As Chapter Five argued, beginning in the 1970s, elements of this system began to experience cracks that undermined its political legitimacy and therefore that of the LDP as well. While the *kōenkai* system, and the clientelist politics it fueled may have been highly beneficial to the LDP, it ultimately came to be extremely costly. Over the years, the costs of running *kōenkai* grew, more due to the pressures of intraparty competition than by competition with the JSP, JCP and Kōmeitō. In the process, so too did the risks of corruption, given the tacit assumption that the corporations and organizations (including Nōkyō) funding *kōenkai* would receive payment in kind in return for their contributions. This was manifest in a number of explosive scandals, including most notably the Recruit-Cosmos, Sagawa Kyūbin and Lockheed scandals, each of which sullied the image of politicians in Japan and eventually pushed the door open to change. Moreover, this system, and the clientelist infrastructure spending it required, became increasingly costly. Spending grew steadily in the 1970s, just as Japan's GDP growth rate declined, prompting the onset of a structural deficit. Thus, by the 1980s, the system that had once been the basis for LDP hegemony was now a structural factor behind endemic corruption and inefficient and unaffordable public spending. These dynamics not only undermined political legitimation but also stood increasingly at odds with the interests of capital.

As discussed in Chapter Six, by the 1990s these contradictions had accumulated to the point of sending the system into a crisis. The first signs of this crisis came with the LDP's 1989 Upper House election loss to the JSP. The real push came with the breakaway of the JRP and Sakigake and the subsequent formation of an anti-LDP coalition government in 1993. This coalition government was highly unstable and short-lived but succeeded in passing electoral and campaign financing reform. While these measures were expected to eliminate LDP factions, *zoku* lawmakers, *kōenkai* and corruption more generally, twenty-five years on, the results appear mixed. Moreover, in hindsight the electoral and campaign finance systems were not the only problems with Japan's political system. Indeed, while the LDP returned to power by 1996, the next two major LDP leaders – Hashimoto and Koizumi – each ran on agendas of political reform. Hashimoto's reforms were designed to decisively shift power from the bureaucracy to the Prime Minister and Cabinet, further eliminating structural pressures for clientelist politics and making the system more accountable. Similarly, Koizumi tried to break the LDP from within, crushing the power of *zoku* lawmakers by removing their access to pork-barrel funds through the privatization of the Japan Post Bank. However, despite this apparent resolution to the political crisis, the next three leaders post-Koizumi displayed the same weakness and ineptitude as those of the past. As a result, in 2007 the LDP lost the Upper House election before failing to prevent or swiftly respond to the worst recession of the postwar period in 2008.[1] Then in 2009 it was dramatically swept from power in a landslide election loss to the DPJ. Yet even the DPJ proved incapable of solving the problems of Japan's system, picking a fight with the bureaucracy that it later backed down from before being swept from power in 2012 as dramatically as it had swept to power just three years earlier.

Turning to Chapter Seven and the discussion of the tenure of Abe Shinzō, who succeeded in becoming Japan's longest serving Prime Minister before resigning in 2020, we must ask how Abe addressed the crisis of political legitimacy facing Japan? To that end, political dynamics under Abe were characterized by three main tendencies. First, under Abe the LDP won six consecutive elections with nearly two thirds of total seats, suggesting a categorical return to electoral dominance. Yet these electoral wins came with less than half of the share of the electorate that supported the LDP in the 1960s and were mostly due to the LDP's coalition with Kōmeitō and the lack of unity and coherence of the opposition. Second, Abe won back support from both within and outside of the party through what Gramsci (1992) saw as a Caesarist political strategy that promised to "break the deadlock" of the past twenty years through a bold mix of Keynesian, neoliberal and social democratic policies. Though this program ultimately failed to deliver, it was integral to restoring public trust and optimism initially and thus bringing the LDP back to power. Third, Abe was

---

1 A crisis for which, in fairness, the LDP's long-term neoliberal policies were more to blame than the set of emergency measures they took to address the economic crash immediately after it hit in 2007–8.

effective in exerting control over forces that challenged his power. This included both the State Secrets Act, which put a damper on press critical of the government and the revision of the Civil Service Act, which enabled Abe to do what the DPJ failed to do in gaining control over the bureaucracy by centralizing administrative power in the hands of the *kantei*. In contrast to his Caesarist economic and social policies, Abe's administrative and security policies thus stayed true to his original conservative and even soft authoritarian impulses and can be understood as examples of what Gramsci called passive revolution. Yet while they may have succeeded in stifling opposition to the LDP and Abe – whether from the media, bureaucracy or opposition – they did so at the expense of liberal democracy in Japan, further undermining rather than restoring the basis for the LDP's political legitimacy (at least as a "liberal democratic" party) in the long run. Such moves might work in creating what Jessop (1983) has termed a "two nation hegemony" where conservatives, nationalists, revisionists and LDP sycophants are represented but everyone else is silenced, but this would be very different from the "one nation hegemony" discussed in Chapter Four that existed until the 1990s.

Looking to the future, then, as Chapter Eight argued, we can predict that efforts to restore conditions for political legitimation will be various. Indeed, these will likely range from calls to push for a neoliberal pluralism based on personal responsibility, an emphasis on a truly democratic, pluralist pacifism via the social democratic model, a deepening of neo-conservative nationalism *a la* Abe, and a return to the golden age of clientelism and personal network-based support. However, all these projects face challenges politically and potentially suffer from contradictions of their own.

2   Conditions for Hegemonic Order: Capital Accumulation

We can also see how dynamics of capital accumulation impacted the post-war hegemonic order in varying ways over time. Again, as explored in Chapter Four, Japan of the 1950s and 1960s experienced unprecedented, sustained and stable growth, not only in GDP but also in real wages and labour productivity, while income and wealth disparities declined. While many factors account for this success, I argued that four, in particular, were of note. First, there was the favorable international context. This not only included the benefits of the US-Japan security alliance (Anpo), which ensured Japanese security under the American nuclear umbrella, guaranteed a stable and amicable trading relationship with the US and allowed the Japanese state to divert attention away from foreign policy and towards economic and industrial policy. It also included the post-war global political economic order of embedded liberalism, which combined a liberal trading order with domestically rooted, Fordist economies and strongly complemented the Japanese industrial policy of export-oriented developmentalism. Second, as Johnson (1982), Okimoto (1989) and others have discussed in greater detail, there was the Japanese model of developmentalist industrial policy, whereby state intervention was used to promote infant industries, maximizing export competitiveness. Third, the *keiretsu* system further served as the basis for stable, trust-based relations among firms (and between firms and the state), providing another anchor for the high degree of stability that accompanied rapid growth. Finally, Japan's labour regime of lifetime employment, the seniority wage system and enterprise unionism served as the backbone for a highly productive and docile workforce, at least while the average worker was still young.

However, as discussed in Chapter Five, changing structural conditions posed new challenges for Japan's regime of accumulation, forcing adjustment by both the state and capital. Internationally, these changes included the end of the Dollar-Gold standard and the wider decline of the embedded liberal system as well as the two oil shocks. These structural changes led to mounting trade frictions with the US and eventually the Plaza Accord, which played a role in the development of the bubble economy in the late 1980s. In response, the state, particularly under Nakasone, made major policy adjustments to enable Japanese capital to benefit from globalization, including through various neoliberal measures aimed at financial and trade liberalization, labour market deregulation and privatization. Japanese firms, for their part, sought to maximize the benefits of an increasingly deregulated (or more precisely, liberalized) global economic order. Japanese corporations developed transnationalized accumulation strategies that included significant outflows of capital into production facilities in both low-wage production zones in Asia[2] and the lucrative (and increasingly insecure) American export market, while also introducing novel production techniques such as the "Just In Time" production of Toyota in order to increase competitiveness in world markets. While all these market-expanding dynamics ensured that Japanese capital could benefit from the 1980s' economic globalization, they also led to heightened volatility and insecurity as labour and capital alike were increasingly exposed to the vagaries of market forces.

Out of these conditions of volatility and insecurity, as Chapter Six argued, the turn to the Heisei era in 1989 brought an abrupt end to the speculative real

---

2 Here (and below) I use Asia as shorthand for East and Southeast Asian developing countries other than China, including South Korea, Taiwan, Hong Kong, Singapore, Thailand, Malaysia and Indonesia.

estate and asset bubble and ushered in a period of prolonged economic crisis and stagnation. While interpretations of the causes of this prolonged crisis vary, I have argued, following Gramsci's (1992) understanding of the organic and conjunctural, that it can best be explained by considering a range of both organic and conjunctural dynamics that undermined conditions for capital accumulation. At the conjunctural level, the speculative bubble had led to a high volume of debt held by banks that became bad debt after the stock market crashed. Indeed, it took until the early 2000s for this bad debt problem to finally be resolved. Later on, hopes of recovery were dashed by Japan's entanglement in global economic crises, including the 1997 Asian Financial Crisis and the 2008 Global Financial Crisis, which were exacerbated by Japanese capital's growing integration with global markets and the enduring frailty of the Japanese economy more generally. Yet these conjunctural dynamics were overshadowed by a range of organic conditions that prevented any escape from the crisis despite numerous reform measures and extensive (debt-funded) recovery packages. These include the increasing outflow of Japanese capital away from the domestic economy and towards Asia and later China, decreased consumer spending and debt deflation driven partly by growing poverty, economic precariousness and labour market deregulation; and population aging, which turned many of the advantages of Japan's lifetime employment system into disadvantages. Overall, while the period of the 1990s and 2000s saw many large Japanese firms continue to be competitive in a range of industries, under conditions of globalization the strength of Japanese capital was increasingly disconnected from the frailty of the Japanese domestic economy.

In the context of this prolonged organic crisis, Chapter Seven considered how Prime Minister Abe Shinzō tried to solve the crisis through his Abenomics agenda, a rhetorically bold program based on a mix of neoliberal and Keynesian economic policies as well as ostensibly progressive social policies that I have framed as an example of Caesarism. However, while Abenomics' inflation-targeting monetary policy and corporate tax cuts were successful in spurring a stock market boom in its first few years, Abenomics ultimately failed to live up to expectations. Neither inflation nor GDP growth targets were met, and perhaps most significantly the frailty of the Japanese economy led Abe to postpone a consumption tax hike on two occasions (before finally implementing it in 2019), leading the public debt to grow further even as GDP growth remained near zero. While Abe pushed for a range of labour market reforms, including those aimed at bringing more women into the workforce as well as a major increase in the admission of migrant workers, the majority of these jobs have been in low-paying and insecure sectors of the economy. This has meant that despite labour shortages (due to population aging and decline), real wages remained stagnant, and the share of economic output that went to workers declined. Abe's own goal of a permanent economic recovery driven by a virtuous cycle of increased consumer spending leading to increased investment (and in turn to further wage increases) thus failed to materialize even before the economy was derailed by the 2020 COVID-19 pandemic and the worst recession of the postwar era.

Finally, looking ahead to the future post-Abe, Chapter Eight suggested that efforts to restore conditions for capital accumulation will be fought over between three main visions for society. Leading the charge, and already in the drivers' seat for most of the past twenty years, are more market-friendly approaches, whether neoliberal or neo-conservative, which seek to make Japanese capital more competitive globally, whatever the effects for workers and small businesses likely to be displaced in the process. However, competing with this program is a long-standing force within the LDP's coalition: the neo-communitarian approach and its attachment to the interests of small businesses, even if they can only be defended through market-restricting measures. Alternatively, though currently a highly disfavoured position, coming decades may see a rise of more labour-centric approaches to political economy, which may include social-democratic or Keynesian measures to restore conditions for economic growth by boosting demand. Finally, lurking just beyond the horizon of our imaginations, the prospects for a more radical socialist project that calls for an abandonment of the prioritization of capital accumulation altogether in favor of other means of achieving conditions of material security and a high quality of life for the majority of people can never be dismissed, at least as long as we retain some element of Gramsci's "optimism of the will."

3 Conditions for Hegemonic Order: Social Reproduction

Along with these long-term trends in dynamics relating to the maintenance of conditions of political legitimation and capital accumulation, we can also see the various ways through which dynamics of social reproduction affected hegemonic order. As discussed in Chapter Four, the post-war regime of social reproduction was rooted in what Miura (2012) has called the gender dual system, which involved a rigid division between stable male breadwinners and female housewives who also filled gaps in the economy under temporary, insecure, and low-paying conditions. Moreover, this regime of social reproduction also included a welfare regime that involved minimalist explicit welfare programming on one hand, and extensive policies geared at maintaining full male employment on the other, which generally included generous corporate welfare provisions. A third condition of Japan's regime of social reproduction was the persistence of extended family households, with three generations living under one roof, which placed the burden of eldercare on households (and usually on women), excusing the state from having to invest heavily in pension and care programs. A final condition of this regime of social reproduction lay at the level of culture and society, whereby a new variety of nationalism combined a commitment to pacifism with a continued attachment to Japan as a homogenous ethno-nation (and thus excluded ethnic minorities from the national community). Overall, though this regime of social reproduction was rigid, highly restrictive to both women and men and exclusionary for some citizens, especially single women and minorities, it provided conditions for stable and secure social reproduction without a significant cost to the state. The fertility rate remained high enough to ensure a sizeable workforce, while the lack of welfare spending enabled the state to prioritize industrial policy and as well as policies aimed at curbing underdevelopment in the countryside.

However, this regime of social reproduction started to face challenges beginning in the 1970s, particularly as prevailing structural economic and demographic conditions necessary for it began to shift. As Chapter Five showed, in the 1970s Japan's population started aging rapidly, while urbanization and the rise of individualistic cultural attitudes drove a shift away from extended family households. At the same time, as gender norms slowly started to change, more women entered the workforce, challenging the basis for a model of reproduction that relied more heavily on women's unpaid domestic labour rather than public provisioning of a range of services. In this context, the period beginning in the early 1970s saw a significant shift towards increased welfare spending, particularly on pensions. However, in the context of declining economic growth these spending increases prompted the onset of a fiscal deficit. Unwilling to introduce unpopular tax increases to restore a fiscal balance, the LDP of the 1980s halted welfare spending increases under the slogan of "fiscal consolidation without tax increases." While this approach proved immediately popular (and fit well with the increasingly ascendant global neoliberal paradigm), it ultimately proved to be a missed opportunity to adapt Japan's regime of social reproduction to the demographic and economic changes that were poised to come.

By the 1990s, these (largely predictable) demographic changes began to accelerate, just as the state was forced to deal with not only the post-bubble economic crisis but also the political crisis brought on by the Recruit Cosmos and Sagawa Kyūbin scandals. As Chapter Six argued, the 1990s saw a rapid decline in the fertility rate, due as much to the declining economic conditions as to the lack of a safety valve in Japan's regime of social reproduction.

Indeed, childrearing was still thought of as a private domain and measures to address it remained inadequate (Osawa 2013). While women continued to enter the workforce both by choice and by necessity, they lacked supports to help them balance family and work, and many forewent the former out of necessity (Schoppa 2006). During this period, insecurity and poverty markedly increased due to neoliberal labour market deregulation, structural changes in the economy and the decline of lifetime employment. Moreover, population aging continued to place a burden on the state and economy, and depressed economic conditions and neoliberal policies led to increased social insecurity that exacerbated the demographic crisis. While a number of measures were introduced to provide piecemeal supports to families, these proved to be woefully inadequate, and the fiscal crisis of the state and depressed economic conditions more generally precluded a more comprehensive solution to the crisis of social reproduction. Furthermore, while the decline in the fertility rate during the 1990s was not unique to Japan, and occurred in several European countries as well, Japan's enduring cultural nationalism and ideology of ethnic homogeneity precluded any serious consideration of immigration as a solution to the mounting demographic crisis.[3]

In the context of these crisis conditions for Japan's regime of social reproduction, Chapter Seven showed how Abe tried to solve the crisis through a range of policies aimed at promoting women in the workforce, increasing daycare spaces, and even admitting migrant workers in order to alleviate the extreme labour shortage. However, while the government has been effective in creating new daycare spaces and facilities, it has failed to meet its targets for the elimination of wait lists. Moreover, while a record proportion of Japanese women now work outside the home (even passing the US in 2018), most of the new jobs created for women workers have been insecure and low-paying, and targets for the appointment of women to top positions in the private sector have been significantly underperformed. However, perhaps the biggest limitation of all has been the lack of significant increase in Japan's fertility rate, which, at 1.39 in 2020, was even lower than below Abe took office. Even the government's bold new migrant worker program, in its current form, cannot be a permanent

---

3 While automation and robotics are often touted as possible solutions to the chronic labour shortage, it is important to remember that despite centuries of ongoing labour saving technological innovation since the beginning of the Industrial Revolution, more people today are employed in the capitalist economy than ever before in history. If all hitherto labour saving technological innovations have only served to increase the demand for human labour on aggregate, there is little reason to expect that emerging technologies will do anything to reverse this basic dynamic of capitalism.

solution to the labour shortage, since most of the migrant workers admitted through the program face legal obstacles to permanent settlement, and only permanent immigrants can provide a solution to the demographic crisis in the long term. In all these ways, it is clear that Abe's social policies ultimately failed to resolve Japan's crisis of social reproduction.

Looking ahead to the prospects for social reproduction in post-Abe Japan, Chapter Eight considered what future attempts to solve the crisis of social reproduction might involve. It argued that these attempts will vary between neo-communitarian, neo-conservative, neo-liberal and social democratic approaches. The neo-communitarian, and to some extent the neo-conservative approach as well, seek to restore the old, gendered division of labour through a return to active (male-oriented) employment maintenance programs on one hand and policies that incentivize women's roles as mothers (and secondarily as part-time workers) on the other. In contrast, neoliberal solutions to the crisis of social reproduction imply further efforts to mirror Japanese society after those of the neoliberal heartland in the US, Canada and Britain. In that sense they seek to erase the ethnic nationalist discourse and replace it with a hegemonic discourse of personal responsibility (*jiko sekinin*) for economic security and life chances. At the same time, the neoliberal project sees immigration as a means of furnishing capital with unbridled access to cheap labour at domestically, solving the labour shortage if not wider socio-cultural elements of Japan's crisis of social reproduction, including many of the dynamics of growing social isolation and *anomie* experienced by increasing numbers of people. Finally, a fourth vision for the solution to Japan's crisis of social reproduction is characterized by a social democratic or democratic socialist project that is unapologetically feminist. Such a project would place at its core the restoration and expansion of welfare institutions, social and community supports so that all people have the livelihood security needed to start families and so that women (and men) can comfortably balance the responsibilities of family and work. It would also eschew ethnic nationalism for a more pluralist and solidaristic ethos that emphasizes the dignity and uniqueness of all people, while encouraging immigration, less for the benefits that accrue to corporations and more for the cultural enrichment that people of diverse backgrounds might bring to Japanese society.

While this section has thus far examined these three dynamics – capital accumulation, political legitimation, and social reproduction – in isolation, we must also consider how these three dynamics interact dialectically. In that regard, we can see how while initially reproduction, accumulation and legitimation were maintained in complementary ways, beginning in the 1970s we began to see contradictions among them due to structural, institutional and policy changes. Attempts to resolve flagging conditions in one area only led to more problems in another, and by the 1990s all three became dysfunctional. In particular, by the 2000s there was a vicious cycle between reproduction and accumulation. While poor accumulation conditions (such as depressed GDP growth) led to declining reproduction dynamics (including the sharp decline in the birth rate), attempts to restore conditions for profitable accumulation, through neoliberal deregulation in particular, proved futile partly because they only served to exacerbate the crisis of social reproduction, thus undermining conditions for stable accumulation in the long-term. At the same time, attempts to restore conditions for stable social reproduction were largely avoided as they would have involved high costs to capital, undermining conditions for profitable accumulation. As a result, the crisis lurched forward, only temporary deferred through growing public debt.

4 Overarching Theoretical Implications of the Argument

The above section has provided an overarching review of the ways in which dynamics relating to the three major requirements for stable hegemonic order – political legitimation, capital accumulation and social reproduction – have changed over the course post-war Japan. In light of these findings, what general conclusions can we make about the nature of hegemonic order, its contradictions and its relationship with organic crisis in capitalist societies? At its best, a capitalist hegemonic order can maintain all three of these things at the same time – though perhaps not for very long. Economic growth and capitalist profitability are fundamentally necessary conditions for capitalism in general. Moreover, as O'Connor (2003) has argued, capital accumulation is not only necessary for the capitalist class to maintain their power but also for the state to maintain its legitimacy, as the capitalist state requires economic growth to generate tax revenue necessary for all its functions. Similarly, social reproduction is necessary for the long-term viability of the system, as without an adequate labor force, both in quantity and quality, capital accumulation is impossible. Political legitimacy is of course necessary to ensure conditions necessary for capital accumulation over the long term: the threat of revolution or serious resistance to the established economic order significantly undermines conditions of credibility, consistency and confidence necessary for capital to invest (Bakker and Gill 2003a).

When some, but not all, of these three conditions can be maintained, there may appear contradictions within the system and the potential for a crisis. However, it is important to note that while an economic or political crisis is immediate and pressing in its consequences for hegemonic order, a crisis of social reproduction occurs over a much longer time frame, or it may be compressed into one or two generations. It may display what Gramsci (1992) termed "morbid symptoms" (276) in the interim, while the most acute effects of the crisis might not occur for a generation. An abrupt decline in economic growth or political legitimacy is thus already a crisis situation and a real danger to hegemonic order. In contrast, a temporary increase in inequality or a dysfunction of social reproduction mechanisms is more likely to manifest beneath the surface, with its negative socio-economic effects postponed temporally and hidden behind women's unpaid and paid social reproductive labour. Either way, we use the term conjunctural crisis to refer to the first type of crises that occur on relatively short time horizons. In some cases, a conjunctural crisis can be easily rectified without opening new contradictions. For example, a crisis of economic accumulation can be solved without the solution itself causing a crisis of social reproduction. The Keynesian model of counter-cyclical fiscal policy was designed to achieve this. However, in many cases, the solution to one conjunctural crisis will structurally necessitate the onset of another in a different area; in this case the crisis is not solved but merely displaced. The most common way is for an economic crisis of over-production or political legitimation to be solved through policies that themselves lead to crises of reproduction or legitimation.

When most, or all, of these conditions become dysfunctional simultaneously, we can observe conditions of organic crisis: an economic, demographic social, political and even cultural crisis with no easy solution. In this situation, not only do solutions to any single element of the crisis usually lead to a deepening of contradictions impacting other elements of the crisis, the solutions themselves may be largely ineffective given how deep the crisis is and how the centrifugal forces behind various elements of the crises coalesce. For example, with a combined crisis of capital accumulation and crisis of social reproduction, a solution to the crisis of accumulation might be to further deregulate conditions for labor while making corporate tax cuts in order to shore up conditions for profitable accumulation. But these pro-capital measures will only further exacerbate the crisis of reproduction by undermining the livelihood security experienced by workers and the fiscal capacity of the state to fund social programs. The ensuing crisis of social reproduction then might dampen consumer spending, business confidence, and investment, leading to a renewed market downturn. In this way, we can see the complex dialectical relationship between the various requirements of hegemonic order.

Overall, then, contemporary Japan's organic crisis has appeared intractable thus far because of how its various dimensions overlap in complex ways, while attempts to address each element have only exacerbated other elements of the crisis. However, we must understand Japan's organic crisis as fundamentally a crisis of a capitalist society and of an economic system inherently beset by contradictions that can ultimately only be displaced but never completely transcended (see also Federici 2012). While some of the capitalist programs to solve the organic crisis (whether neo-liberal, neo-conservative, or social democratic) may succeed in temporarily displacing elements of the crisis, it is unlikely that a permanent, lasting solution is possible under capitalism. For this reason, it is only the democratic socialist option, which offers a qualitative break from the capitalist basis for Japanese political economy entirely, that offers a permanent solution to the conditions of crisis and contradiction facing Japanese society.

5 Towards a Gramscian Political Economy of Modern States

While this book should be thought of primarily as a contribution to the field of Japanese political economy, I have tried to write it not only as a study of post-war Japan but also as a rigorous (though at times generous) application of many of the key theoretical concepts developed by Antonio Gramsci, and thus in a way that is relevant to wider discussions within critical and Gramscian political economy outside Japan. Indeed, Gramsci's theory is of critical importance to the analysis of this book for several reasons. First, as the leading theorist of hegemony, Gramsci's thought enables us to understand the dialectical relationship between coercion and consent, and thus more widely between politics and culture. Gramsci's expanded understanding of hegemony has long been useful for explaining the persistence of support for class-based systems of authority even in an era of liberal democracy and mass politics, and is perhaps even more relevant today, in the context of deepening crisis and renewed populism around the world.

Second, Gramsci's understanding of hegemony also enables us to explore the contradictory relationship between capitalist regimes of economic accumulation and political ruling regimes, and how within liberal democracy patterns of capital accumulation must serve to reproduce class-based rule while ensuring conditions necessary for political legitimacy. Third, Gramsci's dialectical understanding of the relationality both between consent and coercion and more abstractly between economy, politics, society, culture and religion is not only a crucial starting point for understanding conditions necessary for hegemony, but also for theorizing conditions of crisis through the lens of organic crisis. Thus, and as this study of Japan has shown, while hegemonic order is dependent on the concurrent maintenance of conditions necessary for economic accumulation and political (and thus cultural) legitimacy, organic crises such Japan's are manifest as a concatenation of various economic, political, social and cultural contradictions.

Finally, the theoretical framework developed here to explore conditions of hegemony and crisis in post-war Japan may also be a useful point of departure for those studying conditions of hegemony and crisis in other countries, as many of underlying structural dynamics and contradictions inherent in Japanese political economy and society are not unique to Japan. Indeed, my hope is that this book will not only serve to inspire wider interest in contemporary Japanese political economy and society, but that it will also facilitate the development of a wider debate over conditions of hegemony and organic crisis in other industrialized countries, and that out of that debate a twenty-first century "philosophy of praxis" may emerge. No doubt, in an era of deepening organic crisis around the world, such an effort is of increasing urgency to ensure that this generation's organic crisis does not lead to the same fate that befell Gramsci's generation.

Bibliography

Abegglen, J. (1958) *The Japanese factory*. Glencoe, IL: Free Press.

Akashi, J. (2014) New aspects of Japan's immigration policies: Is population decline opening the doors? *Contemporary Japan, 26*(2), 175–196.

Anchordoguy, M. (2005) *Reprogramming Japan: The high tech crisis under communitarian capitalism*. Ithaca, NY: Cornell University Press.

Asahi Shimbun [Asahi] (2018a) Concerns rise over Abe's 'hasty' push to overhaul Broadcast Law. *The Asahi Shimbun*. (Date accessed: 19/3/2019).

Asahi Shimbun [Asahi] (2018b) Abe seeks to remove 'balance' requirements in broadcast news. *The Asahi Shimbun*. (Date accessed: 19/3/2019).

Asahi Shimbun [Asahi] (2019) Taiki jidō mondai "mieruka" purojekuto. *Asahi Shimbun*. (Date accessed: 22/3/19). Available at: http://www.asahi.com/special/taikijido/.

Asao, Y. (2011) Overview of non-regular employment in Japan. In The Japan Institute for Labour Policy and Training (Eds.) *Non-regular employment – Issues and challenges common to the major developed countries: 2011 JILPT Seminar on non-regular employment*, 1–42.

Avenell, S. A. (2010) *Making Japanese citizens: Civil society and the mythology of the shimin in postwar Japan*. Berkeley, CA: University of California Press.

Babb, J. (2005) Making farmers conservative: Japanese land reform and socialism. *Social Science Japan Journal, 8*(2), 175–195.

Baehr, P. (1999) An 'ancient' sense of politics? Weber, Caesarism and the republican tradition. *European Journal of Sociology, 40*(2), 333–350.

Bakker, I. (2007) Social reproduction and the constitution of a gendered political economy. *New Political Economy, 12*(4), 541–556.

Bakker, I. (2003) Neo-liberal governance and the reprivatization of social reproduction: social provisioning and shifting gender orders. In I. Bakker and S. Gill (Eds.) *Power, production and social reproduction: Human in/security in the global political economy*. Basingstoke, UK: Palgrave Macmillan, 66–79.

Bakker, I. and S. Gill (2003a) Global political economy and social reproduction. In I. Bakker and S. Gill (Ed.) *Power, production and social reproduction: Human in/security in the global political economy*. Basingstoke, UK: Palgrave Macmillan, 3–16.

Bakker, I. and S. Gill (2003b) Ontology, method and hypotheses. In I. Bakker and S. Gill (Ed.) *Power, production and social reproduction: Human in/security in the global political economy*. Basingstoke, UK: Palgrave Macmillan, 17–46.

Bakker, I. and R. Silvey (Eds.) (2008) *Beyond states and markets: The challenges of social reproduction*. London: Routledge.

Bamkin, S. (2018) Reforms to strengthen moral education in Japan: A preliminary analysis of implementation in schools. *Contemporary Japan, 30*(1), 78–96.

Barrett, M. (1988) *Women's oppression today: The Marxist/feminist encounter.* London: Verso.

Befu, H (2009) Concepts of Japan, Japanese Culture and the Japanese. In Y. Sugimoto (Ed.) *The Cambridge companion to modern Japanese culture.* Cambridge, UK: Cambridge University Press.

Befu, H. (2001) *Hegemony of homogeneity: An anthropological analysis of nihonjinron.* Melbourne: Trans Pacific Press.

Befu, H. (1993) Nationalism and nihonjinron. In H. Befu (Ed.) *Cultural nationalism in East Asia: Representation and identity.* Berkeley, CA: Institute of East Asian Studies, University of California at Berkeley, 107–135.

Berggren, C. (1995) Japan as number two: Competitive problems and the future of alliance capitalism after the burst of the bubble boom. *Work, Employment & Society,* 9(1), 53–95.

Biglobe (2019) *Rekidai NHK Taiga dorama: Shichōritsu suii gurafu.* (Date accessed: 6/9/2019). Available at: http://www7b.biglobe.ne.jp/~yama88/taiga.html.

Bloomberg (2014) Gohsn to top executive pay scale again. *The Japan Times.* (Date accessed: 4/4/2019). Available at: https://www.japantimes.co.jp/news/2014/06/24/business/corporate-business/ghosn-top-executive-pay-scale/#.XKWkpWQzZz-.

Blumenthal, T. (1985) The practice of amakudari within the Japanese employment system. *Asian Survey,* 25(3), 310–321.

Boyer, R. (2014) Foreword: From 'Japanophilia' to indifference? Three decades of research on contemporary Japan. In S. Lechevalier (Ed.) *The great transformation of Japanese capitalism.* New York: Routledge, Japan Series, xiii–xxxv.

Braudel, F. (1980) "History and the social sciences: The *longue durée*". In *On history.* Chicago, IL: University of Chicago Press, 25–54.

Brenner, N.; J. Peck and N. Theodore (2010) Variegated neoliberalization: Geographies, modalities, pathways. *Global Networks,* 10(2), 182–222.

Burrett, T. (2017) Abe Road: Comparing Japanese Prime Minister Shinzo Abe's leadership of his first and second governments. *Parliamentary Affairs,* 70, 400–429.

Cabinet Office, Government of Japan [CAO] (2018) Dai-isshō: Shōshika taisaku wo meguru genjō. *Sōshika shakai taisaku hakusho: Gaiyōhan.* (Date accessed: 4/4/2019). Available at: https://www8.cao.go.jp/shoushi/shoushika/whitepaper/measures/w-2018/30pdfgaiyoh/pdf/s1-1.pdf.

Cabinet Office, Government of Japan [CAO] (2016) Shakai hoshō kyūfuhi no suii tō. *Jimukyoku shiryō: Shōshikōreika – shakai hoshō.* (Date accessed: 6/9/2019). Available at: https://www5.cao.go.jp/keizai-shimon/kaigi/special/2030tf/281020/shiryou1_2.pdf.

Cabinet Office, Government of Japan [CAO] (2015) Shiryō 1–2 zaimushō teishutsu shiryō III: Kōkyō jigyō kankei hi no hōkōsei. *Hi shakai hoshō wākingu gurūpu: Dai-yonkai kaigi shiryō*. (Date accessed: 4/4/2019). Available at: https://www5.cao.go.jp/keizai-shimon/kaigi/special/reform/wg2/271028/shiryou1-2-3.pdf.

Cabinet Office, Government of Japan [CAO] (2012) Kōrei shakai taisaku setsumei 2/4. *Heisei 24 nendo kōrei shakai fōramu hōkokusho*. (Date accessed: 4/4/2019). Available at: https://www8.cao.go.jp/kourei/kou-kei/24forum/pdf/tokyo-s3-2.pdf.

Cabinet Office, Government of Japan [CAO] (2006) Kosodate katei wo torimaku jōkyō to kazoku wo meguru henka. *Dai-goshō: Shakai zentai no ishiki kaikaku*. (Date accessed: 11/10/2018). Available at: https://www8.cao.go.jp/shoushi/shoushika/whitepaper/measures/w-2006/18webhonpen/html/i1511110.html.

Calder, K. (2013) Beyond Fukushima: Japan's emerging energy and environmental challenges. *Orbis, 57*(3), 438–452.

Carroll, M. (2019) From nationalist communitarianism to fragmentary neoliberalism: Japan's crisis of social reproduction. *Capital & Class, 43*(4), 637–652.

Carroll, M. (2018) Production, reproduction and crisis in Heisei Japan. *The Japanese Political Economy, 42*(1–4), 53–71.

Cerny, P. (2005) Capturing benefits, avoiding losses: The United States, Japan, and the politics of constraint. In G. Menz, P. Cerny and S. Soederberg (Eds.), *Internalizing globalization: The rise of neoliberalism and the decline of national varieties of capitalism*. Basingstoke, UK: Palgrave Macmillan, 123–148.

Chapman, W. (1978) Japanese politician is implicated in Lockheed scandal. *Washington Post*. (Date accessed: 6/8/2019). Available at: https://www.washingtonpost.com/archive/politics/1978/10/27/japanese-politician-is-implicated-in-lockheed-scandal/083c07f2-f72e-4aa2-8a18-c59b01643152.

Chiang, H. and Ohtake, F. (2014) Performance-pay and the gender wage gap in Japan. *Journal of the Japanese and International Economies, 34*, 71–88.

Chiavacci, D. and S. Lechevalier (2017) Japanese political economy revisited: diverse corporate change, institutional transformation, and Abenomics. *Japan Forum, 29*(3), 299–311.

Cowling, K. and Tomlinson, P. (2011) The Japanese model in retrospective: Industrial strategies, corporate Japan and the 'hollowing out' of Japanese industry. *Policy Studies, 32*(6), 569–583.

Cox, R. (1987) *Production, power and world order: Social forces in the making of history*. New York: Columbia University Press.

Cox, R. (1996) *Approaches to world order*. Cambridge, UK: Cambridge University Press.

Cox, R. (1992) Multilateralism and world order. *Review of International Studies, 18*(2), 161–180.

Curtis, G. (1999) *The logic of Japanese politics: Leaders, institutions and the limits of change*. New York: Columbia University Press.

Curtis, G. (1988) *The Japanese way of politics*. New York: Columbia University Press.

Dalton, E. (2017) Womenomics, 'equality' and Abe's neo-liberal strategy to make Japanese women shine. *Social Science Japan Journal, 20*(1), 95–105.

Dian, M. (2015) Interpreting Japan's contested memory: Conservative and progressive traditions. *International Relations, 29*(3), 363–377.

Dobson, H. (2017) Is Japan really back? The "Abe Doctrine" and global governance. *Journal of Contemporary Asia, 47*(2), 199–224.

Dore, R. (1986) F*lexible rigidities: industrial policy and structural adjustment in the Japanese economy, 1970–1980*. London, UK: Athlone Press.

Du Bois, C. (2019) The two prices of soy. *History Today 69*(5). (Date accessed: 6/8/2019). Available at: https://www.historytoday.com/archive/behind-times/two-prices-soy.

Easley, L. (2017) How proactive? How pacifist? Charting Japan's evolving defense posture. *Australian Journal of International Affairs, 71*(1), 63–87.

Economic Planning Agency [EPA] (1981) *Nenji keizai hōkoku: Nihon keizai no sōzōteki katsuryoku wo motomete*. (Date accessed: 6/9/2019). Available at: https://www5.cao.go.jp/keizai3/keizaiwp/wp-je81/wp-je81–02401.html.

The Economist (2015) Speak no evil: Japan's media are quailing under government pressure. *The Economist*. (Date accessed: 19/3/2019). Available at: https://www.economist.com/asia/2015/05/14/speak-no-evil.

Envall, H. (2011) Abe's fall: Leadership and expectations in Japanese politics. *Asian Journal of Political Science, 19*(1), 149–169.

Esping-Andersen, G. (1990) *The three worlds of welfare capitalism*. Cambridge, UK: Polity Press.

Estevez-Abe, M. (2008) *Welfare and capitalism in post-war Japan*. New York: Cambridge University Press.

Evron, Y. (2017) China – Japan interaction in the Middle East: A battleground of Japan's remilitarization. *The Pacific Review, 30*(2), 188–204.

Facker, M. (2015) Effort by Japan to stifle news media is working. *New York Times*. (Date accessed: 19/3/2019). Available at: https://www.nytimes.com/2015/04/27/world/asia/in-japan-bid-to-stifle-media-is-working.html.

Facker, M. (2016) The silencing of Japan's free press. *Foreign Policy*. (Date accessed: 3/19/2019). Available at: https://foreignpolicy.com/2016/05/27/the-silencing-of-japans-free-press-shinzo-abe-media/.

Federici, S. (2012) *Revolution at point zero: Housework, reproduction, and the feminist struggle*. Oakland, CA: PM Press.

Feldhoff, T. (2017) Japan's electoral geography and agricultural policy making: The rural vote and prevailing issues of proportional misrepresentation. *Journal of Rural Studies, 55*, 131–142.

Flath, D. (2000) *The Japanese economy*. Oxford, UK: Oxford University Press.

Fraser, N. (1995) From redistribution to recognition? Dilemmas of justice in a 'post-socialist' age. *New Left Review, 1/212*, 68–93.

Fraser, N. (1997) *Justice Interruptus: Critical reflections on the "post-socialist" condition.* London: Routledge.

Fukuoka, K. (2018) Japanese history textbook controversy at a crossroads?: Joint history research, politicization of textbook adoption process, and apology fatigue in Japan. *Global Change, Peace & Security, 30*(3), 313–334.

Fuse, K. (2013) Daughter preference in Japan: A reflection of gender role attitudes? *Demographic Research, 28*(1), 1021–1052.

Gao, B. (2001) *Japan's economic dilemma: The institutional origins of prosperity and stagnation.* Cambridge: Cambridge University Press.

Gender Equality Bureau Cabinet Office [GEB] (2016) I − 2 − 1 zu: josei no nenrei kaikyū betsu rōdōryoku ritsu no suii. (Date accessed: 22/3/2019). Available at: http://www.gender.go.jp/about_danjo/whitepaper/h27/zentai/html/zuhyo/zuhyo01-02-01.html.

Gereffi, G., Humphrey, J. and Sturgeon, T. (2005) The governance of global value chains. *Review of International Political Economy, 12*(1), 78–104.

Germann, J. (2014) Capital-driven? The fall of Bretton Woods and the currency float reconsidered. *New Political Economy, 19*(5), 769–789.

Gill, S. (2012) Towards a radical concept of praxis: Imperial 'common sense' versus the post-modern prince. *Millennium – Journal of International Studies, 40*(3), 505–524.

Gill, S. (2008) *Power and resistance in the new world order* (2nd edition). Basingstoke, UK: Palgrave Macmillan.

Gill, S. (2000) Toward a postmodern prince? The battle in Seattle as a moment in the new politics of globalization. *Millennium – Journal of International Studies, 29*(1), 131–140.

Gill, S. (1998) New constitutionalism, democratization and global political economy. *Pacifica Review, 10*(1), 23–38.

Gill, S. (1993) Epistemology, ontology and the "Italian School." In S. Gill (Ed.) *Gramsci, historical materialism and international relations.* Cambridge, UK: Cambridge University Press, 21–48.

Gill, S. and D. Law (1989) Global hegemony and the structural power of capital. *International Studies Quarterly, 33*(4), 475–99.

Gordon, A. (2003) *A modern history of Japan: From Tokugawa times to the present.* Oxford, UK: Oxford University Press.

Gotoh, F. and T. Sinclair (2017) Social norms strike back: Why American financial practices failed in Japan. *Review of International Political Economy, 26*(6), 1030–1051.

Gottfried, H. (2015) *The reproductive bargain: Deciphering the enigma of Japanese capitalism.* Leiden: Brill.

Gottfried, H. (2008) Pathways to economic security: Gender and nonstandard employment in contemporary Japan. *Social Indicators Research, 88*(1), 179–196.

Gramsci, A. (1992) *Prison notebooks.* J. A. Buttigieg (Ed.), Trans. J. A. Buttigieg and A. Callari. New York: Columbia Press.

Grbic, D. (2007) The source, structure, and stability of control over Japan's financial sector. *Social Science Research,* 36(2), 469–90.

Grimes, W. (2012) Japan's fiscal challenge: The political economy of reform. In B. Youngshik and T. J. Pempel (Eds.) *Japan in crisis: What will it take for Japan to rise again?* New York: Palgrave Macmillan, 81–103.

Grimes, W. (2001) *Unmaking the Japanese miracle: Macroeconomic politics 1985–2000.* Ithaca: Cornell University Press.

Hacker, J.; P. Pierson and T. Thelen (2015) Drift and conversion: Hidden faces of institutional change. In J. Mahoney and K. Thelen (Eds.) *Advances in comparative-historical analysis.* Cambridge, UK: Cambridge University Press, 180–208.

Haeber, J. (2007) Japan's palace grounds once more valuable than California. *CBS News.* (Date accessed: 19/11/2019). Available at: https://www.cbsnews.com/news/japans-palace-grounds-once-more-valuable-than-california/.

Hall, D. (2009) Pollution export as state and corporate strategy: Japan in the 1970s. *Review of International Political Economy,* 16(2), 260–283.

Hall, P. and Soskice, D. (2001) *Varieties of capitalism: The institutional foundations of comparative advantage.* Oxford, UK: Oxford University Press.

Hamaguchi, K. (2015) A welcome revision of the Worker Dispatch Act. *Nippon.com.* (Date accessed: 22/3/2019). Available at: https://www.nippon.com/en/currents/d00203/a-welcome-revision-of-the-worker-dispatch-act.html.

Hanochi, S. (2003) Constitutionalism in a modern patriarchal state: Japan, the sex sector and social reproduction. In I. Bakker and S. Gill (Eds.) *Power, production and social reproduction: Human in/security in the global political economy.* Basingstoke, UK: Palgrave Macmillan, 83–97.

Harada, Y. (1999) *Nihon no ushinawareta junen: Shippai no honshitsu, fukkatsu e no senryaku.* Tokyo: Nihon Keizai Shinbunsha.

Harvey, D. (1996) *Justice, nature and the geography of difference.* Malden, MA: Blackwell Publishers.

Hasegawa, N., H. Kim and Y. Yasuda (2017) The adoption of stock option plans and their effects on firm performance during Japan's period of corporate governance reform. *Journal of the Japanese and International Economies,* 44, 13–25.

Hashimoto, K. (2001) *Class structure in contemporary Japan.* Melbourne: Trans Pacific Press.

Hayakawa, H. (2015) *Abenomikusu shin 'sanbon no ya:' so no haikei to imi* [Abenomics' new three arrows: Background and meaning]. *Fujitsu Research Institute,* 10 November 2015. (Date accessed: 16 December 2015). Available at: http://www.fujitsu.com/jp/group/fri/column/opinion/201511/2015-11-1.html.

Hayes, J. and Kawaguchi, H. (2015) Economics, culture, and electoral reform: The case of Japanese agricultural trade negotiations. *The Japanese Political Economy*, 41(3–4), 80–111.

Heino, B. (2020) A modern day Caesar? Donald Trump and American Caesarism. *Journal of Historical Sociology*, forthcoming. https://doi.org/10.1111/johs.12280.

HighCharts (2019) "Shuyō nanasha" konbini no kokunai tenposū suii wo gurafuka (1983~) *HighCharts FreQuent*. (Date accessed: 26/9/2019). Available at: http://frequ2156.blog.fc2.com/blog-entry-106.html.

Honma, M. and Hayami, Y. (1988) In search of agricultural policy reform in Japan. *European Review of Agricultural Economics*, 15(4), 367–395.

Hook, G; Gilson, J., Hughes, C. and Dobson, H. (2011) *Japan's international relations: Politics, economics and security*. London: Routledge.

Hook, G. (2005) Japan's role in the east Asian political economy. In G. Hook and H. Hasegawa (Eds.) *The political economy of Japanese globalization*. London: Routledge, 38–51.

Hosono, Y. (2011) Nihon Firipin keizai renkei kyotei wo tsujita kangoshi kaigoshi ukeire kosho katei. *Yokohama kokusai shakaikagaku kenkyu*, 15(5), 67–89.

Hutchison, M. (1993) Structural change and the macroeconomic effects of oil shocks: Empirical evidence from the United States and Japan. *Journal of International Money and Finance*, 12, 587–606.

Ikeda, S. (2011) *Gendai nihon seijishi 2: Dokuritsu kansei no kutō, 1952–1960*. Tokyo: Yoshikawa Kōbunkan.

Immigration Bureau of Japan [IBJ] (2018) Points-based system for highly skilled foreign professionals. (Date accessed: 4/10/2018). Available at: http://www.immi-moj.go.jp/newimmiact_3/en/system/index.html.

Ishihara, S. (1991) *The Japan that can say no: Why Japan will be first among equals*. Trans. F. Baldwin. New York: Simon & Schuster.

Itoh, M. (1990) *The world economic crisis and Japanese capitalism*. London: Palgrave Macmillan.

Itoh, M. (1992) The Japanese model of post-Fordism. In M. Storper and A. Scott (Eds.) *Pathways to industrialization and regional development*. London: Routledge, 102–120.

Itoh, M. (2000) *The Japanese economy reconsidered*. Basingstoke, UK: Houndmills.

Japan Institute for Labour Policy and Training [JIL] (2016) Labor situation in Japan and its analysis: General overview 2015/2016. *Japan Institute for Labour Policy and Training*. (Date accessed: 2/4/2019). Available at: https://www.jil.go.jp/english/lsj/general/2015-2016/2015-2016.pdf.

Japan Times (2013) Mr. Abe stacking the deck at NHK. *The Japan Times*. (Date accessed: 19/3/2019). Available at: https://www.japantimes.co.jp/opinion/2013/11/06/editorials/mr-abe-stacking-the-deck-at-nhk/#.XJCPMGQzZuU.

Japan Times (2015) Abe's new package lacks roadmap. *Japan Times (Editorial)*, 1 December 2015. (Date accessed: 16 December 2016). Available at: http://www.japantimes.co.jp/opinion/2015/12/01/editorials/abes-new-package-lacks-road-map/#.VnLvqNCdLzJ.

Japan Times (2017) The Kake and Moritomo scandals and the bureaucracy. *Japan Times*. (Date accessed: 1/4/2019). Available at: https://www.japantimes.co.jp/opinion/2017/10/20/editorials/kake-moritomo-scandals-bureaucracy/#.XKHG4GQzZz8.

Japan Tourism Board (JTB) (2019) Japanese outbound tourist statistics. *JTB Tourism Research and Consulting Co.* (Date accessed: 18/9/2019). Available at: https://www.tourism.jp/en/tourism-database/stats/outbound/.

Jayasuriya, K. (2018) Authoritarian statism and the new right in Asia's conservative democracies. *Journal of Contemporary Asia*, 48(4), 584–604.

Jeong, D. and R. Aguilera (2008) The evolution of enterprise unionism in Japan: A socio-political perspective. *British Journal of Industrial Relations*, 46(1), 98–132.

Jessop, B. (2012) "Marxist approaches to power." In E. Amenta; K. Nash and A. Scott (Eds.) *The Wiley-Blackwell companion to political sociology*. Oxford, UK: Blackwell, 3–14.

Jessop, B. (1983) Accumulation Strategies, State Forms and Hegemonic Projects, *Kapitalistate*, 10–11, 89–111.

Johnson, C. (1995) *Japan: Who governs? The rise of the developmental state.* New York: Norton Press.

Johnson, C. (1982) *miti and the Japanese miracle: The growth of industrial policy, 1925–1975.* Stanford, CA: Stanford University Press.

Jun, J. and H. Muto (1998) The politics of administrative reform in Japan: More strategies, less progress. *International Review of Administrative Sciences*, 64, 195–202.

Kameyama, Y. (2017) *Climate change policy in Japan: From the 1980s to 2015.* London: Routledge.

Kamikawa, R. (2016) The failure of the Democratic Party of Japan: The negative effects of the predominant party system. *Social Science Japan Journal*, 19(1), 33–58.

Kaneshiro, K. (1998) Kindai nihon ni okeru kazoku kōzō no hen'yō. *Okinawa Daigaku Kiyō Dai 15 Gō*. (Date accessed: 13/8/2021). Available at: http://okinawa-repo.lib.u-ryukyu.ac.jp/bitstream/20.500.12001/5849/1/No15p249.pdf.

Kantei (2013) Todōfuken betsu shōrai suikei jinkō (kōserōdōshō teishutsu shiryō). *Shakai hoshō seido kaikaku suishin honbu.* (Date accessed: 4/4/2019). Available at: https://www.kantei.go.jp/jp/singi/shakaihoshoukaikaku/wg_dai2/siryou4.pdf.

Katada, S. (2013) Financial crisis fatigue? Politics behind Japan's post-global financial crisis economic contraction. *Japanese Journal of Political Science*, 14(2), 223–242.

Kato, S. (2018) Balancing political leadership and bureaucratic autonomy: Scandals highlight the need for a correction. *The Tokyo Foundation for Policy Research*. (Date accessed: 1/4/2019). Available at: https://www.tkfd.or.jp/en/research/detail.php?id=25.

Katz, R. (1998) *Japan, the system that soured and the rise and fall of the Japanese economic miracle*. Armonk, NY: M. E. Sharpe.

Kawai, Y. 2009. "Neoliberalism, nationalism, and intercultural communication: A critical analysis of Japan's neoliberal nationalism discourse under globalization." *Journal of International and Intercultural Communication*, 2(1): 16–43.

Kay, M. (1996) Toys "R"Us Japan and the global toy business. *Nanzan Review of American Studies*, 18, 89–99.

Kerbo, H. R. and J. A. McKinstry (1995) *Who rules Japan? The inner circles of economic and political power*. Westport, CT: Praeger.

Khilji, F. (2015) Whither Mr. Abe's Japan? *Asian Affairs*, 46(3), 424–457.

Kingston, J. (2019) Revisionists' meddling backfires. *Critical Asian Studies*, 51(3), 437–450.

Kitaoka, S. (2013) The Abe administration: Beyond 100 days. *Asia-Pacific Review*, 20(1), 1–12.

Koike, O. (1996) Seisaku tankan to kanryo no beheibia: Gaikokujin rodosha mondai wo jirei ni. *Seikei Gakkai Zasshi*, 64, 17–35.

Komine, T. (2018) A retrospective view of the Heisei economy. *Asia-Pacific Review*, 25(1), 19–37.

Komiya, R. and Wakasugi, R. (1991) Japan's foreign direct investment. *Annals of the American Association of Political and Social Science*, 508(1), 48–61.

Koyama, K. (2013) Japan's post-Fukushima energy policy challenges. *Asian Economic Policy Review*, 8(2), 274–293.

Krauss, E. S. and R. J. Pekkanen (2010) *The rise and fall of Japan's ldp: Political party organizations as historical institutions*. Ithaca, NY: Cornell University Press.

Krugman, P. (1998) It's baaack: Japan's slump and the return of the liquidity trap. *Brookings Papers on Economic Activity*, 2, 137–205.

Lebra, T. S. (2004) *The Japanese self in cultural logic*. Honolulu: University of Hawaii Press.

Lechevalier, S. (2014) *The great transformation of Japanese capitalism*. New York: Routledge Japan Series.

Lechevalier, S. and Monfort, B. (2018) Abenomics: Has it worked? Will it ultimately fail? *Japan Forum*, 30(2), 277–302.

Liberal Democratic Party [LDP] (n.d.a) Chapter 4: Period of President Ikeda's leadership. *A history of the Liberal Democratic Party*. (Date accessed: 9/7/2019). Available at https://www.jimin.jp/english/about-ldp/history/104281.html.

Liberal Democratic Party [LDP] (n.d.b) Chapter 6: Period of President Tanaka's leadership. *A history of the Liberal Democratic Party*. (Date accessed: 24/10/2018). Available at https://www.jimin.jp/english/about-ldp/history/104281.html.

Liddle, J. and S. Nakajima (2004) States of distinction: Gender, Japan and the international political economy. *Women's History Review*, 13(4), 521–540.

Lucarelli, B. (2015) The crisis of over-accumulation in Japan. *Journal of Contemporary Asia, 45*(2), 311–325.

Mackie, V. (2013) Gender and modernity in Japan's "long twentieth century." *Journal of Women's History, 25*(3), 62–91.

Maclean, J. (1981) Political theory, international theory, and problems of ideology. *Millennium, 10*(2), 102–125.

Mainichi (2016) Abenomikusu "minaoshi" 61% naikaku shijiritsu 7 pointo gen. *Mainichi Shimbun.* (Date accessed: 8/10/2021). Available at: https://mainichi.jp/articles/20160620/ddm/001/010/155000c.

Marx, K. and F. Engels (2008) *The manifesto of the Communist Party.* D. McLellan (Ed.). Oxford: Oxford University Press.

Marx, K. (1990) *Capital: A critique of political economy, Volume I,* Trans. Ben Fowkes. London: Penguin Books.

Marx, K. (1977) *The 18th Brumaire of Louis Bonaparte.* In D. McLellan (Ed.) *Selected writings,* New York: Oxford University Press.

Masujima, T. (2005) Administrative reform in Japan: Past developments and future trends. *International Review of Administrative Sciences, 71*(2), 295–308.

Miliband, R. (1969) *The state in capitalist society.* London: Basic Books.

Minami, R. (2008) Income distribution of Japan: Historical perspective and its implications. *Japan Labour Review, 5*(4), 5–20.

Ministry of Education, Culture, Sports, Science and Technology [MEXT] (2006) 1: School education. *Japan's education at a glance 2006.* (Date accessed: 4/4/2019). Available at: http://www.mext.go.jp/component/english/__icsFiles/afieldfile/2011/03/07/1303013_005.pdf.

Ministry of Finance [MOF] (2017) Japanese public finance fact sheet. (Date accessed: 13/8/2021). Available at: https://dl.ndl.go.jp/view/download/digidepo_11096623_po_04.pdf?contentNo=1&alternativeNo=.

Ministry of Finance [MOF] (2016) "Heisei 28 nendo kokusai kanri seisaku no gaiyou." (Date accessed: 12/12/2017). Available at http://www.mof.go.jp/jgbs/issuance_plan/fy2016/gaiyou151224.pdf.

Ministry of Finance [MOF] (n.d.) Total value of exports and imports (1950-) – Trade Stastistics Japan. *Trade Statistics of Japan – Ministry of Finance.* (Date accessed: 17/4/2019). Available at: http://www.customs.go.jp/toukei/suii/html/nenbet_e.htm.

Ministry of Health, Labour and Welfare [MHLW] (1996) Daiisshō: Sengo nihon no kazoku hendō – sengo, kazoku ha do no yō ni hen'yō shita ka. *Kōsei Hakusho Dai Ippen: Dai ichibu kazoku to shakai hoshō – kazoku no shakaiteki shien no tame ni.* (Date accessed: 22/3/2019). Available at: https://www.mhlw.go.jp/toukei_hakusho/hakusho/kousei/1996/dl/03.pdf.

Ministry of Health, Labour and Welfare [MHLW] (2010) Introduction to the revised Child Care and Family Care Leave Law. (Date accessed: 6/9/2019). Available at: https://www.mhlw.go.jp/english/policy/affairs/dl/05.pdf.

Ministry of Health, Labour and Welfare [MHLW] (2012) "Gōkei tokushu shusseiritsu ni tsuite." (Date accessed: 20/4/2017). Available at http://www.mhlw.go.jp/toukei/saikin/hw/jinkou/kakutei12/dl/14_tfr.pdf.

Ministry of Health, Labour and Welfare [MHLW] (2018a) Press release: Hoikujotō kanren jōkyō torimatome (heisei 30 nen 4 gatsu 1 nichi) kōhyōshimasu. (Date accessed: 22/3/2019). Available at: https://www.mhlw.go.jp/content/11907000/000350592.pdf.

Ministry of Health, Labour and Welfare [MHLW] (2020) Chiiki betsu saitei chingin no zenkoku ichiran. *Seisaku ni tuite*. (Date accessed: 13/8/2021). Available at: https://www.mhlw.go.jp/stf/seisakunitsuite/bunya/koyou_roudou/roudoukijun/minimu michiran/.

Ministry of Internal Affairs and Communications [MIC] (n.d.) Shiryoshu: Senkyo Seiji Shiryo. Date accessed: 10 August 2021. Available at: https://www.soumu.go.jp/sen kyo/senkyo_s/data/shugiin/ichiran.html.

Ministry of Land, Infrastructure, Transport and Tourism [MLIT] (2010) Shakai shikin seibi kankei: Sankō shiryō. *Kokudo kōtsūshō*. (Date accessed: 17/4/2019). Available at: http://www.mlit.go.jp/common/000121595.pdf.

Mishima, K. (2017) A big bang for Japanese mandarins? The civil service reform of 2014. *International Journal of Public Administration, 40*(13), 1101–1113.

Miura, M. (2012) *Welfare through work: Conservative ideas, partisan dynamics, and social protection in Japan*. Ithaca, NY: Cornell University Press.

Miyamoto, T. (2008) *Fukushi seiji: Nihon no seiji hoken to demokurashii*. Tokyo: Yuikaku.

Mizoguchi, T. and V. Ngyuen. (2012) Amakudari: The post-retirement employment of elite bureaucrats in Japan. *Journal of Public Economic Theory, 14*(5), 813–847.

Mochizuki, M. and S. Porter. (2013) Japan under Abe: Toward moderation or nationalism? *The Washington Quarterly, 36*(4), 25–41.

Mulgan, A. G. (2015) Shinzo Abe's 'glass jaw' and media muzzling in Japan. *The Diplomat*. (Date accessed: 3/19/2019). Available at: https://thediplomat.com/2015/05/shinzo-abes-glass-jaw-and-media-muzzling-in-japan/.

Mulgan, A. G. (2018) What's wrong with Japan's bureaucrats. *East Asia Forum*. (Date accessed: 1/4/2019). Available at: https://www.eastasiaforum.org/2018/05/03/whats -wrong-with-japans-bureaucrats/.

Murakami, S (2019) On Constitution Day, Abe again vows to revise Japan's top law, aiming for enactment in 2020. *Japan Times*. (Date accessed: 11/19/2019). Available at: https://www.japantimes.co.jp/news/2019/05/03/national/politics-diplomacy/constitution-day-abe-renews-pledge-enact-revised-top-law-2020-despite -resistance-diet/#.XdQPnGRKi8o.

Murakami, Y. (1996) *An anticlassical political-economic analysis: A vision for the next century*. Trans. K. Yamamura. Stanford, CA: Stanford University Press.

Murakami, Y. (1984) *Shin-chūkan Taishuu no Jidai*. Tokyo: Chūō Kōronsha.

Nakajima, T. (2011) *Gendai nihon seijishi 3: Kōdoseichō to Okinawa hensen, 1960–1972*. Tokyo: Yoshikawa Kōbunkan.

Nakakita, H. (2017) *Jimintō: "Ikkyō" no jitsugen*. Tokyo: Chūkō Shinsho.

Naver Matome (2013) *Nihon no rekidai terebi shichō: Besto 10*. (Date accessed: 6/9/2019).

Nemoto, K. (2013) Long working hours and the corporate gender divide in Japan. *Gender, Work and Organization*, 20(5), 512–527.

Nemoto, K. (2008) "Postponed marriage: Exploring women's views of matrimony and work in Japan." *Gender and Society*, 22(2): 219–237.

Nenji Toukei (2014) Kanzen shitsugyōritsu. *Nenji Toukei*. (Date accessed: 4/4/2019). Available at: https://nenji-toukei.com/n/kiji/10046/%E5%AE%8C%E5%85%A8%E5%A4%B1%E6%A5%AD%E7%8E%87.

New York Times (1973) Japanese upset by U.S. soybean ban. *New York Times*. (Date accessed: 6/8/2019). Available at: https://www.nytimes.com/1973/07/07/archives/japanese-upset-by-us-soybean-curbs-u-s-ban-on-soybean-exports-is.html#story-continues-1.

Nikkei (2015) Japanese CEO pay roughly 10% that of US counterparts. *Nikkei Asian Review*. (Date accessed: 4/4/2019). Available at: https://asia.nikkei.com/Business/Japanese-CEO-pay-roughly-10-that-of-US-counterparts.

Noble, G. (2012) Japan's economic crisis: More chronic than acute – so far. In B. Youngshik and T. J. Pempel (Eds.) *Japan in crisis: What will it take for Japan to rise again?* New York: Palgrave Macmillan, 53–80.

Noda, T. and D. Hirano (2013) Enterprise unions and downsizing in Japan before and after 1997. *Journal of the Japanese and International Economies*, 28, 91–118.

North, S. (2009) Negotiating what's 'natural': Persistent domestic gender role inequality in Japan. *Social Science Japan Journal*, 12(1), 23–44.

O'Connor, J. (2003) *The fiscal crisis of the state*. New Brunswick, NJ: Transaction Publishers.

OECD (2019) Elderly population (indicator). *OECD Data*. (Date accessed: 9/6/2019). Available at: https://data.oecd.org/pop/elderly-population.htm.

Oguma, E. (2002) *A genealogy of 'Japanese' self-images*. (Trans. D. Askew). Melbourne: Trans Pacific Press.

Okimoto, D. (1989) *Between miti and the market: Japanese industrial policy for high technology*. Stanford, CA: Stanford University Press.

Osaki, T. (2018) Japan passes controversial immigration bill paving way for foreign worker influx. *Japan Times*. (Date accessed: 27/3/2019). Available at: https://www.japantimes.co.jp/news/2018/12/07/national/politics-diplomacy/japan-set-enact-controversial-immigration-bill-paving-way-foreign-worker-influx/#.XJsseGQzZz8.

Osawa, M. (2013) *Seikatsu hoshou no gabanensu: Jendaa to okane no nagare de yomitoku* [Governance of livelihood security]. Tokyo: Yuuhihaku.

Osawa, M., M. Kim and J. Kingston. (2012) Precarious work in Japan. *American Behavioral Scientist, 57*(3), 309–334.

Park, G. and E. Ide (2014) The tax-welfare mix: Explaining Japan's weak extractive capacity. *The Pacific Review, 27*(5), 675–702.

Pempel, T. (2010) Between pork and productivity: The collapse of the Liberal Democratic Party. *Journal of Japanese Studies, 36*(2), 227–254.

Pempel, T. (1998) *Regime shift: Comparative dynamics of the Japanese political economy.* Ithaca, NY: Cornell University Press.

Pempel, T. (1982) *Policy and politics in Japan: Creative conservatism.* Philadelphia, PE: Temple University Press.

Pollack, A. (1996) Shin Kanemaru, 81, kingmaker in Japan toppled by corruption. *New York Times*. (Date accessed: 18/9/2019). Available at: https://www.nytimes.com/1996/03/29/world/shin-kanemaru-81-kingmaker-in-japan-toppled-by-corruption.html.

Posen, A. (1998) *Restoring Japan's economic growth*. Washington, DC: Institute for International Economics.

Pugliese, G. (2017) Kantei diplomacy? Japan's hybrid leadership in foreign and security policy. *The Pacific Review, 30*(2), 152–168.

Ramseyer, M. and F. Rosenbluth (1993) *Japan's political marketplace*. Cambridge, MA: Harvard University Press.

Ratherford, R.; N. Ogawa and R. Matsukura (2001) Late marriage and less marriage in Japan. *Population and Development Review, 27*(1), 65–102.

Reitan, R. (2012) Narratives of "equivalence": Neoliberalism in contemporary Japan. *Radical History Review, 112*, 43–64.

Reporters without Borders [RSF] (2018) Index details: Data of press freedom ranking 2018. *Reporters without Borders*. (Date accessed: 20/3/2019). Available at: https://rsf.org/en/ranking_table.

Revell, L. (1997) Nihonjinron: Made in USA. In P. Hammond (Ed.) *Cultural difference, media memories: Anglo-American images of Japan*. London: Cassell, 49–81.

Ritchie, H. and M. Roser (2018) Urbanization: Japan. *Our World in Data*. (Date accessed: 19/11/2019). Available at: https://ourworldindata.org/urbanization.

Rosenbluth, F. M. and M. F. Thies. (2010) *Japan transformed: Political change and economic restructuring*. Princeton: Princeton University Press.

Royle, T. and Urano, E. (2012) A new form of union organizing in Japan? Community unions and the case of the McDonald's 'McUnion'. *Work, Employment and Society, 26*(4), 606–622.

Ruggie, J. G. (1982) International regimes, transaction and change: Embedded liberalism in the postwar economic order. *Internaitnal Organization, 36*(2).

Sadoh, A. (2012) *Gendai nihon seijishi 5: "Kaikaku" seiji no konmei, 1989~*. Tokyo: Yoshikawa Kōbunkan.
Sakoh, K. (1990) Economic implications of enterprise unionism. *Journal of Labor Research*, 11(3), 257–267.
Saltzman, I. (2015) Growing pains: Neoclassical realism and Japan's security policy emancipation. *Contemporary Security Policy*, 36(3), 498–527.
Sasada, H. (2015) The "third arrow" or friendly fire? The LDP government's reform plan for the Japan agricultural cooperatives. *The Japanese Political Economy*, 41(1–2), 14–35.
Schoppa, L. (2006) *Race for the exits: The unraveling of Japan's system of social protection*. Ithaca, NY: Cornell University Press.
Schwarcz, E. (2018) Making sense of Japan's new immigration policy. *The Diplomat*. (Date accessed: 27/3/2019). Available at: https://thediplomat.com/2018/11/making-sense-of-japans-new-immigration-policy/.
Seccombe, W. (1974) The housewife and her labour under capitalism. *New Left Review*, 1/83.
Sekai Keizai (n.d.) Nihon no GDP no Suii. *Sekai Keizai no Netacho*. (Date accessed: 19 December 2016). Available at: http://ecodb.net/country/JP/imf_gdp.html.
Shibata, S. (2017) Re-packaging old policies? 'Abenomics' and the lack of an alternative growth model for Japan's political economy. *Japan Forum*, 29(3), 399–422.
Shimada, H. (2017) Abenomikusu: Daini no ya to zaisei saiken. *Huffington Post*. (Date accessed: 22/3/2019). Available at: https://www.huffingtonpost.jp/haruo-shimada/abenomics-second-arrow_b_9322686.html.
Shimotsu, K. (2014) The effect of large-scale retailers on price level: Evidence from Japanese data for 1977–1992. *RIETI Discussion Paper Series, 14-E-013*. (Date accessed: 2/4/2019). Available at: https://www.rieti.go.jp/jp/publications/dp/14e013.pdf.
Shinoda, T. (2013) *Seijishugi vs. kanryōshihai: Jiminseikenn, minshuseiken, seikan 20 nen tōsō no naimaku*. Tokyo: Asahi Shimbun Shuppan.
Shiratori, R. (1995) The politics of electoral reform in Japan. *International Political Science Review*, 16(1), 79–94.
Shire, K. (2008) Gender dimensions of the aging workforce. In F. Coulmas; H. Conrad, A; Schad-Seifert and G. Vogt (Eds.) *The demographic challenge: A handbook about Japan*. Leiden: Brill, 963–978.
Shire, K. and K. Nemoto (2020) The origins and transformations of conservative gender regimes in Germany and Japan. *Social Politics*, 27(3), 432–448.
Statistics Japan (n.d.) Chapter 2 population and households. *Statistics Japan*. (Date accessed: 27/3/2019). Available at: http://www.stat.go.jp/english/data/nenkan/1431-02.html.
Steinmo, S. (2010) *The evolution of modern states: Sweden, Japan, and the United States*. New York: Cambridge University Press.

Stockwin, J. (2006) To oppose or to appease? Parties out of power and the need for real politics in Japan. *Japan Forum, 18*(1), 115–132.

Sudo (2014) Japan weighs cutting tax break for housewives. *The Wall Street Journal: Japan Real Time*. (Date accessed: 4/10/2018). Available at: https://blogs.wsj.com/japanrealtime/2014/06/17/japan-weighs-cutting-tax-break-for-housewives.

Sugimoto, Y. (2010) *An introduction to Japanese society*. Port Melbourne, Australia: Cambridge University Press.

Takahashi, N. and K. Mizuno (2013) *Abenomikkusu ha nani wo motarasu ka*. Tokyo: Iwanami Shoten.

Takeda, H. (2005) *The political economy of reproduction in Japan: Between nation-state and everyday life*. London: Routledge.

Tanaka, K. (2010) *Shōshikōrei shakai no shakai hoshōron*. Tokyo: Chūō Hōki.

Thelen, K. (2012) Varieties of capitalism: Trajectories of liberalization and the new politics of social solidarity. *Annual Review of Political Science, 15*, 137–159.

Tiberghien, Y. (2014) Thirty years of neoliberal reforms in Japan. In S. Lechevalier (Ed.) *The great transformation of Japanese capitalism*. New York: Routledge, Japan Series, 26–55.

Tokumoto, E. (2016) Lockheed scandal 40 years on: The downfall of Prime Minister Tanaka. *Asia Times*. (Date accessed: 6/8/2019). Available at: https://www.asiatimes.com/2016/12/article/lockheed-scandal-40-years-downfall-prime-minister-kakuei-tanaka/.

Tokyo Broadcasting Corporation [TBS] (2018) Keiki kaifuku no jikkan ha aru? *JNN Yoron chōsa*. (Date accessed: 7/8/2019). Available at: https://news.tbs.co.jp/newsi_sp/yoron/backnumber/20180901/q4-1.html.

Usui, C. and R. Colignon (1995) Government elites and amakudari in Japan, 1963–1992. *Asian Survey, 35*(7), 682–698.

Van der Pijl, K. (1998) *Transnational classes and international relations*. London: Routledge.

Vogel, E. (1979) *Japan as number one: Lessons for America*. Cambridge, MA: Harvard University Press.

Vogel, L. (1983) *Marxism and the oppression of women: Toward a unitary theory*. London: Pluto Press.

Vogel, S. (2006) *Japan remodeled: How government and industry are reforming Japanese capitalism*. Ithaca, NY: Cornell University Press.

Vogel, S. (2018) Japan's labor regime in transition: Rethinking work for a shrinking generation. *The Journal of Japanese Studies, 44*(2), 257–292.

Wakatabe, M. (2015) *Japan's great stagnation and Abenomics: Lessons for the world*. Basingstoke, UK: Palgrave Macmillan.

Wakatsuki, H. (2011) *Gendai nihon seijishi 4: Daikoku nippon no seiji shidō, 1971–1989*. Tokyo: Yoshikawa Kōbunkan.

Watanabe, O. (2007) Characteristics of neoliberalism in Japan: Late start and different modality. *Japonesia Review*, 3, 8–18.

Weiss, J. (1986) Japan's post-war protection policy: Some implications for less developed countries. *Journal of Development Studies*, 22(2), 385–406.

Williams, R. (1983) "History". In *Keywords: A vocabulary of culture and society*. London, UK: Fontana Press, 146–148.

World Bank (2019) GDP growth (annual %) – Japan. (Date accessed: 19/11/2019). Available at: https://data.worldbank.org/indicator/NY.GDP.MKTP.KD.ZG?locations=JP.

World Nuclear Association [WNA] (2019) Nuclear power in Japan. (Date accessed: 26/9/2019). Available at: https://www.world-nuclear.org/information-library/country-profiles/countries-g-n/japan-nuclear-power.aspx.

Yoda, T. (2006) The rise and fall of maternal society: Gender, labor, and capital in contemporary Japan. In T. Yoda and H. Harootunian (Eds.) *Japan after Japan: Social and cultural life from the recessionary 1990s to the present*. Durham: Duke University Press, 239–274.

Index

Abe Shinzō 1, 10–11, 59–61, 140, 149, 154, 159, 176–96, 198–207, 212, 233–34, 236–37, 239–40
   administration 176, 183, 206
   Caesarism 177, 186, 196
   Keynesian policies 181, 182
   militarist agenda 189
   neoliberal reforms 183–84
   passive revolution 193
Abegglen, James 15, 21
Abe government 11, 184, 195, 199, 204, 210, 230
Abenomics 11–12, 179, 181–82, 185–86, 188, 196, 200, 236
accumulation 20, 30–32, 46, 48, 51–52, 66, 76, 202, 204, 235, 240–42
administrative reforms 120, 134, 145–47, 151, 158–59, 161, 176, 186–87, 190, 193, 218
aging society 26, 32, 115, 145
agricultural cooperatives 96 (see also Association of Japan Agriculture Cooperatives; Nōkyō)
agricultural deregulation 12
agricultural subsidies 37, 166
aikokushin 189, 204, 206
Ainu 107
amakudari 86–88, 126–27
Anchordoguy, Marie 28–29, 90–91, 129, 160, 210
Angel Plan 123, 147
Anpo 74–77, 80, 87, 113, 122, 144, 154, 223, 234 (see also US-Japan Security Treaty)
Arubaito 163
Asian Financial Crisis 24, 146, 150, 155, 236
Asō Tarō 150, 159, 205
Association of Japan Agriculture Cooperatives 95 (see also Nōkyō)
authoritarian 60, 74, 103, 190, 203, 206
   soft 186–87, 234

Bakker, Isabella 4–5, 8, 48–50, 52, 66, 72, 241
Barrett, Michele 48, 50
birth rate 36, 66, 98, 139, 173, 174, 179, 186, 214, 241

falling 135, 174
low 32, 147, 169
Boyer, Robert, 32, 92, 155, 162
Braudel, Fernand 44–45
Bretton Woods System 31, 77–79, 109, 111, 118, 136
bubble economy 10, 24, 26–27, 30, 32–33, 109, 112, 114–15, 133, 137, 141–42, 145, 154–55, 174, 215, 236
burakumin 107

Caesarism 7, 11, 43, 59–60, 176–201, 233–36
capital 17–18, 31–32, 48–49, 52–53, 66–67, 72–73, 91–93, 128, 134, 160–61, 214–15, 218, 221–22, 226–30, 235, 240–41
capital accumulation 7–8, 10, 48–52, 66–68, 70–71, 99, 105, 130, 132–33, 171–72, 180, 194, 206–7, 213–15, 219–20, 227–31, 234, 236–37, 240–43
capitalism 27, 29, 34, 40, 42, 46–50, 61–62, 71–72, 239, 241, 243
Childcare Leave Act 147
China 74–76, 103, 111, 122, 152, 154, 156, 204, 209–10, 217, 235–36
Chūritsu Rōren 93
Civil Service Act 234
civil society 3, 46, 56–57, 61, 170, 187, 195–96, 205, 208, 225
class 5, 48, 60, 64, 67, 95, 101, 176, 200
   nobility 101
   peasant 95, 101
   samurai 94
   working 6, 8, 29, 33, 46, 60, 67–68, 91, 96, 102, 209, 219, 225
class compromise 99, 219, 227–28
class struggle 46, 69, 72, 93–94, 219, 228, 229
clientelism 19, 37–38, 57, 68, 83, 94, 131, 134–35, 145, 147, 151, 212, 218–19, 231–34
climate change 1, 43, 62, 170–71, 224
coalition 52, 70, 106, 139, 143–45, 147, 150, 158, 195, 211, 218
   LDP-Kōmeitō 147
   proto-DPJ 147
   seven-party 143

coalition agreement   146
coalition cabinet   143
coalition government   37, 143–44, 150, 156, 232
Cold War   74–77, 153–54
Communist Party   47, 62
Companies Act   160
Constitutional Democratic Party   152, 195, 222
Construction Ministry   39, 96, 131, 218
contradictions   2–7, 11–12, 19–21, 26–27, 31–33, 37–38, 55–56, 63, 65–68, 108–9, 174–75, 199–200, 213–14, 228–32, 240–41, 243–44
Copenhagen Accord   151
corporate paternalism   93
Cox, Robert   4–5, 42, 50, 56–57, 59, 68, 77
crisis of capital accumulation   172, 229, 242
crisis of political legitimacy   214, 233
crisis of social reproduction   139, 173, 199–200, 239–42
Curtis, Gerald   2, 22, 81

Dai-ichi Kangyo   161
Democratic Party (post-war conservative)   86n.1
Democratic Party of Japan   1, 145, 152n. (see also DPJ)
Democratic Party for the People   212
Democratic Socialist Party   76, 80, 150 (see also DSP)
demographic crisis   123, 139, 147, 153, 167–70, 179, 185, 198, 239–40
deregulation   29, 120, 127, 162, 164, 166, 172, 200, 209, 212, 214
    commercial   166
    financial   112, 114, 128–29, 137, 155, 211
developmentalism   4, 19, 78, 88, 173, 215–16, 235
developmental state   14, 16–18, 86
Doi Takako   141
Dokō Toshio   120
Dollar-Gold Standard   9, 30, 109–10, 235
Dōmei   224
Dōyūkai   212
DPJ   1, 10, 12, 37–38, 149–54, 157–59, 166, 174–75, 180, 190, 195, 197, 212, 222, 225, 233–34

DSP   76, 80–81, 84, 93, 143, 158, 221 (see also Democratic Socialist Party)

Edano Yukio   152
enterprise unionism   15, 17, 93–94, 102, 122, 131, 235
Equal Employment Opportunity Law   130
Esping-Andersen, Gøsta   34–35, 38, 118
Estevez-Abe, Margarita   36–38, 90, 92, 96, 99, 106, 118–19, 123, 126, 146–47, 165, 168, 173
Etsuzankai   124
extended family households   98–99, 115–16, 135–36, 217, 220, 238

factions   19, 23, 82–84, 124–26, 137, 143, 147–50, 157, 213
Fair Trade Commission   27
Family Care Leave Law   147
Financial Activities' Management and Reform   148
fukoku kyōhei   196, 203
Fukuda Takeo   149
Fukuda Yasuo   149, 150, 159

gakubatsu   64
Gill, Stephen   5, 8, 15n., 42, 49–52, 57, 62, 66, 134, 226
Gold Plan   147
Gordon, Andrew   71, 73, 89
Gramsci, Antonio   2–4, 7, 40, 42–43, 46, 52, 55–56, 58–60, 62, 68, 174, 176, 179, 233–34, 236–37, 242–43
Gulf War   141–42, 153

Hanshin Earthquake   144
Hashimoto Ryūtarō   10, 95, 107, 140, 145–47, 151, 159, 161, 165, 215, 218, 233
Hatoyama Ichirō   86
Hatoyama Yukio   150–53, 159
hegemonic order   7–10, 42, 47–48, 50–56, 59, 61, 63, 67–68, 70–71, 73–74, 108–10, 133–34, 136–37, 140, 175–77, 193–94, 231, 237, 241–42
hegemonic project   42, 60–61, 64, 180, 186, 209
hegemony   3–5, 7–8, 42–43, 46–47, 50, 53, 56, 59–60, 63, 67–68, 209, 214, 243–44

INDEX

one nation   106, 234, 209
two nation   209, 234
hikikomori   167, 173
Hokkaido Takushoku Bank   139, 146
Hosokawa Morihiro   143–44

Ikeda Hayato   75, 77, 80, 104
Ishiba Shigeru   178, 202
Ishihara Shintarō   204
Itoh, Makoto   1–2, 4–7, 14, 24, 29–33, 36, 65, 67, 71, 105, 129

Japan Airlines   120
Japanese Business Federation   5, 86, 91, 105
Japanese Communist Party   12, 76, 195
Japanese Federation of Trade Unions   222
Japanese National Railways   130
Japanese Socialist Party   12, 76 (see also JSP)
Japanese Teachers' Union   189
Japan Import-Export Bank   127
Japan Inc   15, 21
Japan Medical Association   95
Japan New Party   145, 150
Japan Nurses Association   95
Japan Post Bank   233
Japan Renewal Party   143, 145, 150
JCP   12, 75, 80–81, 83, 87, 93, 130, 197, 221, 225, 232 (see also Japanese Communist Party)
Johnson, Chalmers   4, 14–18, 20–21, 24, 29, 64–66, 77, 86, 93, 104, 130, 190, 235
JSP   75–77, 80–81, 83–84, 87, 93, 96, 118, 130, 132, 134, 141, 143–45, 147, 158, 221, 232 (see also Japanese Socialist Party)

Kaifu Toshiki   141–42, 153
kaizen   130
Kake Gakuen   191, 195
Kanemaru Shin   142, 156
Kan Naoto   151–52, 159
kansei dangō   88
kantei   123, 145, 168, 234
karōshi   92, 173
Katz, Richard   1, 4–5, 15, 24, 26–29, 31, 64, 66, 112, 128, 132
Keidanren   5, 86, 91, 120, 160, 198, 205, 211–12, 219, 224

keiretsu   5, 16–20, 28, 64–65, 86, 88–91, 128–29, 139–40, 160–61, 235
Kishi Nobusuke   177
kōenkai   23, 82–83, 96–97, 124–26, 131, 135, 137, 142, 157, 231–33
Koizumi Jun'ichirō   10, 12, 140, 147–49, 155, 157, 159–60, 165, 178, 180, 183, 203, 208, 210, 230, 233
Kōmeitō   11, 76, 80, 83, 143, 145–47, 150, 156, 195, 197, 218, 221, 225, 232–33
Kōno statement   178
Krauss, Ellis   2, 23, 82–85, 125–26, 131, 157, 166 (see also Pekkanen, Robert)

Large-Scale Retail   131, 146, 165
Large Scale Retailers Law   162
LDP   17–20, 22–23, 37–38, 70–71, 75–77, 80–87, 95–96, 104–6, 118–20, 131–32, 134–35, 137, 141–47, 149–52, 156–59, 165–66, 169–72, 174–206, 211–13, 231–34
Lechevalier, Sebastien   32–33, 91, 112, 114, 120, 130, 133, 155–56, 160–61, 165, 194, 200
Liberal Democratic Party   1 (see also LDP)
liberalization   25, 28, 71, 121, 127, 129, 137, 147, 160, 165, 184, 199
Liberal Party   85, 150
lifetime employment   32, 35, 64, 67, 91–92, 97, 129, 131, 162, 208, 210, 235, 239
lifetime employment system   1, 19–20, 28–30, 35, 40, 66–67, 91–92, 99, 121–22, 129–30, 163, 216, 218
Lockheed corruption scandal   124, 232
Lucarelli, Bill   113–14, 128, 142, 182

Maekawa Commission   120
Maekawa Report   114, 121
Manchuria   78, 89, 177
Marx, Karl   7, 44, 46, 48, 52
M-curve   36
Meiji Restoration   61, 100–101, 148, 203
MHLW   36, 116–17, 147, 170, 185 (see Ministry of Health, Labor and Welfare)
migrant workers   169, 198, 208, 229–30, 236, 239–40
Miike mine strikes   72
Miki Takeo   122, 124, 141
militarism   103, 122, 89, 186, 188, 203, 207, 223
Minamata disease   104

Ministry of Agriculture   218
Ministry of Defense   205
Ministry of Economy, Trade and Industry   5, 161, 212
Ministry of Education   105, 205
Ministry of Finance   5, 16, 86, 88, 105, 212 (see also MOF)
Ministry of Fisheries   218
Ministry of Health, Labor and Welfare   224 (see also MHLW)
Ministry of Health and Welfare   105, 123, 147
Ministry of International Trade and Industry   5, 16 (see also MITI)
Ministry of Justice   205
Ministry of Land   218
Ministry of Posts and Telecommunications   126 (see also Postal Ministry)
MITI   15–16, 18–20, 27, 64–65, 78, 86, 88, 105, 126, 128–29, 146 161 (see also Ministry of International Trade and Industry)
Miura, Mari   2, 29, 33–39, 62, 64, 66, 97–98, 167, 215–16, 237
Miyamoto, Tarō   118–19, 121, 131–32, 215–16
Miyazawa Kiichi   142–43
modern prince   7, 43, 46, 61–62, 68
Ministry of Finance   1, 5, 16, 32, 64, 79, 112
Mori Yoshirō   146
Moritomo Gakuen   190, 195
Murakami, Yasusuke   4, 17, 21–22, 24, 89–91, 95, 100–102, 188
Murayama Tomiichi   144

Nakasone Yasuhiro   9, 12, 32–33, 112, 120–23, 130, 137, 203, 235
Nanking Massacre   189
National Association of Special Postmasters   95
National Federation of Small Business Associations   95
nationalism   101, 103, 203, 212, 223, 229, 238
  cultural   102, 169, 239
  developmentalist   118
  ethnic   240
  soft   216
nationalist   61, 188, 193, 196, 199, 203, 205–6, 208, 214–15, 234
nationalist communitarianism   70, 109

National Public Service Law   190–91, 205
neo-communitarian   217, 240
neo-communitarianism   215–16, 218, 220, 226
neo-conservatism   12, 203–4, 207, 215, 222, 226, 229
neoliberal   38, 40, 43, 142, 145, 149–50, 170, 172, 203, 210, 214–15, 230, 233, 236–37
neoliberal deregulation   129, 147, 154, 156, 160–61, 167, 173, 181, 212, 218, 241
neoliberalism   3, 33, 66, 135, 160, 209, 212–15, 222, 226–29
New Frontier Party   145, 150, 158
Nixon Shocks   70, 110–11, 136
Noda Yoshihiko   152, 159, 162, 164, 212
Noda Seiko   226
Nōkyō   95, 184, 213, 232 (see also Association of Japan Agriculture Cooperatives)

Obuchi Keizō   146
O'Connor, James   7–8, 42, 47–48, 51, 241
Ōhira Masayoshi   112, 120, 123, 125, 148
Oil Crisis   110, 112 (see also oil shocks)
oil shocks   30–31, 112–13, 125, 136, 235 (see also Oil Crisis)
  First Oil Shock   27, 70, 112, 118
Okimoto, Daniel   4–5, 18–21, 24, 29, 64, 84, 86, 90, 92, 128, 235
Okinawa   70, 74–75, 77, 151, 168
organic crisis   2, 5–7, 10–11, 45, 55–56, 61–62, 74, 139–76, 179–81, 186, 199, 202, 206–7, 219, 226–27, 229, 236, 241–44
Osaka Restoration Party   205
Osawa, Mari   1–2, 38–39, 66, 107, 123, 147, 153, 163–64, 239
Ozawa Ichirō   140–145, 150, 151, 154, 169, 212

Pacific War   74, 103, 148
pacifism   75, 103, 223, 238
pacifist constitution   154, 208
pacifist nationalism   101, 103, 169, 219
parasite singles   167, 173
PARC   23, 82, 84–85, 125–26, 131, 137 (see also Policy Affairs Research Council)
passive revolution   7, 11, 43, 59–61, 68, 176–201, 206, 234
pāto   163

Pekkanen, Robert   2, 23, 82–85, 125–26, 131, 157, 166 (see also Krauss, Ellis)
Pempel, TJ   4, 17–19, 21, 24, 26, 64
petit bourgeoisie   5, 8–9, 94–96, 106, 117, 120, 132, 134, 162, 165–66, 210, 213, 216, 219, 228
Plaza Accord   31, 110, 113–14, 235
Policy Affairs Research Council   23, 84 (see also PARC)
political legitimation   7–10, 12, 46–48, 51–52, 54, 68, 71–72, 172, 174, 195, 206, 213, 219, 231, 240–42
Political Reform Committee   142
population aging   1, 3, 115, 117–19, 147, 153, 163, 168, 173, 217–18, 220, 236, 239
Postal Ministry   131, 218 (see also Ministry of Posts and Telecommunications)
postal privatization   12, 147–49, 159, 218
protectionism   29, 113, 212, 216
public debt   1–2, 24, 26, 32, 120, 145, 173, 200, 211, 220, 236
Public Highway Corporation   148
public works spending   37, 96, 99, 106, 118–19, 121, 126–27, 132, 145, 159, 165–66

Reagan, Ronald   122
Reagan administration   112
Reagan-era policies   114
Recruit-Cosmos   141, 232, 238
regime of accumulation   20, 31, 51
regime of social reproduction   51, 99, 135–36, 138, 202, 237–38
regulation school   7, 32–33
relations of force   7, 10, 42–43, 58–59, 61, 202, 204, 206, 211, 213, 218, 224, 226
Rengō   130, 164, 224
Rikken Minseitō   89
Rikken Seiyūkai   89
Rinchō   12, 120–22, 135, 145, 155
Rosenbluth, Frances   22–23, 75, 105
ryōsai kenbo   107

Sagawa Kyūbin   142, 144, 156–57, 232, 238
Sakigake   143–45, 150, 232
Satō Eisaku   70, 77n., 111 177
Schoppa, Leonard   1–2, 4, 14, 18, 29, 31, 36, 64–65, 127, 129, 180

SDF   141, 144, 188, 210, 223 (see also Self-Defense Forces)
Seccombe, Wally   48–50
Second Oil Shock   114
Second World War   78, 88, 102, 122, 166
seikatsusha   222
Seiwa Seisaku Kenkyūkai   204
Self-Defense Forces   141, 144, 205 (see also SDF)
shōshika   166
shōshikōreika   1
Small Business Associations   95
Socialist Democratic Federation   143
social reproduction   3–8, 10, 33, 39–40, 42, 48–52, 65–68, 70–74, 97–99, 108–10, 135–36, 138–40, 166–67, 169, 173–74, 198–202, 213–15, 226–27, 230–31, 237–42
Sōhyō   93n.1, 130, 164 224
South Korea   3, 74, 210, 217, 235
Specially Designated Secrets Protection Law   192–93
stagflation   24, 134
stock market   97, 112, 114, 128, 139, 142, 171, 236
Suga Yoshihide   1, 188, 199, 202
Suzuki Zenkō   9, 120

Taishō democracy   89
Takeshita Noboru   123, 135, 141
Tanaka Kakuei   9, 70, 118–19, 124–26, 131, 148–49
tan'itsu minzoku   2, 5, 101, 169, 174, 184, 198–99, 204, 217
Toyota   17, 66, 86, 120, 128, 130, 160, 235
Toyotism   130
trade liberalization   121, 209, 235
   agricultural   132, 184
trasformismo   7, 43, 59, 61, 68, 200
Trilateral Commission   142
Trump, Donald   215

unions   17, 93–94, 130, 142, 164, 226
US-Japan Security Treaty   72, 74–76 (see also Anpo)

welfare   37, 40, 85, 91–92, 98–99, 105, 119, 123, 136, 199, 215–16, 219–20, 224
welfare reform   145

welfare regime 237
welfare states 14, 34, 51, 91, 119, 205, 214
   minimalist 17, 136
   welfare through work 33–35, 39, 64, 215
   womenomics 183
   Worker Dispatch Law 121–22, 130

Yasukuni Shrine 122, 148, 203
Yoshida Shigeru 75, 85
Yoshida Doctrine 74–77

zaibatsu 16, 19, 88–90
zoku 84–85, 95, 125–27, 131, 134, 137, 146, 148, 177, 218, 232–33

www.ingramcontent.com/pod-product-compliance
Lightning Source LLC
Chambersburg PA
CBHW071232070526
44583CB00017B/2151